LITERATURE, SCIENCE AN
IN THE ROMANT
Bodies of Knowledg

In 1768, Captain James Cook made the most important scientific voyage of the eighteenth century. He was not alone: scores of explorers like Cook, travelling in the name of science, brought new worlds and new peoples within the horizon of European knowledge for the first time. Their discoveries changed the course of science. Old scientific disciplines, such as astronomy and botany, were transformed; new ones, like craniology and comparative anatomy, were brought into being. Scientific disciplines, in turn, pushed literature of the period towards new subjects, forms and styles. Works as diverse as Mary Shelley's *Frankenstein* and Wordsworth's *Excursion* responded to the explorers' and scientists' latest discoveries. This wide-ranging and well-illustrated study shows how literary Romanticism arose partly in response to science's appropriation of explorers' encounters with foreign people and places and how it, in turn, changed the profile of science and exploration.

TIM FULFORD is Professor in the Department of English and Media Studies at Nottingham Trent University. He is the author of *Landscape, Liberty and Authority: Poetry, Criticism and Politics from Thomson to Wordsworth* (Cambridge, 1996) and *Romanticism and Masculinity* (1999) and co-editor with Peter J. Kitson of *Romanticism and Colonialism* (Cambridge, 1998).

DEBBIE LEE is Professor of English at Washington State University. She is the author of *Slavery and the Romantic Imagination* (2002) and co-editor with Peter J. Kitson of *Slavery, Abolition and Emancipation: Writings in the British Romantic Period* (2000).

PETER J. KITSON is Professor in the Department of English at Dundee University. He is co-editor with Tim Fulford of *Romanticism and Colonialism* (Cambridge, 1998).

CAMBRIDGE STUDIES IN ROMANTICISM

General editors
Professor Marilyn Butler   Professor James Chandler
University of Oxford   *University of Chicago*

Editorial board
John Barrell, *University of York*
Paul Hamilton, *University of London*
Mary Jacobus, *University of Cambridge*
Kenneth Johnston, *Indiana University*
Alan Liu, *University of California, Santa Barbara*
Jerome McGann, *University of Virginia*
David Simpson, *University of California, Davis*

This series aims to foster the best new work in one of the most challenging fields within English literary studies. From the early 1780s to the early 1830s a formidable array of talented men and women took to literary composition, not just in poetry, which some of them famously transformed, but in many modes of writing. The expansion of publishing created new opportunities for writers, and the political stakes of what they wrote were raised again by what Wordsworth called those 'great national events' that were 'almost daily taking place': the French Revolution, the Napoleonic and American wars, urbanisation, industrialisation, religious revival, an expanded empire abroad and the reform movement at home. This was an enormous ambition, even when it pretended otherwise. The relations between science, philosophy, religion and literature were reworked in texts such as *Frankenstein* and *Biographia Literaria*; gender relations in *A Vindication of the Rights of Woman* and *Don Juan*; journalism by Cobbett and Hazlitt; poetic form, content and style by the Lake School and the Cockney School. Outside Shakespeare studies, probably no body of writing has produced such a wealth of response or done so much to shape the responses of modern criticism. This indeed is the period that saw the emergence of those notions of 'literature' and of literary history, especially national literary history, on which modern scholarship in English has been founded.

The categories produced by Romanticism have also been challenged by recent historicist arguments. The task of the series is to engage both with a challenging corpus of Romantic writings and with the changing field of criticism they have helped to shape. As with other literary series published by Cambridge, this one will represent the work of both younger and more established scholars, on either side of the Atlantic and elsewhere.

For a complete list of titles published see end of book.

LITERATURE, SCIENCE AND EXPLORATION IN THE ROMANTIC ERA

Bodies of Knowledge

TIM FULFORD, DEBBIE LEE
AND
PETER J. KITSON

CAMBRIDGE UNIVERSITY PRESS
Cambridge, New York, Melbourne, Madrid, Cape Town, Singapore, São Paulo

Cambridge University Press
The Edinburgh Building, Cambridge CB2 8RU, UK

Published in the United States of America by Cambridge University Press, New York

www.cambridge.org
Information on this title: www.cambridge.org/9780521829199

© Tim Fulford, Debbie Lee and Peter J. Kitson 2004

This publication is in copyright. Subject to statutory exception
and to the provisions of relevant collective licensing agreements,
no reproduction of any part may take place without the written
permission of Cambridge University Press.

First published 2004
Third printing 2006

A catalogue record for this publication is available from the British Library

Library of Congress Cataloguing in Publication data
Fulford, Tim, 1962–
Literature, science and exploration in the Romantic era : bodies of knowledge / Tim
Fulford, Debbie Lee and Peter J. Kitson.
p. cm. – (Cambridge studies in Romanticism ; 60)
Includes bibliographical references and index.
ISBN 0 521 82919 4
1. English literature – 19th century – History and criticism. 2. Literature and
science – Great Britain – History – 19th century. 3. Discoveries in
geography – British – History – 19th century. 4. British – Foreign countries – History – 19th
century. 5. Science – Great Britain – History – 19th century. 6. Great Britain – Intellectual
life – 19th century. 7. Learning and scholarship in literature. 8. Romanticism – Great Britain.
9. Explorers in literature. 10. Geography in literature. 11. Science in literature.
I. Lee, Debbie. II. Kitson, Peter J. III. Title. IV. Series.
PR468.S34F85 2004 820.9'36 – dc22 2003063280

ISBN 978-0-521-82919-9 hardback
ISBN 978-0-521-03995-6 paperback

Transferred to digital printing 2008

Contents

List of illustrations	*page* ix
Acknowledgements	xii
A note on the text	xiii
Frequently cited texts	xiv

	Introduction: bodies of knowledge	1

PART I: EXPLORATION, SCIENCE AND LITERATURE

1	Sir Joseph Banks and his networks	33
2	Tahiti in London; London in Tahiti: tools of power	46
3	Indian flowers and Romantic Orientalism	71
4	Mental travellers: Banks, African exploration and the Romantic imagination	90
5	Banks, Bligh and the breadfruit: slave plantations, tropical islands and the rhetoric of Romanticism	108
6	Exploration, headhunting and race theory: the skull beneath the skin	127
7	Theories of terrestrial magnetism and the search for the poles	149

PART II: BRITISH SCIENCE AND LITERATURE IN THE CONTEXT OF EMPIRE

8	'Man electrified man': Romantic revolution and the legacy of Benjamin Franklin	179

9	The beast within: vaccination, Romanticism and the Jenneration of disease	198
10	Britain's little black boys and the technologies of benevolence	228
	Conclusion	271
Notes		274
Index		313

Illustrations

1. W. Watts, engraving after a drawing by W. Hodges, 'The Island of Otaheite', from James Cook, *A Voyage Towards the South Pole* (London, 1777). By permission of the Syndics of Cambridge University Library — *page* 19
2. A specimen collected on the *Endeavour* voyage. Courtesy of Marina Warner — 36
3. James Sowerby, 'Banksia Spinulosa', from James Edward Smith, *A Specimen of the Botany of New Holland* (London, 1794). By permission of the National Library of Australia — 37
4. Engraving, 'Sir Joseph Banks at Dinner', from Peter Pindar, *Peter's Prophecy* (London, 1788). By permission of the British Library — 40
5. Engraving, 'Omai, A Native Of Otaheite brought to England by Captain Fourneaux' (1774), from *London Magazine*, August 1774. By permission of the Syndics of Cambridge University Library — 50
6. Benjamin West, portrait of Sir Joseph Banks (1771). By permission of Lincolnshire County Council, Usher Gallery — 51
7. Johann Jacobe, engraving, after Sir Joshua Reynolds, 'Omai, a Native of the Island of Utietea [i.e. Ulietea]' (1780). By permission of the National Library of Australia — 52
8. William Parry, oil, 'Sir Joseph Banks with Omai, the Otaheitian Chief and Dr Solander' (*c.* 1776). Private collection — 54
9. J. Caldwall, engraving, 'Omai' (1777), published in James Cook, *Voyage Towards the South Pole*. By permission of the Syndics of Cambridge University Library — 55
10. Royce, engraving, 'Omai's Public Entry on his First Landing at Otaheite' (1781), after a drawing by Robert Dodd, in John Rickman, *Journal of Captain Cook's Last Voyage* (London, 1781).

By permission of the Syndics of Cambridge University
Library 61
11 Engraving, 'Semecarpus Anacardium Nella-jiedy of the Telingas'
(1795), from a drawing by an Indian artist, in William Roxburgh,
Plants of the Coast of Coromandel (London, 1795). By permission
of the Syndics of Cambridge University Library 76
12 John Frederick Miller, engraving after Sidney Parkinson, 'A
Branch of the Bread-fruit Tree with the Fruit' (1773) from John
Hawkesworth, *An Account of the Voyages Undertaken by the Order
of his Present Majesty for Making Discoveries in the Southern
Hemisphere* (London, 1773). By permission of the National
Library of Australia 111
13 Engraving, from *The Works of the Late Professor Camper,
On the Connexion between the Science of Anatomy and the
Arts of Drawing, Painting, Statuary* (London, 1794).
By permission of the Syndics of Cambridge University
Library 130
14 John Webber, watercolour, 'A Human Sacrifice at Tahiti' (1777).
By permission of the British Library 136
15 Michael Dahl, 'Edmond Halley (1656–1742)'. By permission of
the Royal Society 152
16 Halley's Atlantic Chart of 1701, illustrating magnetic variation.
By permission of the Royal Astronomical Society 153
17 John R. Wildman, 'Captain Sir James Clark Ross (1800–62)'.
By permission of the National Maritime Museum 167
18 Engraving, 'Sarah Nelmes's Hand' (1798), from Edward Jenner,
An Inquiry into the Causes and Effects of the Variolae Vaccinae
(London, 1798). By permission of the Jenner Museum, Berkeley,
Gloucestershire 200
19 James Gillray, 'The Cow Pock, or, The Wonderful Effects of the
New Inoculation' (1802). By permission of the Jenner Museum,
Berkeley, Gloucestershire 205
20 Engraving, 'Galvanic Experiments upon the Head and Trunk of
an Ox' (1803), from Giovanni Aldini, *An Account of the Late
Improvements in Galvanism* (London, 1803). By permission of
the British Library 206
21 Engraving, 'The Ox-Faced Boy' (1805), from William Rowley,
Cow-pox Inoculation No Security Against Small-pox Infection
(London, 1805). By permission of the British Library 208

22 Engraving from the *Report of the Royal Commission on the Employment of Children in Mines and Manufacturies* (1842), XVII. By permission of the Syndics of Cambridge University Library 232
23 James Gillray, caricature, 'The Comforts of a Rumford Stove' (12 June 1800). Copyright the British Museum 237

Acknowledgements

Early versions of some of the arguments contained herein have appeared previously as articles. The authors thank, for permission to rework these articles here, the editors of *Nineteenth-Century Contexts*, *Studies in Romanticism*, *Cultural Critique*, *Literature and History*, *European Romantic Review*, *Eating Romanticism*, *Coleridge and the Sciences of Life*, *The Wordsworth Circle*.

The British Academy awarded Tim Fulford a grant, which made it possible to carry out some of the research. Nottingham Trent University also provided financial support. Staff at the following libraries made our work easier: Cambridge University Library, the Sidney Jones Library, Liverpool, the John Rylands Library Manchester, the National Maritime Museum, the British Library, University of Dundee Library, St Andrews University Library, the National Library of Scotland. We thank the following for help and advice: Alan Bewell, Carol Bolton, Anthony Bowen, Neil Chambers, Nora Crook, Michael Franklin, Marilyn Gaull, Jan Golinski, John Goodridge, Peter D. Hingley, David Knight, Myron and Stephanie Lee, Trevor Levere, Philip Martin, Anne Mellor, Rob Mitchell, Timothy Morton, Morton Paley, Andrew Plowman, Lynda Pratt, Alan Richardson, Daniel Roberts, Nicholas Roe, Sharon Ruston, Tami Spector, Jane Stabler, Anya Taylor, Marina Warner, Timothy Webb, Peter, Bonnie and Madge Williams.

We are grateful to the following museums and galleries for permission to publish images in their possession: the British Library, the British Museum, Cambridge University Library, the Franklin Collection, Yale University Library, the Jenner Museum, the Mitchell Library, the State Library of New South Wales, the National Library of Australia, the National Maritime Museum, Greenwich, the National Portrait Gallery, the Royal Astronomical Society, the Royal Society, the Science Museum, the Usher Gallery, Lincoln.

A note on the text

This book was conceived by all three authors; it is not a collection of essays by different hands. Nevertheless, different chapters reflect the original research of different writers. Chapters 2, 3, 8 and the conclusion originated in research by Tim Fulford, chapter 7 in research by Peter Kitson and chapters 1 and 4 in research by Debbie Lee. Chapter 6 originated with Tim Fulford and Peter Kitson and the introduction, chapters 5, 9 and 10 with Tim Fulford and Debbie Lee.

Frequently cited texts

The following texts are commonly cited in the abbreviated form shown below:

Bewell	Alan Bewell, *Romanticism and Colonial Disease* (Baltimore and London, 1999)
BJHS	*British Journal for the History of Science*
BL	Samuel Taylor Coleridge, *Biographia Literaria*, ed. J. Engell and W. Jackson Bate, 2 vols. (London and Princeton, N.J., 1983). *CC*, VII
BL Add MS	Banks Correspondence, in British Library Additional Manuscripts
BPW	George Gordon, Lord Byron, *The Complete Poetical Works*, ed. Jerome McGann, 7 vols. (Oxford, 1980–6)
Carter	H. B. Carter, *Sir Joseph Banks, 1743–1820* (London, 1988)
CC	*The Collected Works of Samuel Taylor Coleridge* Bollingen Series LXXV (Collected Coleridge)
CL	*The Collected Letters of Samuel Taylor Coleridge*, ed. E. L. Griggs, 6 vols. (Oxford, 1956–71)
CM	S. T. Coleridge, *Marginalia*, ed. George Whalley, 5 vols. (London and Princeton, N.J., 1980–). *CC*, XII
CN	*The Notebooks of S. T. Coleridge*, ed. Kathleen Coburn, 5 vols. (London and Princeton, N.J., 1957–)
CPW	*The Complete Poetical Works of Samuel Taylor Coleridge*, ed. E. H. Coleridge, 2 vols. (London, 1912)
CSF	James Montgomery, *The Chimney Sweeper's Friend and Climbing Boy's Album* (London, 1824)
Curry	*New Letters of Robert Southey*, ed. Kenneth Curry, 2 vols. (New York and London, 1965)

DTC	Banks Correspondence, Dawson Turner Copies, in the Natural History Museum, London
EOT	S. T. Coleridge, *Essays on his Times*, ed. David V. Erdman, 3 vols. (London and Princeton, N.J., 1978). *CC*, III
Erdman	*The Complete Poetry and Prose of William Blake*, with commentary by Harold Bloom, newly rev. edn (Berkeley, Calif., and Garden City, N.Y., 1982)
Frankenstein	Mary Shelley, *Frankenstein or the Modern Prometheus*, ed. Nora Crook. Volume 1. *The Novels and Selected Works of Mary Shelley*, 8 vols. (London, 1996)
Friend	S. T. Coleridge, *The Friend*, ed. B. Rooke, 2 vols. (London and Princeton, N.J., 1969). *CC*, IV
Gascoigne 1994	John Gascoigne, *Joseph Banks and the English Enlightenment: Useful Knowledge and Polite Culture* (Cambridge, 1994)
Gascoigne 1998	*Science in the Service of Empire: Joseph Banks, the British State and the Uses of Science in the Age of Revolution* (Cambridge, 1998)
Golinski	Jan Golinski, *Science as Public Culture: Chemistry and Enlightenment in Britain, 1760–1820* (Cambridge, 1992)
H Works	*The Complete Works of William Hazlitt*, ed. P. P. Howe, 21 vols. (London, 1930–4)
Jones	*The Works of Sir William Jones*, 13 vols. (London, 1807)
Keats	*Keats: The Complete Poems*, ed. John Barnard (Harmondsworth, 1973)
Kew BC	Banks Correspondence, Royal Botanic Gardens, Kew
KL	*The Letters of John Keats, 1814–21*, ed. Hyder E. Rollins, 2 vols. (Cambridge, Mass., 1958)
Latour	Bruno Latour, *Science in Action: How to Follow Scientists and Engineers through Society* (Milton Keynes, 1987)
LB	W. Wordsworth and S. T. Coleridge, *Lyrical Ballads 1798*, ed. W. J. B. Owen, 2nd edn (Oxford, 1969)
Leask	Nigel Leask, *British Romantic Writers and the East: Anxieties of Empire* (Cambridge, 1992)

Lects 1795	S. T. Coleridge, *Lectures 1795 on Politics and Religion*, ed. L. Patton and P. Mann (London and Princeton, N.J., 1971). *CC*, I
Lects 1808–19	S. T. Coleridge, *Lectures 1808–19 on Literature*, ed. R. A. Foakes, 2 vols. (London and Princeton, N.J., 1987). *CC*, V
Levere	Trevor H. Levere, *Poetry Realized in Nature: Samuel Taylor Coleridge and Early Nineteenth-Century Science* (Cambridge, 1981)
McCormick	E. H. McCormick, *Omai Pacific Envoy* (Auckland and Oxford, 1977)
Pratt	Mary Louise Pratt, *Imperial Eyes: Travel Writing and Transculturation* (London and New York, 1992)
Prelude	William Wordsworth, *The Prelude, 1799, 1805, 1850*, ed. Jonathan Wordsworth, M. H. Abrams and Stephen Gill (New York and London, 1979)
Rennie	Neil Rennie, *Far Fetched Facts: The Literature of Travel and the Idea of the South Seas* (Oxford, 1992)
Schiebinger	Londa Schiebinger, *Nature's Body: Gender in the Making of Modern Science* (Boston, 1993)
Shelley	*Shelley's Poetry and Prose*, ed. Donald H. Reiman and Sharon B. Powers (New York and London, 1977)
SiR	*Studies in Romanticism*
SL	*The Letters of Percy Bysshe Shelley*, ed. Frederick Jones, 2 vols. (Oxford, 1964)
Smith	Bernard Smith, *European Vision and the South Pacific 1768–1850* (Oxford, 1960)
SWF	S. T. Coleridge, *Shorter Works and Fragments*, ed. H. J. Jackson and J. R. de J. Jackson, 2 vols. (London and Princeton, N.J., 1995). *CC*, XI
Task	*The Poems of William Cowper*, vol. II: *1782–1785*, ed. John D. Baird and Charles Ryskamp (Oxford, 1995)
TT	S. T. Coleridge, *Table Talk*, ed. Carl Woodring, 2 vols. (London and Princeton, N.J., 1990). *CC*, XIV
TWC	*The Wordsworth Circle*
Visions	*Visions of Empire: Voyages, Botany, and Representations of Nature*, ed. David Philip Miller and Peter Hanns Reill (Cambridge, 1996)

Watchman	*The Watchman*, ed. Lewis Patton (London and Princeton, 1970). *CC*, II
WProse	*The Prose Works of William Wordsworth*, ed. W. J. B. Owen and J. W. Smyser, 3 vols. (Oxford, 1974)
WPW	*The Poetical Works of William Wordsworth*, ed. E. de Selincourt and Helen Darbishire, 5 vols. (Oxford, 1940–9)

Introduction: bodies of knowledge

As an undergraduate at Oxford, Percy Bysshe Shelley, just as he was forming his literary identity, became fascinated by science, exploration and poetry. According to his friend Thomas Jefferson Hogg, Shelley enthused about amazing discoveries that would give humankind a power it had never possessed before, a power to command the elements in even the remotest parts of the globe. With this power, he prophesied, life on earth could be transformed for the better, if only Europe would project its new technologies into foreign lands: 'The balloon', he declared, 'will enable us to traverse vast tracts with ease and rapidity, and to explore unknown countries without difficulty. Why are we still so ignorant of the interior of Africa? – Why do we not dispatch intrepid aeronauts to cross it in every direction, and to survey the whole peninsula in a few weeks? The shadow of the first balloon, which a vertical sun would project precisely beneath it, as it glides silently over that hitherto unhappy country, would virtually emancipate every slave, and would annihilate slavery forever.'[1]

It was not just the newly invented balloon that intrigued Shelley: advances in controlling water, fire and air all suggested ways of spreading civilisation and liberty across the world. 'What a mighty instrument would electricity be in the hands of him who knew how to wield it . . . by electrical kites we may draw down the lightning from heaven,' he exclaimed. Technology promised to make intervention in nature possible on a scale never before dreamed of: 'The galvanic battery is a new engine, what will not an extraordinary combination of troughs of colossal magnitude, a well arranged system of hundreds of metallic plates effect?'

Shelley's questions heralded a new age, an age in which we are still living today – a globalised age in which space, time, geography – life itself – have been transformed by science. As he foresaw, science would change Britain and transmit European power into the furthest regions of the world. It would do so because many of the inventions that excited him – Count Rumford's heating devices, Benjamin Franklin's lightning conductors, Volta's battery and the Montgolfiers' balloons – were turned into technologies for commanding not only the elements but also people's lives at home and abroad. Shelley was right to link them with each other and with exploration, for at the Admiralty, the Royal Society and the African Association fellow Britons shared his dreams and had the power to make them a reality.

This book is about a three-fold relationship between exploration, science and literature that not only underpinned Shelley's youthful ideas, but also spread deep into British culture during the years when Britain expanded its colonial possessions further across the globe than ever before. This relationship had significant effects on the British empire and on the attitudes of British people to that empire, changing Britons' understanding of themselves and of foreigners. This relationship also changed the discourses involved: what we term exploration, science and literature were areas of activity that, while largely distinct from each other, were not always wholly separate or utterly unitary fields.

A few words at the outset about terms. Before the professionalisation of disciplines in the later nineteenth century, there were few hard-and-fast barriers between intellectual discourses and fewer blanket designations. What we call 'science' was, in practice, a number of areas of enquiry, which did not necessarily all share common goals and methods. Nevertheless, there were institutional parameters, and bodies concerned with enforcing them, ensuring that intellectuals could, in practice, define what was, and was not, acceptable as a proper scientific discourse. The sanction of the Royal Society and the Royal College of Physicians was important, and both these bodies preferred work that followed inductive method and used an empiricist and realist style. The narratives of explorers, for example, were accepted as valid scientific documents if they followed a 'plain, unvarnished' style in which the explorer's impressions were represented as objectively observed 'evidence'. If they did not, they might be dismissed as travellers' tales – fanciful fictions.[2] It was also the case, however, that the explorer's – or experimentalist's – political opinions and professional associations influenced the reception of his work: the definition of the properly scientific was, in part, a political and social construct. In fact, 'science' and 'scientist' were concepts under construction in the period. Discoveries were not automatically established as truths or universally hailed as works of genius, for what was granted the authority of demonstrable fact depended on the person's ability to shape his practice so that it satisfied the needs, or spoke to the anxieties, of groups within his culture. Focusing people's hopes and fears within a persuasive explanatory frame was a rhetorical, and often political, activity. The way in which men of science represented their experiments and theories, the alliances they made with patrons, press and public all affected the way their activity was seen. So did their gender: the few women who had the opportunity to practise science were mostly presented as assistants to their male relatives or explicators of the original research of men. Effectively, what was accepted as scientific truth depended on its observation (or, in some cases, its defiance) of social conventions about what truth looked and sounded like and where it proceeded from.

Similarly, 'exploration' was – and is – a social and political construct, one that is bound up with the history of imperialism. The people whom Britons called heroic explorers were often, to indigenous peoples, something much more mundane: travelling traders, suspicious vagrants, helpless visitors or unwelcome invaders. In using the term here, then, we do not intend to uphold uncritically the mythmaking that defined travelling Britons as intrepid adventurers but categorised the people they met (and, in practice, depended upon) as primitive savages. Instead, we wish to investigate the voyaging of men such as Captain Cook as a process not dissimilar – or necessarily superior – to the voyaging of the indigenous people who themselves travelled – sometimes to guide the very white men who were later called explorers. We use the term exploration, accepting that it was not only white men who explored and that it did not consist of discovering uninhabited blanks on the map. It was a form of travel, engaging with unfamiliar people in places that were their homes.

While exploration embodied the activities of travelling and visiting, it also carried the freight of conquest and colonisation. We reflect all of these activities in our use of the term. Thus, we prefer 'exploration' as a concept to 'travel' since we do distinguish – as Britons in the period did – between the kind of travelling performed by men such as Cook, William Bligh, Mungo Park and Francis Masson and the kind that gentlemen performed on their tours of Europe, Scotland and Wales. Although it is true that travellers on the Grand Tour sometimes reported back upon the rustic 'natives' in similar manner to travellers in Africa, India and the Pacific, it remains the case that these European 'natives' had been known for centuries. The people whom Cook met and described, on the other hand, were unknown to Britons, and it is this encounter that we examine under the term 'exploration'.

If 'science' and 'exploration' were not simple or wholly separate entities, neither was literature. Yet it too had parameters, patrolled by arbiters of the literary. Newly powerful critics such as Francis Jeffrey defined, in the influential journals that served the expanding public sphere, what was and was not acceptable as literature. Their critical definitions, ostensibly made on aesthetic grounds, were also shaped by class-consciousness and political bias. Though relatively narrow, such definitions did not categorically separate the literary from the non-literary by equating the literary with fiction, and the non-literary with fact, or by separating aesthetic writing from scientific writing. And even when iconic poets themselves – Wordsworth and Coleridge, for example – distinguished poetry from science, they accepted that the two discourses were polar opposites and thus shared certain characteristics. They were both forms of literature, parts of a Janus-faced enquiry into the principles that animate both mind and nature.[3] In fact, it was not customary formally to divide fictional from factual writing until De Quincey in 1848 made fiction a defining characteristic of the 'literature of power' and claimed it was distinct from the 'literature of knowledge'.[4] By this distinction he fenced off travel writing, natural history, political journalism, to name but a few genres, from the realm of 'high' literature – that which communicated across time, through the aesthetic mode of the sublime.

It is the period before De Quincey's distinction between the literature of power and the literature of knowledge that we cover in this book. In this Romantic era, writers such as Coleridge and Wordsworth did not oppose their journalism or their travel writing to their fiction categorically. For Coleridge, literature could include a Theory of Life, an essay on criticism, and articles on William Pitt as well as poems, and all could work through the sublime and the beautiful. We reflect this practice in our construction of what constituted literature and the literary in the period, using the terms to designate poetry most frequently but not excluding the other discourses that writers such as Erasmus Darwin, Joseph Priestley and De Quincey himself wrote so voluminously.

Explorers such as Mungo Park and William Bartram also wrote texts that were of value both to naturalists and to poets. In effect a number of explorers were both literary and scientific writers simultaneously. Their writing reveals the overlaps between what we today designate as separate things. Obviously, though, overlaps do not constitute identity: it remains the fact that there are differences between sailing to the Pole, dissecting a corpse and writing a poem. The terms exploration, science and literature designate sometimes overlapping areas of thought and practice, which were sometimes performed by the same people, yet retained distinct cores and skills.

Our study begins with one significant date in the history of the Romantic era, and ends with another. The first, 1768, is the year that Captain James Cook embarked on the most important scientific voyage of the eighteenth century, sailing for Tahiti, New Zealand and Australia and returning to Britain with an unprecedented number of botanical specimens as well as charts, journals and calculations that put parts of the world on European maps for the first time. Cook was accompanied by a retinue of naturalists and astronomers – but not 'scientists' – since the word 'scientist' did not exist in 1768. It was coined the year our study ends – 1833 – in a historic meeting of a body that also did not exist when Cook set sail – the British Association for the Advancement of Science. 1833 was also, significantly, the year that Britain moved to ban a practice that, in 1768, was the bedrock of the national economy – colonial slavery. Clearly, between the two dates a major conceptual shift had occurred in the way Britons conceived of themselves and the world. We describe this shift as 'looking beyond to see in'.

By 1833 science had transformed European understanding of the natural and human worlds and simultaneously transformed European modes of acting in those worlds. In the process, it had itself been changed: it had gained immensely in authority and power, was acquiring institutional and professional status, and was recognisable as a distinct and coherent body of knowledge and practice. Quite simply, 'science' had come of age as a European discourse and the 'scientist' was a new species with more social authority than his forebear, the 'natural philosopher' or 'man of science',[5] had ever possessed.

What in 1768 was largely amateur natural philosophy performed by men (and not women)[6] of science had, by 1833, begun to turn into institutionalised disciplines, some staffed by paid professionals, most with their own learned societies. The Royal Society was no longer the only major scientific body, for new societies such as the Linnean (1782), the Geological (1807) and the Wernerian (1808) flourished. So did new journals, especially after the invention of the steam press, with *Nicholson's Journal*, the *Philosophical Magazine*, the *Annals of Philosophy* and the *Edinburgh* all giving sciences a much larger place in a public sphere that, indeed, they were helping to form. From 1825 that sphere began to widen still further, as Whig reformers responded to Henry Brougham's calls to educate the labouring classes by founding Mechanics' Institutes. These were intended to spread useful sciences, and within a few years were teaching chemistry and electricity in Newcastle, Derby, Edinburgh and many other towns. From 1828 the Society for the Diffusion of Useful Knowledge backed them up with a series of publications.

More than anything else, science's profile was raised by astonishing discoveries made in the far Pacific. Cook returned with strange fruit plucked from tropical trees, with still stranger beasts from the antipodean bush and, most marvellous of all, a living 'Indian' from an island so remote that white men had not visited it before 1767. Old scientific disciplines such as botany and natural history were transformed as a result, while more recent ones such as race theory and comparative anatomy gained new scope. Meanwhile, armed with new instruments which, like Cook's marine chronometer and Gowin Knight's compasses, made exploration feasible, astronomers saw planets and inconceivably remote clusters of stars, navigators hunted the mysterious force that lay at the poles, while chemists harnessed gas and electricity, making the secret of life itself seem within reach. These scientific activities, in turn, pushed literary writing towards new subjects and styles. Works as diverse as Shelley's *Prometheus Unbound* and Wordsworth's *The Excursion* responded to the latest discoveries as they looked out across the seas in order to probe into Britons' inner selves. Thus, what scholars have called 'Romanticism' arose partly as a response in writing (travel writing, scientific writing, literary writing) to encounters with foreign people and places. These encounters were seminal: they shaped not only the discourses that explicitly addressed distant cultures, but also those that concerned themselves with matters closer to home.

The relationship between exploration, science and literature cannot be addressed outside the contexts of colonialism and cultural imperialism. As many critics have emphasised in the past ten years, explorers often travelled in order to spread British dominion over new lands and seas. When science codified explorers' journeys, it acquired authority. When Romantic literature responded to this codification, it gained power. Science and literature thus increased their social status as they processed information that was acquired as part of an effort to exploit foreign peoples. As bodies of knowledge, they grew strong by acquiring knowledge of new bodies. In turn, both science and literature gave Britons confidence to imagine and to execute further exploration for the benefit of empire.

The reverse was also true: throughout this book we show that the movement from exploration to science, to literature and back was not always one by which Britain's imperial priorities were confirmed. The acquisition of information about new worlds and new peoples, and the use made of that information back in Britain, did not necessarily assist in the extension of British power across the world. What many writers learned led them to question the utility and morality of colonialism: Cook's descriptions of the Society Islands, for example, gave Coleridge a utopian image, in contrast to which he could show Britain's Caribbean slave islands to be dystopias. Other writers saw exploration and experimentation as a relentless pursuit of nature's secrets that was a new and socially dangerous form of male egotism: Mary Shelley indicted the comparative anatomist Victor Frankenstein, the polar explorer Captain Walton and the Orientalist Henry Clerval. What she had read of contemporary scientific quests effectively led her to doubt the benefits of scientific knowledge as it was currently being constructed. Blake, meanwhile, linked exploration with militarisation, writing 'he who shall train the Horse to War/ Shall never pass the Polar Bar' (Erdman, p. 491). And even those, such as Robert Southey, who did not oppose *per se* the idea that the exploration and classification of the world should be a national goal, nevertheless gained leverage to attack particular colonial policies and specific justifications of empire.

In exhibiting a range of responses to the expansion of empire, Romantic-era writers helped shape a debate. The dominant imperialist ideology of the late Victorian period had not yet emerged; scientific and literary writers were part of a contest in which ideologies and stereotypes were in the process of being formed, often in conflict with each other and in contradiction with themselves. In this relatively early period of what became the nineteenth-century empire, travellers of different perspectives – men, women, deists, evangelical missionaries, slavers, abolitionists, doctors, generals, botanists and ethnographers – were debating with each other, and for the benefit of their readers (including their governments), the nature and usefulness of what (and who) they saw and collected. Writers used what explorers showed them to argue about the reasons and the ends for which Britain should be subjecting remote parts of the world to its scrutiny. Deskbound writers, men as diverse as the surgeon J. C. Prichard and the poet William Cowper, used the latest scientific surveys of indigenous peoples as evidence that Britain should found an empire dedicated to missionary proselytism rather than commercial profit. In other words, they developed a new and (as they saw it) more ethical vision of empire as a result of what natural historians wrote.

One of the things natural historians wrote was that indigenous people's very bodies revealed their natural inferiority to whites. It is in reference to this that we have subtitled our book *Bodies of Knowledge*. Our story is about the ways in which certain discourses – structures of knowledge – gained definition, coherence and authority in relationship to the bodies of the indigenous peoples with whom Britain's explorers and colonisers were in contact. And although that contact took place on the plains of America, in the deserts of Africa, in Indian villages and on tropical beaches, it was largely back in their mother country that Britons described and depicted it. Nevertheless, the representations made in the countries that Britons visited and colonised were also significant, affecting the views that visitors and visited had of themselves and each other and influencing the actions of both. So powerful were the representations of contact that Britons' perceptions of their place at home as well as of their role in the world were changed (as were native peoples').

What explorers and scientific and literary authorities declared about the people of remote lands made Britons see themselves in a new context so that even discourses that did not originate in direct response to indigenous people were affected by them. Thus, we examine some of those discourses, showing how sciences that had intrinsically little to do with foreign places were defined, by poets and public, in relationship to the black and brown bodies which explorers and colonists had brought into Britons' consciousness. Vaccination (one of the most significant medical advances of the time) and the new chemistry of heat acquired unexpected public profiles because they became implicated in debates in which the relationship of Britons at home to the peoples of the empire was central. In many cases it was the writers we now call Romantic who implicated them: men such as S. T. Coleridge and Thomas Clarkson seized on new scientific discoveries to dramatise what they had come to see as the major moral problem facing Britons – the problem of exploitation of native peoples across the world. Science in Britain, it follows, often acquired its position in the contemporary public sphere as literary writers responded to it in their own discourses. Conversely, those literary writers found their own characteristic voices as they developed what they had read of contemporary exploration and science into works that made Britons peer into their consciences as they looked out towards the peoples of the empire.

Literature, Science and Exploration is divided into two sections. The first deals with the effects of overseas exploration and colonisation on scientific and literary discourses that spanned the empire, the second with the ways in which science and literature interacted in a British context, where exploration had opened up debates about Britons' relationship to 'foreign bodies'. Running through both sections are two common threads, or rather two substantial figures. The first, Sir Joseph Banks, himself an explorer, was one of the most influential men of science of the time. His influence, often neglected by historians of science as well as by scholars of Romanticism, was pervasive in the scientific and literary culture of the period. The second, Samuel Taylor Coleridge, was a theorist of science and a mentor of its practitioners as well as one of the most incisive analysts, as a journalist and poet, of the effects of exploration and empire at home and abroad. Although they never met, these two men were affected by each other again and again: Banks was an unwitting begetter of the Romanticism for which Coleridge is best known; Coleridge helped shape the public profile of the scientific practices that Banks had fostered.

In what follows, we summarise the developments in exploration, science and literature that form our subject, giving a schematic overview of the relationship that we assess in detail in the book as a whole.

EXPLORATION

Between 1768 and 1833 exploration transformed Britain's position in the world. When Cook set sail for Tahiti, Britain had only recently wrested control of Quebec from France. It still ruled its American colonies from London. Spain was the imperial power in Mexico and 'Louisiana' – a vast area whose extent was a matter of imagination, for parts of America's northwest coast had still to be charted. Britons knew still less of Africa, and were second to the Dutch in the exploration of South East Asia.

By 1833 the picture had changed vastly: Britain had lost its first (American) empire and, after fifty years of intense exploration and conquest, acquired a new one. It had colonised Australia, spread its missionaries to Polynesia, and planted its manufacturers in South America. It had penetrated Africa, and charted much of the polar seas and America's west coast. It had crossed Canada, taken possession of India, occupied Burma and founded Singapore. Though challenged by Russian voyages of discovery and commerce, its navy was the most powerful in the world and its explorers were national heroes.

No explorers seemed more heroic than those who travelled to the Pacific and Africa. They fascinated the public because they endured great dangers and encountered people who had previously been so little known. But it was, more than any other single person, Sir Joseph Banks who made them fascinating, since he not only combined exploration with science but also represented the expeditions for public consumption. Banks was an explorer himself: in 1768–72, as a member of Cook's voyage, he visited Tahiti and charted much of the New Zealand and Australian coasts. It was a major scientific achievement because Banks, on board as a gentleman of science with a retinue of botanists and assistants, increased the number of plant species known to science by 25 per cent. A second voyage was planned, but, after a disagreement, it left without Banks. Cook commanded, returning to Tahiti before pushing further south than ever before towards Antarctica (1772–5). The third, 1776–80, sailed through the Pacific to Alaska in search of the Northwest Passage. Cook, however, was killed at Hawaii.

Cook's achievements were celebrated at home because they suggested that Britain's culture of invention and manufacture allowed it to do what no other nation could. Science assisted exploration, which in turn provided men of science with opportunities to test their ideas in demanding conditions. It was his use of the newly invented chronometer for determining longitude, for example, and of the latest medically approved agents against scurvy, that allowed Cook to chart the furthest-flung regions of the globe.

The relationship between science and exploration appeared mutually beneficial and the voyages seemed free of the rapacious self-interest that characterised Britain's colonies in India, America and the West Indies. In the words of his elegist Anna Seward, Cook had voyaged not in aid of war or exploitation, but from benevolence (although in fact he had secret instructions to claim land for the Crown as well as to test the latest scientific instruments).[7] Cook, in other words, made Britons feel good about their global power, at a time when many were ashamed about the imperial violence their nation was inflicting in America, India and the slave islands of the Caribbean. He advanced geographic and scientific knowledge, without, it seemed, colonising or subjugating indigenous peoples. But after Cook died, Banks turned his legacy in a more nakedly imperialist direction. Essentially, our discussion of exploration tells the story of how he did so and to what effect.

By 1778 Banks had the scientific authority and political influence, as the President of the Royal Society and as a confidant of the King and his ministers, to initiate explorations that aimed to increase imperial profit as well as to further scientific knowledge. He became the shadowy orchestrator of a campaign of exploration designed not just to map but also to colonise the remotest parts of the world. He sent the very men who had sailed with Cook on a series of journeys of major importance in the history of science and exploration. Matthew Flinders circumnavigated Australia, showing it to be a single landmass, while his botanists collected and classified native species. William Bligh went to Tahiti to uproot the breadfruit trees that grew so plentifully there and take them to the West Indies, where they would provide a cheap food for slaves. After Bligh's eventful voyage on the *Bounty*, Banks had him sent to Australia to govern the penal colony that had been established there as a result of his lobbying. George Vancouver, meanwhile, retraced Cook's route along America's west coast, claiming territory and seeking the Northwest passage that would, if found, permit speedy communication with Britain's lucrative colonies in Asia. Vancouver did not find the passage, and neither did the later explorers whose expeditions Banks influenced: William Scoresby, James Ross, John Franklin,

William Edward Parry. But the fact that they travelled at all owes far more than has often been realised to Banks's power and to his vision. More than any other Briton, Banks had the combination of authority and imagination to hitch scientific exploration to colonial expansion.

It was not only to the South and Northwest Pacific that Banks projected British power. As adviser to the East India Company he seeded botanists across the subcontinent. As organiser of the African Association, he sent explorer after explorer into the continent least known to white people. John Ledyard, Frederick Hornemann, Joseph Ritchie and, most famously, Mungo Park were all selected by Banks with the aim of opening African geography, flora, fauna, customs, trades and languages to British eyes. What they discovered, however, was of more than purely scientific interest. Park brought back news of gold and soon Banks was organising military expeditions intended to bring the goldfields under British control. In Africa, as in Australia and Canada, Banks was determined to make exploration pay for itself – and more – in colonial wealth.

Such are the outlines of our presentation of exploration. We aim to reveal the extent to which it was linked to colonial expansion and to show the degree to which Banks, working behind the scenes, drove it forward. Banks, we show, was an impresario of empire as well as a doyen of science. We are still living with the material and cultural consequences of his vision.

SCIENCE

Science assisted exploration, as the chronometer, as dip compasses, as antiscorbutics, for example, reveal. But how did it benefit from exploration? Here we consider the effects of explorers' findings on the practice of science in Britain. Once again, Sir Joseph Banks is at the centre of our account, for he was one of the pioneers of the systematisation of knowledge through which the enquiries of gentlemen amateurs began to increase their disciplinary coherence and social authority, began, that is, to become the modern professional practice of the institutionalised 'scientist'.

Banks was no Romantic. In taste, outlook and *modus operandi* he was an Enlightenment gentleman who numbered such un-Romantic figures as Samuel Johnson and Joshua Reynolds among his friends. It was not Banks's character but his collection that nurtured the transformations in science which we today call Romantic. When Banks returned to Britain from his voyage round the world with Cook in 1772, he had with him a massive haul of things he had gathered up. But without a method of ordering them, and of displaying that order in intelligible form to others, his things would remain a heap of mementoes or, at best, a cabinet of curiosities. Banks, however, building on established Royal Society procedures,[8] would find both an order and ways of making it public. As a result he (among others) would stimulate men of science from all over Europe into developing new ways of conceptualising the world.

The French geographer-theorist Bruno Latour has argued that collections such as Banks's convinced Europe that it already *knew* the cultures it was exploring even before explorers returned to the places from which specimens had been brought. This was because the systematisation that took place in such collections gave Europe power to act from a distance, for they produced bodies of knowledge which reconstructed from the metropolis the time, space, history, geography, people and landscape of remote areas (Latour, p. 230). Exploration was tied to scientific zones in Europe where information would be categorised, catalogued and shrunk. One of the main purposes of these scientific zones was to provide a workplace for extending the empire. An explorer going into Egypt, or Brazil, or even the South Pacific, could visit one of Europe's scientific zones to examine maps, read previous travellers' accounts, even press his cheeks against Tahitian cloth or let African sand run through his fingers. Latour calls these scientific zones 'centres of calculation' and the way in which information was shuttled into these zones and then used by Europeans for subsequent voyages he calls the 'cycle of accumulation'.[9]

This book builds on Latour's insights by suggesting that these 'centres of calculation' and 'cycles of accumulation' were all part of complex *networks* connecting scientific zones around the world, and making them more and more dependent on dissemination. Banks, we reveal, manipulated one of the largest of these networks for the benefit of science but also on behalf of Britain's empire. He succeeded in doing so on an unprecedented scale because he mastered all the available techniques of dissemination and organisation. For instance, Banks helped make exploration writing into a scientific subdiscipline, a body of knowledge with an internal order that led men of science to trust it although they had no means of checking it. Many travel accounts included separate sections containing a generalised and supposedly objective account of some aspect of the country on which the traveller could speak with authority. Most common was a formal description of the flora and fauna, or of the customs of the native peoples. William Marsden's *History of Sumatra*, a book which exemplified the scientific style and which Banks sponsored, included both. As Mary Louise Pratt has argued, these 'manners and customs' sections often allowed a generalised stereotype about 'the Indian' to survive when the closer encounters recorded in the narrative proper tended to undermine that stereotype (Pratt, pp. 33–5). Even when the explorers were relatively sympathetic, the very form of the 'manners and customs' section suggested that the indigenous people were less than fully human. Like flora and fauna, it suggested, they could properly be assessed *en masse*, displaying the characteristics of a species rather than the complexities of human character and society. Thus, the 'manners and customs' section not only gave the writer 'scientific' authority but ensured that his specific dealings with individual native people would not, in the end, lead him to 'go native'. By such means exploration accounts prepared the way for colonisation. They made remote places imaginatively familiar enough to seem a possible and rightful home. Thus they often precipitated the subordination, removal or death of the native inhabitants on whom they lavished such minute attention. Though explorers often showed considerable empathy with the native people they discussed, and criticised the colonising culture from first-hand experience of its effects, they nevertheless for this reason served the purposes of the men who held power at the imperial centres of Europe.

It was by the classification, display and dissemination of exploration, in museum, correspondence and book, that Banks linked his scientific zones into a network. But which sciences, specifically, did this network affect? First, botany. We show that a vast trawl of plants came from the newly explored lands to London and to Kew, where Banks turned the royal gardens into a centre for classification and cultivation. These specimens gave botanists their first encounter with thousands of plants that had previously been unknown to them. Banks was helping pioneer what is now known as economic botany.[10] His network of botanic gardens that spread across the empire allowed plants to be taken from one colony and then cultivated under scientific supervision so that they could transported to another colony. This scientific practice was to intervene in global agriculture on a systematic pattern never before seen by white people. It harnessed exploration and pure science to imperialist priorities.

The Banksian network was most beneficial to the study of natural history. Armed with the host of specimens that Banks and others had placed at their disposal, natural historians were able to take their discipline into new areas. At the same time, they were able to pretend to a greater empirical accuracy than ever before. A prime instance of this occurs in the careers of the great French natural historian the Comte de Buffon and his successors. In the 1750s he had been forced, through lack of evidence, to speculate about the fauna of North America. After explorers of the 1770s had stocked their centres of calculation, Buffon's followers could access the skin and bone they needed to slot the animals of new regions into their universal systems of nature. And they did not just leave those specimens in drawers, but began to build new methodologies, and ultimately disciplines, upon them. Georges Cuvier in France, John Hunter in Britain, and J. F. Blumenbach in Germany became the leaders of a technique with enormous interpretive power – comparative anatomy. Poring over the bones that Banks and other travellers retrieved from Australia, Tahiti and North America, they learned to infer the shape and scale of the whole skeleton. Examining the internal organs too, they discovered a new way of arranging animals. Displayed in the anatomists' museums, the similarities and differences of a range of bodily structures revealed a rank order in nature.

Empowered by their technique, natural historians scrutinised both the animals and the indigenous people whom explorers had encountered. They collected and then measured their bodies and bones and some of them used these data to divide humankind into a catalogue of races that distinguished 'Caucasians' as superior and ranked 'negroes' nearer to animals than other races. Racial theory and the related disciplines of ethnology and craniometry (the measurement of skulls) gathered strength because explorers had encountered native peoples and because men such as Banks had the networks to ship these people back to Europe in the form of specimens for study – alive or dead. We devote a chapter to examining the rise of racial theory, demonstrating for the first time the extent to which it depended on a skull-collecting scheme organised by Banks. Race theory, frequently pernicious in its implications for indigenous people, depended on an international trade in their body parts.

Indigenous people came to London whole and living as well as in severed parts. In a chapter devoted to the first living Pacific islander to land in Britain, we consider the consequences for Banks's network of the visit of Omai (Mai).[11] Arriving in London with a ship from Cook's second voyage, Omai, we suggest, was Banks's chief specimen and, as such, a prize which greatly increased his prestige as a man of science. The real indigene, live in London, built the reputation of Banks's centre of calculation. But Omai also destabilised it, precisely because he was no inert object but a man, who asked questions and entered relationships. Omai would not sit still to be classified and his activity put Britons' assumptions of centrality and superiority in doubt. His exploration of Britain, we suggest, was a complex phenomenon both provoking anxieties and liberating fantasies, a phenomenon too multiple and too slippery, as human encounters are, to be easily labelled like the items hanging on the walls and stuffed into the drawers of Banks's house. As such it reveals the limitations of the centre/periphery self/other model that natural historians constructed from their collections, however powerful those collections were, in practice, at giving men of science confidence to pronounce on places they had never visited.

Banks was not stopped by the limitations of his model, but continued to accrue power. The prestige that his network brought helped Banks dominate the Royal Society and thereby impose his will over which scientific enquiry received its validation. In the 1790s, in the wake of the French Revolution, Banks refused the Society's patronage to a number of experimentalists whose politics were radical. Among these were several men who themselves influenced Romantic poets: Joseph Priestley, Thomas Beddoes and Humphry Davy, denied the Society's imprimatur, attempted instead to disseminate their work on an alternative network – provincial not metropolitan, dissenting rather than Anglican, middle-class professional rather than upper-class amateur, reformist rather than conservative.[12] Banks had once supported this network; now, distrustful of its politics, he withdrew. Yet it was on this network that the young Coleridge and Southey, for example, first broadcast their literary work, which, as a consequence, stood against the established authorities in science, state and church. The politics of literary Romanticism, in its early years, were, in effect, conditioned by the social context in which Banks, among others, forced radical natural philosophers to operate.

By the end of the eighteenth century, the alternative networks operated by Priestley, Beddoes, Darwin and others were close to collapse. Virulent attacks by the politician Edmund Burke, the satirists of the *Anti-Jacobin*, and the Edinburgh professor John Robison, made the reformist middle classes less and less prepared to welcome radical innovation. Without an audience to support their researches, young experimentalists dropped their association with radicalism and strove for a *rapprochement* with Banks and access to the metropolitan and European contexts that he influenced. So began a second phase for Romantic science and literature, as provincial radicals repositioned themselves (and their thought) so as to achieve authority in anti-Jacobin London. Such was the case with vaccination. Seen as a dangerously radical practice, vaccination was initially rejected by British scientific and medical bodies. Edward Jenner, its pioneer, was refused access to Banks's network: the Royal Society would not give his work its sanction. But soon, with the help of Romantic writers, Jenner was given a public image that had been previously developed for explorers such as Cook. It was a patriotic, rather than oppositional, image: Jenner as a *British* genius. It was Romantic but not radical: Jenner, it suggested, had been able to harness nature's powers because he was himself so attentive to nature. Jenner tried to prove as much, staging a special experiment solely to win Banks over. Impressed, Banks retracted his opposition and vaccination was loaded on to the network of imperial science, transmitted across and then beyond Britain by colonial doctors and surgeons (often of Banks's choosing) to America, India and the South Pacific. Disseminated on the scientific network, it was only subsequently adopted by colonial government. By 1833 this discovery, which had been made in a rural backwater of provincial England, had spread across the globe from London as an imperial cure and thus as a symbol of the benefits of British rule.

If the reception of vaccination was conditioned by politics within Britain as well as by the networks that spanned the empire, so, after the 1790s, was that of electrochemistry, which came to symbolise revolution because it was associated with republican France. Banks's determination to dissociate the Royal Society from radical science precipitated an alteration in the practice and political symbolism of electrochemical research, as the career of Humphry Davy reveals. From 1798 the young Davy was the assistant at the reformist medical centre Beddoes had created in Bristol. Working there, Davy operated in a context both radical and Romantic: Coleridge and Southey were his strongest supporters and viewed him as a genius capable of amending society by liberating nature's hidden healing forces. Davy followed their agenda, writing both verse tributes to the power of genius and prose speculations on the ultimate unity of mind and matter.

By 1801, Davy was on the way to London, tired of working in a situation that left him without the Royal Society's approval but with the vilification of the conservative press. He was ready to remodel his activities so as to make himself popular and powerful in the capital. He went to work at the Royal Institution, which Banks, with others, had set up. There, Davy staged spectacular demonstration lectures for fashionable audiences, placing his electrochemical researches at the heart of the establishment. He presented himself, as before, in Romantic terms – as a sublime figure working with, rather than against, nature's own powers. But there were no references to revolutionary levelling or radical mentors. He had realigned his science and its Romantic associations, in response to the institutional context that Banks had helped produce. And this makeover worked so well that in 1820, after Banks's death, it was Davy, now famous and well connected, who succeeded him as President of the Royal Society.

It is with another researcher at the Royal Institution that we conclude our book. In a discussion of the heat-saving technology that Count Rumford derived from his theoretical work, we show how the Count, along with

Banks, founded the Royal Institution as a new centre of calculation. The Institution was a design museum and research centre combined, and it was intended to gather the latest inventions into one forum. It became a centre for Romantic science whose oppositional politics had been displaced into fashionable philanthropy. It was there that Davy staged the demonstrations that made him seem a genius to the public, and it was Davy who won plaudits for turning his genius to philanthropic ends when he invented the safety lamp to stop miners being killed by underground gas. Coleridge and Southey hailed him for this achievement, for they now welcomed a project that replaced social revolution with targeted relief. In this respect, these literary Romantics of the 1790s, like their scientific peers, acclimatised themselves to the prevailing conditions that Banks and other conservative loyalists helped create. In the Royal Institution and the Royal Society, innovations that demonstrated science's beneficence towards the labouring classes, while preserving the social order unchanged, were embraced. It was in this spirit that the heat-saving technology which the Institution was founded to show off reached the public, because campaigners adopted it as a means of obviating the need to use little children as chimney sweeps. Heat-saving devices would reduce the amount of fuel burned and soot deposited, freeing the children (whom William Blake was to make so grimly famous in his *Songs of Innocence and Experience*) from the slavery of climbing up narrow and filthy chimneys until they died from accidents or of cancer. Science would facilitate social reform, the campaigners hoped, removing the guilt-inducing likeness between the soot-covered 'climbing boys' and the black West Indian slaves. Science, that is to say, was enlisted to help extirpate an exploitation of human bodies that had begun abroad, when explorers had linked Africa and the Caribbean in the colonial slave system.

LITERATURE

What led Britons, between 1768 and 1833, after two hundred years of exploring distant lands and enslaving their peoples, to campaign against slavery in the empire and exploitation at home? Religious and economic arguments played vital parts; another factor, however, was the way literary writers awakened an expanding reading public to what explorers and natural philosophers told them about the inhabitants of faraway places. *Literature, Science and Exploration* investigates this literary response in each of its chapters, revealing a central paradox: literary writers saw through the eyes of explorers and scientific writers who worked in the service of empire, yet they often used what they saw to question the material and ideological processes of imperialism. They accessed the foreign through Banks's network, yet unsettled the aims that the network was designed to serve.

But how did they do so? As they learned to look beyond British shores, some writers discovered new ways of seeing into their own humanity. They found themselves acknowledging their human kinship with the people whom Britons had, hitherto, been exploiting with few qualms. In the process they pioneered new forms of literature, forms which placed the British self in uncomfortable dialogue with the subjects of exploration and empire. Banks hitched exploration and science to empire, but the information released in the process made it possible to question empire in previously unthought-of terms. It was now possible, in short, not only to imagine a relationship with people one would never meet, but to see how such imaginary relationships could conjure up alternatives to those that pertained in most of Britain's older colonies. For these imaginary relationships had flesh-and-blood models in at least some of the explorers' encounters. Repeating Cook's journey in their mind's eyes as they read the narrative of his voyages, readers imagined his vulnerability before, shared his respect of, and acknowledged his dependence on the indigenous people he met. This was a process of imaginative participation that led readers, vicariously, to a relationship with indigenous people that, while not without its biases and blind spots, was humanitarian. By contrast, the treatment of Caribbean slaves by their fellow Britons seemed callous, brutal and shameful.

One keen opponent of colonial slavery was the poet William Cowper. As he stated in 1784, it was the virtual journey on which the narratives of Cook and Banks sent him that took him beyond the narrow perspective of self-interest.

> He travels and I too. I tread his deck,
> Ascend his topmast, through his peering eyes
> Discover countries, with a kindred heart
> Suffer his woes and share in his escapes,
> While fancy, like the finger of a clock,
> Runs the great circuit, and is still at home.
> (*Task*, book IV, lines 114–19)

Here Cowper defines the appeal of the exploration narrative with great precision. Through words and pictures (Fig. 1), it offers a virtual reality: he feels himself *there* on Cook's ship, *there* in the newly discovered country sharing the explorer's feelings and adventures. Yet he is not there, but 'still at home' – at the centre of the circle whilst 'fancy', like Cook,

Figure 1. Viewing a new country through the voyager's eyes. One of the illustrations Cowper saw. W. Watts, engraving after a drawing by W. Hodges, 'The Island of Otaheite', from James Cook, *A Voyage Towards the South Pole* (London, 1777).

circumnavigates the periphery. Cowper shows himself to be drawn imaginatively beyond himself even while he remains fixed physically at a central vantage point:

> Thus sitting and surveying thus at ease
> The globe and its concerns, I seem advanced
> To some secure and more than mortal height,
> That liberates and exempts me from them all.
> It turns submitted to my view, turns round
> With all its generationsp; I behold
> The tumult and am still.
> (*Task*, book IV, lines 94–100)

Cowper is a voyeur extraordinaire, empowered by exploration writing to occupy the still point of the turning world.

It is no coincidence that Cowper's godlike perspective on the world, gleaned from explorers' texts, appeared at the same time as Jeremy Bentham was planning a social regime based on Panopticons. These buildings were intended to produce social order by constructing an architecture that allowed inspection from a central vantage point. Seated at that point, an observer would be able to oversee the activities of the people who were placed in rooms around him. Bentham designed Panopticons for prisons, poorhouses and schools, intending to reform Britain by creating institutions that built surveillance into the social fabric.[13]

Cowper had no such scheme, yet his characterisation of reading travel narratives puts him in the same position as Bentham's central observer, not just with regard to Britain, but to the whole world. Cowper, in other words, had made a brilliant diagnosis of the way in which exploration was precipitating the technologisation of viewing from a distance. Henceforth, virtual overview would develop into a discourse of social control on an imperial as well as national scale (an essential step in the process of globalisation from which the West continues to benefit today). Reading Joseph Banks's publication,[14] he instinctively understood that printed explorations placed him, as well as men of science in London, at the centre of calculation from which overall views and so-called objective truths emanate. This made him complicit with the process by which the new world was reconstructed from afar, for the benefit of European systems of knowledge and power. But it also took him beyond the local view to which he would otherwise be limited. By giving him an extensive view of Britain's activities in the world, a view in which he had nothing personal to gain, exploration narrative enlarged Cowper's concerns.

Cowper did more than analyse exploration narratives' effects on him as a reader. He showed how they changed his practice as a writer. Throughout his work he credited travel writing with enabling him to imagine disinterested, though vicarious, relationships with people unlike himself. He described these relationships at length so that his readers could share them, and then he explicitly contrasted them to the exploitative treatment that British traders and colonisers meted out to the people of established colonies. Cowper, in other words, not only branded colonial exploitation and enslavement as the products of a national self-interestedness but imagined a disinterested alternative. He offered the ethical relationship exemplified in his own poetry as a counter example to the immoral relationships that prevailed in the existing empire.

Cowper's was a seminal achievement. The poets who succeeded him were to intensify his process of imagining disinterested relationships with the foreign. Like Cowper, they were to identify their own poetry – their own imagination, in fact – as a counter example to the self-interested discourses that sustained colonial exploitation. They understood that, given the history of exploitation of which they were conscious, it was already too late to conceive of interracial relationships wholly outside the context of colonialism, and so they pitched their imaginary scenarios as alternatives to (but also critiques of) subjection and enslavement. In this book we examine how they did so in direct and indirect reply to the view of indigenous people that was given by Banks's network. We show how Keats, Shelley and Leigh Hunt followed the gaze of Banks's African explorers only to turn the landscapes they saw into moral allegories. Responding to Park, Hornemann and Ritchie, they imagined the allure of the explorer's quest and the danger that quest turned into conquest.

So did Wordsworth, although his response to explorers was less to imagine foreigners and more to find new terms to see into himself. Exploring within, Wordsworth changed English poetry forever. *The Prelude*, as the first long poem on the growth of the poet's own mind, both revolutionised the epic and pioneered a psychoanalytic turn that no subsequent literature would ignore. Wordsworth, in effect, explored his mind while his compatriots were exploring the world. He did so, however, not in rejection of but in reflexive relation to the exploration of men such as Cook and Mungo Park. Indeed, the very form and style of his verse, as well as its narrative pulse, may, as Heather McHugh has suggested,[15] have derived from scientific exploration. Wordsworth may have owed to the chronometer that Cook used for calculating longitude his breakthrough insight into mental time. Wordsworth, like Cook reading 'the watch', locates himself in space by referring time in his present location back to time elsewhere. In *The Prelude*, time elsewhere was not time at Greenwich, but the time of his boyhood. Nevertheless, as for Cook, both times are in play at once and both are necessary for Wordsworth, emotionally and intellectually, to find his place and feel at home. He is 'two consciousnesses'; his onward journey through time and space anchored (but also directed) by the present consciousness of time past, or what he terms 'those days/ Which yet have such self-presence in my mind' (*Prelude* (1805), book II, lines 29–30).

Within Wordsworth's prosody, presence is registered by the use of parenthetic and appositional phrases that interrupt the main flow of a sentence written in the past tense. So vivid are these phrases that the reader visualises the events they narrate, making them present to the mind. The description of skating is a perfect example: the main thrust of retrospection is carried by past-tense main verbs, but it is repeatedly diverted by phrases which make the deeds of the past, boy Wordsworth, visually present. Using present participles and infinitives, Wordsworth puts the events of his childhood into potentially unlimited motion. The past is not only not finished, but it so overtakes the present narrator that it becomes as much (or more) *him* as is the adult consciousness that governs the main, retrospective, verbs.

Furthermore, because the subject of the description is motion, and the surprising insight into one's place in the world that comes when motion is arrested, the prosody effectively mirrors in its organisation of time what the verse's semantic import says about the experience of space.

> Not seldom from the uproar I retired
> Into a silent bay, or sportively
> Glanced sideway, leaving the tumultuous throng,
> To cut across the image of a star
> That gleamed upon the ice. And oftentimes
> When we had given our bodies to the wind,
> And all the shadowy banks on either side
> Came sweeping through the darkness, spinning still
> The rapid line of motion, then at once
> Have I, reclining back upon my heels,
> Stopped short – yet still the solitary cliffs
> Wheeled by me – even as if the earth had rolled
> With visible motion her diurnal round!
> Behind me did they stretch in solemn train,
> Feebler and feebler, and I stood and watched
> Till all was tranquil as a dreamless sleep.
> (*Prelude* (1805), book I, lines 474–89)

To put it simply, the boy voyages to discover his own centrality in space. He becomes, Wordsworth's final metaphor implies, a king progressing through his realm. The man, reliving the boy's progress, voyages too, overcoming his isolation in a purely present space/time by carrying in his head what Cook carried on his ship – a ceaselessly working monitor of time as it was/is in the place from which he came.

It is impossible to be certain that Wordsworth owed his stunningly original understanding of time and the self to Cook and the chronometer. There is no direct evidence to prove McHugh's stimulating speculation. It is clear, however, that explorers gave Wordsworth terms to describe mental introspection and to evoke the creative results of such introspection: in his tribute, for instance, Isaac Newton becomes a Cook of inner space, 'voyaging through strange seas of thought, alone' (*Prelude* (1850), book III, line 63). It is also clear that explorers provided him with terms for making himself at home in strange and unfamiliar territories. Carol Bolton has shown how the fourth poem in the Naming of Places sequence that appeared in *Lyrical Ballads* (1800) 'narrates a process of naming very like Cook's, where a landmark is identified in terms of Wordsworth's emotional and moral reaction to discovering it'.[16] Here is the passage concerned:

> My Friend, Myself, and She who then receiv'd
> The same admonishment, have called the place
> By a memorial name, uncouth indeed
> As e'er by Mariner was giv'n to Bay
> Or Foreland on a new-discovered coast;
> And POINT RASH-JUDGMENT is the Name it bears.
>
> (lines 81–6)[17]

Cook frequently named the islands he visited not as their native inhabitants did but so as to relate them to his own, his crew's, and his country's enterprise. Wordsworth echoes the captain and for a similar reason: he makes alien land, land already dwelt upon by others, into a place that feels to him, his companions and readers, like his own. Furthermore, by publishing that name in a poem, Wordsworth seeks to make his own designation, and his own emotional investment, supersede whatever designations and investments preceded it. 'A private name,' as Bolton puts it, 'endowed with emotional significance, claims the importance of a common universal currency.'[18] As Bolton also notes, this process is akin to the renaming that colonisers engaged in when occupying the lands that explorers had mapped out. For Wordsworth it is the Lake District, rather than Tahiti or Australia, that he wishes to occupy, but in both cases it is necessary to ignore the prior names of the existing occupants. It was arguably easier for a 'mariner', looking from a small ship at a distant coast, to name in ignorance than it was for Wordsworth, walking across a landscape owned by a few local magnates. But it was precisely for this reason that Wordsworth made the comparison. Making a language of possession stick was much easier when he could imagine himself on 'new-discovered', rather than long-appropriated, soil. And Wordsworth wanted, above all, a language of possession that would emotionally return to him the homeland from which he had been exiled. For the Lake poet, the end of exploration was to colonise the place that, when found, seemed always to have been one's own.

For Southey, Coleridge and Byron it was the later voyage of Cook's subordinate, William Bligh, that was most intriguing. We reveal how they responded to Bligh's breadfruit voyage and the mutiny on his ship, the *Bounty*. They imagined loving partnerships between the British mutineers and Tahitian women and opposed these partnerships to the tyranny they detected in the British colonies in India and the Caribbean. In other words, their poems had as their source Bligh's imperialist voyage, but derived from that source imaginary relationships that acted as contrasts to the exploitative relationships of Britain's established colonies. It was poets' capacity to imagine worlds that they had never seen, but to know that these imaginary worlds had a basis in the real – a capacity dependent on explorers' narratives – that led them to do this. And it was, in turn, these processes that Shelley had in mind when he called poets the unacknowledged legislators of the world. By imagining utopias of love, poets set out a moral, political and social model to correct the dystopian present.

Coleridge is at the centre of *Literature, Science and Exploration* as the literary writer who was most deeply engaged in contemporary science and exploration. As early as 1797 he was planning the course of this engagement, writing that 'I would thoroughly know Mechanics, Hydrostatics, Optics, and Astronomy, Botany, Metallurgy, Fossilism, Chemistry, Geology, Anatomy, Medicine – then the *Mind of man* – then the *minds of men* – in all Travels, Voyages and Histories' (*CL*, vol. VI, p. 1009). We assess his interests in many of these areas, beginning with his response to South Sea narratives, showing that he too used what Cook and Bligh wrote about Tahiti to imagine a utopia that was intended to show Britain's West Indian colonies, by contrast, to be dystopias. But we also show that Coleridge gradually turned his view of the Pacific islands in less radical directions. Our story, here, is about Romantic writers' retreat, about the later revision of their imaginary alternatives to empire into a modified imperialism. Thoroughly conversant with the natural history that Banks and his network were fostering, Coleridge became a theorist of race who argued for the natural inferiority of Pacific islanders and Africans to Caucasians. Coleridge added a twist to the theories that anatomists were building on the evidence of people's skulls. As he saw it, race relations constituted a divinely ordained interplay of natural processes working itself out in history's slow movement towards a millennial reconciliation of all humanity.

By 1833 Coleridge had put his imagination into the service of a conservative view of empire. His racial theory was his contribution to a science that was growing in power and it stood behind his suggestion that it was Britain's divine mission to colonise the inferior races: 'Colonisation', he declared, 'is not only a manifest expedient – but an imperative duty on Great Britain. God seems to hold out his finger to us over the sea' (*TT*, vol. I, p. 369). Coleridge in effect was one of the founders of Victorian imperialism. Having once seen the empire as the rape of indigenous people, having campaigned against slavery, he now, as slavery was being abolished in Britain's colonies, justified empire as the white man's god-given burden to civilise black people.

Coleridge combined an intense interest in the knowledge produced by exploration with a close awareness of the latest science in Britain. We show him linking the two in his insistence that it was creative thought, of which both science and poetry could be examples, that could direct society, opening new and prophetic routes to worlds not yet realised. Excited by Humphry Davy's electrochemistry and Edward Jenner's vaccination, Coleridge elevated the experimentalist to the level of imaginative genius. Great experimentalists and great poets, Coleridge told the public, put the imagination into concerted action. Their achievements sprang from the same mental process – a blend of meditation and observation. By exercising these faculties in tandem, they brought new bodies of knowledge into being. In the case of, say, Shakespeare, these bodies were dramas. In the case of Davy they were calculations and theories that could be checked against nature by further experiment (see *Friend*, vol. 1, pp. 470–1). This argument was, in turn, to inspire Shelley, in his *Defence of Poetry*, to claim that poets apprehend in their imaginations the relationships between elements that men of science then arrange into order.

The effect of Coleridge's psychological analysis of the creative process was to bring science and poetry into methodological proximity. Men such as Davy and Jenner were awarded Shakespearian status, their mental processes shown to be decodings of processes that were inherent in nature itself. Having defined this role for them, Coleridge declared them to be worthy to represent Britain at its best. Because Jenner and Davy willingly adopted the Romantic role Coleridge set out, and because his writings had authority in the public sphere, Coleridge shaped science's methodology and its very profile.

Although Coleridge is central to our account, he is surrounded by many others, including writers from beyond the traditional literary canon. We investigate once popular poets including Robert Bloomfield and Mary Howitt and examine campaigning balladeers such as James Montgomery and Samuel Roberts, showing how they used current science as they looked at events within Britain through eyes that explorers had opened to issues in the empire. Concluding with William Blake's juxtaposition of the British boy chimney sweep with the little black boy of Africa, we present a wide-ranging view of the literary writing that intrigued Britons between 1768 and 1833. Equally, we demonstrate how the scientific network that Banks built from Cook's legacy informed a movement that, in radically new ways, looked beyond to see within. This movement changed the course of literature so that it confronted colonial exploitation and, if it did not ultimately reject imperialism, nevertheless demanded its redefinition.

OUR METHODOLOGY AND ITS PRECURSORS

This book contributes to the interdisciplinary enquiry, involving literary critics, geographers and historians of science that has flourished since

Edward Said's *Orientalism* (1978) brought about a major shift in critical focus.[19] Two seminal post-Saidian works were Mary Louise Pratt's *Imperial Eyes* and Peter Hulme's *Colonial Encounters*.[20] Pratt and Hulme showed that, in an era of unprecedented European expansion to the East and West, exploration writing provided not just the factual data but many of the imaginative topoi which aided the development of imperialist knowledge and power. Their work has been taken up in studies such as John Barrell's *The Infection of Thomas De Quincey* and Nigel Leask's *Romantic Writers and the East*, and more recently in *Romanticism, Race and Imperial Culture* and *Romanticism and Colonialism*.[21] Together, these works show not only the increased scholarly interest in the issues surrounding exploration literature and empire in the Romantic period, but a consensus that the issues are particularly important because there was at this time no fully formed single version of imperialism and no fully crystallised stereotype about the peoples who were subjected to empire. They also show a growing scholarly dissatisfaction with the binaries of opposition into which Said's discourse organised the representations that arose out of empire and exploration. Leask and Barrell proposed a three-fold model ('this, that and the other') to replace the rigidity of what Abdul R. JanMohamed termed the 'Manichean allegory' of the binary opposition.[22] Homi K. Bhabha, meanwhile, introduced the concepts of mimicry and hybridity, arguing that the coloniser's construction of himself in opposition to the colonial other is always unsettled by that subject's mimicry of the coloniser's discourse. A disturbing hybridity haunts the colonial encounter, preventing it from ever ossifying into a settled binary and ensuring that the coloniser's assumption of centrality and superiority is continually under threat.[23]

This book also begins from the premise that the complexity and variety of representations of indigenous people cannot be accounted for by a binary model. Such a model constructs the colonising and the colonised as single, stable entities. It derogates voices of difference and criticism on both sides and has all too often been applied, with little justification, to discourses it was never intended to describe. In *Orientalism*, Said was criticising a western academic tradition that, he argued, saw itself as consistent and viewed the East as a single and stable object of enquiry. Orientalism made its own binary oppositions. The related discourses of literature, exploration and science that we investigate in this volume were not necessarily engaged in this Orientalist process.

In pursuing a post-Saidian approach to these discourses, we look to build on the work of a critic who is neglected by many literary critics of imperialism. Bruno Latour, like Michel Foucault, showed that the eighteenth-century Enlightenment produced a series of interlocking intellectual disciplines that empowered those who mastered them to reduce the world to order. But whereas Foucault portrayed these disciplines as means by which a bureaucratised state was created, a state that surveyed and controlled its individual subjects, Latour considered the way they linked individuals and centres across national boundaries.[24] He saw these disciplines as creating, rather than a centralised state, a series of dispersed centres that collected information, organised it and then disseminated it as knowledge. This knowledge was instrumental as much as theoretical: it told people how to repeat what others had already done. In particular, it showed them how to go to foreign places and to come back safely – by systematising what the first successful explorers had done and seen and so helping them predict and avoid dangers.

We build on Latour's model for several reasons. First, it is more flexible and sophisticated than that of a binary opposition, because it reveals how explorers' encounters were cycled and recycled through different, but interconnected, information-systems. Second, it allows literary and visual representations to be considered as intimate parts of a process of exploration that was both materialist and representational from the start. Very often the point of a voyage was not simply to ship materials to and retrieve commodities from a new world, but to make representations of the world so that others could visit it and know what to do when they got there. On Latour's model, narratives are not merely secondary to, or reflective of, a colonial encounter that occurs beyond and before them. They contribute to that encounter, preparing the explorers' views, shaping their motives, influencing their actions.

Latour's 'centres of calculation' produced, among other information, writings that he has taught us to see as handbooks or manuals for accessing the remote, rather than as exhaustive and accurate systematic knowledge. And although men of science such as Banks manipulated these writings so that they did fit into exhaustive and accurate systems (by editing them, by building theories from them), it nevertheless often remained possible to read them differently. Cowper could read the exploring Briton's marginality and vulnerability in Cook's description of Tahiti even though, at the same time, theorists of race were using the same account as evidence of the islanders' inferiority to whites.

While we develop Latour's approach in our study of exploration and science, we also address questions that neither Latour nor many of the historians influenced by him consider. In this respect we aim to add another element to the groundbreaking work of H. B. Carter, D. L. Mackay and John

Gascoigne, critics who have rescued Joseph Banks from neglect.[25] Carter provided a massively detailed summation of Banks's activities; Mackay discussed his imperial projects, but it was Gascoigne who found in Latour the means to see Banks as the creator of centres and networks of calculation. In extending Gascoigne's work, we aim to put Banks at the forefront of an area of scholarship that is growing fast.

Centres and networks of calculation are powerful tools for examining Banks's achievements. They are not, however, sufficient in themselves to account for all the relationships produced by exploration, especially when we turn from their effects in Britain to the events that occurred in the places the explorers visited. While from London these places appeared as a periphery reached, studied and known from an imperial metropolis that commanded it, they did not appear so to the people who lived there, people who were often considerable voyagers themselves. As Nicholas Thomas has argued,[26] the centre/periphery model fails to account for inter-island relationships, for the local interactions of indigenous and visiting people or for the revaluation of one culture by another. The Pacific islanders, for example, were accomplished improvisers and traders who put the objects they got from Banks's explorers to new uses, giving them roles and meanings never dreamt of in London. In the period covered by this book, a period before colonial government was established in the South Pacific, islanders were able to turn their relationship with visitors to strategic use. They were neither simply primitives to the civilised Britons nor victims of colonial dominance nor passive others for active exploring selves. Their activities, that is to say, eluded the centralised view that the centre of calculation offered, however efficacious that view was in allowing Britain to plan further exploration and colonisation. Here we give credit to those activities by showing how Omai, after returning to the Pacific, exchanged the tools given him in Britain for Tongan goods that he judged more likely to impress Tahitians. By a shrewd assessment of their exchange value Omai demonstrated his independence: he would not return to his native island simply to show off the objects the British had given him so as to reveal the superiority of their culture.

The cultural impact of South Sea exploration on Britain, if not in the South Seas themselves, was first treated in depth by Bernard Smith, who wrote from an art historian's perspective but considered literature too.[27] A later generation, including Philip Edwards, Neil Rennie and Rod Edmond, have brought a more incisive approach to the rhetoric of explorers and of literary writers.[28] Meanwhile, Greg Dening and Nicholas Thomas[29] have examined the relationship of textual depictions to the material expropriation of the South Pacific. Drawing on their work, and on the anthropological studies of Marshall Sahlins and Gannath Obeyesekere, we aim to produce an approach that unites sophisticated literary analysis with a materialist investigation of the means by which Britain commodified the South Pacific and the South Pacific, Britain.[30]

Recent work by James Walvin and by Henry Hobhouse, though not specifically concerned with the South Seas, shows how the study of imperial commodities can clarify the complex cultural, as well as the mercantile, relationships between coloniser and colony.[31] In studying the circulation of breadfruit and native skulls, as objects and as images, we take their work on tea, sugar and coffee as a point of departure.

One of the more popular areas of investigation for recent historians is the commodification of people's bodies in pursuit of profit. We have benefited from the work of Hugh Thomas, Philip Curtin and James Walvin on the colonial slave trade.[32] We have learned from the writing of Catherine Hall on exploitation within Britain.[33] Still more influential has been the work of historians of science who reveal how the emerging disciplines of the eighteenth century grew strong on their ability to categorise and discipline the body in systematised forms. Barbara M. Stafford, Ludmilla Jordanova and Londa Schiebinger have investigated these aspects of medicine and natural history.[34] Stephen Jay Gould has discussed the rise of craniometry.[35] Their work makes it possible to understand the emergence of racial theory in the period. It was a 'science' predicated upon ownership and objectification of the foreign bodies which, when first seen by explorers, had been fascinatingly, but also worryingly, unfamiliar. Explorers brought the bodies back; men of science measured, dissected and catalogued them. It was this process, we show, that underpinned the elaborate discussions of race that have been studied, in the contexts of philosophy and theology, by Nicholas Hudson, Robert Young, David Theo Goldberg, Hannah Augstein, David Bindman and Roxann Wheeler.[36]

In assessing the ways in which empire and exploration affected the practice and reception of science in Britain, we build on the approaches of several especially illuminating scholars. Working on chemistry and on medicine, Simon Schaffer, Jan Golinski, Patricia Fara and others have formulated a new historicism, in which science is neither viewed in isolation as a series of works of genius nor presented as a progress from incorrect to correct theories, but is studied as a collection of practices and rhetorics competing for authority in a complex social and political context.[37] Roy Porter's example[38] is also significant here: his investigations of 'quack' or pseudo-science, of, for example, Mesmerists in Britain and Thomas Beddoes's atmospheric medicine, stand behind our own discussions.

Our approach is indebted to several writers who have addressed the relationship of science with literature explicitly. It has been a topic of interest since Carl Grabo's innovative discussion of Shelley and science in 1930.[39] In the 1970s, Desmond King-Hele returned Erasmus Darwin to critical attention; subsequently David Knight explored Davy's connections with Southey and Coleridge.[40] But it was the 1981 publication of Trevor H. Levere's *Poetry Realized in Nature* that uncovered the sheer extent and depth of Coleridge's involvement in science.[41] Levere's book remains a resource, and a model, for investigation of the most scientific of all the Romantic poets. Nevertheless, there are areas of importance, to the study both of Coleridge and of Romantic-era literature in general, that Levere did not consider. Most importantly, the origin of the Romantic imagination in Coleridge's response to what explorers and men of science said of foreign bodies was beyond Levere's remit. It was left to a more recent book to broach that topic – Alan Bewell's *Romanticism and Colonial Disease* (1999).[42] This fertile study saw literary Romanticism as a reaction to anxieties about empire that centred on sickness. Disease, Bewell showed, was a material product of exploration and empire: sickness was exported round the globe by colonisers. It was a threat to Britons abroad and at home. As such, it became an apt symbol of empire's effects too. Romanticism, Bewell suggested, arose as a response to a real and symbolic empire of disease, a response that was, from its beginnings, interwoven with the discourse of contemporary medicine.

Bewell's work opened new issues for literary critics of Romanticism to consider. It is in our enquiry into Romanticism's relationship to foreign bodies, as those bodies were represented by explorers and men of science, that we develop the implications of Bewell's writing. As our subtitle *Bodies of Knowledge* indicates, the aim is to make us understand the Romantic imagination and its relationship to others in a way that is not possible without grasping, as Bewell and Latour have done, the roles of science and exploration. Our book, taking theirs as its precursors, is itself an exploration of a new kind in a still incompletely charted field.

PART I

Exploration, science and literature

CHAPTER I

Sir Joseph Banks and his networks

Many men were influential in augmenting the diet of imperialism; none more so than Sir Joseph Banks (1743–1820), a botanist, collector, traveller, adviser of monarch and ministers and President of the Royal Society. Banks combined roles formerly occupied by a number of men. He was a botanical collector on a greater scale than his predecessors James Petiver and Hans Sloane.[1] An explorer and publisher in the manner of the French Louis Antoine de Bougainville and the German Alexander von Humboldt, he had an institutional power greater than theirs. As a longer-serving President of the Royal Society than previous incumbents, he stood astride British science's most prestigious body. A Privy Councillor and adviser to the Admiralty and the East India Company, he wielded political influence as only Count Rumford among contemporary men of science (and that briefly and on a small scale) was able to do. Banks, in fact, was an embodiment of the informal power and influence that, in eighteenth-century society, a wealthy and disinterested gentleman could achieve. Belonging to no profession, dependent on no patron, employed by no company, Banks was an amateur whose vision was that science should continue to flourish as a broad, amateur practice, of immediate practical benefit to agriculture and manufactures if possible. Opposed to professional languages that excluded educated laymen, he disliked the creation of institutions outside the Royal Society that represented narrow specialisms. He was determined that gentlemen who did not themselves pursue enquiry actively should remain members, and presided over science that was researched either by gentlemen or by men whom those gentlemen patronised. By 1833 this approach had come, to new generations of professionalising and institutionalising 'scientists', to seem outdated and haphazard, hence the coining of a new name for the enquirer and the establishment of a new national body to direct research – the British Association for the Advancement of Science. The freshly named scientists, men who felt Banks had paid them and their disciplines insufficient notice, also struggled to control the Royal

Society. Eventually, they succeeded, and reform took place. That the struggle occurred and was so difficult, however, indicates both that Banks had successfully shaped the Society in his image and that by doing so he had so maintained its prestige that it was worth fighting over.

Strong in Britain's chief scientific institution, Banks was still more influential, though less visible, beyond the nation's borders. He was the unseen hand, the shadowy impresario of Britain's colonial expansion in the era before the state had created an administrative machine to run the empire. What academies and institutes did in continental Europe, Banks did for Britain. He sent explorers out to Africa, Australia, China and the North Pole. He prepared their journals for publication. He collected, classified and disseminated data and specimens, turning Kew Gardens and his Soho Square house into centres of a network that spanned the empire. It was a network designed to shape the circulation of both literary and scientific 'knowledge' about remote places and unfamiliar cultures.

The network aimed to globalise economic progress too – on the pattern of the agricultural improvement that had benefited landowners at home. As *de facto* director at Kew Gardens, Banks imported plants and seeds from remote climes, studied and propagated them in the name of science and exported them again to feed Britain's new colonies. He helped form the patterns of colonial capitalism that still shape our world today: he it was who first sent sheep and vines to Australia and organised the smuggling of tea plants from China to British India. However unlikely the product, however remote the source, Banks, it seemed, could procure it. He supplied the drugs with which Coleridge experimented: 'We will have a fair Trial of *Bang*,' wrote the poet after Sir Joseph had sent him some he had obtained from Barbary. Coleridge also intended to try opium, hensbane and Nepenthe, 'a preparation of the Bang known to the Ancients' according to Banks. Sir Joseph gave him a social and historical geography of the drug: 'The Bang, you ask for, is the powder of the Leaves of a kind of Hemp that grows in Hot Climates. It is prepared, and used . . . in all parts of the East, from Morocco to China. In Europe, it is found to act very differently on different Constitutions. Some it elevates in the extreme: others it renders torpid & scarcely observant of any evil that may befall them.'[2] The productive torpidity that released 'Kubla Khan' had, Banks's words remind us, material and Oriental origins.

For Banks, supplying drugs for Coleridge and his friends was a tiny part of his massive and lifelong project. With endless energy, he harnessed his political influence to his scientific curiosity, spanning the world with a web of colonial sites dedicated to furthering scientific knowledge. And this network, in a period marked by Britain's loss of the lucrative American colonies and by its global struggle with France, helped to spread an empire based on the desire to profit. Building on the collecting and classifying operations of predecessors such as Sloane, dedicated, like the East India Company, to expanding British commerce, it nevertheless constituted an alliance of scientific enquiry with policy and administration on an unprecedented scale. Banks created an unofficial ministry of science, empire and exploration, which anticipated the future organisation of government.[3] He shaped the imaginary of the Romantic period because he manipulated processes by which far-flung countries were made available for penetration by European commerce and colonisation. Importer of drugs, plants and seeds, publisher of explorers' narratives, he gave Britons a taste of exotic lands and then sent them out to conquer the places they had consumed from afar. He opened mental geographies within the minds of Britons that seemed to place foreign realms within their knowledge and power.

Banks's power grew from a small seed – from his schoolboy hobby of botany. The fertile ground was provided by the Chelsea Physic Garden and the British Museum, where he absorbed the knowledge of the foremost botanists and scholars in Britain. Nourishment came from Banks's wealth: at twenty-one he inherited 10,000 acres of rich agricultural land. Equipped to turn his hobby into a vocation, Banks set out for the coast of Newfoundland and Labrador where he collected 340 species of plants and 91 of birds, besides fishes, insects and soil.[4] His intention was to make his name by advancing the burgeoning science of natural history.

As it turned out, the Newfoundland journey was just a practice run, for in 1768 Banks used his money and influence to get himself a place on the most ambitious scientific expedition Britain had ever mounted. He announced, 'my grand tour shall be one round the whole globe': he would complete his education by sailing with Captain Cook through the South Pacific, exploring Tahiti, circumnavigating New Zealand and landing at Botany Bay for the first time.[5] The voyage became as much Banks's as Cook's, for he took with him a retinue of botanists, collectors and artists with the aim of netting and recording every new species within reach. The results were spectacular: Banks and his employees gathered 30,000 specimens of plants and 1,000 of animals, all carefully preserved, drawn, painted and listed.[6]

Collections need classification if they are to attain the status of systematic knowledge. In the eighteenth century, no system had more followers than that of the Swedish botanist Linnaeus, 'that God of my adoration' as Banks

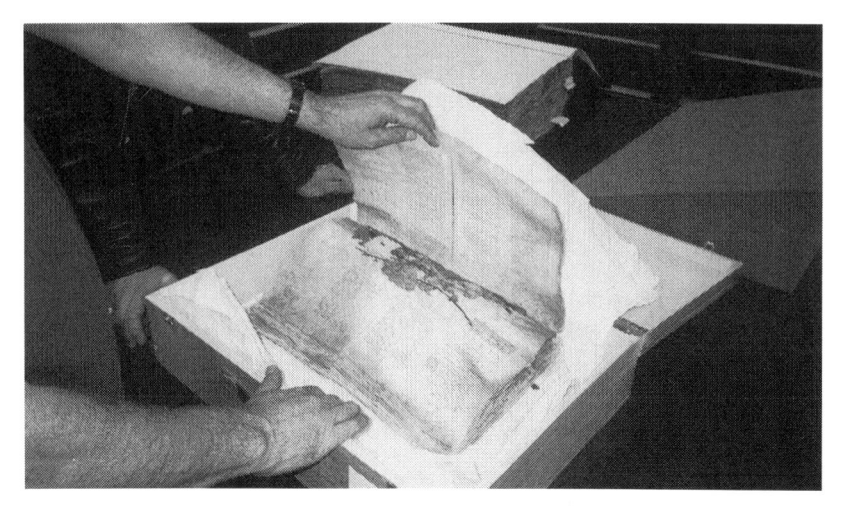

Figure 2. A specimen collected on the *Endeavour* voyage, preserved between proof sheets of Addison's *Spectator* essay on *Paradise Lost*. In the herbarium, Natural History Museum, London.

called him.[7] Linnaeus set the natural world in order in his *Systema naturae*. This system, a procedure of classifying plants and animals into genera and species, enabled European scholars to navigate with relative ease the tangled mass of information compiled in voyage after voyage to the new world and the East.[8] Linnaeus's method turned Banks the collector into Banks the systematiser:[9] when the South Sea specimens were classified (with the help of one of Linnaeus's students), Banks had increased the number of known plant species by nearly 25 per cent, introducing such plants as *Gaultheria mucronata* and the everlasting flower *Helichrysum bracteatum* (Fig. 2). He had discovered 110 new genera, one (*Banksia*) named after him to this day (Fig. 3). The great Linnaeus himself was overwhelmed. Banks's collection, he wrote, was 'matchless and truly astonishing'.[10]

Banks's collection thus gave him the admiration of international science. But what gave him his lasting importance was his ability to set it up in a web of classified information centred on himself, a web dedicated not just to spreading scientific knowledge but to fostering Britain's international growth. It was a web that depended on an established Royal Society practice that Banks dramatically expanded – correspondence.[11] Banks sent over 20,000 letters across Europe, America and the colonies in his efforts to bring the natural productions of the entire globe – and the profits that might accrue from them – within his view.[12] Even more than on correspondence,

Figure 3. A contemporary engraving of a *Banksia*. James Sowerby, 'Banksia Spinulosa', from James Edward Smith, *A Specimen of the Botany of New Holland* (London, 1794).

however, Banks's web relied on publication. A letter from Linnaeus's son clearly reveals Banks's determination to use his resources to give systematic science widespread appeal:

> [my purpose] is only to continue the system, only to determine the plants' genera and species and thereby preserve the already started central book [*Systema naturae*] . . . but Banks, who has money, wants to illustrate these with descriptions and figures.[13]

The younger Linnaeus was referring to the *Florilegium*, Banks's attempt to publish the botanical collections of the Cook voyage in fourteen volumes of illustrations.[14] Deploying his great wealth, Banks turned his house into a workshop of reproduction. For close on twenty-seven years, as many as ten engravers worked in a back room experimenting with the latest methods. They were striving to achieve the most accurate and beautiful reproduction possible of the visual record of the Cook voyage – '987 plants drawn and coloured by Parkinson; and 1300 or 1400 more drawn with each of them a flower, a leaf, and a portion of the stalk, coloured by the same hand; besides a number of other drawings of animals, birds, fish, etc'.[15] Their work would let Banks turn Linnaeus's system sensual, would supplement description with depiction, delighting European eyes by representing the exotic flora of the South Seas in its overwhelming entirety. The latest technologies of reproduction would bring unfamiliar plants, in all their sensual beauty, within Europe's imaginative grasp.[16]

It was not only through sumptuously illustrated science like the *Florilegium* that Banks sought to open new continents to the European imagination. It was also through the publication of popular narratives of the explorations that he sponsored. His own journal of the Cook voyage formed the core of the account written by John Hawkesworth (1773). Hawkesworth, however, embarrassed the voyagers by spicing the account with hints that Banks, amongst others, had sampled the varied sexual, as well as botanical, delights of Tahiti. And he alienated the public by adding his own, speculative, views. As a result, Banks became an object of satirical attacks. He also became a public symbol of the explorer 'gone native', the gentleman whose scientific desire to record an exotic place led him into adopting the 'primitive' and immoral customs of its inhabitants.[17]

Banks took steps to ensure he never again lost control of the way exploration of the new world was presented to western eyes. He ensured that he had a supervisory role over all the narratives of the expeditions with which he was associated – effectively over most of the major British expeditions between 1774 and 1820, whether to Africa, Australia, China, North America or the North Pole.[18] The travel books were carefully prepared to excite public interest without embarrassing the explorers. The dignity of the aim of increasing scientific knowledge had to be protected from the temptation to pander to a mass reading public which craved sensation. For the burgeoning publishing industry was marketing remote regions to the European public on an unprecedented scale. Readers consumed travel narratives, and devoured danger from the comfort of their homes. William Cowper summed up the excitements of this mental travel:

> He travels and expatiates, as the bee
> From flower to flow'r, so he from land to land;
> The manners, customs, policy of all
> Pay contribution to the store he gleans,
> He sucks intelligence in ev'ry clime,
> And spreads the honey of his deep research
> At his return, a rich repast for me.
> (*Task*, book IV, lines 107–13)

Cowper's poem exemplifies what, according to John Gascoigne, was a conceptual shift. It shows 'the extent to which the natural world [was] refashioned in a scaled-down', and thus accessible, form.[19] The world could be shrunk to a quarto, a map, a botanical engraving sitting on a desktop, and the traveller's fame was directed, like it or not, by the homebound public's hunger for geographic novelty, as Robert Montgomery suggested in *The Age Reviewed* (1827).

> Columbian deeds in story scarcely reign,
> E'en Cook and Otaheite are on the wane:
> So fast learn'd vagabonds defame the earth,
> So fast their blund'ring quartos spring to birth!
> (lines 103–6)[20]

Banks felt the hunger for new discoveries. But, rather than be consumed by it, he fed it. In London, Banks's 'centre of calculation', Banks imported data and objects through which 'some traces of the travel . . . [went] back to the place that sent the expedition away'.[21] He classified, depicted and reproduced these returned fragments of foreign cultures, so that they became a code that could be used, again and again, to make the distant appear familiar. His systematised, illustrated and published collection allowed natural philosophers and explorers to access specimens of foreign cultures, specimens that, having been classified and reproduced, could be compared and contrasted with each other in a way not possible within each of the cultures from which they had been derived. Prepared and guided by this virtual experience, explorers could then go abroad again, exporting to those foreign cultures the versions of them they had constructed at home.

NETWORK CENTRES

Banks's main 'centre of calculation' was his house. If France had the Institut national for the scientific study of other cultures, Britain had Banks's backyard – or rather the complex of offices and storerooms built over his backyard to preserve his collection. No. 32 Soho Square, a house just 18 feet

Figure 4. Banks's home as a warehouse of the exotic. Engraving, 'Sir Joseph Banks at Dinner', from Peter Pindar, *Peter's Prophecy* (London, 1788).

wide, defied its dimensions. It was Banks's home, but it was also an Aladdin's cave of the exotic (Fig. 4). In one room, Banks had 'warlike instruments, mechanical instruments and utensils of every kind, made use of by the Indians of the South Seas'; in another his herbarium – thousands of dried plants preserved in purpose-designed cases and painstakingly catalogued.[22] The house was a bustle as Banks's staff and protégés reproduced the fruits of his travels and arranged the seeds and specimens, the letters and documents that poured in from gardeners, politicians and men of science from all over the world. A librarian worked full-time to catalogue what has been called the greatest natural history library in the world of its time, containing at least 22,000 items.[23] Fully open to scholars, it also held hundreds of maps and travel narratives, effectively becoming a repository of remote places as reconstructed by European knowledge-systems. As if finding the world in a grain of sand, natural philosophers, dignitaries, politicians and explorers discovered there a microcosm of the nature and culture of distant lands. When they travelled to those lands, when they wrote about them, when they colonised them, their view was already shaped by the perspective they had acquired in Soho Square. Mungo Park spent weeks there poring over travel books, maps and manuscripts that presented the latest European view of Africa's hidden interior. The settlement of Australia was planned in Soho Square. Close to the British Museum and to Westminster, Banks's home gave him a semi-institutional position not only as patron of European science but as adviser to government. His 'perfect museum' made him the most powerful man of science living.[24]

Power grew not just in Soho but at Kew. A friend of the King, Banks had at his disposal the Royal Gardens. Here he cultivated seedlings from around the world – increasing the species held from 3,400 to 11,000 – and watched as Britain's knowledge expanded by way of foreign 'growth'. At this central point plants were classified ready for redistribution across the world.

NAVIGATING THE NETWORK

Banks's network extended across the world along its rivers. From Soho Square and Kew Gardens, on the banks of the Thames, it flowed up river valleys into the heart of lands uncharted by Europeans. In Tahiti Banks had explored the Vaipopoo river into the interior. There, the islanders fished with baskets and nets in the stream as he was later to do in Lincolnshire. Not only did Banks import fishing technology from the Vaipopoo: he also brought back rocks which mineralogical analysis showed to be volcanic. Thus the very origin of this unfamiliar land was opened to European knowledge by Banks's trip up-river. The flow of knowledge was reversible: rivers opened the island to European ideas and technologies. In 1777 shaddock trees were planted in the upper Vaipopoo valley. These had been imported from the Friendly Islands by David Nelson, the gardener Banks had chosen to accompany Captain Cook's third Pacific voyage. In 1792 these shaddocks were 'teeming with fruit'.[25] Banks's river-system flowed both ways: the shaddocks brought up-river were part of his effort to increase Tahiti's prosperity by extending its food supply, goals he pursued actively on his own farms in Lincolnshire. Not for the last time, the islanders proved less open to Banks's imports than were their river valleys. They were reluctant to eat the shaddocks, careless of the English passion for agricultural improvement.

Improvement remained, despite all setbacks, Banks's obsession. He developed on an intercontinental stage agricultural schemes like those that had brought wealth to his fellow landowners in England's eastern counties. Central to those schemes was the introduction of new crops. In 1798 he had eighteen boxes of plants, intended to equip the first colonists of Australia, carried from Kew Gardens down the river Thames to Long Reach, where HMS *Porpoise* lay at anchor. One of the boxes contained the 'Wooginoos', a plant the Abyssinians used against dysentery. The Wooginoos had been brought to Britain by James Bruce, who had encountered it on his exploration of the Blue Nile. Banks had cultivated it at Kew and given it a Linnaean name, *Brucea antidysenterica*. Imported to Britain from an African river, re-exported round the world from the Thames, the plant would, Banks hoped, spread the colony up the river valleys of Australia: 'it is impossible to conceive', he wrote to the colony's prospective governor, 'that such a body, as large as all Europe, does not produce vast rivers, capable of being navigated into the heart of the interior'.[26]

Rivers were routes for exploration and streams of information linking Soho and Kew with the Pacific islands, with the river valleys of Australia and with the great rivers of Africa. They made the world a navigable network centred on the banks of the Thames. Banks kept a jar of Nile sediment at Soho Square: it was a souvenir of Bruce's successful exploration of that mighty river, and a symbol of the secrets of nature that his chosen explorers might bring back from those other African rivers, the Niger and the Congo.

SPREADING THE SEEDS

Banks's influence extended across the globe along rivers, but to flourish and multiply it required gardens and gardeners.[27] 'Imperial Kew', as Erasmus Darwin called it, formed a centre of the overlapping networks of men and materials on which Banks's empire of knowledge, and the British empire of commerce, depended.[28]

The men were as important as the materials they manipulated. And Banks was just as careful to control them personally. He disseminated botanists like the seeds they tended: 'I can always', he wrote, 'supply a Kew Gardiner in half a week.'[29] In 1791 gardeners from Kew were sent to collect breadfruit for transplantation to the West Indies, where the planters needed an inexpensive food source for their slaves. The ministry gave Banks his choice of commander as well as gardeners. Captain Bligh was accompanied by James Wiles and Christopher Smith. Banks gave the gardeners detailed instructions to ensure the success of the plant transfer. They were to bring plants back to Britain as well as the West Indies. And they were to ensure that they remained in the hands of the authorities, for the plants were essential to the future prosperity of a British empire that was competing with the French:[30] 'never quit them', Banks wrote, 'till you have delivered them to his Majesty's Botanic Gardener at Kew, who will be ready at Kew bridge to receive them; & you are particularly to take notice that no plant, cutting, layer, sucker, or part of Plant, be, on any condition whatever, taken away by any other person, but that the whole be safely & carefully delivered to his Majesties use'.[31] In the event Wiles was allowed to stay in the West Indies to supervise the growth of the breadfruit there: thus Banks exported expertise from his network centre even as he imported plants back to Kew.

As a landowner, gentleman and Knight of the Bath, Banks assumed that it was his prerogative to direct the lives of those in his employ. He could, and did, 'supply' Kew gardeners, trained botanists, explorers, ships' captains and even colonial governors to staff his spreading network. The Banksian empire extended across the globe the systems of stewardship and patronage by which the eighteenth-century aristocracy administered Britain. At the same time, it pioneered the development of bureaucratic data-gathering structures by which nineteenth-century imperial government was to extend its power at home and abroad. The men who worked on Banks's behalf around the globe acted very much as did the steward of his estates at Revesby Abbey, James Roberts (who had himself been round the globe with Banks on the *Endeavour*).[32] Characteristically, Banks expected thoroughness: in 1797 the agricultural writer Arthur Young was staggered by the extent and order of the records kept at Revesby. Banks's steward held catalogued information in 156 drawers of Banks's own design. 'Whether', Young declared, 'the enquiry concerned a man, or a drainage, or an enclosure, or a farm, or a wood, the request was scarcely named before a mass of information was in a moment before me.'[33]

Banks expected detailed reports from his steward so that, although he visited Revesby for only a few weeks each year, he retained effective control of what went on there. He was an absentee landlord who, by virtue of the statistics and observations communicated to him by mail, became a *deus ex machina*. But he was a benevolent (or paternalist) god, who rewarded men who served him well. So too in his worldwide botanical network. A 1796 letter from Francis Robson, deputy governor at St Helena, revealed Banks's postal system in action. Robson reported 'with the greatest regret and concern' the 'death of my valuable acquaintance, Colonel Gordon at the Cape, who shot himself, this has cut off all my resources of Plants from thence. All my Plants of Fern Trees are also dead'.[34] Despite Gordon's inconsiderate interruption of the network, and four months of drought, Robson was, he assured Banks, still planting. And in return for his loyal service he asked Banks to influence the East India Company to procure his son 'a writer's appointment either to Madras or Bombay'.

Banks's influence, like his plants, spread from Africa to India, from London to St Helena. Robson and the other botanic gardeners nurtured Banks's transplanted seedlings in the hope that one part of Britain's empire might grow fat (and rich) on the plants native to other parts. Vines and Merino sheep went to New South Wales. Date trees were brought to India from Persia with the aim of protecting Britain's colonies from famine. Tea plants were smuggled to India in the hope of breaking Britain's financially ruinous dependence on China for its favourite drink.[35] All were to be nurtured in the botanic garden specially established by the East India Company for the purpose of 'promoting the cultivation of articles useful to the manufacturers of Great Britain & consequently important to the Investments of India'.[36] Banks's botanic gardens were seedbeds for a newly global capitalism. They were designed for 'the aggrandisement of the power and commerce of Great Britain', by giving the nation a commercial advantage over its trading rivals.[37]

The East India Company's garden hit a snag. The proposed site in Calcutta was already occupied by local widows who resisted the Company's efforts to move them.[38] The widows were paid off and moved whether they liked it or not. Banks and the Company got their garden where they wanted it. Sometimes, however, the peoples who were subjected to imperialism threatened Banks's network by active as well as passive resistance. In the West Indies slave rebellions made the botanic gardens contested ground. In 1796 Banks's man in St Vincent, Alexander Anderson, was forced to abandon his plot. He wrote to Banks like an anxious steward reporting to an exacting landowner who he fears will not be inclined to accept war and rebellion as adequate reasons for neglect of duty:

> The unhappy situation of this Island for 12 months past has made me remiss in my duty to you, but I am sure, when you consider the anxiety's and miserys, I, as well as every one else has experienced here, your goodness will forgive my seeming inattentions, and you will certainly be happy in hearing that the Garden has remained safe, & is now in the most flourishing state: as it is my charge & almost only concern you can easily judge my feelings when three times obliged to abandon it with little hopes of ever seeing it more, but at a distance a mass of ruins.[39]

Banks used his influence to ensure Anderson received recognition for his efforts. He was given the Silver Medal of the Society of Arts and was praised by the Royal Society as a result of a report communicated to it by Banks, its president.[40] Banks's network was sustained by such methods, by the ability of Sir Joseph himself to pull enough strings at the imperial centre to keep his far-flung estates and their stewards, as well as the plants they tended, in flourishing condition.

Banks was a dominant figure in science in Britain as well as across the empire. It is, however, the far-flung estates that we are concerned with in this first section of *Literative, Science and Exploration*. In the following chapters, we investigate Banks's explorers and gardeners spreading his network into Africa, India and the West Indies. We show him shaping the course of botany, natural history and race theory, as well as influencing colonial trade and administration. We show him collecting artefacts and people from the Pacific islands, forging his reputation as a man of science in the years after the *Endeavour* voyage. And we examine the effects of this collecting on the Tahitians he collected and on Britons back home. Both in the Pacific and in Britain, the people who responded to his activities gave them unexpected twists, enhancing their power in their own cultures by turning their encounters with Banksian knowledge in directions Sir Joseph himself did not take. Thus, in Britain, Banks's projects helped give rise to literary Romanticism (inflecting its political concerns, its symbolism, its very content) while in Tahiti they gave some islanders opportunities to voyage, explore and build their own centres of calculation. It is on one such islander, Omai, that we focus next.

CHAPTER 2

Tahiti in London; London in Tahiti: tools of power

Sir Joseph Banks was fortunate. In the late eighteenth century no city on earth was better placed to give an explorer fame and fortune, or to house a centre for accessing remote cultures, than Britain's capital. In London, the exotic was already at home; feeding on the wealth gleaned from tropical lands, its shops offered spectacular displays of 'absolutely everything one can think of . . . in such abundance of choice as . . . to make one greedy'.[1] Visiting Europeans were amazed: London made their own metropolises seem dull. It was a 'continuous fair', overflowing with 'the whim-whams and fribble-frabble of fashion'.[2] By the 1770s, colonial commodities had made the city a catwalk for commercial capitalism. The newspapers then spread the fashions through the country. When what came to be called 'Polynesian'[3] costumes collected by Cook were exhibited in Leicester Square, within days their cut and colour was being discussed in the drawing rooms of middle England.

To London came the fruits of exploration and empire, and the profits that stemmed from those fruits. From at the end of the seventeenth century, and gathering pace as the eighteenth wore on, sugar, tobacco, tea, coffee and chocolate changed British society from its capital outwards. Coffee shops and chocolate houses became the new social centres for gentlemen, while ladies made tea and sugar the focus of a social ritual over which they presided.[4] Many of these polite classes gained their wealth, directly or indirectly, from the very imperial commodities they liked to taste. This wealth allowed them to spread a commercial culture of conspicuous and fashionable consumption.

If the new London consumed colonial crops, it also featured live imports. Fruits and spices were displayed in shops and on stalls; so were exotic animals, as Wordsworth discovered on his first visit to the city in 1791. Foreign people appeared in this great exhibition too – dead or alive. Londoners could ogle shrunken heads collected from Maori warriors or stare, as Wordsworth did, at the visitors who walked the streets:

>   from remote
> America, the hunter-Indian; Moors
> Malays, Lascars, the Tartar and Chinese,
> And Negro Ladies in white muslin gowns.
>   (*Prelude* (1805), book VII, lines 240–3)

Like explorers in a remote island, visitors to the metropolis were spectators of powerfully strange peoples. Indian jugglers swallowed swords; Mohawks performed the war-whoop. Black people feigned the bewitching bodies of West Indian obeah-men. To Wordsworth the city was a 'raree-show' of 'specimens' (*Prelude* (1805), book VII, lines 236, 190), to Cowper a 'resort and mart of all the earth', a 'crowded coop' holding 'all complexions of mankind' (*Task*, book III, lines 834–6). Likewise, to the Unitarian poet Anna Barbauld, London was a place of racial diversity 'where the turbaned Moslem, bearded Jew,/ And woolly Afric, met the brown Hindu' (lines 165–6).[5]

If London was a showhouse of the exotic accessed by British voyagers, the colonies were themselves becoming saturated by British manufactures. In the process indigenous peoples learnt to become consumers. As James Walvin has shown, the 'first people to experience a consumer revolution, the first to devour European goods on a prodigious and transforming scale', were Africans and North American Indians.[6] Buying British knives, pots, hatchets and guns, these people were no longer subsistence farmers or hunters but commercial traders. In Canada some tribes ceased hunting almost completely and became middlemen, buying pelts from remote tribes and selling them on to the British at their forts on Hudson's Bay. The Indians took firearms, utensils and knick-knacks back to their homelands: their 'desire of new-fangled novelties' changed their society, and its relationship to the land and its animals, irrevocably. A culture of consumption and display spread back from Britain to the countries it explored and exploited so that by 1821, when John Crawfurd travelled to Siam (a country scarce visited by Britons for 150 years) he saw Buddhist monks decorating their monasteries with prints of foxhunting in the English shires.

The mutual influence between Britons and indigenous peoples – where goods, and thus representations, were cycled and recycled, where centre and periphery both shaped the process of globalisation and, in the process, changed their relationship – is our subject in this chapter. We focus, in particular, on two encounters, one between the colonialist Stamford Raffles and the people of Java, another between a Pacific islander and the British public. Both encounters spanned distant islands and the metropolis of London.

It is in the capital that we begin, with the visit of a South Sea 'specimen' that did not arrive pressed between the pages of a book or pinned to a board, a 'specimen' that lived, breathed and talked – the human 'specimen' Omai (Mai)[7] – a real islander who voyaged to Britain, explored it and returned, changed, to Tahiti. Omai, we suggest, was far more than another 'curiosity' in Banks's collection. He was a discoverer for himself – and for his own culture – just as Banks and Cook were for themselves and for British culture. And what he discovered (and what Britons discovered by encountering him) altered not just each people's relationship with the other but also their attitudes and actions towards themselves. Here, we retrace Omai's view of Britain before assessing what different Britons made of him (McCormick, p. 20).[8] We focus on the literary responses to his visit, showing that he provoked a range of works that criticised British culture in his name – the most searching of which was *The Task*, in which William Cowper used him to make the era's most prescient critique of the globalising capitalism that drove exploration.

If Britons made much out of Omai, so did he out of them. His voyage empowered him just as theirs did Cook and Banks, who won prestige and promotion in Britain as a result of what they saw and described in the South Seas. And Omai was only one of the first of many islanders to effect changes at home by his use of the opportunities that a rapidly developing intercultural knowledge provided.[9] For example, not only Britons but also Tahitians collected newly encountered objects, practices and ideas – and put them to unexpected uses. In effect, the implements of each culture became what we call 'power tools' in the other. By 'power tools' we refer to the practices, ideas and objects that gave those who acquired them cultural capital or allowed them to make social interventions. And we intend by the concept to address an issue that is not addressed in Bruno Latour's model of scientific exploration (detailed in chapter 1). Latour's emphasis on centre and periphery takes little notice of the effects (either for the individuals concerned or for larger groups) that using these power tools had within each culture. Here we supplement Latour's model by making a detailed investigation of these effects at their most human (and therefore most complex). In short, we examine Omai in order to open Banks's network, and the globalising capitalism that it assisted, to a critique from the stance of an indigenous person who used it for his own ends.

A youth when the *Endeavour* arrived in 1769, Omai did not at first come to the notice of the British. He was was not from the high-ranking *arii* class but the less important *raatira*, and was, in any case, a landless refugee who had fled from the neighbouring island, Raiatea, when the Boraborans invaded. Indeed, it was not until Cook returned, without Banks, on his second circumnavigation in 1773, that Omai came to his attention. On leaving Huahine (Tahiti's neighbouring island), Cook discovered that the young man had been on board the ship of his second-in-command, Captain Furneaux, since it first arrived on 3 September. With Furneaux's approval, Omai was allowed to remain on the *Adventure* and to sail with the expedition towards New Zealand, Antarctica and Britain.

Omai's motives for putting himself in the Britons' hands related to his status as a refugee on Tahiti.[10] He wanted to end his landless exile there. He had witnessed the effect of British guns at first hand and now said he was 'going to *Britannia* to get poopooe's [guns] of the Aree [chiefs]'.[11] With these ultimate power tools he would re-take his native island from the Boraborans, gaining land, status and a home in the process. For Omai, it seems, exile in Tahiti was less comfortable than he wished. If British reports are correct, then he was trying to escape Tahitian prejudice, having left the island 'because his countrymen teised him about his Nose being flatter than other peoples'.[12] Out of place, resentful, Omai was determined to transform his situation by using Britain's superior technology of violence.

Once on board, Omai became the subject of prejudiced comments from the voyagers. Cook termed him 'dark, ugly and a downright blackguard' while the naturalists Johann and Georg Forster thought him of 'the darkest hue of the common class of people'.[13] To the officers and gentlemen, used to socialising with the *arii*, who took care to avoid the sun, Omai's blackness marked him out as vulgar. He was not an honoured guest but a common 'Jack', like one of the rough, brown seamen who worked Cook's vessels.

Omai arrived in London on 14 July 1774 and was delivered into the care of the by now acknowledged expert on the newly explored Pacific – Banks. At first, Sir Joseph shared Cook's view of the man. In the words of Daniel Solander, Banks's fellow voyager and curator of his collection, Omai was neither handsome nor high-ranking:

He is very brown, almost as brown as a Mulatto. Not at all hansome, but well made. His nose is a little broadish, and I believe that we have to thank his wide Nostrils for the visit he has paid us – for he says, that the people of his own country laughed at him upon the account of his flattish Nose and dark hue, but he hopes when he returns and has many fine things to talk of, that he shall be much respected.[14]

Banks and Solander knew enough Tahitian to learn from Omai that he had voyaged, just as they had done, not just from curiosity but to win respect at home. He intended to use his trip as a tool to overcome the colour prejudice that, he felt, led islanders to look down on him. And if initially his hosts shared this prejudice, they soon revised their judgement as it became clear that in Britain Omai was the opposite of what he was

Figure 5. Omai as public figure in London. Engraving, 'Omai, A Native Of Otaheite brought to England by Captain Fourneaux' (1774), from *London Magazine*, August 1774.

Figure 6. Benjamin West, portrait of Sir Joseph Banks (1771).

in Tahiti. On the Pacific island he was unremarkable, unnoticed by the chiefs and British commanders. In Britain he was the only Pacific islander ever to have appeared in the flesh. Everyone of note in London wanted to meet him, and Banks, with Omai's eager co-operation, exploited his rarity value, becoming the impresario of his tour of high society. Omai was soon Banks's prize specimen, the crown jewel of his Pacific collection as a living representative of a culture that had previously been accessible in the artefacts that Banks was still classifying in his museum and illustrating in engravings (Fig. 5). If one wanted to meet, measure or examine Omai – and men of science from all over Europe did want to – one approached Banks. In a mutually advantageous relationship, Banks used Omai, the most powerful tool yet retrieved from the Pacific, to establish himself as *the* pre-eminent British expert through whom Tahiti could be accessed. Omai, for his part, received the attention, respect and weapons that he desired.

The nature of the relationship shines out of two portraits that Banks commissioned: one of Omai (from his friend, the society painter Sir Joshua Reynolds), one of himself (from the fashionable portraitist Benjamin West). In the West picture (Fig. 6), the young explorer appears romantically posed

Figure 7. Johann Jacobe, engraving, after Sir Joshua Reynolds, 'Omai, a Native of the Island of Utietea [i.e. Ulietea]' (1780).

full-length, clothed in a Maori mantle, and surrounded by the indigenous objects that he, and nobody else in Britain, possessed. These rare commodities not only exoticise Banks but signify his claim to public notice. Ordinary in Tahiti, they are precious in Britain for they give Banks credibility as an expert on Pacific cultures. Thus they are not neutral or static objects, of interest only in providing anthropological knowledge of a faraway culture, but tools with which Banks could gain leverage in the scientific culture of Britain. It was, in part, because of his ability to display his expertise on far-flung places that Banks won, in November 1773, election to the Council of the Royal Society.

Banks enhanced his reputation still further because he could present Omai to men of taste as well as science, and he did so with care, as Reynolds's idealised portrait reveals (Fig. 7). Here Omai is no 'ugly, dark blackguard' but an eastern prince, a noble savage dressed to look Romantic rather than to be accurate. Like Banks in the companion portrait, Omai stands full length in exotic surroundings yet in classical pose. He is a figure of dignity to be admired rather than a native to be condescended to or a specimen to be measured.[15] Reynolds exhibited the picture at the Royal Academy in May 1776, showing that he considered it worthy to stake his artistic reputation upon. Together, the Tahiti-ised Banks and classicised Omai gave their subjects comparable aesthetic and social stature.

As if to ram the message home, Banks commissioned a former pupil of Reynolds, William Parry, to make a portrait featuring both voyagers, as well as Banks's assistant. In 'Sir Joseph Banks with Omai, the Otaheitian Chief and Dr Solander' (1776) (Fig. 8), the baronet and the Polynesian dominate the picture together. They are linked by their similar poses and by Banks's hand, which almost touches Omai's. The islander's white robes and Banks's black suit show them as complementary opposites, men of command from different cultures whose significance is joined, hand to hand. The picture represents what, by its very existence, it is designed to promote – the authority of the two men and the dependence of that authority on their mutual relationship. Solander, seated, is by comparison a subordinate figure, though the fact that Banks is looking towards him rather than at Omai indicates that Sir Joseph remembers his scientific interests. It is to the botanist Solander, Linnaeus's student, that Banks is displaying Omai's tattoo (one of the Tahitian features that most intrigued Britons).[16] Solander, presumably, is copying the tattoo onto the paper lying on the desk – capturing the symbols on a European medium, but divorcing them from the body that, in the Pacific, gave them their cultural meaning. Omai, in effect, is Banks's partner but also, as his prime specimen,

Figure 8. William Parry, oil, 'Sir Joseph Banks with Omai, the Otaheitian Chief and Dr Solander' (c. 1776).

the unique tool with which he and Solander demonstrate their scientific expertise.

Banks's publicity pictures worked, for it was to him as guardian of Omai that natural historians applied. One picture of the visitor went to the anatomist John Hunter, who collected likenesses of native peoples so as to catalogue humanity into races (Fig. 9). Another went to Germany when, in 1794, J. F. Blumenbach wrote asking for a 'striking characteristical likeness' of a Tahitian to use as supporting evidence in his latest book-project – the anatomical illustration of his classification of humanity into five distinct races.[17] Banks sent him an original miniature painted during Omai's stay in London. Using this and an engraving of Reynolds's idealised portrait, Banks was able to illustrate the typical Tahitian racial type in his

Figure 9. An engraving of Omai after a drawing made by William Hodges in preparation for the oil portrait that still hangs in the Hunterian Museum at the Royal College of Surgeons. J. Caldwall, engraving, 'Omai' (1777), published in James Cook, *Voyage Towards the South Pole*.

Objects of Natural History Illustrated (this despite the fact that those who lived on or travelled to Tahiti abused Omai for his abnormally dark colour and flat nose). Omai, as the only living Tahitian accessible through the London centre of calculation, was made to embody a whole, anatomically determined race, a race that, as London surgeon William Lawrence argued when reproducing an engraving of Omai as an illustration of the 'Malay Variety' of mankind, was agreed to be inferior to the white, Caucasian, one.[18]

Men of science were not alone in wanting to see Omai. The islander had arrived in London at the right time. The narrative of Cook's and Banks's voyage was just published, making Tahiti hot news. The reading public was fascinated by three aspects of Tahitian culture. First, its abundant fruit, which seemed to free the inhabitants from the biblical injunction that man should work for his bread. 'These happy people', Banks wrote, 'may almost be said to be exempt from the curse of our forefather; scarcely can it be said that they earn their bread with the sweat of their brow when their chiefest sustenance Bread fruit is procurd with no more trouble than that of climbing a tree and pulling it down.'[19] Tahitians, it was believed, simply plucked their food fresh from the trees. Second, its sexual freedom – Cook and Banks described exotic dances followed by lovemaking with supple maidens who seemed free to sleep with whomever they chose. Third, its apparently noble savages. Free from work, free (it seemed) from war, strikingly handsome, Tahitians seemed to be blessed inhabitants of a sensual Eden, a new Cytherea, free from the vices of civilisation. The Tahitian was a living embodiment of the 'happy man', the fortunate rustic idealised by Virgil and Horace and, with specific reference to Indians, the Abbé Raynal.

Banks took advantage of the vogue that the narrative of his voyage created. He found that Omai was so fascinating that the King himself gave them an audience (on 17 July – only three days after Omai's arrival). Accounts of the meeting appeared in the *London Chronicle*, ensuring that royal interest in the visitor and his guardian was widely publicised. The King's example set a trend that the establishment followed – the Duke of Gloucester, the Royal Society and the 'Doctors and Professors' of Cambridge University entertained Omai to dinner.

As well as the institutions of state, church and scholarship, Omai visited the most eminent literary men of the time. Even the crusty Samuel Johnson was impressed, saying of Omai that

Lord Mulgrave and he [Omai] dined one day at Streatham; they sat with their backs to the light fronting me, so that I could not see distinctly; and there was so little of the savage in Omai, that I was afraid to speak to either, lest I should mistake one for the other.[20]

Omai's perceived nobility made him the lion of London society; crowds cheered as he went past, delighted by this human exotic, this living evidence of London's pre-eminence as the centre to which all the world gravitated.

Banks used Omai to get himself prestige, yet the relationship was not simply cynical and exploitative. Banks came to respect Omai and enjoy his company, taking him on vacation to Scarborough, botanising and sharing campfire cookery with him, and introducing him to his closest friends, including Lord Sandwich, who declared, 'I own I am grown so used to him, and have so sincere a friendship for him, from his very good temper, sense, & general good behaviour, that I am quite distressed at his leaving me.'[21]

English gentlemen liked Omai, but what did Omai think of them and their country? And what did he do, of his own accord, while in Britain? As far as we can tell from the numerous records of his broken English conversation, Omai was no overwhelmed ignorant 'savage' but an enthusiastic yet shrewd judge of Britons with a keen sense of the ridiculous: for example, spotting the Duchess of Devonshire (perhaps the most fashionable and wealthiest noblewoman in the land) with her hair dishevelled, Omai 'asked her why she let her hair go in that manner? Ha, Ha, Ha, – don't you laugh at her having a Lesson of Attention from *an Otaheitian*?'[22] A conscious satirist, Omai was quick to point out discrepancies between the aristocracy's supposed deportment and its actual behaviour.

Omai respected his hosts when they treated him with courtesy, willingly undergoing alien scientific procedures after their efficacy had been explained. For example, because he trusted Banks's advice, he accepted immunisation for smallpox in 'good spirits' despite his fear that 'every person buried [in a local graveyard] had died under inoculation'.[23] However, when used as a mere specimen for experiment, he rebelled, for 'when Omai was at the Duke of Manchester's he was Electrified which frightened him so much he ran out & would not come back till . . . persuaded . . . he should have no more tricks played him'.[24] In effect, Omai insisted on retaining his agency by the only means available to him, by showing his hosts he was no toy to be played with or specimen to be tested by the latest scientific machines. His own words (reported by J. E. Gambier) declare his sense of himself as an active and daring explorer acting from friendship rather than under coercion or in servitude:

He resolved to see ye Country of white man – & to trust white men because he Loved two white men – Banks & Solander (by ye way neither of ym very white) and he was resolved to die or to know the truth of the white men's story for himself.[25]

Gambier's comment on this statement is to be endorsed: '*All things considered* – does the History of ye world produce a parallel instance of intrepidity & Curiosity? I think not.'[26]

Omai had his own views and his own motives. In the eyes of the British press, however, he was a perfect vehicle for making criticisms of high society. As in Montesquieu's *Persian Letters*, a foreign character allowed one's homeland to be viewed through (supposedly) alien eyes. Omai was described as a noble savage condemning London's luxury in topical satires. In *Seventeen Hundred and Seventy Seven; or, a Picture of the Manners and Character of the Age. In a Poetical Epistle from a Lady of Quality*, Omai was portrayed exploring not only the palace but also the brothels with the royal princes. Fashionable London society, the poem concluded cynically, found Tahitian sensuality all too much to its liking:

> Our silken youths for you shall cross the line,
> To dress your females and your boards refine;
> Each travell'd peer shall bless you in his tour
> With arts of play, and secrets of amour.
> Yours, be our feathers, tinsels, paints and lies,
> Our playful frolicks, and our deep disguise:
> Ours, be that want of feeling, or that pride,
> Which bravely boasts what common mortals hide.
> In pleasure's sources, what a gainful trade!
> Of mutual science, what exchanges made!
> Then shall perfection crown each noble heart,
> When southern passions mix with northern art;
> Like oil and acid blent in social strife,
> The poignant sauce to season modish life.[27]

Here Omai is at home in the immorality of London because it resembles the savage excess of Tahiti. Apparently, sexually transmitted diseases and unwanted pregnancy were the spectres that haunted both societies. The poem ends by picturing Vauxhall Gardens, a pleasure resort south of London in which fashionable society congregated and made assignations. The Gardens become a Tahitian grove where promiscuity, and the attendant danger of venereal disease, haunt the leafy shade:

> May no disease th'unbounded joys invade,
> Nor ghastly surgeon haunt the blissful shade!
> Let male and female, old and young resort
> To woo the goddess of nocturnal sport.
> (*Seventeen Hundred and Seventy Seven*, p. 23)

Satires such as this were the most biting of the literary responses to Omai. Although they took little interest in the real islander and failed even to try to explore his experience, they succeeded in disturbing cosy assumptions about Britons' superiority to 'savages' and forced a scrutiny of mores at home and in the Pacific. Tahiti, in these verses, was no longer idealised as a Cytherea or Eden before the fall. Violence and suffering were located there, just as in Britain. By implication, the value of exploration was called into question.

Satires used Tahiti to criticise; shows, meanwhile, used it to make money. Vauxhall Gardens, as it turned out, was not the only London location that, in the wake of Omai, became a 'Tahitian' fantasy zone. The famous madam Charlotte Hayes advertised to her exclusive clientele a private performance. Her live show starred 'a dozen beautiful Nymphs, unsullied and untainted... who breathe health and nature and who will perform the celebrated rites of Venus, as practised at Tahiti'.[28] After witnessing the nymphs dance, the paying voyeurs were invited to sample their fleshly delights, just as Banks had done according to the narrative of Cook's first voyage.

By 1786 Hayes's was only the most erotic of the many exhibitions that had cashed in on the vogue for the Pacific. In Leicester Square tourists could feed their eyes, for the price of 2/6, on the heads of two cannibal warriors from New Zealand.[29] Having satisfied their appetite for the gruesome, they could, half a mile away at the British Museum, refresh their palates by admiring the delicate weaving of the feather-garment of a Tahitian chief. Or they could walk a few blocks east and peruse the artefacts assembled by Georg Forster, who had voyaged, with Omai, on Cook's second expedition.

The most lucrative and spectacular Tahitian show of all occurred not in a museum but a theatre. The pantomime *Omai, Or a Trip Round the World* seemed, in the words of a *Times* reporter, 'a beautiful illustration of Cook's Voyages' – a 'virtual voyage' (to quote historian Iain McCalman).[30] It featured elaborate scenery, colourful costumes and replica dances, all, the public was assured, accurate copies of the real originals seen by the explorers. John Webber, artist on Cook's second voyage, advised on detail and the resultant combination of apparent verisimilitude with awesome spectacle made the production a huge success. As Marina Warner has observed, 'practical objects became theatrical curiosities, and other, sacred instruments tools of the ... stagecraft that excited so much admiration'.[31] Thus, too, Banks's project of assembling artefacts to access Tahiti from afar achieved truly popular form. His science became spectacle, his classified collection a pantomime show.

The show featured no cutting satire. It had a cheerful plot, showing Omai visiting Britain, wooing and winning 'Londina' and returning to live with her as a sovereign of Tahiti. And it ran for over fifty performances, including one by royal command. Both people and king liked its sunny and sentimental depiction of Anglo-Tahitian relations.

Omai the pantomime played after the real Omai's return to Tahiti. By 12 July 1776 the visitor was on his way to Tahiti with Cook's third expedition. He took with him a supply of tools designed to increase his status, some at his own request, others, like the dolls' houses intended to show how Britons lived, suggested by his hosts.[32] There was a Bible and a jack-in-the-box, port-wine and a hand-organ, crockery and kitchenware, a bed, table and chairs (all unheard of in Tahiti), a large globe, an electrical machine and, as Omai had always wanted, muskets, shot and gunpowder. There was also a coat of armour and a horse.

When the *Resolution* arrived at Tahiti on 12 August 1777, Omai was eager to put his tools to use. He went ashore and set up house in a European-style building left by Spanish sailors, using a bed 'put up after the English fashion'.[33] And he staged a demonstration of horse-riding that was intended to, and did, impress the islanders – a demonstration in which he was dressed to kill, 'cap-a-pie in a suit of armour ... mounted and caparisoned with his sword and pike, like St George going to kill the dragon' (Fig. 10).[34] Omai fired his pistol over the heads of the crowd to keep the eager viewers at a respectful distance but also, less impressively, fell off his steed. To some of the voyagers, the whole performance seemed a naïve travesty of the British military might of yesteryear, with Omai an enthusiastic but clumsy imitator – a latter-day Don Quixote. As an act of mimicry by a native person it did not, *pace* Homi Bhabha, destabilise the visitors' assumptions of centrality and superiority. Omai's faulty horsemanship reminded them that their own riding was secure by comparison, while the islanders' excitement confirmed that a man in the saddle was a man fit to command. 'Nothing', said Cook, who repeated the demonstration daily, gave the people 'a better idea of the greatness of other Nations'.[35]

As the expedition's visit to the island continued, it became clear that the British wanted Omai, their protégé, to succeed in impressing the locals on their behalf and on their terms. Omai was both their responsibility and an ambassador who might embody the benefits of British civilisation to the South Seas. In this diplomatic role Omai proved frustrating: when Cook used his influence to get Omai married into a chief's family he found that Omai had taken up instead with 'refugees and strangers whose sole Views were to plunder him'.[36] Omai missed the chance, preferring to spend

Figure 10. Royce, engraving, 'Omai's Public Entry on his First Landing at Otaheite' (1781), after a drawing by Robert Dodd, in John Rickman, *Journal of Captain Cook's Last Voyage* (London, 1781).

his time with his sister, whose husband seemed to the British to be an untrustworthy parasite.

If Omai's return seemed embarrassing to the hardy sailors, it evoked a deeper insight from a sensitive poet. William Cowper, unlike most of his contemporaries, strove to imagine how it might feel to be the Omai who had toured Britain only to return to his Pacific island. Cowper had his own reasons for thinking about Omai's return to a remote home after experiencing London society, for he himself had fled the capital for a rural retreat. Cowper lived in retirement and cultivated his garden, in conscious withdrawal from the London of consumption and sin. Remote from the city and from the empire that centred on the city, Cowper, as we showed in chapter 1, nevertheless became an avid consumer of the exploration narratives that were published in the metropolis. In his poem *The Task*, he enthused about the new worlds that Cook's and Banks's voyages opened up for him, writing of the Captain, 'he travels and I too. I tread his deck,/ Ascend his topmast, through his peering eyes/ Discover countries' (*Task*, book IV, lines 114–16). Yet he simultaneously luxuriated in his own safe distance from the scene: reading, rather than doing, let him share Cook's 'woes', yet retain a critical remove. And for all his enthusiasm, Cowper was indeed critical of what Cook – or rather Banks – had done with Omai. 'We brought away an Indian,' he wrote, 'and having debauched him, we sent him home again to communicate the infection to his country.'[37]

Omai had led Cowper to change his mind about exploration. After reading, in 1784, details of Omai's return to Tahiti in Cook's last voyage-narrative, Cowper declared 'these volumes furnish much matter of philosophical speculation'.[38] Formerly, he had seen Tahitians as noble savages; after reading Cook's descriptions of Tahitian dance, however, he decided that they possessed a sophisticated culture:

it seems wonderful, that they should arrive at such perfection . . . which some of our English gentlemen, with all the assistance of French instruction, find it impossible to learn. We must conclude, therefore, that particular nations, have a genius for particular feats, and that our neighbours in France, and our friends in the South Sea, have minds very nearly akin, though they inhabit countries so very remote from each other.[39]

Here Cowper does away with the civilised/savage opposition on which most thought about 'Indians' was predicated. Tahitians were as trained and skilled in physical arts as the refined French.

What followed from this realisation was disenchantment. Cowper admitted that 'my imagination is captivated' by reading about 'discoveries', but tried to undo the spell. He decided that the discoveries of Cook were not worth making since the discoverers debauched the people they discovered. Omai seemed a living example of this process. For Cowper, he was not a savage visiting civilisation but an islander whose uncommercial yet refined culture was spoilt by the London culture of conspicuous consumption, which turned the sophisticated Tahitian dances into cheap pantomimes or titillating shows. It was this very culture, dependent on the visualisation of the exotic, that Banks's collection had assisted and flourished in. Cowper's Omai, like Cowper himself, stood for rural culture against the capitalistic commercialism that London was spreading across the world. The fictionalised islander was part of the poet's opposition between country and city and between the cultures for which country and city stand.

And so Cowper put Omai into *The Task*, imagining him having left 'our palaces, our ladies, and our pomp' for his 'bananas, palms and yams' (*Task*, book 1, lines 643, 640). In the poem, he imagines Omai as a rustic isolated by a brief taste of city sophistication and by the consciousness of difference which that taste produces. Omai is not like his 'simple friends' (645) any more – but not like a native Londoner either. He is at home yet out of place, and consequently 'sad' and forlorn (658):

> She tells me too that duely ev'ry morn
> Thou climb'st the mountain top, with eager eye
> Exploring far and wide the wat'ry waste
> For sight of ship from England. Ev'ry speck
> Seen in the dim horizon, turns thee pale
> With conflict of contending hopes and fears.
> But comes at last the dull and dusky eve,
> And sends thee to thy cabbin, well-prepar'd
> To dream all night of what the day denied.
> (*Task*, book 1, lines 663–71)

Here Cowper, with profound sympathy, articulates a depression that affects people who are displaced in the aftermath of global exploration. Like few others at the time, Cowper had understood the mental consequences of the cultural disturbance that the spread of British power across the world was to bring. His version of Omai is a uniquely serious and prophetic one for it configures the alienation that millions of indigenous people were to suffer as a result of contact and colonisation by Europeans.

But the Omai of *The Task* is always an imaginative projection of Cowper himself. He is an enthralling figure because he is distant enough for Cowper to delineate in him what he could not comprehend in himself: invested in Omai are contradictions, both personal and public, which Cowper could not resolve in the first person. If Omai is a foreigner in his own land, so is Cowper himself: the poet overwrites the real man so that he becomes the bearer of Cowper's own burdens. Chief among those burdens is Cowper's own mental alienation from his countrymen, an alienation that took religious form and also appeared in his contradictory fascination with and hatred of London and its culture. Throughout *The Task*, Cowper condemns London from afar. He cannot leave it alone, viewing it through newspapers, books and letters. His absorption in its arts, ideas and refinements separates him from the Buckinghamshire peasants whose life he imagines as being free of the restless desire born of city-knowledge. The local 'peasant's' cottage, seemingly 'tranquil and secure', is, for Cowper himself, too remote from the conveniences of civilised urban living: 'farewell', he says, 'envy of the *peasant's nest.*/ If solitude make scant the means of life,/ Society for me!' (*Task*, book 1, lines 236, 247–9). Cowper is caught between country and city, rustic independence and urban consumerism.

Ironically enough – and this is a sign of the enormous transformation of space and time wreaked by exploration and empire – Cowper sees more of himself in a South Sea islander than he does in an English farm labourer. Cowper's Omai is no other to his British self, no savage to his civilised gentleman, but a fellow foreigner who is at home in neither country nor city. Cowper's Omai is conscious of his difference from his fellow islanders, a difference that registers as the desire to revisit London (as these lines from *The Task* reveal):

> And having seen our state,
> Our palaces, our ladies, and our pomp
> Of equipage, our gardens and our sports,
> And heard our music; are thy simple friends,
> Thy simple fare, and all thy plain delights
> As dear to thee as once? And have thy joys
> Lost nothing by comparison with ours?
> Rude as thou art (for we return'd thee rude
> And ignorant, except of outward show)
> I cannot think thee yet so dull of heart
> And spiritless, as never to regret
> Sweets tasted here, and left as soon as known.
> Methinks I see thee straying on the beach,
> And asking of the surge that bathes thy foot
> If ever it has wash'd our distant shore.
>   (*Task*, book 1, lines 642–56)

Here Cowper suggests that capitalist globalisation functions as a fall from self-sufficiency. And what supersedes that self-sufficiency is a longing, a lust, a carnal desire to possess things that collapses distinctions between races, peoples and classes. For Cowper, this is reprehensible, dizzying and exciting all at once. Omai lets him name what he hates to admit of himself – that he longs for the 'queen of cities' that he condemns (*Task*, book 1, line 727).

Cowper punishes Omai – and himself – for his longing, in the voice of one who knows from bitter experience that it is not worth it. Don't expect British ships to visit, he tells Omai:

> We found no bait
> To tempt us in thy country. Doing good,
> Disinterested good, is not our trade.
> We travel far 'tis true, but not for nought;
> And must be brib'd to compass earth again
> By other hopes and richer fruits than yours.
> (*Task*, book 1, lines 672–7)

Commercial exploitation is the name of London's game. Hope as Omai may, he will be disappointed because his rural retreat has no fruit worth sending ships to collect and no market on which to sell British wares. Tahiti will not become an agricultural colony like the West Indies and Omai will be left alone but unhappy. Here Tahiti is like Cowper's rural England and vice versa – both are remote but not remote enough from the metropolitan and imperial centre. They are too far away to be part of that centre but close enough to be tainted by knowledge of it. That is their fate, but also their blessing – and Cowper remained deeply divided and ambivalent about it. Self-exiled, he continued to yearn for the city-sophistication that he continued to mistrust.

Cowper's Omai was a product of the poet's reading of exploration narratives and newspaper reports. But if Cowper depended on what the explorers and the journalists wrote, he also questioned it. In Omai he imagined a figure through whom he could unsettle the assumptions of the narratives he was reading. What resulted was not a clear-cut rejection of exploration or travel writing but a profound pondering of the moral dilemmas and mental instabilities that they produced. In the same moment, Cowper also reached an uneasy understanding of their complicity – and that of scientific advance in general – with consumer capitalism. Science fuelled a global circulation of wealth and power, a circulation of which London was, in Cowper's ambivalent metaphor, the beating but engorged heart:

> In London; where her [science's] implements exact
> With which she calculates computes and scans
> All distance, motion, magnitude, and now
> Measures an atom, and now girds a world.
> In London; where has commerce such a mart,
> So rich, so throng'd, so drain'd, and so supplied,
> As London, opulent, enlarg'd and still
> Increasing London? Babylon of old
> Not more the glory of the earth, than she
> A more accomplish'd world's chief glory now.
> (*Task*, book 1, lines 715–24)

Cowper, in effect, had made an incisive analysis of two vital eighteenth-century developments – globalising capitalism and the colonialism to which exploration often led. Home and abroad, he saw, were placed in a new relationship to each other since both were now peripheries to the metropolitan centre. The commercialism that was radiating from London across the landscape of Britain was the same process as that which was centring the Pacific on Britain's imperial capital. And the anxieties that this process produced in a Tahitian were akin to those experienced by a rural Englishman. Not just physical but mental space was being globalised as exploration spread consumerist desire across land and seas.

Or was it? Although the returned Omai provoked sympathy in Cowper and anxiety in Captain Cook, he did not in fact linger passively longing for what he had experienced in London. Back in Tahiti, Omai acted resourcefully with the things he had wanted – and acquired – in Britain, using them to fulfil desires that sprang from his situation in island society. He was not simply a creature of his longing for capitalist London but an agent putting to use the tools his world tour had given him. Globalisation, Omai's actions show, would arise not simply as a universal consumerist desire of country for city, periphery for centre but also as technology transfer and transformation, allowing new modes of social action. He was neither an innocent victim of city life nor a jaded tourist, but a resourceful actor in his own reoccupation of his culture. Omai, in fact, was an independent trader who, *en route* to Tahiti, sold to the Tongans the British goods for which he had no use, and got in return feathers that proved of enormous exchange value back home (where feathers were used in ceremonial garments but where the red kind available in Tonga were not to be found). On first approaching Tahiti, Omai gave some to a chief who came out to the *Resolution* by canoe. Immediately, the chief's indifference turned to friendliness and he gave Omai a pig. Soon the ship was surrounded by eager Tahitians who spurned the British nails and beads (the staples of trade on previous visits) in favour of Omai's red feathers. The British had been outsold and were left incredulous. Cook noted 'not more . . . than might be got from a Tom tit would purchase a hog of 40 or 50 pound weight'.[40] Omai had a monopoly and found himself sought out by chiefs for special favours: one, to the disgust of the officers, spent hours showing off his feather-adorned body from the cabin windows 'like some eastern Monarch adored by his Subjects'.[41] It all seemed, as the Orientalist comparison suggested, alien and un-British. Omai was succeeding neither as an ambassador for British civilisation nor as a demonstrator of British wares, but as an inter-island merchant with a working knowledge of what Pacific island culture most valued. He had found his most effective power tools, trading away the British goods that Britons so much wanted him and the islanders to prize.

Omai traded his British goods with Britons as well as Tongans. He exchanged his crockery and kitchenware with crewmen on the *Resolution* in return for hatchets and iron tools. Again, Omai's views diverged from those the officers thought proper. Cook negotiated for him a grant of land on the island of Huahine and the ship's carpenters built a timber house there. Omai, however, thought it as mean as a British pigsty. And even as Cook negotiated, Omai was mistranslating his words, telling the Huahine chiefs that he and the British would invade Raiatea and expel the Boraborans. Cook refused to do so and tried to ensure Omai's safety by threatening the inhabitants that he would punish anyone who harmed Omai when he again returned to the island.

Cook never did return, but when Captain Bligh reached Tahiti on his breadfruit voyage, he enquired after Omai. It turned out that Omai had not, once his feathers ran out, elevated his status into the chiefly class. But in one respect he had changed his position, having realised the ambition that had originally led him to travel to Britain:

Soon after Captn. Cook left Huaheine there were some disputes between the people of that Island and those of Ulieta, in which also the Natives of Bola-bola or Borabora took a part. Omai now became of consequence from the possession of three or four Muskets and some Ammunition, & he was consulted on the occasion. Whatever were the motives, such was Omai's opinion and Assurance of Success, that a War was determined on, and took place immediately. Victory soon followed through the means of those few Arms and many of the Ulieta & Bora-bora men were killed.[42]

Omai died of natural causes some months later, having shown the islanders the power of one aspect of British civilisation – its armaments. He had set a precedent that would later change Tahitian society irrevocably, when, in 1819 the chief Pomare, by converting to Christianity, won the armed support of the British missionaries and conquered all his rivals. British 'civilisation' and Christian religion spread because Tahitians wanted firepower for their wars rather than because they believed in its doctrines or its values.

With Omai dead, the British-style house was left to fall down. Omai's hand-organ and the electrical machine disappeared, but some of the items sent to represent British culture still survived in 1818. They survived in the collection of a chief, a collection that uncannily mirrors Banks's collection of Tahitian artefacts in London: 'A few of the trinkets, such as a jack-in-a-box . . . were preserved with care by one of the principal chiefs, who . . . considered them great curiosities, and exhibited them, as a mark of his condescension, to particular favourites.'[43] Scientific Britons were clearly not the only ones who had learned that to display sundry objects of another culture gave one glamour and status in one's own, even if the process yielded, at best, fragmentary knowledge.

Such was the case in the islands of the East Indies, particularly the events in the career of Sir Stamford Raffles, from 1805 to 1824.[44] Raffles's correspondence with the local princes and sultans of Java – the 'Native Powers', as he called them – demonstrates that the collecting of the Tahitian chief was just one example of a process of exchange that Banksian exploration stimulated, a process in which items from one culture were transformed and thus took on symbolic significance when deposited in another. In the letters Raffles wrote to and the seventy-three replies he received from the indigenous Javanese between 1810 and 1811, his main purpose was to get them to pledge loyalty to the East India Company, to denounce their loyalty to the Dutch, and to promise support of British troops in the form of rice, livestock and naval supplies. Finally, Raffles wanted the princes and sultans to send him as many original documents of Malay and Javan origin as possible. The answers to these letters show that Raffles was far from successful. He received few promises but many requests for items of British manufacture. Raja Ali of Pedas, for instance, wrote to Raffles thanking him for the 'European painted cloth-fabric and a keg of gunpowder', and although he acknowledged Raffles's request for 'the laws' of Pedas, the 'Hykayats', or prose poems, and 'tales of ancient men', Ali regretted he could not send these along. He added, however, 'if it is possible I would like my friend to send me a rifle of my friend's own wearing'.[45] Similarly, Ratu Gusti Wiyahan Karang Asam of Bali wrote asking Raffles for 'twenty kegs of gun powder, two kegs of priming powder, a one-tiered Camera obscura, with a reflecting glass complete with its two hundred pieces of new picture paper and of the best kind, a burning glass which when exposed to the sun's rays will produce a flame, all at a reasonable price'. In return, he sent Raffles a token of his sincerity: 'an eight-year-old boy and a seven-year-old girl'. Ratu had one final request: 'Could my brother help to get me a small entertainment boat of about six fathoms in length and of the best kind that has two masts and with furniture of English style?'[46]

Ironically, if the Malaysian royalty wanted furniture of English style, the royalty of England wanted furniture in Malay style. When Raffles returned to London in 1817, one of the first things he did was attend a dinner at the home of Princess Charlotte (the Prince Regent's daughter), where he presented her with a table and chairs made of richly textured *kayubuku* wood from Java. Immediately, King George's consort, Queen Charlotte, wrote to Raffles, saying she had 'heard so much of the curious and precious things which he had brought' from Java, and that 'everybody is in raptures with the beautiful tables, &c. which you have given to Princess Charlotte'. The news was not so great for Banks, however. Raffles ordered a pair of tables, which had been reserved for Sir Joseph, to be 'sent immediately to Frogmore', residence of Queen Charlotte; the result was that Raffles himself received an invitation to dine – in English style on Javan furniture.[47]

Yet Raffles's collecting and categorising of Malaysia from 1805 to 1824 was far more systematic than the few trade items the Javans sent to him and the items he provided local powers, and this made all the difference in the use to which trade and collections were ultimately put. From the moment Raffles set foot in Malaysia, he began a massive natural history hoard, all the while corresponding regularly with Banks as well as Orientalists such as William Marsden (author of the *History of Sumatra*).[48] Banks was happy to receive and share information with Raffles, but at least one Malaysian, Abdullah bin Abdul Kadir Munsyi, who described in minute detail Raffles's scientific activity, wondered apprehensively how all this collecting would affect the Malay people:

There were four men whom Raffles employed at different occupations: one he sent into the jungle to look for various herbs and flowers and fungus and mosses, and anything that showed diversity of form; and another man he sent to look for grubs and grasshoppers and various butterflies and beetles, and all kinds of insects, and cicadas and centipedes and scorpions, etc.; and he gave him pins, and told him to pin these creatures. Another man he sent to look for things on the reefs, such as various kinds of whelks and mussels and cockles and oysters, etc., which he brought in a basket, with various kinds of fish. Then another man went to look for wild animals and birds, jungle fowl and all kinds of deer, etc. [Raffles] had a large book made of thick paper, and he used to put in it all kinds of leaves and flowers, etc. And if there was anything which he could not put in it, he had a chinaman, a Cantonese, who was very clever at drawing pictures of either fruits or flowers, which he painted like life, and he told him to paint all these things. Besides all this, he had a barrel which was full of either arrack or brandy, I don't know which, into which he put such creatures as snakes and centipedes and scorpions; he put them alive, and after two days he took them out, and put them in bottles, where they looked as if they were alive. The people of Malacca were astonished to see all this. At this time many people in Malacca earned money hunting for various creatures in the air, on the earth, or in the sea, in the country or in the town, or in the forest, flying things and creeping things, and things which grow and spring from the ground; all the things which I have mentioned meant money. Then other people brought Malay books and histories, I don't remember how many hundreds of them; almost all the Malay writings of ages past the property of our forefathers were sold, and people brought them from various places, because they fetched a good price; they were all sold, because people did not realise that afterwards they would become ignorant, not having a single book to read in their own language. For those books were all manuscripts; if they had been printed books it would not have mattered, but now there are not copies left to be reproduced.[49]

Raffles loaded his collections onto the Banksian network where they became the foundation for the Zoological Society of London (which Raffles established with Sir Humphry Davy), and later, the London Zoo.[50] But more importantly, Raffles's natural history and Orientalist pursuits gave him such extensive local knowledge that they enabled him to purchase Singapore in 1819 in the name of the British Government and the East India Company: Britain's Malaysian collections – as opposed to Malaysia's British collections – were thus the basis of extending commerce and empire.[51]

CHAPTER 3

Indian flowers and Romantic Orientalism

By the time Sir Stamford Raffles turned his hungry eyes towards Java, Sir Joseph Banks had long experience of directing the East India Company's gaze at the cultures and crops of Bengal and beyond. Since the 1780s, Banks had been prodding the Company (Britain's most powerful colonial body) to recognise that the interests of science and empire coincided: gathering seeds and plants from all over the world would not only augment botanical knowledge but also increase colonial profit. Banks's botany was imperial and commercial: by exchanging plants he would give the empire new and lucrative crops.

In this chapter, we examine the operation of Banks's network in the East Indies, showing how Sir Joseph used his political influence to spread botanical gardens into the subcontinent. We also investigate not only the Indian botany that he stimulated but also its effects on imperialist thought and its influence on literature. Banks, we show, helped precipitate new kinds of Orientalist scholarship and the new forms of verse that have come to be called Romantic. He stood behind the writings of Sir William Jones, who in turn influenced Robert Southey and Thomas Moore. All three of these poets, and others like them, imagined flowers as poetic symbols in which Britons' attitudes to their Indian colonies could be contemplated.

We begin with one such poetic symbol – a verse flower that grew from the colonial habit of sending flowers, roots, and even pictures and poems about such flowers, between the motherland and the foreign places it colonised. James Montgomery's poem 'The Daisy in India' describes this activity, even as it also contributes to it. For Montgomery, it is the daisy's very survival, despite its fragility and isolation, in a land of giant plants that makes it a symbol of the immigrant colonist.

Thrice welcome, little English flower!
My mother-country's white and red,
In rose or lily, till this hour,
Never to me such beauty spread:
Transplanted from thine island-bed,
A treasure in a grain of earth,
Strange as a spirit from the dead,
Thine embryo sprang to birth.

Thrice welcome, little English flower!
Whose tribes, beneath our natal skies,
Shut close their leaves while vapours lower;
But, when the sun's gay beams arise,
With unabash'd but modest eyes,
Follow his motion to the west,
Nor cease to gaze till daylight dies,
Then fold themselves to rest.

Thrice welcome, little English flower!
To this resplendent hemisphere,
Where Flora's giant offspring tower
In gorgeous liveries all the year:
Thou, only thou, art little here,
Like worth unfriended and unknown,
Yet to my British heart more dear
Than all the torrid zone.

Thrice welcome, little English flower!
Of early scenes beloved by me,
While happy in my father's bower,
Thou shalt the blithe memorial be;
The fairy sports of infancy,
Youth's golden age, and manhood's prime,
Home, country, kindred, friends, – with thee
I find in this fair clime.

Thrice welcome, little English flower!
I'll rear thee with a trembling hand:
Oh, for the April sun and shower,
The sweet May dews, of that fair land,
Where Daisies, thick as star-light, stand
In every walk! – that here may shoot
Thy scions, and thy buds expand,
A hundred from one root.

Thrice welcome, little English flower!
To me the pledge of hope unseen:

> When sorrow would my soul o'erpower,
> For joys that were, or might have been,
> I'll call to mind, how, fresh and green,
> I saw thee waking from the dust;
> Then turn to heaven with brow serene,
> And place in God my trust.[1]

Sentimental and pious, Montgomery uses the daisy to symbolise the vulnerability but also the godliness of the colonists. His flower is an emblem for Christian missionaries, a sign that they should trust in the God of their own shores though faced with the overwhelming difference (and indifference) of native India.

Montgomery focuses on flowers. The transplantation he longs for and (in the form of images) achieves is an aesthetic one. Nevertheless, to the extent that it reduces colonists' feelings of otherness, it has material consequences. It helps to sustain the men who make their business the conversion of India into mercantile wealth for Britain. Much of the mercantile wealth, of course, stemmed from the transportation of plants in the other direction – from the East to Europe. The administrators and missionaries consoled by Montgomery's beautiful daisy would not have been in the East at all had their country not benefited by a plant exchange that was not aesthetic but commercial. Montgomery's symbolic poem, in effect, ignores its own relationship to the primary significance of plants in colonial India. Pepper, nutmeg, coffee, tea, opium, cotton and sugar were the plants that flowered for Britain's empire.

Montgomery's poem is Romantic in that it treats nature symbolically in order to explore personal emotions that cannot be articulated directly. And in putting Romantic motifs into the context of colonial flora it opens up the areas we wish to explore in this chapter – namely, what relationships do cultural artefacts (poems and other literary texts) have to the export of plants on which colonial wealth depended? In particular, what was the impact on these relationships of the reorganisation of colonial trade by the botanical science that Joseph Banks began to spread across India?[2]

In the late eighteenth century, few India-hands had much scientific training and fewer still had either the inclination or the linguistic skill to discover what Indian scholars knew about their native flora. To Banks in London, this situation was regrettable: 'Bengal and its dependencies', he told the East India Company in 1787, 'form a vast blank in the book of information, which no one hitherto has attempted to fill up.'[3] India must be brought within the horizon of scientific scrutiny, Banks advised, and the foundation of a botanic garden in Calcutta was the best means of achieving it.

The East India Company had mixed motives in trying to incorporate India in Banks's network.[4] One was what we now call imperial guilt, for it was in the conscience of a colonist that the proposal for the botanic garden originated. Lieutenant Colonel Robert Kyd had suggested the idea in 1786. His letter to the Company's Board of Directors explains his feelings: 'I have', he wrote, 'been sometimes betrayed into reflections on the comparative benefit which we have conferred on the nations of India . . . the balance will stand greatly against us.' The British, he continued, had done little to prevent 'the greatest of all calamities, that of desolation by famine, and subsequent pestilence'. This neglect entailed upon them 'the imputation of inhumanity, and improvidence from the enormity of misery and wretchedness, which inevitably continues to impend over the Natives'.[5] But the imputation could be turned aside if the Company established a garden for imported plants: 'these trees or their seeds to be procured & by authority of Government disseminated over the Country, that each village may have a reserve of them in case of necessity'.[6]

When the Company submitted Kyd's idea to Banks for his opinion, he agreed. Importing sago trees from Malaya, date palms from Persia and breadfruit from Malabar, and then cultivating them in a Calcutta garden, would show that the British had 'nobler prospects in view than the mere attempt of Filching from another country its commercial advantages'. Banks described the 'Disinterested humanity' and 'exalted benevolence' of saving people from famine by seeking 'to exchange between the East and West Indies the productions of nature useful for the support of mankind'.[7]

In 1787 the East India Company's rule of India was under severe attack in London. While Banks wrote, Sir Warren Hastings, the former Governor General, was being impeached for misgovernment. His prosecutors, including some of the most powerful politicians in the land, gave the public lurid details of the 'filching' and looting of Indians' property by the Company and its minions. In this context, Banks's letter displays his acute political nous. The botanic garden would, he reassured the Company, make its government humane and benevolent, just when it was being branded greedy and exploitative. At the same time, the garden would make Britain even richer. 'Nor', Banks continued, 'can it fail of drawing from the Jungles and deserts hitherto unexplored articles of Commerce, which Europe, China, & even Bengal itself now receive from other Countries & promoting the cultivation of articles useful to the manufacturers of Great Britain & consequently important to the investments of India.'[8] Banks argued that botany made economic as well as political sense for an imperial nation: if it was neglected, then rival empires would leave Britain's behind. The French had already created a system for transferring lucrative crops to their colonies. Britain must imitate them before it was too late.[9] The Company was persuaded and in 1787 the garden was established.

By 1794 it was flourishing: its superintendent William Roxburgh had, in Britain's richest colony, official resources at his disposal and was able to employ Indian artists whom he had trained to meet the requirements of European science. Banks praised

The skill with which the drawings are made, the accuracy with which the parts illustrative of the sexual system are delineated, the intelligence with which interesting views of these parts are selected, and the patience and detail with which the descriptions are drawn up.[10]

Indians were co-opted in the process of categorising native flora.[11] They drew the plants that Roxburgh cultivated and he exported the drawings to London, where Banks employed Daniel Mackenzie to engrave them (Fig. 11). When Banks had them published as part of the comprehensive *Plants of the Coast of Coromandel* (1805–20), they allowed the nature of India to be known from Europe in a way that was not possible within Indian tradition. This was a process akin to the colonial export of wealth, as a letter that German botanists wrote to Roxburgh's successor indicates. Thanking Nathaniel Wallich for sending them plants, the botanists added, 'we have become as rich as nabobs and vie with them in treasures. And it is you who made us so rich and glorious . . . What a new world you have conquered for science and mankind.'[12]

The Germans were right to connect botanists with nabobs and conquerors. Ultimately, the networks pioneered by Banks would bring tea plants from China and coffee from Java, and spread them over the colonial hills, changing world trade and enriching Britain. For all the genuine advances in nutrition and medicine that it allowed, colonial botany was at root a plant of imperial commerce.

The first poets to respond to botany's imperial role saw that Kew Gardens was at the centre of a new phenomenon. Kew was a royal research station,[13] run by Banks, to collect, display and profit from Britain's command of foreign lands. In 1767 Henry Jones declared that at Kew 'an image of our conquest wide appear[s],/ Our added empire, and our Indian world'.[14] Kew illustrated Britain's successful harnessing of the 'richest growth' of the East:

Figure 11. Engraving, 'Semecarpus Anacardium Nella-jiedy of the Telingas' (1795), from a drawing by an Indian artist, in William Roxburgh, *Plants of the Coast of Coromandel*, published by the order of the Hon. Court of Directors of the East India Company, under the direction of Sir Joseph Banks, Bart. PRS (London, 1795).

> From Indian gardens, and from Eden's groves,
> To Britain's cold adopting climate brought;
> Nor there shall die, nor disappoint his hope,
> Whose patriot heart and powerful hand are stretch'd
> From pole to pole for happy Britain's good.
> (canto 1, lines 159–63)

Governed by the British monarch's protective hand, Oriental luxuriance would be brought under control.

It was left to Erasmus Darwin to versify the imperial symbolism of botany more fully. In doing so, he brought Banks's network out of the herbarium and the East India Company and into the drawing rooms of the middle classes. Darwin was a polymath, a theorist as well as botanist, a doctor as well as inventor, who numbered James Watt and Joseph Priestley among his friends. He was also an acquaintance of Banks and sought Banks's help when making his monumental translation of Linnaeus's works, *The System of Vegetables* and *The Families of Plants*.[15] Banks gave advice and lent books; Darwin credited him and his librarian.[16]

As a translator, Darwin marshalled the best available botanical scholarship to present Linnaeus as accurately as possible to the British public. But it was as a poet that he succeeded in popularising the science. *The Botanic Garden* (1791) was both about botanic gardens and was itself a botanic garden of verse – a collection of subjects and motifs brought from all over the world. Darwin, that is to say, was to his poem as Banks was to the real garden at the centre of it – Kew. Kew, Darwin wrote, was the perfect emblem of the imperial science that his poem celebrated and symbolised:

> So sits enthron'd in vegetable pride
> Imperial Kew by Thames's glittering side;
> Obedient sails from realms unfurrow'd bring
> For her the unnam'd progeny of spring.[17]

The 'unnam'd progeny' was contained by a botanical order within which it received its designation and rank. In other words, because it divided flora into species and genus and allotted names to each plant, the Linnaean system was a microcosm of the political order that was the British empire.[18]

Darwin celebrated both the garden and the botanical and political empires that it represented. The whole poem was a tribute to the power of the Linnaean system since, like the Swedish botanist, Darwin defined plants by their sexual characteristics. He also personified them so that he could portray their reproduction by analogy with human behaviour. Darwin's plants loved, courted, married and had sex with each other, sometimes in groups, sometimes in what he called 'promiscuous marriage', as in this passage:

> A *hundred* virgins join a *hundred* swains,
> And fond Adonis leads the sprightly trains;
> Pair after pair, along his sacred groves
> To Hymen's fane the bright procession moves;
> Each smiling youth a myrtle garland shades,
> And wreaths of roses veil the blushing maids;
> Light Joys on twinkling feet attend the throng,
> Weave the gay dance, or raise the frolic song;
> – Which, as they pass, exulting Cupids sting
> Promiscuous arrows from the sounding string;
> On wings of gossamer soft Whispers fly,
> And the sly Glance steals side-long from the eye.
> – As round his shrine the gaudy circles bow,
> And seal with muttering lips the faithless vow,
> Licentious Hymen joins their mingled hands,
> And loosely twines the meretricious bands. –
> Thus where pleased Venus, in the southern main,
> Sheds all her smiles on Otaheite's plain,
> Wide o'er the isle her silken net she draws,
> And the Loves laugh at all, but Nature's laws.
> (canto IV, lines 489–508)

A footnote explained the analogy between the plant and human worlds. Just as 'many males and many females live together in the same flower', so 'the society called the Areoi in the island of Otaheite consists of about 100 males and 100 females who form one promiscuous marriage'.[19] This was to pay tribute to Banks's network, for it was Banks and the later explorers whom he sent to Tahiti who reported the sexual customs of the 'Areoi' society. It was Banks, too, who brought Linnaean system to Tahitian, as well as African and Indian, flowers. In his highly allusive style, Darwin had erected a monument – or rather built a garden – in verse to celebrate the knowledge and power that Banks's enterprises produced.[20]

The Botanic Garden proved so popular that, in the view of historians of botany Ann B. Shteir and Janet Browne, it made the science a fashionable pursuit.[21] Soon the English countryside would be sprinkled with young ladies and gentlemen armed with trowels, satchels and botanical manuals. They were not the poem's only fans: Blake, Coleridge, Crabbe and Wordsworth all took ideas and images from it, as biographer Desmond King-Hele has shown.[22] What they did with their borrowings was, however, very different from what Darwin had done. *The Botanic Garden* was not a Romantic poem. Its style was an ornamented derivative of Pope's wit; its couplet form and mythological apparatus were also neo-classical. Darwin wrote playfully but made no attempt to explore the inward self in relation to what scientific exploration revealed about the world outside. This was a matter of choice not just of chronology. Cowper's *The Task*, which was published five years before *The Botanic Garden*, did explore the self in these terms. Darwin, regarding himself as a man of science, saw his verse as the amusing illustration of scientific discoveries rather than as a deeper investigation into their effect. It was not he but another friend of Banks, Sir William Jones, who was to write a botanical poetry that opened the paths that Romantic poets were to tread.

By 1788 Jones had known Banks for many years. A fellow member of the Literary Club that included Samuel Johnson and David Garrick, Jones had entertained the visiting Omai at Banks's entreaty. Now he was in India, his brilliance as a scholar of Persian and Arabic repaid with a position in Bengal's supreme court. As a judge, he studied Sanskrit in order to codify the legal tradition he was required to use, and this study led him to the linguistic thesis that gave him lasting fame – that European and Indian languages were connected and descended from a common archetypal language, now lost.[23]

Jones's studies of India were not confined to its ancient language. In 1784 he had instituted the Asiatic Society, a group of colonial scholars whose investigations were, from 1788, published annually in the *Asiatick Researches*. These investigations included astronomy, natural history and botany. Jones himself called botany a 'bewitching study' and termed Linnaeus's *Philosophica botanica* 'a masterly work'.[24] He welcomed the Calcutta Garden and collaborated with Roxburgh on identifying Indian plants. By 1788 he was a supplementary branch of Banks's network, sending Dacca cotton seeds and roots of the medicinal 'Pee-arunga' plant to Kew. In reply, Banks asked for Jones's help in procuring plants to send to the botanic garden at St Vincent, while Jones encouraged him to publish all the botanical manuscripts he had received from India.

Publication mattered to Jones, for he was anxious that as much of Indian culture and nature should be represented to Europe as possible. In 1790 he published his own *Design of a Treatise on the Plants of India*, sounding an imperialistic note at the outset: '*Give us time* . . . for our investigations, and we will transfer to Europe *all the sciences, arts and literature of Asia*.'[25] Here Jones was perfectly in tune with Banks. Botany would be part of a colonial enterprise that aimed to export Indian knowledge, just as merchants exported Indian goods, to Europe. Linnaean classification would put it in order, fitting the overwhelming variety of Indian flora into a familiar scheme. Jones's botany, as Edward Said wrote of Orientalist scholarship in general, would constitute a western style for dominating, restructuring and having authority over the Orient.[26]

And yet, despite his stated desire, Jones's botany neither simply exported India to the West nor solely enclosed it within a European knowledge-system. Jones was not, in fact, wholly content with Linnaean method. He accepted its usefulness in classifying plants, but thought Linnaeus's 'diction barbarous and pedantic'.[27] Jones regretted the Linnaean custom of naming plants after the first Europeans to describe them and preferred local Indian names, provided that the names were recorded 'in *Sanscrit* preferably to any vulgar dialect; because a learned language is fixed in books'.[28] In his next publication on the subject, *Botanical Observations on Select Indian Plants* (1795), he recorded the Sanskrit name alongside the Linnaean classification. He also argued that botanists who ignored local names were like an exploring 'geographer, who, desiring to find his way in a foreign city or province, should never inquire by a name for a street or a town, but wait with his tables and instruments, for a proper occasion to determine its longitude and latitude'.[29] In this argument, Jones agreed with several other colonial botanists who were also using local knowledge in order to identify plants that might have medical uses. But Jones went further, informing readers that the plants included in the volume were chosen for their significance in Indian culture.

Jones's fascination with the ancient arts and sciences of India had moved him away from botany as practised by Linnaeus, Banks and Darwin. Although he still shared most of their aims and methods, he also insisted on the significance of local knowledge for its own sake. In the event, his collection of that local knowledge from Brahmins was to be an influential intervention in both cultures; Jones collated oral traditions about plants with Sanskrit manuscripts, codifying Indian discourses in print for the first time. This codification, as Nehru said in 1946, was a vital step for Indians for it made their ancient knowledge available to Hindus on a new scale.[30] At the same time, Jones was presenting to the West what amounted to an eco-anthropology of India, displaying in intricate detail a flora that was not solely marked by Linnaean tags, but inflected by its traditional use in Indian medicine, mythology and literature. Jones's botany, in short, was an unexpected hybrid of European science with Indian discourses, a plant never seen before that could not have existed without his considerable scholarship in botany and in Sanskrit. Both Linnaeus and Banks, on the European side, and the learned Brahmins whom Jones consulted on the Indian, were its progenitors. And while it was not innocent of imperialist aims (as a colonial governor Jones could never be that), it was nevertheless significantly different from both commercial exploitation and Banks's scientific exploration. Jones gave British science a more detailed and respectful engagement with Indian knowledge traditions than ever before.

What made the deepest impact on Europe was not Jones's botany itself, but the use he made of it in his language studies. Garland Cannon has argued that it was Jones's immersion in Linnaean classification of plants that enabled him to arrive at his breakthrough theory that Indo-European languages were a family, divided into different species that descended from the same archetype.[31] In other words, allotting Indian flowers into genera and species helped Jones to imagine a methodology for judging relationships between whole languages. This put philology on a new footing, for until Jones introduced this systematic approach it had often comprised merely the subjective assertion of similarities in sound between individual words.

Jones's language theory had a dramatic impact, especially in Germany, where it precipitated linguistic and cultural research into an India that was now taken to be the origin of Europe – a huge shift in consciousness. But Jones's translations from Sanskrit were still more important, for they caused a sensation, showing Europeans that Hindu civilisation was capable of producing poets as great as Shakespeare. To Goethe, the translations established their author as 'the incomparable Jones'.[32] Particularly successful was *Sacontalá* (1789), a drama written by Kalidasa in the fifth or sixth century. Goethe declared that, 'when I mention Sakuntala, everything is said'.[33]

Part of *Sacontalá*'s success stemmed from its flowers. Jones showed that Kalidasa had used Indian flora as symbols not only of characters' appearance but also of their moral states and psychological relationships. They were visibly growths of a sophisticated and native poetic tradition, and, therefore, far removed from Darwin's personified plants. Where Darwin simply applied Linnaean categories to his poetic flowers, Jones brought both European science and Hindu learning to his translation of *Sacontalá*. For example, he depicted the heroine tending a garden, and compared her to a particular plant, a creeper called the 'Delight of the Grove': 'her lip glows like the tender leaflet; her arms resemble two flexible stalks; and youthful beauty shines, like a blossom, in all her lineaments'. The creeper twining around the Amra tree was made emblematic of Sacontala hoping for a bridegroom to embrace lovingly: 'the Amra tree seems wedded to you, who are graceful as the blooming creeper which twines around it'.[34]

Jones rejected Darwin's and Linnaeus's 'allegory of sexes and nuptials', calling it 'wantonly indecent'.[35] His own poetry offered, instead, the reverse of Darwin's; plant life illustrated human love rather than human sexuality illustrating plant sexuality. Jones's Indian plants, moreover, depicted loving monogamy rather than sexual promiscuity. In his *Botanical Observations* he commented of the 'Atimucta': 'This was the favourite plant of Sacontala, which she very justly called the *Delight of the Woods*; for the beauty and fragrance of its flowers give them a title to all the praises, which Calidasas and Jayadeva bestow on them: it is a gigantick and luxuriant climber.'[36] In Indian poetry, Jones found a floral language both more decent and profound, since he saw the Hindu 'allegory of sexes' as an expression of a creation myth that resembled Platonism. Despite his admiration for this myth, however, he omitted some of the erotic passages of Jayadeva's *Gitagovinda* for fear of offending British taste. If this, by twenty-first-century standards, resembles bowdlerisation, nevertheless what remained impressed a new generation of British poets for whom orthodox literary style and established forms of knowledge seemed tainted by their association with political conservatism and colonial exploitation. Coleridge, Shelley and Thomas Moore all borrowed from Jones in their efforts to write a new kind of poetry, but it was Southey who drew on him most heavily, creating works that seemed revolutionary in form as well as style.

The Curse of Kehama (1810), as Southey stated in the preface, 'took up that mythology which Sir William Jones had been the first to introduce into English poetry', not just to add a dash of local colour but also 'to construct a story altogether mythological'.[37] In developing Jones's presentation of Hindu myth, Southey aimed to reinvigorate what he regarded as the exhausted western genre of epic. The 'moral sublimity' of Indian myth would supply the great theme and lofty subject-matter that eighteenth-century imitators of 'the great poets of antiquity' so clearly lacked.[38] By combining an Oriental content with an older western style, Southey hoped to achieve what his fellow poets had not – an epic for an age in which Britain was in contact with eastern cultures to a degree never before seen.

The finished work bore traces of the revolutionary politics that Southey had not entirely discarded by 1810. Its hero abhors the self-destructive and superstitious loyalty of people to the godlike tyrants who hold them in thrall, very much as Southey imagined himself and his fellow radical intellectuals doing in the British climate of the 1790s. In *Kehama*, though, radical resistance to superstition is set in an India derived from Jones's appreciation of the flowers he had studied botanically.

One God alone, with wanton eye,
Beheld them in their Bower;
O ye, he cried, who have defied
The Rajah, will ye mock my power?
'Twas Camdeo riding on his lory,
'Twas the immortal Youth of Love;
If men below and Gods above,
Subject alike, quoth he, have felt these darts,
Shall ye alone, of all in story,
Boast impenetrable hearts?
Hover here, my gentle lory,
Gently hover, while I see
To whom hath Fate decreed the glory,
To the Glendoveer or me.

Then, in the dewy evening sky,
The bird of gorgeous plumery
Poised his wings and hover'd nigh.
It chanced at that delightful hour
Kailyal sate before the Bower,
On the green bank with amaranth sweet,
Where Ganges warbled at her feet.
Ereenia there, before the Maid,
His sails of ocean blue display'd;

And sportive in her sight,
Mov'd slowly o'er the lake with gliding flight;
Anon, with sudden stroke and strong,
In rapid course careering, swept along,
Now shooting downward from his heavenly height,
Plunged in the deep below,
Then rising, soar'd again,
And shook the sparkling waters off like rain,
And hovering o'er the silver surface hung.
At him young Camdeo bent the bow;
With living bees the bow was strung,
The fatal bow of sugar-cane,
And flowers which would inflame the heart
With their petals barb'd the dart.

The shaft, unerringly addrest,
Unerring flew, and smote Ereenia's breast.
Ah, Wanton! cried the Glendoveer,
Go aim at idler hearts,
Thy skill is baffled here!
A deeper love I bear that Maid divine,

> A love that springeth from a higher will,
> A holier power than thine!
>
> A second shaft, while thus Ereenia cried,
> Had Camdeo aim'd at Kailyal's side;
> But lo! The Bees which strung his bow
> Broke off, and took their flight.
> To that sweet Flower of earth they wing their way,
> Around her raven tresses play,
> And buzz about her with delight,
> As if with that melodious sound,
> They strove to pay their willing duty
> To mortal purity and beauty.
>
> Ah! Wanton! cried the Glendoveer,
> No power hast thou for mischief here!
> Choose thou some idler breast,
> For these are proof, by nobler thoughts possest.
> Go, to thy plains of Matra go,
> And string again thy broken bow!
>
> (part x, stanzas 19–23)[39]

The meaning of this passage turns upon knowing the role of Camdeo, and so Southey provides an explanation in a footnote:

> Eternal CAMA! Or doth SMARA bright,
> Or proud ANANGA, give the more delight?
> Sir W. Jones.
>
> He was the son of MAYA, or the general *attracting* power, and married to RETTY, or *Affection* and his bosom friend is BESSENT, or *Spring*. He is represented as a beautiful youth, sometimes conversing with his mother and consort in the midst of his gardens and temples; sometimes riding by moonlight on a parrot or lorry, and attended by dancing girls or nymphs, the foremost of whom bears his colours, which are a *fish* on a red ground. His favourite place of resort is a large tract of country round *Agra*, and principally the plains of *Matra*, where KRISHEN also, and the nine GOPIA, who are clearly the *Apollo* and *Muses* of the Greeks, usually spend the night with music and dance. His bow of sugar-cane or flowers, with a string of bees, and his *five* arrows, each pointed with an Indian blossom of a heating quality, are allegories equally new and beautiful.

Here Southey was reworking Jones's own adaptation of Hindu myth in his *Hymn to Camdeo* (1784). Camdeo, Jones tells his readers, is the Indian 'Eros'. He goes on to give the exact Indian names of the blossoms with which Camdeo tipped his arrows of love:

> He with five flow'rets tips thy ruthless darts,
> Which thro' five senses pierce enraptur'd hearts:
> Strong *Chumpa*, rich in od'rous gold,
> Warm *Amer*, nurs'd in heav'nly mould,
> Dry Nagkeser in silver smiling,
> Hot Kiticum our sense beguiling,
> And last, to kindle fierce the scorching flame,
> *Loveshaft*, which Gods bright *Bela* name.
> ('A Hymn to Camdeo', lines 54–61)[40]

Jones had researched these plants himself. In his *Botanical Observations* he classified them according to the Linnaean system but also discussed their significance in Indian medicine and mythology, noting of the Nagkeser that 'the tree is one of the most beautiful on earth, and the delicious odour of its blossoms justly gives these a place in the quiver of Cámadéva'.[41] Furthermore, Jones's *Hymn* explained the allegorical import of Camdeo's blossom: his arrows of desire would keep mortals enchanted with the world, maintaining creation eternally.

Jones's Camdeo was a hybrid who grew from European botany and neo-classical verse on the one hand and from Indian writings on the other. In developing the figure, Southey hybridised western forms still further by making the action of the most important genre of all – epic – depend on him. Southey's Camdeo may have been derived second-hand from Jones's versions of Sanskrit but he, and other gods derived from Jones, were essential to *The Curse of Kehama*'s action. Jones's Orientalism enabled Southey to produce a strange new poetry, one that took Hindu myth more seriously than ever before. Southey took the epic eastwards and asked readers to see Hindu culture not just as an exotic other, nor just as a decorative veneer, nor even, as in Jones's own verse, as a fascinating anticipation of western tradition. More radical than Jones, Southey treated it as a subject-matter, belief-system and poetic style as appropriate for the epic as were Trojan wars to Homer and the Biblical fall of man to Milton. *The Curse of Kehama* constituted the apogee of the kind of Orientalism precipitated by Jones – a kind that neither solely appropriated the East and exported it westwards nor simply categorised it according to European knowledge-systems, but used it to question the cultural forms that Europeans saw as proof of their superiority. By making the epic Hindu (albeit pseudo-Hindu) Southey left it radically altered.[42] He had looked beyond, through the eyes of the latest scholarship and science, and learned to question the primacy of his own culture. Jones's and Banks's Orientalism had let him break with

European neo-classical poetic tradition and, at the same time, see past the assumption that Indian culture was unworthy of serious rendition. He had made an imaginative leap beyond British convention and, even if he could not produce an authentic representation of Hindu scripture, the hybrid that he did create demanded that British readers be moved and awed by their likeness to the foreign.

The reviewers saw what Southey was doing and hated it. John Foster worried about the credibility conferred on 'false religions'; *The Monthly Review* remarked on the 'utter depravity of his taste'.[43] Southey, they recognised, was deliberately innovative: he had 'his own system of fancied originality, in which every thing that is good is old and every thing that is new is good for nothing'.[44] This system was not his alone. Southey's 'gross extravagancies' typified a 'school of poetry' of which Wordsworth and Coleridge were members.[45] To contemporary reviewers, in effect, Romantic literature was a dangerous new movement epitomised by Southey's Jonesian and Hindu epic.

Ironically enough, Southey half agreed with his reviewers, for he was not always prepared to endorse the innovations of his own text. He referred to the 'monstrous . . . deformities' of the Hindu mythology that supplied his plot and his symbolism. He also attacked Jones, calling him in 1808 'one of the show-books of fashion' with a reputation 'far above his deserts'.[46] It was as if Southey fought shy of the affiliation to a Jonesian India into which the imaginative process of writing verse led. Something of his ambivalence is detectable even in his portrayal of Camdeo. Southey's heroine Kailyal, who has faith in her spiritual destiny and rejects Camdeo's sensuality, resists the flower-wielding god. Unlike Jones then, Southey did not endorse the sensuality of Hindu myth as an allegory of creation, but preferred what amounted to a Protestant spirituality displaced to India. This was in line with his support of attempts by English missionaries to convert Hindus and destroy the caste system.

Southey's ambivalence did not save him from being critically attacked. The reviewers were right to view him, despite himself, as a founder of a school. It was the radicalism that Shelley detected in Southey's epics that won the admiration of the young atheist and revolutionary. Byron also learned from Southey's example, though he took it in a less revolutionary direction than Shelley. 'Stick to the East,' he told Thomas Moore, 'the public are Orientalising.'[47] Southey had opened a new field but his own works were 'unsaleables', being too long and too dense. Moore took Byron's advice and followed in Southey's footsteps, carefully avoiding, however, the error of making his poems depend on a complicated and unfamiliar mythology. The result, *Lalla Rookh* (1817), was enormously popular but also far less demanding than Southey's works. Moore used Orientalist texts to provide accurate local colour, but did not ask readers to step outside their religious beliefs or poetic expectations, though he did endorse rebellion against tyrannical government, displacing his sympathies with Irish nationalism and Whig radicalism to the ancient East.[48] Moore's story revolved around conventional romantic love and moral conflict rather than around a mythical interpenetration of human and divine, as in *Kehama*.

Moore's Orient was a fashionable commodity, an imitation East manufactured in London with as much colourful detail as possible. Like Southey, Moore gave references to prove that his eastern flora really existed. Unlike Southey, however, he used botanical discoveries to supply exotic costume rather than action and style. He dutifully included footnotes to Jones on Indian botany, giving the Linnaean classification, but the flowers themselves were decoration, for Moore's was a watered-down Orientalism that avoided the risks that Southey took. Moore plundered Jones, and what the Brahmins told Jones, to add a touch of realism to his picture of the East as a composite exotic bower of love. What flowers signified in different eastern cultures was subordinate to the impression they jointly gave that the Orient was a perfumed garden of desire. And this garden, Moore assured readers, really exists because it could be visited and studied. He located it near Kashmir and pictured his protagonists travelling there:

In an evening or two after, they came to the small Valley of Gardens, which had been planted by order of the Emperor, for his favourite sister Rochinara, during their progress to Casmere, some years before; and never was there a more sparkling assemblage of sweets, since the Gulzar-e-Iram, or Rose-bower of Irem. Every precious flower was there to be found, that poetry, or love, or religion, has ever consecrated; from the dark hyacinth, to which Hafiz compares his mistress's hair, to the Cámalatá,* by whose rosy blossoms the heaven of Indra is scented.

* The Cámalatá (called by Linnaeus, Ipomaea) is the most beautiful of its order, both in the colour and form of its leaves and flowers; its elegant blossoms are 'celestial rosy red, Love's proper hue', and have justly procured it the name of Cámalatá, or Love's Creeper. Sir W. Jones.[49]

By 1817, then, the botany that Banks and Jones had helped to project eastwards had returned, changed, to Britain in the verbal flowers of poetry as well as the seeds and roots brought back to Kew. Botany had stimulated a radical engagement with Hindu culture, an engagement that epitomised the new poetic school we now call Romantic. But the hostility that Southey's Orientalism had met led his successors to produce a more conventional and decorous version of the East. Yet their Orientalism was still a changed one: after Jones, and Southey's adaptation of Jones, the Romantic Orientalists prided themselves on proving the accuracy of their details by giving chapter and verse in footnotes. Jones was so clearly a master of both western and eastern forms of knowledge that he was quoted more than anyone else. With his own authority established by his use of the familiar European system of Linnaeus, Jones was trusted as a source on the East as well. He and his hybrid botany became the guarantor of the new – Romantic – kind of writing.

How did that writing fare in the colonies it described? We began this chapter with Montgomery's botanical antidote to the colonist's sense of alienation in the face of Indian flora. We end it with another lonely traveller, the Indian army officer, poet, and friend of Shelley, Lieutenant Thomas Medwin. In his narrative *The Angler in Wales* (1834), Medwin adopts a quintessentially late Romantic pose. Like Moore and Shelley himself in 'Ozymandias', Medwin muses in melancholy fashion on human vulnerability in general and the fragility of empire in particular. One of the sites that prompt these musings is a fenced-off botanic garden in a fenced-off East India Company cantonment where he had been stationed in 1817. A sensitive traveller, Medwin sees in that garden an image of colonial India that runs contrary to the norm. He exults in neither its scientific nor its commercial value. Nor does he present it as a sensuous bower. Its Orientalist pleasures are not for him. What he discovers there, instead, is an India of exotic imports, both from East and West, whose hold on the land is tenuous and short-lived:

Below, is a beautiful botanical garden, composed of the choicest plants and shrubs, from all parts of the Eastern, and some from the Western world, and laid out in the European manner. I could not but help reflecting, that we are exotics in the animal, as many of them are in the vegetable kingdom . . . I sighed and exulted over the concluding paragraph from Gibbon, whilst speaking of the overthrowal of the Moghul Empire 'Since the reign of Aurungzebe, their empire has been dissolved – their treasures of Delhi rifled by a Persian robber, and the riches of their kingdom are now possessed by a company of Christian merchants, of a remote isle in the *Northern* ocean'. The train of thought engendered by the recollection of this remarkable sentence, threw a gloom over my mind, that had till then been pretty tranquil. I sate down for some time in the garden. The air was filled with the odours of the aromatic blooms, and the branches were full of 'bulbools', but neither had any sweets or music for me.[50]

It was the optimistic vision of empire shared by Banks and Jones that led to the laying out of botanic gardens in the subcontinent; thirty years on, however, Medwin sees in one such garden the vanity of that vision. Unlike Montgomery, Medwin finds no security in science, no consolation in the flowers. He cannot see the botanic garden as another knot in Britain's world-encompassing net, but only as a reminder that he and his nation are alien to this soil and vulnerable in this land. He internalises Gibbon's warning to his fellow countrymen: what the author of *The Decline and Fall* discovered in imperial history, Medwin now rediscovers in imperial botany.

Medwin's garden should remind us that the relationship between imperial science and Romantic literature was highly unstable. Medwin is far removed from Southey's enthusiastic but ambivalent embrace of Hindu culture. The path from Banks, through Jones, to *Kehama* seems not to have guided Medwin's view of Indian flowers. Not for him a study of Sanskrit, of sexual symbolism or a Hinduisation of the epic. Yet, for all his difference, Medwin is recognisably in debt to a Romantic conception of the Orient as the zone where the sensitive traveller enjoys lamenting over the futility of his own and his fellows' ambitions. Unlike Europe, where, after Waterloo, Britain was dominant, the East was potentially large and different enough for a limit to the triumph of British power to be imagined. Medwin followed Byron in seeing the East in these terms, but it was Southey who pioneered the use of the East as a stage on which to enact the disenchantment that came from the failure of revolution in Britain and Europe. For Medwin, the disenchantment is personal, a matter of grief but also of exaltation as he imagines the doom that he thinks empire deserves. The end of British power comes to seem inevitable: Medwin, bolstered by Gibbon, becomes a prophet of imperial ruin. To Medwin and the other 'prophets of nature', the imperial system of which Banks's network, Linnaeus's botany, Jones's scholarship and Montgomery's verse were all parts was ultimately a flower transplanted into a land where it did not belong.[51] Without the special and artificial treatment that the botanic garden symbolised, it was, they saw, bound to fail. It is a fragrant irony that Medwin, who had learned to see botany as a symbol because of the power of the networks – scientific, imperial, scholarly – that had applied it to the nature of India, should now use it to show that these networks were doomed to wither and die.

CHAPTER 4

Mental travellers: Banks, African exploration and the Romantic imagination

The new – Romantic – writing did not solely spring from India. Exploration of Africa was equally influential on the forms and figures developed by writers at the turn of the eighteenth century. In this chapter we examine Banks's role in organising the scientific exploration of Africa, and in publishing the explorers' narratives that placed the continent within Europeans' imaginative reach for the first time. We look first at the botanical travels of Francis Masson, before assessing Banks's most successful African explorer, Mungo Park. Park, we show, achieved such authority and such popularity that he effected major changes in natural historians' views of Africans and sent poetry in new directions. Sub-Saharan Africa, after Park and the explorers whom Banks sent to follow in his footsteps, was to become one of the places in which literary Romanticism staged its journeys into the self.[1] It also became a place that Park opened up to colonial desire: both literary and scientific Britons followed Banks's lust to possess the continent's inmost secrets. In Banks's own case, this lust also took the form of a desire to colonise territory and exploit its riches. Some literary writers were to question the morality of this colonialism.

In 1783 François Le Vaillant, exploring Africa from the Cape of Good Hope, came upon a welcome sight and recorded it in his narrative: a 'verdant carpet embroidered with flowers; the surrounding hills, covered with shrubs and beautiful plants, displayed to my eyes a delightful shelter in every thicket: it was a garden in the bosom of a desert'.[2] The blooms were lovely, but they made Le Vaillant regret his lack of botanical knowledge:

How many did I see, which, were they transplanted into the richest gardens of Europe, would constitute their chief ornament! And how often did I regret, that I was not a skilful botanist! Who knows, said I to myself, whether among this number art might not find some that would impart to our manufactures those beautiful and unfading dyes which we have hitherto deemed the exclusive property of India?[3]

For Le Vaillant there was little gap between aesthetics, science and commerce. He was delighted by floral beauty because it contrasted with the surrounding 'desert', but his very next impulse was to regret his botanical ignorance because it might mean a lost opportunity to enrich French manufacturers at India's expense. The beauty of flowers and the beauty of wealth were linked, or would have been linked if Le Vaillant had been able to bring scientific knowledge with him on his travels.

What Le Vaillant lacked, Sir Joseph Banks was determined to provide. Having botanised at the Cape himself on his voyage with Captain Cook, he knew that African flora was an untapped resource. Once back in Britain he used his new prestige to persuade the King of 'the advantage which might accrue from sending a smart under-gardener to the Cape to collect seeds and send home living plants'.[4] The gardener selected was Francis Masson and when he set sail with Cook in 1772 he was the first of the many explorers that Banks would send to Africa. Cook left Masson at the Cape, where he was to spend the next three years making trips into the interior to collect many plants that were to become staples of Victorian gardens, including Cape heaths and Pelargoniums (which were bred into the garden geranium).[5] Seeing 'the whole country enamelled with flowers',[6] Masson had the training to turn beauty into order. He was, Banks noted, 'sufficiently instructed in the science of Botany for the purposes of his Mission'.[7] That mission, as Banks also recorded, was amply fulfilled. By means of the 'profusion of plants' that Masson sent to London, 'Kew Gardens has in great measure attained to that acknowledg'd superiority which it now holds over every similar Establishment in Europe'.[8]

Imperial superiority was important to Banks, so, having projected botanical science to the African colony that Britain would take from the Dutch in 1795, he cultivated Masson's seeds at Kew. The results were catalogued and disseminated to the scientific world in William Aiton's *Hortus Kewensis* (1789). Masson's report on his expedition was published in the Royal Society's transactions (1776).[9] Finally, in 1796, engraved illustrations of some of Masson's findings appeared under the title *Stapeliae Novae; or, A Collection of several New Species of that Genus; discovered in the Interior Parts of Africa*. With these publications, Banks ensured that no educated European ever need feel alienated by the unfamiliar flora of southern Africa again. Its abundance and beauty, as well as its economic value, were now reorganised by Linnaean classification. Cultivated, categorised and illustrated in Britain, African plants were accessible on Banks's network, without the need to travel. They had been put in their places in a Europe-centred science that, in both material and conceptual terms, stretched across the world.

Banks's network did more than classify and publish Masson's plants. In 1787 Masson, back in the Cape, supplied 'trees, plants, and seeds of every sort'[10] to the First Fleet sailing to colonise Australia. The following year, he assisted Captain Bligh, who stopped en route to Tahiti, where he was to collect breadfruit trees and take them to the West Indies. By this time Masson had, at Banks's request, established a botanic garden so that he could nurture the plants he collected before sending them back to Kew or out still further across the world. Thus the Cape, perhaps *the* most vital port for colonial shipping, became a remote node of Banks's world-wide scientific network. It was a network of which explorers like Masson were each a small part.

Masson could rest assured that if he observed and collected diligently, then Banks would employ him again and again. So it proved: he collected in the Azores, the Canaries, the West Indies and Canada. Often alone, he nevertheless had the emotional protection of knowing he was part of Banks's network and could operate an intellectual system that would allow him to place each strange plant that he encountered. Botany connected him to the European centres of calculation even in the African bush.

Masson's exploration brought the natural history of southern Africa into Banks's grasp. But the Africa of the centre remained a tantalising blank that haunted Banks's imagination precisely because so few westerners had brought knowledge back from its deserts and jungles. Banks was determined to turn imagination into reality. In 1788 he set up another informal network to do so. The African Association was a private club of lords, bishops and MPs, influential enough to persuade the government to send its Oriental interpreter, Simon Lucas, to the interior of Africa. Lucas, however, found it too risky to venture far inland from Tripoli, and returned having accomplished little. John Ledyard and Daniel Houghton tried harder on the Association's behalf, but died in the process. Undeterred, Banks and company sent out Frederick Hornemann in 1797 and Johan Ludwig Burckhardt, disguised as an Arab, in 1809. Dysentery killed both. In 1818 Joseph Ritchie followed in their footsteps: he too was to die in Africa's unhealthy interior.[11]

Yet the mortality rate was not total. Burckhardt and Ritchie were inspired to travel because one explorer had returned alive. They were following in the footsteps of Banks's greatest success, a man who seized the British public's imagination – Mungo Park. Banks prepared and sent Park out in 1794 as a 'Geographical Missionary to the interior countries of Africa'.[12] Banks told him that he would explore the Niger valley with the aim of 'rendering the geography of Africa more familiar to my countrymen, and in opening to their ambition and industry new sources of wealth, and new channels of commerce'.[13] Park's mission was as imperialistic as it was adventurous.

When Park reached central Africa, he found that opening new commercial channels carried appalling risks. He was vulnerable to local chiefs, who imprisoned him, and at the mercy of brigands, who stripped him of his clothes. After one brutal attack, when he had been robbed and left for dead, he lamented, 'I saw myself in the midst of a vast wilderness in the depth of the rainy season, naked and alone; surrounded by savage animals and men still more savage . . . I had no alternative but to lie down and perish.'[14] He did not perish, though, but restored his resolution by a desperate measure of which Banks the botanist would have been proud: he inspected a plant.

At this moment, painful as my reflections were, the extraordinary beauty of a small moss, in fructification, irresistibly caught my eye. I mention this to show from what trifling circumstances the mind will sometimes derive consolation; for though the whole plant was not larger than the top of one of my fingers, I could not contemplate the delicate conformation of its roots, leaves and capsula, without admiration. Can that Being (thought I) who planted, watered, and brought to perfection, in this obscure part of the world, a thing that appears of so small importance, look with unconcern upon the situation and sufferings of creatures formed after his own image? – surely not! Reflections like these would not allow me to despair. I started up, and disregarding both hunger and fatigue, travelled forwards, assured that relief was at hand; and I was not disappointed.[15]

Botany restored his Christian faith, and Park, like a pilgrim sorely tested, resumed his quest. Sustained by his God, he returned safely to London, and duly reported to Soho Square, to load his precious knowledge of the African interior onto Banks's network.

Banks and the African Association soon set about shaping his experiences into a publication designed to open the unknown continent to the eyes of European readers. They trod carefully as they did so, for they wanted to enthral the public without alienating men of science for whom travellers' narratives were a major, but frustratingly unverifiable, source of information. Banks had not forgotten the derision poured on John Hawkesworth's account of Tahiti. Explorers of Africa had met similar scorn. In 1790 James Bruce's *Travels to Discover the Source of the Nile* had been disbelieved because it had included so many unlikely stories.[16] Banks, who had audited the notes from which Bruce compiled it, had been forced to defend it against sceptical comments from his scientific friends. If Park also failed to convince, then African exploration, the African Association, and Banks himself would be discredited. Banks recruited Bryan Edwards, who had already written the influential *History Civil and Commercial of the British . . . West Indies*, to supervise the first-time author.[17] Edwards edited Park's text to ensure it was 'interesting and entertaining' and had Banks 'cast [his] eye' over each chapter for final approval.[18] Together, they ensured it used a style that was trusted by men of science, a style associated with the Royal Society of which Banks was President. That style, as Steven Shapin has argued, was one in which theoretical investments were precluded. It was empiricist, uncontroversial and polite, intended to persuade readers that the writer was a reliable witness because he was a disinterested gentleman, free from the desire to gain personally from his testimony.[19] Park had to be encouraged to write like a gentleman-amateur so that men of science, themselves often amateurs, would trust his testimony when they had no means of checking it. Only then would his claims be believed, only then his text be accepted as truth and accorded the status of 'knowledge'.

Park's narrative begins by alerting readers to its truthfulness. Park, says the Preface, can be trusted because he is faithful to experience: readers will be disappointed if they demand 'discoveries to be unfolded which I have not made, and wonders to be related of which I am utterly ignorant'.[20] His narrative 'has nothing to recommend it but *truth*. It is a plain unvarnished tale'.[21] Trustworthiness, it seems, is an effect of plain 'unvarnished' realism. Realism, however, is a style, and Park, according to Edwards, was a quick learner. 'Park goes on triumphantly,' he wrote to Banks in 1799, characterising the writing of the narrative in terms appropriate for the journey itself. 'He improves in his style so much by practice that his journal now required but little correction; and some parts, which he has lately sent me, are equal to anything in the English language.'[22] The public – general and scientific – thought so too, for when *Travels to the Interior Parts of Africa* was published in April it became an instant success, necessitating two more editions of the book after the first sold out within a week, and German, French and American editions by 1800.[23]

THE SCIENTIFIC RESPONSE

As Banks intended, contemporary men of science accepted Park's trustworthiness. They validated his traveller's tales and turned them into scientific 'truth'. This had important consequences for their work: Park soon became a major source for natural historians and theorists of racial difference. With Park travelling for them, bringing 'facts' to their desks, men of science were able to 'read' the 'natives' without leaving home. Natural historians built theories about Africans' relationship to Europeans on what they found – or thought they found – in Park. These theories, apparently as disinterested as Park's 'facts', were less innocent and value-free than they seemed. They made racial inferiority, on Park's authority, seem an objective fact of nature. William Lawrence, the surgeon and comparative anatomist, cited him on African appearance as he argued that heredity, and not climate, was responsible for racial difference. Africans were of the same species as Caucasians, but 'the Negro is more like a monkey than the European'.[24] J. C. Prichard, also an eminent surgeon and theorist, agreed, and based his entire 'proof' on Park's account of tribal distribution:

> The tribes who inhabit the countries bordering on the Senegal and Gambia rivers, have been described by Mr. Park. He divides them into four principal nations, the Mandingoes, Feloops, Jaloffs and Foulahs. The two former have the Negro characters in the greatest degree. The Jaloffs are of the deepest shade, or of a jet black in their complexion, but their features approach more to the European model than the rest of these nations. But the Foulahs are distinguished in several respects from the other natives in this part of Africa. They are not black but of a tawny colour, which is lighter and more yellow in some states than in others. They have small features, and soft silky hair, without either the thick lips or the crisp wool which are common to the other tribes . . . These tribes inhabit the same latitudes, and are indeed interspersed through the same territories. The variety which subsists among them must therefore depend on some other influence than that of climate.[25]

Prichard spoke confidently for Africans, and generalised from them to humanity at large. He explained racial variety by hereditary modification, preparing the ground for the theories of evolution with which, in a later century, social Darwinists argued that racial difference corresponded to evolutionary development (although Prichard himself came to doubt whether science could draw up any fixed lines of difference between peoples). Blacks were less evolved than whites. Prichard's explanation, established in a language of generality, objectivity and logic, depended nevertheless on a traveller's tale carefully prepared for its readers. Indebted to Park, the men of science were also indebted to the promoter of his *Travels*. It was the virtual travel ushered in and manipulated by Sir Joseph Banks that gave them new terms in which to talk about the outer human.

THE POETIC RESPONSE

Poets were more concerned with the inner human, and they responded differently. The *Travels'* sensational content, combined with its literary form, allowed writers of fiction to imagine exploration as a quest romance.[26] Park became, by association, a holy pilgrim or at least a somewhat Quixotic adventurer, who pursues his promised task with a faithfulness that exposes him to adventures both heroic and comic. Like a knight of medieval romance, Park reaches the object of his quest only after many trials and misadventures. He is attacked by wild beasts, lost, betrayed, struck down by disease. He is imprisoned in a Moorish kingdom and subjected to anti-Christian humiliations which leave him despairing. Finally reaching the Niger, Park thanks his God: 'I hastened to the brink, and, having drank of the water, lifted up my fervent thanks in prayer to the Great Ruler of all things, for having thus far crowned my endeavours with success.'[27] Having reached it with him, the reader has become a mental traveller, only to discover that the river was not after all the real end of his journey. The real end, the narrative suggests, was a discovery made in the interior of the self as well as in the heart of Africa. It was the discovery that a 'civilised' man could be alone, abandoned and destitute in the heart of the overwhelming otherness of a 'savage' country, without losing his faith, his self-command or his resourcefulness. Park is no Kurtz, no Marlow either: he is infected neither by what he calls the fanaticism of the Moors nor by the 'superstitious' fatalism of the Negroes. A practical European, he survives when deprived of his scientific armoury (his compass, his thermometer) because, for him, scientific observation leads to a sustaining faith. After he has restored his belief by observing the fructifying moss he is, it appears, rewarded. A Bushreen trader offers him an escape to the coast because he can read the copy of the Book of Common Prayer that the trader owns.

God, Park's *Travels* implies, moves in mysterious ways to save those pilgrims whose faith and humanity have been deepened by their experiences of vulnerability. Not surprisingly, this implication made the book appeal to a British public for whom the Book of Common Prayer and *Pilgrim's Progress* were foundational parts of the cultural fabric. Park's narrative made a huge impact on contemporary society, not least because it showed that poor African blacks, themselves vulnerable to enslavement by Muslim Moors, repeatedly took pity on him in his hour of need. One woman sheltered him from a storm in her hut. Having fed him, she and 'the female part of her family' laid him down to sleep whilst they spun cotton.

They lightened their labour by songs, one of which was composed extempore: for I was myself the subject of it . . . The air was sweet and plaintive, and the words, literally translated, were these: 'The winds roared, and the rains fell. The poor white man, faint and weary, came and sat under our tree. He had no mother to bring him milk; no wife to grind his corn.' Chorus 'let us pity the white man; no mother has he,' etc. etc. Trifling as this recital may appear to the reader, to a person in my situation, the circumstance was affecting in the highest degree.

I was oppressed by such unexpected kindness; and sleep fled from my eyes. In the morning I presented my compassionate landlady with two of the four brass buttons which remained on my waistcoat; the only recompense I could make her.[28]

The Duchess of Devonshire rewrote the African women's words under the title 'Favourite Song from Park's Travels' and they became a text for campaigners against the slave trade. James Montgomery quoted them in his popular abolitionist poem 'The West Indies' (1809), contrasting Park with the slavers who had destroyed the 'blest' life of the 'hospitable' Africans. The slavers were 'spoilers' who would be punished on Judgement Day by the slaves they had killed. Park, by contrast, was a 'Pilgrim' lost in Africa who deserved divine reward: 'in heaven or earth, wher'er thou be,/ Angels of mercy guide and comfort thee!'[29] Mary Russell Mitford took a similarly Evangelical view in her 'Lines, Suggested By the Uncertain Fate of Mungo Park' (1811): Park's journey was a pilgrimage on behalf of 'Religion' and 'philanthropy', bringing the benefits of British commerce and Christianity 'to meliorate the lot of savage man'. Reaching the Niger was a Christian quest:

> Delighted of the mystic wave he drank,
> Hail'd that bright flood, and dropt upon the bank;
> And on that spot, then first by Christian trod,
> Pour'd forth thanksgiving to the living God.[30]

Park's very vulnerability made him pitiable; Mitford allied herself with the Duchess of Devonshire in praising, on behalf of 'the gentler sex', the African women who sheltered him. Unthreatening and helpless, yet triumphant,[31] Park symbolically purged Britain of the guilt of the slave trade,[32] as a white man feminised by his dependence on, rather than exploitation of, blacks. His experiences proved the truth of his grateful assertion that there was no difference between 'the Negro and European . . . in the genuine sympathies and characteristic feelings of our common nature', despite the apparent primitiveness of African civilisation.[33] In effect, Park both popularised abolitionism and inflected its rhetoric. His words helped redefine Britain's imperialist ideology, becoming powerful tools in the hands of those who argued that the slave colonies must be replaced with a benevolent paternalist empire designed to enlighten and to Christianise black people.

Park's popularity survived the abolition of the slave trade in 1807. His influence remained powerful – but also intriguingly divided on gender lines. Park was particularly attractive to women poets, who used his isolation in the African landscape to offer ways of dramatising – and assuaging – the vulnerability and tenderness nineteenth-century culture defined as feminine. Mary Howitt fixed upon the incident in which Park overcame despair by observing the fructifying moss:

> when sore distress
> O'ertook him in the wilderness;
> When courage failed, and dark Despair
> Scowled on him in the withering air,
> And home-thoughts in his heart sprung up –
> The bitterest drops in his bitter cup;
> As then – a little flower could reach
> His spirit's core, and proudly preach
> Of Him whose eye-lids never fall: –
> Of Love, which watcheth over all.[34]

Here the vulnerable traveller is comforted by the flower because it is still more insignificant than he. If an object so 'little' survived 'the withering air', then there must be a God who would protect him – and all other Englishmen and women living in 'alien' lands. This sentimental Christian comfort reinterpreted Park's own narrative, in which it is not the flower's smallness, but its scientifically observed design, that assures him of God's presence. Park's vulnerability had sponsored a sentimental poetry that offered women spiritual consolation. African nature, as represented by Howitt's sentimental Christianity, could contain secret sources of spiritual comfort for weakness. It could, thanks to Banks, now be known – in imagination at least – since botanical exploration had rendered it familiar enough to be appropriated.

Park's exploration inspired male poets too. To the male Romantics, African travel narratives were foundational texts because they brought the unknown and exotic tantalisingly almost within reach. In doing so, they gave the poets not only a new subject-matter, but contributed a new poetic: they stimulated them to convert material journeys into mental travel, to turn the world outside in. And most stimulating of all was African travel, as Wordsworth revealed when in 'Peter Bell' (1798) he made the centre of the continent into a location where the never-never land of fantasy might come true:

> I know the secrets of a land
> Where human foot did never stray
> Fair is that land as evening skies
> And cool, though in the depth it lies
> Of burning Africa.   (lines 90–4)

This land, the poem suggests, can be reached only by liberating the play of imagination. In other words, for the footwork of men such as Bruce and Park, Wordsworth substitutes the poet's flights of fancy:

> Or, if you thirst with hardy zeal
> Less quiet regions to explore
> Prompt voyage shall to you reveal
> How earth and heaven are taught to feel
> The might of magic's lore!
>
> (lines 106–10)

The mind soars into new realms, whereas Banks's protégés trudged. Yet Wordsworth, although ultimately elevating the poet's imagination over the explorer's determination, takes his metaphors from the explorer. He is enough of a respecter of the common ordinary world in which we live and have our being to show that, without the 'hardy zeal' which footslogging exemplifies, the poet's airy flights are just hot air. Wordsworth's images, that is to say, reveal his admiration for recent African travellers as well as reserve the greater exploration for the poet. Ultimately it is the poet's mind, having undergone a spiritual journey as severe and self-disciplined as an explorer's physical trek, that is able to know the secret that is Africa – the secret which the explorer had reached but not quite grasped – the secret of a paradise beyond suffering and beyond pain.

That it was Park who prompted Wordsworth to picture the poet as an explorer and Africa as the location of a peace that passeth conventional understanding is clear in an 1804 draft of *The Prelude*.[35] In this draft, Park features as one of a number of explorers Wordsworth had been reading who had, he thought, shown how nature ministers to man in moments of extreme suffering. These explorers include Columbus and Dampier, and they appear just after Wordsworth, climbing Snowdon, has himself experienced the climactic revelation of the whole poem – the discovery, as he hiked up the mountainside, that in rare, unexpected epiphanies, nature discloses to man 'the Soul, the Imagination of the whole' (*Prelude* (1805), book XIII, line 65). What Wordsworth discovers by accident among the Welsh crags, he finds, reading travel narratives, explorers to have discovered among the perils of the sea and amid the dangers of the African desert. Here is what Wordsworth says about Park:

> Doth that Land Traveller living yet appear
> To the mind's eye when, from the Moors escap'd
> Alone & in the heart of Africa,
> And having sunk to earth worn out with pain

> And weariness that took at length away
> The sense of Life, he found when he awaked
> His horse in quiet standing at his side
> His arm within the bridle & the Sun
> Setting upon the desert.[36]

For Wordsworth this is an exemplary moment. Park collapses helpless, utterly subject to nature's power. But he is neither abandoned by his horse nor shrivelled by the sun. Prone on the desert earth, Park, like Lear on the heath, is bare natural man, all defence mechanisms, all accoutrements of civilisation, gone. Ready to die, he loses consciousness only to awake, refreshed, in the cooler evening, as if rewarded by nature for giving himself over to it. In effect, Wordsworth rewrites Park's narrative as a spot of time in which the power of nature is 'felt along the heart' because the solitary walker is completely vulnerable to that power. Africa, then, is the place where a 'living' Englishman has, like Wordsworth himself, most recently stepped beyond the social networks in which our personality is normally constructed, to find, *in extremis*, his deeper selfhood, a selfhood whose kinship with nature's power is simultaneously revealed.

The discussion of Park reveals Wordsworth's sense of himself as an explorer. It shows that Africa was one of the grounds on which he learnt that inner discovery depended on outer journeys. It discloses, that is to say, the constitutive influence of Banksian exploration – and the travel writing arising from that exploration – on the central topos of Wordsworthian Romanticism.

Nevertheless, Wordsworth did not in the end include the Park passage in book XIII of *The Prelude*. Why not? Perhaps because the implicit comparison of himself climbing Snowdon with a heroic explorer alone in Africa too clearly revealed his egotism. Perhaps, also, because he wanted to emphasise still more strongly than in *Peter Bell* that the deep self which nature revealed, in spots of time, to men such as Park could be discovered, by men of 'higher minds', in and by themselves. Ultimately, for Wordsworth, the inner discoveries made by travellers o'er land and sea were preparatory for those made by mental explorers of their own minds.

Wordsworth may have had another reason for excluding his Park passage from *The Prelude*. The very same incident from Mungo's *Travels* was cited at length in the notes to an equally ambitious quest romance that had been published in 1801. *Thalaba*, by Wordsworth's friend and neighbour Southey, quoted Park's collapse and recovery for two reasons. First, Southey wished to persuade readers that the hardships by which *Thalaba*, his fictional hero, deepened his faith had their parallels in empirical fact. Second, he also wanted to show that his hero – a young Arab Muslim – was not alien but similar to a stalwart British explorer. Southey's recourse to Park, in other words, not only anticipated Wordsworth's (and may have prompted it) but occurred for similar reasons: the hardy wanderer through African deserts lent an aura of heroism and realism to the fictional quest. This similarity may have been too close for Wordsworth's comfort, especially because to Francis Jeffrey, the most powerful contemporary reviewer, *Thalaba* seemed to be the defining example of a new poetic movement of which Wordsworth was also a member, a movement we today call Romanticism. According to Jeffrey, *Thalaba* had all the hallmarks of the new school, notably an affected combination of commonplace realism on the one hand and 'wild and extravagant fictions' on the other.[37] One symptom of this awkward marriage was Southey's tendency to support his fantastic tales with factual footnotes. The note citing Park was just one example: Southey, Jeffrey wrote, had 'been as scrupulously correct in the citation of his authorities, as if he were the compiler of a true history'.[38]

Park was one of many travellers whom Southey cited in *Thalaba*. Quoted at length in a note to the fourth book, he appears in order to convince readers that there exists an actual place and a real journey against which the hero's fictional mission might seem believable as fact. That mission is a spiritual one: Thalaba, like the knights of the *Faerie Queene*, travels through an allegorical landscape in which his virtues are tested by encounters with enchanters, demons and witches. The setting is the Arabian desert, but nature continually bends to the will of sorcerers: it is allegorically not naturalistically organised, and is as subject to supernatural beings as it is in the *Thousand and One Nights*. Yet Thalaba himself is naturalistic: he has no magic power but is a common boy of lowly origins, a hero similar, as Jeffrey noted, to those of *Lyrical Ballads*. Southey's verse was also reminiscent of the consciously simple style adopted by Wordsworth and Coleridge and he, like them, used English folk ballads as a source. Confusingly for his readers, Southey had created a strange hybrid of allegorical fantasy and factual naturalism.

Southey's naturalism is an exterior one. He gets the physical details as accurate as possible, but fails to find a way of narrating his hero's interiority. His account of Thalaba wandering in the desert concentrates on the physical effects:

> Still the same burning sun! no cloud in heaven!
> The hot air quivers, and the sultry mist
> Floats o'er the desert, with a show
> Of distant waters, mocking their distress!

> The youth's parched lips were black,
> His tongue was dry and rough,
> His eye-balls red with heat.[39]

'Perhaps', Southey's footnote suggests, 'no traveller but Mr. Park ever survived to relate similar sufferings.' It then quotes at length Park's emotional and spiritual response to those sufferings. Park, and the African desert that Park describes as a real testing ground, are the guarantors of Southey's poetic protagonist and setting. They establish it as a purification zone, a place of inner discovery, rather than a mere exotic backdrop. But to Jeffrey (and perhaps to Wordsworth) Southey's footnotes seemed a mistake. Absurdly, they suggested that Southey thought he could supply the naturalism and interiority that were missing from his implausible plot and flimsy characters by quoting, at the foot of the page, real events described by real travellers. This procedure, Jeffrey thought, typified the new, corrupt, poetry also being written by Wordsworth because it aimed to give the authority of fact to foolish fairy-tales.

Jeffrey was right in his assessment of *Thalaba*; Southey's procedure of backing up his fantastical verse with travellers' sober prose *was* analogous to (though a feeble substitute for) the techniques that the lyrical balladeers used to give their unlikely stories the power of the real. Southey exposed, and reduced to absurdity, the Romantic intention, as Coleridge defined it, to 'procure for these shadows of imagination that willing suspension of disbelief... which constitutes poetic faith' (*BL*, vol. II, p. 6). It was, perhaps, from a wish to differentiate his own quest romance from Southey's and to distinguish his own techniques from those with which Jeffrey had publicly associated him, that Wordsworth dropped his *Thalaba*-esque reference to Park. It remains the case, however, that behind *The Prelude*, just as behind Southey's poem, stands Mungo as one of the explorers who made Africa the place in which a commonplace hero uncovers the hidden depths of human nature.

No one was a greater admirer of *Thalaba* and of Wordsworth than the young Shelley. In 1811, the budding poet made his own pilgrimage to the Lake District to meet his poetic idols. Southey's conservatism did not impress him; he continued, nonetheless, to be fascinated by the poetic Africa that Southey had conjured up in his verse. As a student, Shelley found that his desire to explore the African interior was so great he imagined projecting the latest technology across the continent:

Why are we still so ignorant of the interior of Africa? – Why do we not dispatch intrepid aeronauts to cross it in every direction, and to survey the whole peninsula in a few weeks? The shadow of the first balloon, which a vertical sun would project precisely beneath it, as it glides silently over that hitherto unhappy country, would virtually emancipate every slave, and would annihilate slavery forever.[40]

Keats dreamed of exploring Africa too, stimulated not just by reading Park but also by encountering one of the explorers whom Banks chose to follow Park. In 1818 Keats met Joseph Ritchie, who was shortly leaving for Timbuktu, and was so moved that he asked Ritchie to take with him a copy of *Endymion*. Ritchie agreed, and wrote, in December 1818, 'Endymion has arrived thus far on his way to the Desert, and when you are sitting over your Christmas fire will be jogging (in all probability) on a camel's back o'er those African Sands immeasurable.'[41] Excited by the news, Keats informed his brother that *Endymion* 'is on a camel's back in the plains of Egypt'. His poem was travelling into the heart of the most mysterious continent of all, a place where its exoticism would find a boundless home.

It was in tribute to the importance of exploration in his imagination that Keats sought to send his own Romantic poem back to Africa. Like Shelley, he dreamt, as travel writings encouraged him to do, of 'realms of gold', of lands of drugs and potions so exotic that 'we blend,/ Mingle and so become a part' of them.[42] But the travels that set him dreaming were organised by Banks: the poets' Africa was linked to a process which Britain was spreading across the globe, a process of exploration intended to increase its power and prosperity. Explorers of mental space, the poets followed the remote trails that Banks's men were blazing on behalf of science and empire.

Ritchie never returned, and his copy of *Endymion* was lost with him. But Park's narrative remained inspiring, filled with new metaphors to speak of mental travel, and with an exotic geographic terminology to speak of the mind and of the imagination itself.[43] In 1818, when yet another edition of the *Travels* hit the shelves in London, Keats, Shelley and Leigh Hunt gathered in Hampstead for a sonnet contest. The poets gave themselves fifteen minutes to compose sonnets on the geography of the Nile. They each made use of the popular knowledge of Africa produced by the narratives that Banks had offered to the public: narratives by explorers such as Bruce, Hornemann and Park himself. In Shelley's sonnet, the Nile fertilises the imagination in the same way it nurtures Egypt's 'secret Aethiopian dell' then streams across the continent from the sands of the Sahara to the 'desert's ice-girt pinnacles' in the Atlas mountains.[44] But Keats expresses most explicitly how geographic spaces came to stand for imaginative ones. In his sonnet the map of Africa is also a map of the poet's 'inward span'. Mental travel gives the mind real power, since it opens it up to 'all beyond itself'.[45]

Keats's presentation of Africa mirrors Park's, for Mungo *seems* the most romantic and the least imperialist of explorers. He offers travel as a realistic romance, an exotic quest that actually happened as he described it, a journey of self-discovery rather than conquest. He neither kills Africans nor takes their land. He represents Banks's network at its most apparently benign, shows it, in Keats's terms, as a system giving people paths to travel 'inward' as they go 'beyond'. Hunt, however, took a more ambivalent view than Keats. In his poem the dangers of African exploration are also portrayed. Africa is a mental space, but one discovers there not only images of 'villages ... caves, pillars, and pyramids' but also an emptiness that lies within: the Nile is 'like some grave mighty thought threading a dream' and leading one to an inner desert – 'Then comes a mightier silence, stern and strong,/ As of a world left empty of its throng,/ And the void weighs on us; and then we wake'.[46]

Shelley also gave moral warnings about the inner paths opened by external travel. In his sonnet the Nile 'knowest/ That soul-sustaining airs and blasts of evil/ And fruits and poisons spring where'er thou flowest./ Beware, O Man – for knowledge must to thee,/ Like the great flood to Egypt, ever be' (lines 10–14). Making the unknown known, charting the unmapped deserts of central Africa, Park gave his European readers a double-edged power – a power to know that was also a desire to discover. And that desire, both Shelley and Hunt realised, led Britons onwards because it led them inwards, in pursuit of the unknown that lay always just beyond. The quest for it might lead to isolation, blindness and the sacrifice of others. Africa, that is to say, came in their poetry to symbolise the (self-)explorer's quest to know the darkness that lay always almost within reach, at the centre of their minds.

REALMS OF GOLD

The poets followed in the footsteps of the travellers whom Banks had sent and published. And then, in their turn, new travellers followed in the footsteps of the poets. When Ritchie departed for Africa, he was already an admirer of Wordsworth, Keats and Thomas Moore, precisely because they made imaginary journeys into new realms. His desire to experience the foreign was shaped by reading about it, as he acknowledged in a letter: 'Have you seen Lalla Rookh? I never met with anything that carried me away so completely.'[47] *Lalla Rookh*, as we showed in chapter 3, was itself indebted to the botanical exploration of Banks and Sir William Jones. Ritchie, then, as a traveller sponsored by Banks, was a product of a cycle that had begun with exploration, had continued with the poetry that exploration inspired, and was now issuing in further exploration. It was also inspiring more poetry, for Ritchie was not only a fan of verse travels, but a poet himself. In his 'A Farewell to England' (as Alan Bewell has shown),[48] Ritchie imagined his impending journey into Africa in the Romantic terms made available by Keats's and Moore's depictions of the East. Addressing his mother country, Ritchie asked:

> And what if far from thee my star must set!
> Hast thou not hearts that shall with sadness hear
> The tale – and some fair cheeks that shall be wet,
> And some bright eye in which the swelling tear
> Shall start for him who sleeps in Afric's deserts drear?[49]

Here Ritchie is half in love with easeful death, viewing Africa as the stage on which he will achieve a heroic end. Exploration, as Shelley and Hunt warned in their sonnets, is the seductive route to a doom that, because it lets him discover that he is loved, is also a reward. He anticipates finding abroad what he cannot locate at home – a romantic apotheosis in the tearful sentiments of England's beautiful women.

Ritchie reveals most directly, as a poet, explorer and admirer of poetic explorers, the nature of the process initiated by Banks. Like the male poets he admired, Ritchie mirrors, in verse, Banks's own desire to penetrate the continent. Indeed he shows how poets took Banks's desire a stage further by transferring the glamour of African exploration onto the process of travel into the self. In the poets' words, African journeys became the necessary route into the interior of the soul. And yet, though they were responding to Banks in imagining themselves as mental travellers, the poets were not simply complicit with Banks's network, for they sounded moral warnings about a process that seemed both fascinating and perilous. The poets counted the costs of the desire to penetrate unknown regions – the costs to the explorer and to the region explored, as in *Alastor*, where Shelley depicted 'Dark Ethiopia in her desert hills' (line 116) as the alluring yet dangerous location in which the traveller explores the self. It was in Africa's ruined temples that Shelley's wanderer first 'gazed/ And gazed, till meaning on his vacant mind/ Flashed like strong inspiration, and he saw/ The thrilling secrets of the birth of time' (lines 125–8). By travelling beyond European civilisation and the social limits that civilisation imposed, Shelley's hero was able, in Ethiopia, to look into the self and find the meaning of time. But in this alluring process lay danger, for it led to a fruitless quest into remoter and remoter landscapes that ended ultimately in isolation, sterility and death.[50]

Banks had little time for such warnings, and many explorers and Africans died as a result of his determination that exploration should prompt colonisation. The paths that Banks opened into Africa were, if he got his way, to be commercial ones, for he wanted to turn the lands that Park had brought within his imaginative reach into territorial possessions feeding Britain with commercial and scientific wealth. On 25 May 1799 Banks told the African Association that Park had 'opened a Gate into the Interior of Africa into which it is easy for every nation to enter and to extend its Commerce and Discovery from the West to the Eastern side of that immense Continent'. If Britain did not 'possess' itself of the 'Treasures' of Africa discovered by Park, 'some Rival Nation' soon would. Chief among those treasures was gold, which Park had seen traded as dust. 'Science', Banks stated, 'should teach these ignorant savages that Gold which is Dust at the mouth of a river must be . . . in the form of Pebbles when near the place from whence it was originally washed.' Britain should send troops up the Niger to secure the gold reserves: five hundred, supported by artillery, would overcome 'the whole Forces which Africa could bring against them'.[51] In the event, Britain sent out a more modest expedition. Park led it; he was supported by a troop of soldiers and together they shot their way along until they simply disappeared. Neither Banks nor the public ever heard from them again.

African exploration did not end with Park's disappearance, nor with those of Hornemann, Burckhardt and Ritchie. Banks still wanted to know more, and so did the Britons who were excited by the explorers' narratives he helped publish. If the explorers died and the technology failed, Banks's vision had nevertheless helped set Britain on its imperial path. His network was not powerful enough to give Britain real possession of the space that it brought within mental reach. It was not until the end of the nineteenth century that European governments would seize the interior of Africa, in the name of commerce, science and Christian civilisation. That they were able to colonise Africa in the 1890s was a result of medical advances. But it was also a result of their development of the sorts of network that Banks had pioneered. The organisation of men and materials across the globe, the application of the latest technology to remote areas, the gathering and classification of useful knowledge at the metropolitan centre, the export of explorers and men of science; all these were features of imperialist government developed by Banks. Literature played its part in this process: the travel narratives he shaped placed Africa and other unmapped regions tantalisingly almost within reach, whilst assuring readers that the native inhabitants were naturally inferior and therefore ripe for colonisation. In presenting remote lands to the imagination Banks made them objects of 'knowledge' and desire, objects that literary writers then transformed into the magic places where the furthest recesses of the self could be explored. And these transformations, in turn, inspired further exploration: Joseph Ritchie would not be the last Briton to carry a volume of Romantic poetry into the 'realms of gold'. Soon, new generations of young men – men like the army officer Thomas Medwin – would be taking the words of Byron, Shelley and Keats with them as they crossed the deserts of Arabia and the plains of India.

CHAPTER 5

Banks, Bligh and the breadfruit: slave plantations, tropical islands and the rhetoric of Romanticism

As we have indicated, Banks's botanical network stretched from Africa to India, Australia and back to Britain. It was from the South Pacific, however, that he first made his name, for his descriptions of Tahiti and the visit of Omai made the island and its people a sensation. In this chapter we show that Banks maintained an interest in the island long after Omai's departure from London, and we examine how he aimed to turn a colonial profit from its plants. Pioneering what we now know as economic botany, Banks coupled exploration and pure science with imperialist priorities. The breadfruit that Banks had encountered on Tahiti would, he planned, be transferred to the Caribbean, where it would benefit the sugar planters. Omai's kith and kin – the free islanders of Tahiti – would effectively feed the enslaved Africans in the West Indies.

To a generation of literary radicals, Tahiti, in the person of Omai and later visitors, spelt nature, liberty and equality. To men such as Coleridge, Southey and Byron, a network that tied free Tahiti to the enslaved West Indies was one that united science with tyranny. Disgusted by Banks's scheme, they idealised South Pacific nature in the image of utopian liberty and portrayed the West Indian colonies, by contrast, as dystopias. In effect, their political positions and their abolitionist rhetoric were each influenced by the breadfruit scheme. They looked beyond the horizons of their former knowledge, reading explorers' narratives, and, as a result, entered into an imaginative relationship with islanders, an idealised if vicarious relationship. In contrast to this relationship, the self-interested relationship of the slave owner to the Africans he exploited seemed hellish. By following explorers' narratives, that is to say, they went beyond the narrow perspective of many Britons and the indifference to others that it bred. Imagining 'savage' liberty, they brought the horrors of slavery home to their consciences – something previous generations of Britons had not done. In the process, they established one of the most essential elements of literary Romanticism – the insistence on finding a real, visitable location for the pastoral ideal which previous generations had often placed in the mythical or classical past. In Tahiti's verdant groves, they found, at an early stage of their literary formation, such a location. The island's unfettered nature indicated there was a real, liveable alternative to British rule and to the society it produced. In effect, they thought they saw an extant and equal pastoralism, a community of liberty such as Robert Burns's Scotland and Thomas Gray's Wales. Later, they would locate such a community in England's West Country and Lake District. It was, however, a liberty in which they gradually lost faith, turning instead to a missionary Protestantism that, they hoped, would tame the tropical wilds.

We begin not in Tahiti but in Britain's prosperous slaving port Bristol. Eighteenth-century Bristol was made from sugar. But the purity of this sugar was in doubt. It was produced by slaves, and to many people it made the city red rather than white: 'every brick in the city', went a common saying, 'had been cemented with a slave's blood'.[1] To the young recently arrived radicals, Coleridge and Southey, the city's sugariness was a sign of its sinfulness. Sugar, Coleridge told Bristolians in 1795, was a luxury commodity, an unnecessary sweetener that turned sour in the mouth, for it reeked of the blood of slaves:

Surely if the inspired Philanthropist of Galilee were to revisit earth and be among the feasters as at Cana he would not change Water into Wine but haply convert the produce into the things producing, the occasioned into the things occasioning! Then with our fleshly eye should we behold what even now truth-painting Imagination should exhibit to us – instead of sweetmeats Tears and Blood, and Anguish – and instead of music groaning and the loud Peals of the Lash. (*Lects 1795*, p. 247)

Southey self-righteously contrasted himself with those who didn't taste blood in their teacups:

> Oh ye who at your ease
> Sip the blood-sweeten'd beverage! thoughts like these
> Haply ye scorn: I thank thee Gracious God!
> That I do feel upon my cheek the glow
> Of indignation, when beneath the rod
> A sable brother writhes in silent woe.[2]

Both poets urged Bristolians to boycott sugar, to cleanse their moral palates of the unholy sacrament whose pure whiteness turned blood-red. They campaigned against the slave trade, that is to say, using a Christian rhetoric of transubstantiation, invoking Jesus to show a miracle food embodying the slavery that produced it. Consumption, in this figure, was restored to production: the white gentlefolk of Bristol tasted in their sweetened tea the blood of their black slaves in the West Indies.

Sugar was a symbol of much of what the radicals and Romantics opposed in their society. It made present what was hidden: that a culture of civility at home was dependent on tyranny abroad, that a polite gentleman in Bristol was sustained by the brutal overseer of slave colonies in the Caribbean. Sacramental sugar, as Timothy Morton has shown, brought empire's moral costs as well as money profits back to Britain.[3] Armed with his sugary rhetoric, Coleridge turned his fight against the slave trade into a battle with empire itself. In 'Fears in Solitude', he attacked the imperialism that British voyages of discovery had spread:

> From east to west
> A groan of accusation pierces Heaven!
> The wretched plead against us; multitudes
> Countless and vehement, the sons of God,
> Our brethren! Like a cloud that travels on,
> Steamed up from Cairo's swamps of pestilence,
> Even so, my countrymen! have we gone forth
> And borne to distant tribes slavery and pangs,
> And, deadlier far, our vices, whose deep taint
> With slow perdition murders the whole man,
> His body and his soul!
> (*CPW*, vol. 1, p. 258, lines 43–53)

Coleridge's anti-imperialism made him more radical than most opponents, who merely wished to abolish slavery. Indeed, one of the abolitionists' key arguments was that ending slavery would increase profits from the colonies. Coleridge suggests, however, that the slave trade is not an anomaly in an otherwise peaceful trading empire but the logical consequence of a rapacious drive to exploit native peoples. Britain, in the rhetoric of Coleridge's Bristol years, is bent on an unprecedented project, on world-wide domination designed to guarantee its profits from the labours of others.

If sugar symbolised imperial tyranny, the breadfruit embodied indigenous liberty and natural fertility. Discovered when Captain Wallis visited Tahiti in 1767, the breadfruit became a Europe-wide sensation after the voyage of Cook on the *Endeavour*.[4] It was received, whole, dried and engraved, by a public who saw it as a synecdoche for the Polynesian islands on which it flourished (Fig. 12). Tahiti was imagined as a 'nouvelle Cythère', an exotic garden of Venus, a fertile Eden where far East became far West.[5] Its inhabitants were noble savages living in freedom, so plentifully supplied by nature with breadfruit that they did not need agriculture. Free from

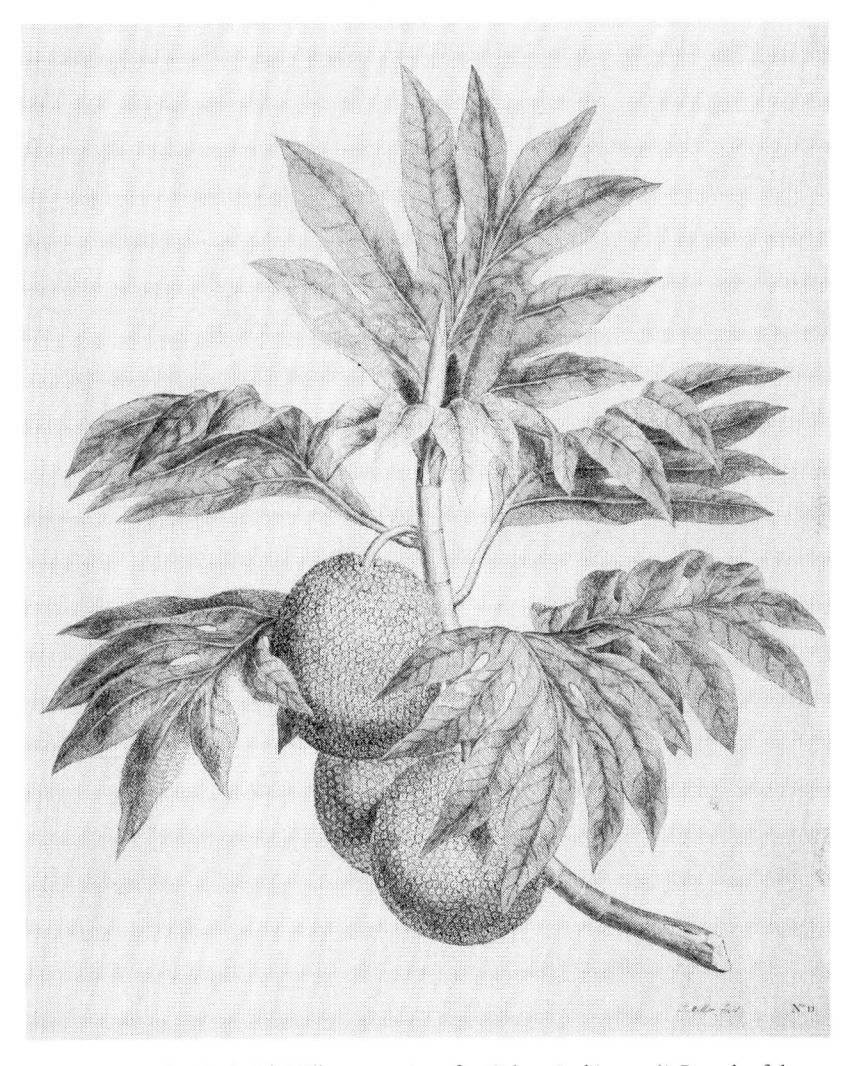

Figure 12. John Frederick Miller, engraving after Sidney Parkinson, 'A Branch of the Bread-fruit Tree with the Fruit' (1773) from John Hawkesworth, *An Account of the Voyages Undertaken by the Order of his Present Majesty for Making Discoveries in the Southern Hemisphere*, 3 vols. (London, 1773).

colonisation, free from labour, they seemed the antithesis of the slaves on the sugar plantations.

To give the cultural history of the breadfruit's impact in Europe is to give the history of a symbol – a political symbol of a life of liberty beyond the grasp of empire. It is to give the history of the production and dissemination of a fruit of Enlightenment ideals. The cultural history of the breadfruit reminds us that the Romantic imagination, and the symbols that characterise it, were elaborated as much in the contexts of scientific exploration and commercial colonialism as they were in response to the politics of France. French politics and their fall-out, however, came to inflect issues from further afield: the breadfruit became poisonous after the French Revolution led many Britons to associate Enlightenment ideals with rebellion and immorality. Coleridge and Southey, we shall see, found their breadfruit tainted by the changing domestic climate, which altered their view of it, and of the Tahitian liberty for which it stood.

Sir Joseph Banks was responsible, more than anyone, for the breadfruit flourishing in the European imagination. Banks first encountered the plant when exploring on Cook's first voyage. On the island Banks and his botanists collected the plant. His artists drew it. Meanwhile, the crew discovered its amazing nutritious properties and experimented with boiling and toasting it. To Banks, it seemed to place Tahitians in Eden before the fall: 'these happy people', he wrote, 'may almost be said to be exempt from the curse of our forefather; scarcely can it be said that they earn their bread with the sweat of their brow when their chiefest sustenance Bread fruit is procurd with no more trouble than that of climbing a tree and pulling it down'.[6] His fellow explorers agreed: breadfruit was prelapsarian, seeding itself everywhere and fruiting often enough to satisfy all the islanders' needs, letting them live in plenty, peace and love.

It was not only in expedition journals that breadfruit became a symbol of paradise islands that seemed to have escaped Adam's curse. It was through Banks's obsession with representation and classification that it became food for the European imagination. Back in London, Banks's efforts made the breadfruit a sign of plenty, an alluring image of paradise regained, to a public that was never likely to see, still less taste, one fresh from the tree. He exhibited specimens of it in his *hortus siccus*. There it could be consulted by botanists from all over Europe, at least in its dried form. He had the drawing of the plant prepared for publication in his *Florilegium*, so that it, along with the other species new to western science, could be disseminated as an image to natural historians unable to examine it in the metropolis.

The breadfruit became the chief delicacy in Banks's Pacific menu, a rare treat for men of science and public alike. They were fed by Banks's ability to supply an empire of knowledge via his power over the processes by which that empire was sustained: he had, as we showed in chapter 1, the resources to maintain a workshop of botanical illustrators and the prestige to shape the printed accounts of the voyages which sold out their editions across Europe. As a friend of ministers and monarch and (from 1778) President of the Royal Society, he also had the influence to ensure that the empire of knowledge remained dependent on him, for he not only shaped the processes of representation, but controlled the means of distribution. In charge of Kew Gardens, he had – or rather could get – the fruit, and men of science who wanted to examine it themselves were reliant on his ability to import it in the flesh just as readers were on his ability to disseminate it as a sign. J. F. Blumenbach, the eminent German professor, asked Banks in February 1794 to send him a breadfruit, since being able to exhibit an actual specimen would be 'exceedingly interesting for my lectures in Natural History' (BL Add MS 8098, p. 215). Banks dispatched some, along with other items from the Pacific, and Blumenbach told him that

their arrival . . . excited the universal curiosity of our little town, (remote in the heart of the continent where such exotic Rarities so seldom arrive –) that I may say there was in the first fortnight a kind of pilgrimage to my house, to see them, & above all that fruit so famous since your voyage round the world & so inestimable for the benefit of mankind. (BL Add MS 8098, p. 218)

Göttingen, Blumenbach's town, may have been little, but its university was at the forefront of contemporary thought, as Coleridge recognised when he chose to study there in 1799.[7] Blumenbach himself was a pioneer both as a natural historian and an anthropologist. He was not a man given to uncritical raptures: his scientific discourse aims at a detached, objective validity by converting particular objects into component signs/parts in a general classification of nature.[8] Yet here his words show the breadfruit as more than an item in an ordered sign-system. In the flesh, the fruit is a holy grail, or a fetish brought from exotic lands. Possession of it makes Blumenbach's house a sacred site and transfers to him the aura of the man who had brought it back from his quest round the world.

Not everyone treated Banks's plant so piously. If the breadfruit embodied the natural fertility of the Pacific islands, it also symbolised the free love that seemed to flourish there. The narratives of Cook's voyages viewed Tahiti through the neo-classical ideals of the explorers. Tahitian women were 'artless nymphs' who were as spontaneously and naturally sexual as the groves in which they disported.[9] And Banks, it was suggested, had indulged himself not only with the island's fruit but with its women.

Indiscreet phrases included in the voyage narrative compiled by John Hawkesworth encouraged satirists to link botanical with sexual discovery. Hawkesworth not only hinted at Banks's sexual encounters but featured his comment that the breadfruit almost exempted the Tahitians 'from the first general curse'.[10] Seizing on this, John Scott had the lovelorn Oberea carving Banks's name, like an Elizabethan sonneteer, on a breadfruit tree:

> Ah! I remember on the river's side,
> Whose bubbling waters 'twixt the mountains glide,
> A bread-tree stands, on which with sharpen'd stone,
> To thy dear name I deign'd unite my own.
> Grow bread-tree, grow, nor envious hand remove
> The sculptur'd symbols of my constant love.[11]

Here Scott makes the breadfruit tree scurrilously phallic. Oberea seems to be tattooing[12] the 'growing' Banks as much as carving her initials on the tree. The tree-like Banks is then imagined back home, spreading his seed over the gardens of Britain's ladies.

The explorers' spreading of their seed rapidly became no laughing matter. What seemed at first to be free love in groves where guilt was unknown soon threatened to destroy the island's reputation as a sensual Eden. Europeans brought not just guilt into Tahiti's sensual bowers, but venereal disease. The voyagers' sexual dalliance corrupted the savage idyll with the infections, physical and moral, of 'civilisation'. Georg Forster, naturalist on Cook's second Pacific voyage, feared

> that hitherto our intercourse has been wholly disadvantageous to the nations of the South Seas; and that those communities have been the least injured, who have always kept aloof from us, and whose jealous disposition did not suffer our sailors to become too familiar among them, as if they had perceived in their countenances that levity of disposition, and that spirit of debauchery, with which they are generally reproached.[13]

Forster was a political radical, an admirer of the French philosophes whose writings helped precipitate the French Revolution. His critique echoed that of Diderot, who adopted the persona of an islander in his discussion of Tahiti. Diderot's islander called European civilisation an infection which blighted his pastoral idyll: 'We knew only one disease, that to which all men, all animals, all plants have been condemned: old age. But you have brought us another; you have infected our blood . . . Our fields will be soaked with the impure blood that has passed from your veins into ours or our children will be condemned to nourish and perpetuate the sickness that you gave to their fathers and their mothers and then to transmit it in their turn, forever, to their descendants.'[14] For Enlightenment radicals, Tahiti's brave new world of noble savagery was already being corrupted by the exploring, and exploiting, Europeans.

Diderot was, of course, bemoaning the destruction of an ideal that was as European as the diseases brought by the explorers. Tahiti, that is to say, served as an imaginary home for social goals which emerged from Europeans' opposition to aspects of their own society. The island became the radical other of the hierarchical old world and the breadfruit the plant that rooted a pastoral utopia of noble savagery into the real soil of the tropics.

Ironically enough, it was Banks, who had done so much to make that utopia grow in Tahiti, who began its final destruction. He planned to uproot the breadfruit, to turn it to commercial, as well as scientific, use. He did not just export the plant in images and specimens for botanists. He exported it for the benefit of Britain, creating in the process a network of institutions and procedures that linked islands and continents. He joined Tahiti to an economic empire by the transportation of plants that were intended to bring plenty of food, and plenty of profit, to those who grew them. But it was this act that changed the image of the breadfruit, and of Tahiti, irrevocably. For Banks's scheme was to use the fruit, symbol of natural fertility and savage liberty, to feed other islands than those of the Pacific. In his hands, the fruit that sustained peace and love in independent Tahiti was to feed slaves in the colonised West Indies.

Banks, a consummate politician, encouraged a campaign to persuade the government that West Indies planters, currently in financial difficulty, were clamouring for the fruit. He helped John Ellis publicise the idea in *A Description of the Mangostan and the Breadfruit*.[15] As President of the Royal Society, he gave the proposals institutional sanction, implying that breadfruit was a miracle cure for the colonies' economic ills: 'the benefits arising from the cultivation of this blessed plant might be very sensibly felt by the English inhabitants of the Sugar Islands, as well as the poor negroes, their slaves; especially in times of scarcity'.[16] The breadfruit was to be Pacific manna for Britain's empire.[17]

By 1787 the campaign had succeeded. A correspondent rejoiced that Banks had 'prevail'd with the Ministry to send for the Breadfruit. This country will also have Reason to bless you'.[18] On Banks's say-so, Captain Bligh was commissioned by the Admiralty to sail to Tahiti, which he had first visited under Cook's command.[19] Bligh was to collect specimens of the breadfruit tree and take them to the West Indies. In 1788 he arrived at Tahiti and collected his trees but found naval discipline collapsing. In January of the next year three of his crew deserted in order to live with the island women. They later took part in the mutiny, which occurred on 28 April after the *Bounty* had sailed away from the island. One of the mutineers' first acts was to throw the breadfruit plants overboard. They would not take the bountiful fruit of the Pacific to the slave colonies of the Caribbean, and returned instead to Tahiti where, Bligh explained, 'they need not labour and where the allurments of dissipation are beyond anything that can be conceived'.[20] It was, of course, the plentifulness of the breadfruit that allowed them to live without labour on the island. The mutineers had 'gone native', sabotaging the imperialist scheme to make the fruit of Pacific freedom into cheap nourishment for Britain's slave labourers. The breadfruit, it seemed, would not after all be absorbed into the commodifying empire that turned places and people into profit-producing sugar.

Banks was not a man to let his appetite go unsatisfied, and a second voyage was prepared in 1791. Bligh, having completed his epic escape in an open boat, found himself returning to the scene of the mutiny. This time he commanded the *Providence*, and successfully reached the West Indies in May 1793 with his breadfruits housed in a plant cabin built to Banks's design. Banks's hand-picked gardeners James Wiles and Christopher Smith were on board, following instructions which Banks had carefully framed with the *Bounty* mutiny in mind.[21]

Banks knew from his friendship with George III that the King took a personal interest in the voyage. It was an interest related to imperial competition: Britain wanted to exploit the commercial opportunities offered by transplantation before the French did. But the French had a head start. On 15 July 1788, French St Domingue received a consignment of plants from Ile de France, including breadfruit. The breadfruit trees were distributed to twelve private and public stations around St Domingue. The French celebrated the breadfruit's arrival[22] while, back in London, Banks fretted but consoled himself that the French consignment was probably from the East Indies, 'where the good sort is not found'.[23]

Banks's botanical network was sophisticated enough to give him a good chance of outdoing the French. He had a back-up system in case the *Providence*, like the *Bounty*, went unexpectedly down. On 28 March 1793, Charles Ker, Army Surgeon, wrote from Calicut about a local source of breadfruit trees, of which he enclosed a drawing. Ker suggested that if the export of the trees from Tahiti failed it would be easy to export the plants from Calicut: 'and as it is a national object, this might be done by a King's ship on its return from this station' (Kew BC, vol. II, p. 94). Banks replied with detailed queries about the situation and soil the trees best thrived in; Ker then informed him that the local Commercial Resident meant to send plants to St Helena to be tried in different soils there. The trading posts and islands of Britain's empire had become research stations, linked by the navy, and dedicated to perfecting the transplantation of crops for commercial and therefore national advantage. Tahiti, like the other remote islands discovered by Britain's navy, could no longer be imagined as innocent and untouched.

The West Indian colonies, on the other hand, did prove independent, in an unexpected way. After all Banks's efforts they remained indifferent to the breadfruit. As a food for empire, it failed, because it fell foul of the complex class and race politics of the slave-islands. The botanic gardener on St Vincent told Banks that 'strange to tell, there are some people who undervalue such a valuable acquisition, & say they prefer a plantain or yam: but, however, these are only some self-conceited & prejudiced Creoles'.[24] The Creoles wanted to insist on their superiority to black people and to Caribs by disdaining food meant for slaves. And the planters, now less pressed by economic difficulties than in the early 1780s, disdained it for economic reasons, as Alexander Anderson remarked:

The breadfruit, although one of the most valuable productions yet sent them, is neglected and despised, unless by a few persons. They say that negroes do not like it, and will not eat it, if they can get anything else; but this is not really the case, as I know, and can declare from experience, that the very reverse is the fact, when once they are a little accustomed to it. The fact is, that the planters hate giving it a place on their estates, as they regard it as an intruder on their cane land, and they dislike any other object but canes. As to futurity, they think nothing of what may be the wants of themselves or negroes three or four years hence.[25]

Banks's scheme had broken, ironically enough, upon the commodity fetishism it had sought to help. Loving profit, the planters treated everything but sugar-cane as an expendable object. Why use land for breadfruit when the slaves it would feed could be replaced by newly imported Africans when they died of overwork and malnutrition?

Back in Bristol, Coleridge and Southey made the planters' indifference to the slaves' welfare central to their campaign against the trade. Coleridge later explained that cruelty was the inevitable outcome of a system of commodification, which loved a thing (sugar-profit) as if it were a person, and treated people as if they were things: 'A Slave is a *Person* perverted into a *Thing*. Slavery, therefore, is not so properly a deviation from Justice, as an absolute subversion of all Morality.'[26] Southey agreed, and went so far as to justify rebellion in his sonnets on the slave trade: 'No more on Heaven he [the slave] calls with fruitless breath,/ But sweetens with revenge, the draught of death.'[27] In an act of poetic justice, the slave kills his master with a drink sweetened with poison rather than sugar. The commodity to which he is enslaved destroys him who profits from it.

Not surprisingly, Southey also showed sympathy towards the *Bounty* mutineers who had sabotaged the commodification of the breadfruit and rebelled against a naval discipline almost as severe as that inflicted on slaves.[28] In a letter he declared:

If the *Bounty* mutineers had not behaved so cruelly to their officers I should have been the last to condemn them. Otaheitia independant of its women had many inducements not only for the sailor but the philosopher. He might cultivate his own ground and trust himself and friends for his defence – he might be truly happy in himself and his happiness would be increased by communicating it to others. He might introduce the advantages and yet avoid the vices of cultivated society. (Curry, vol. 1, p. 19)

Here Southey subscribes to the idealised version of Polynesia that positions it as the opposite of hierarchical and imperialist Britain. The mutineers are not solely motivated by lust: they go where the philosopher wishes to go, escaping the dehumanising discipline of the navy to live in virtue, independence, freedom and peace. Southey envies the mutineers their ability to slip free of the 'vices of cultivated society'. He imagines the *Bounty* affair through the ideal of savage liberty. His view was shaped by reading Hawkesworth, Forster and George Keate's *An Account of the Pelew Islands*.

By 1794, Southey and Coleridge, their conviction that Britain was corrupt growing, were beginning to dream of living in liberty abroad, where they might escape the pressure being exerted upon radicals thought sympathetic to the French Revolution. In February 1793 Southey had imagined a possible location for the commune that he and Coleridge came to term Pantisocracy:

Why is there not some corner of the world where wealth is useless! . . . Is humanity so very vicious that society cannot exist without so many artificial distinctions linked together as we are in the great chain? Why should the extremity of the chain be neglected? At this moment I could form the most delightful theory of an island peopled by men who should be Xtians not Philosophers and where Vice only should be contemptible. Virtue only honourable where all should be convenient without luxury all satisfied without profusion. (Curry, vol. 1, p. 19)

As McKusick argues, here Southey locates his commune on what resembles a Pacific island as described by Keate, Banks, Forster and Hawkesworth.[29]

Such an island would, presumably, be a home for virtue and honour because the abundance of the breadfruit would ensure that all were 'satisfied without profusion'. To Coleridge, revolted as he was by the 'idle gold' whipped by 'Bristowa's citizen[s]' from the bodies of Caribbean slaves, the South Sea islands were moral economies, places where human virtue and natural abundance were in harmony.[30] They were the imagined opposites to 'civilised' Bristol and to the commodified slave islands on which so much of Bristol's 'civilisation' was built. Soon the wilds of America, the valleys of Wales and the hills of Somerset were to fulfil the same function. The Romantic idealisation of rural life, that is to say, moved from Bristol to the South Pacific and back to the British countryside. Looking beyond Britain's shores through the publications that Cook and Banks had inspired led the poets to change their views of their native land and of themselves.

The Pantisocrats decided on the Susquehanna as a more practical destination, but Southey and Coleridge continued to imagine Tahiti as a refuge for liberty. In 1809, Southey wrote of Bligh's 'unendurable tyranny' and added: 'if every man had his due Bligh would have had the halter instead of the poor fellows whom we brought from Taheite' (Curry, vol. 1, p. 519). Southey still regarded the island as an ideal exotic setting for a liberty all too often fettered in Britain by issues of property and propriety.

By the mid-1790s, however, free love had a bad reputation in Britain. In the conservative backlash provoked by the French Revolution, radicals were stigmatised as rebels, traitors and debauchees. Burke portrayed the revolutionary impulse in terms of sexual deviance and monstrosity. Coleridge and Southey saw their friends attacked in similar terms. William Godwin was branded a pander for advocating the end of marriage; Mary Wollstonecraft was called a whore for living out her ideals of sexual equality. Mary Robinson met the same reaction when she became a radical poet. Coleridge himself was accused in *The Anti-Jacobin* of deserting his wife and children. Radicals were ostracised: Thomas Beddoes, their Bristol chemist friend, had his submissions to the Royal Society turned down by none other than Banks, who had already begun, in the words of a contemporary, 'to suppress all *Jacobin innovations*' in science.[31] Soon, Banks was co-operating with an attempt to suppress Pacific liberty too.

That attempt began with the formation in September 1795 of the Church Missionary Society. The Society recruited missionaries from Evangelicals and dissenters. In sermons and articles in the *Evangelical Magazine*, the chief advocate of the scheme, the Revd T. Haweis, sought to attract recruits by depicting the sensual delights of Tahiti. Haweis had never been to Tahiti: it was through reading travel narratives that he knew it. He was sure that missionaries would be able to convert it to Christian morality. Ultimately he was right. But first he had to persuade men to go there. And so he presented it in language which tempted its hearers to plunge themselves in exotic delights, only to reform them. He likened it to the 'gardens of the Hesperides', spoke of the 'fascinations of beauty, and the allurements of the country'.[32] But he identified the abundance of food produced by the breadfruit as an opportunity rather than a blessing. For Haweis, the breadfruit was not nature's but God's gift, given to allow the missionaries the chance to convert the islanders:

The natives not harassed by labour for daily bread, or as slaves, worked under the lash of the whip, are always sure to have abundant time for instruction.

Natives, in this ideology, had to work. Moral instruction would be a holy labour, an alternative to the work discipline that other Britons imposed on other islanders.

When the first missionaries reached the Pacific, instruction began to operate in the opposite direction, as a number of them abandoned their holy work to live on the fruits of the land with local women. By 1809 the problem was bad enough for the Revd George Burder to appeal to Banks on the Society's behalf. He requested Sir Joseph to use his transplantation network for the moral purpose of exporting wives for the missionaries who were facing the temptations of Tahiti.[33] Like a pander for the Church, Banks was to transport women, as he had done plants, for the benefit of the empire. But that benefit was by now defined differently, in terms of decency and propriety rather than scientific advance or commercial profit. The older, more conservative Banks, living down his Enlightenment enthusiasms, had them shipped. It was late in the day, but he had begun to impose Evangelical control over the Tahiti that, represented in travellers' tales, had become an image of liberty, fraternity and love. It was a control for which the Tahitians were to pay dearly.

It was also a control that Southey and Coleridge came to support. Having moved from Bristol by the early 1800s, they were no longer looking for a South Sea idyll to oppose to the islands on which the city's prosperity depended. Self-exiled from that political arena, they were no longer Pantisocrats offering Bristolians a radical other as an alternative to the immoral other of slavery. Under pressure from the anti-Jacobin crackdown in which Banks played a part, they wished to distance themselves from the democratic ideals of those days. And they were influenced by the missionary reports of infanticide, human sacrifice and cannibalism in the Pacific, so that they changed their minds about the islands' supposed harmony and liberty and about the morality of colonisation.[34] Evangelical Christianity offered more successful arguments against slavery, and they even came to accept its emphasis that morality and order proceeded from work. Where once they had idealised the culture produced by the breadfruit, they now condemned it. Tahitians were wicked, Southey wrote in 1803, because they failed to conform to the work ethic: 'when the Creator decreed that in the sweat of his brow man must eat bread, the punishment became a blessing; a divine ordinance necessary for the health of soul as well as body while man continues to be the imperfect being that we behold him'.[35] Coleridge, he added, had a scheme to 'mend' the islanders, 'by extirpating the breadfruit from their island, and making them live by the sweat of their brows'. The two writers, having consumed Tahiti and its fruit through travel narratives, having idealised it in opposition to the bloody islands on which sugary Bristol was built, now wished to see its natural fertility disciplined by Christian colonisation. This was to replace a radical ideal with an Evangelical one, to collaborate with the ideology that an increasingly moralistic age used to reform and to justify Britain's spreading empire.[36] The Tahitians, like West Indians after abolition, were to be Christianised and Anglicised rather than enslaved. Southey declared, 'I want English knowledge and the English language diffused to the east, and west, and the south.' In 1810 Coleridge recommended 'Coercion ... or even compelling' 'Savages into a form of civilisation' through a colonisation which made 'the moral good & personal Happiness of the Savages part of the End' (*CN*, vol. III, entry 3921). For both men, savage liberty and tropical nature were now too wild to be trusted. Uprooting the breadfruit from their political imagination, they turned instead to advocating a reformed imperialism of laboured righteousness and sweated civilisation. Daily bread and not the breadfruit would replace the unholy sacrament of slave-sugar and would symbolise British rule. To be an English writer, for the older Southey and Coleridge, was to accept the task of making the nation, and the world, prefer the communion-wafer of Anglicanism to the fruity flavour of liberty and the sugary taste of profit.[37] By 1833, with the Tahitians Christianised, slavery abolished and missionaries established in India and Africa, they could begin to scent the bland smell of sanctimony successfully spreading across the empire.

No one was a greater enemy of sanctimony than Byron – especially the sanctimony of Southey and Coleridge. In his *Vision of Judgment* (1822) he attacked Southey's vision of order on behalf of the peoples of Britain and – the South Seas (*BPW*, vol. VI). Georgian rule, he declared, would be condemned by all those who had died under its sway, 'From Otaheite's Isle to

Salisbury Plain' (stanza 60). For Byron, Tahiti remained a land of liberty, a Romantic utopia to counteract imaginatively the imperial tyranny by which it was now threatened. In 1822–3, he wrote *The Island*, his poem about the aftermath of the *Bounty* mutiny.[38] Fletcher Christian is its guilty yet defiant anti-hero who goes unrepentant to his death, fighting the British troops who have arrived to arrest him.

Christian dies, purging the guilt of mutiny, that the poem's hero may live. This hero is named Torquil and, deeply in love with an island woman, Neuha, escapes arrest and flees beyond the clutches of the Royal Navy. His love affair is endorsed by Byron. Torquil and Neuha effectively defy British imperialism. They break only one British *tabu* – that against sex outside Christian marriage – whilst they embody the European ideals of romantic love and individual liberty. They also conform to Byron's own stereotypes, to his desire for an unthreatening, because childlike and feminine, savage lover, to his tendency to patronise uncultivated commoners. Neuha is a child of nature, a 'gentle savage of the wild' (canto II, line 123), 'the infant of an infant world, as pure/ From nature – lovely, warm, and premature' (II, 127–8). Like her fertile island and its people, Byron suggests, she is childlike in her innocence: 'she fear'd no ill, because she knew it not' (II, 149). Free of guilt over sexuality, she is nevertheless conveniently sexually mature, 'In growth a woman' (II, 124); in fact, she is a goddess of love the more enchanting for being innocent of her power – 'A form like Aphrodite's in her shell' (II, 132). She is an embodiment of Byron's desire for a liberty that is compliant, simple and unchallenging, for a freedom that can be known in the flesh without loss of innocence.

The Byronic Torquil and his 'South Sea girl' (II, 333) are united 'in one absorbing soul' (II, 305) in a savage marriage blessed by nature rather than a priest. Neuha's 'faithful bosom' unites her solely to him, and their true love match becomes an embodiment of the peaceful and equal union of North and South, Britain and Tahiti. As such it acts as a fantasy that allows Byron to gloss over the more unequal and less idealised transactions that his sources revealed between the two cultures:

> The white man landed! need the rest be told?
> The New World stretch'd its dusk hand to the Old;
> Each was to each a marvel, and the tie
> Of wonder warm'd to better sympathy.   (II, 238–41)

Byron's idealisation is clearly indebted to those of the French philosophes on whose ideas Southey had blamed the French Revolution – Rousseau and Diderot. In Byron's Pacific, desire is not escaped but satisfied, as the symbolically fertile breadfruit reveals:

> The bread-tree which, without the ploughshare yields
> The unreap'd harvest of unfurrow'd fields,
> And bakes its unadulterated loaves
> Without a furnace in unpurchased groves,
> And flings off famine from its fertile breast,
> A priceless market for the gathering guest; –
> These, with the luxuries of seas and woods,
> The airy joys of social solitudes,
> Tamed each rude wanderer to the sympathies
> Of those who were more happy, if less wise,
> Did more than Europe's discipline had done,
> And civilised Civilisation's son! (II, 260–71)

Here the plant is made symbolic of the superior civilisation to be found in the state of nature. Byron thus achieves a late flowering of the symbol of sensual liberty elaborated by his eighteenth-century predecessors – a flowering still more explicitly sexual than its Romantic ancestors. But by 1822 the symbol has a changed context: Byron embraces the breadfruit to display his conscious opposition not only to slave colonies but to the reactionary turn taken by former liberals in Britain. He celebrates the breadfruit to challenge the increasingly received Evangelical wisdom, expressed by Coleridge and Southey, that from the plant grew the vices of a society ignorant of the biblical injunction to work.

But then Byron had never been enthusiastic about work. Yet he was keen on swimming,[39] and that is how he ends his poem. Guided by Neuha, Torquil swims underwater to a sea cave, where the lovers will never be found by the British. There, on the very edge of a world that British sea power was charting and ruling, liberty and free love flourish. The breadfruit, and the ideal of savage liberty it embodies, had been reduced to a narrow strip between land and sea. Menaced by empire, the South Sea home of the Romantic imagination would survive, but only on the margin where missionary colonialism and the ships that spread it could not reach.

What, then, can we conclude about the literary response to Bligh and the breadfruit voyage? Certainly that Romantic literature was shaped by – and in turn shaped – issues arising from exploration, especially as the young Robert Southey sought to locate the age-old pastoral ideal of rural liberty in the actual, present, world. But we can also see that literary Romanticism's relationship with the cultures that Britain was subjecting to its power was never univocal. Coleridge and Southey emerged as writers, in part, through their opposition to slavery[40] and portrayed the sugar islands as shameful dystopias. But this very portrayal was determined by their idealisation of the islands of the South Seas, which became utopias by contrast to the British Caribbean – utopias they abandoned only for Byron to revive them. The process at work here was not a 'Manichean allegory' – not a binary opposition of 'good' coloniser to 'bad' native, as some theorists have characterised imperialist ideology.[41] Rather, three or more terms are in play, and one indigenous culture is idealised in a rhetorical ploy aimed at making the colonisers' despoliation of another seem shameful. In this process, all the terms are in dynamic redefinition: Britain-the-coloniser becomes oppressive and guilty; the West Indies become sadistic labour camps; Tahiti an idyll of pre-colonised indigenous life; revolutionary France a place of illicit freedoms that can be symbolised by Tahiti. But the redefinition takes effect first at the imperial centre: the tropical islands were shaped by the demands of debate back in Britain.

In the Romantic writers' hands, redefinition was ostensibly anti-imperialist. And indeed it did enable them to make a vigorous condemnation of Britain – a condemnation that, historically, helped arouse enough guilt to get the slave trade abolished. But, to a degree, it sacrificed the South Seas in the process. Tahiti, that is to say, was appropriated and commodified as a savage idyll, shaped to serve an argument about Britain and the West Indies. And though this appropriation was, by comparison with the appropriation and commodification of Caribbean islands, relatively benign, it nevertheless had dangerous consequences. Because they were subsumed in the breadfruit, real Tahitians figured in European eyes only in Romantic terms. Their lives and culture were buried beneath the tree that supposedly embodied them, so that they could not figure in other ways. Worse still, because Europeans came to believe that Tahiti Romanticised was Tahiti in real life, they began to turn against it. Ironically and tragically, the Romantic idealisation of the Pacific led to its own extirpation, for had the South Sea islands not been pictured by explorers, scientific and literary writers as sensual Edens, then Evangelical missionaries would not have targeted their culture for 'reform'. And had the islanders not been seen – as Diderot and Byron saw them – as childlike and pliant in their innocence, then the missionaries might not have dared move in. Yet they were so seen, and the missionaries did move in. Thus an anti-colonialist idealisation that was effective in opposing Britain's empire of slavery led to a cultural imperialism with pernicious consequences. There were no innocent fantasies in a world in which Britons could increasingly impose their wills, and repress their desires, at native people's expense.

By 1830, the missionaries had, in uprooting the Romantic image of the islands, succeeded in attacking some of the customs that they found cruel or immoral. They reduced prostitution and attacked infanticide. But they encouraged and participated in wars and effectively destroyed much of the traditional culture that gave Tahitians their identity. The missionaries introduced European dress; they discouraged communal dwelling. They insisted on labour and enforced a strict moral and legal code where they could. In short, they inculcated the regime that Britain's governing classes increasingly sought to instil in the labouring classes at home: Bible learning, handwork, thrift, and monetary payment. Something of the islanders' hybridisation of these imposed systems is evident in an incident remembered by the missionary William Ellis:

On one occasion, a young woman who had been taught the use of the needle, after receiving a number of lessons and attaining some proficiency, applied for payment. 'For what?' asked the teacher. 'For learning', was the answer; 'you asked me to learn and I have learnt.'[42]

The islander's misreading of the missionary's economies of knowledge and money puts the purpose of both into doubt. It mocks them. Yet it also suggests that within the culture controlled by the missionaries she was likely to be permanently disappointed: she would not be paid as she hoped for absorbing European knowledge at the missionaries' behest. Work would not lead to prosperity and neither would knowledge, for her and many of her compatriots, lead to power. Instead, they would lead to alienation and demoralisation. By 1835 the population of Tahiti had fallen by three-quarters; the art of making cloth from tree bark was no longer practised; the great double canoes had been abandoned. A Quaker visitor wrote: 'there is scarcely anything so striking or pitiable as their aimless, nerveless mode of spending life'.[43] The breadfruit would never again, in fantasy or reality, nourish an indigenous culture unmarked by the desires, fears and power of Britain. Scientific exploration had its price, and it was the native people of Tahiti, like the Africans enslaved in the West Indies, who would count its cost as their daily bread.

Not all the native people: if some suffered by the missionaries and their introduction of the work ethic, others profited – at least in the short term. One such was the ambitious chief Pomare who, by converting to Christianity, was able to recruit the missionaries, with their armaments and technological expertise, to assist him in wars that were designed to make him paramount over the other chiefs of the island. With the missionaries' guns and tactics, Pomare gained authority while the missionaries, for their part, got new, official, approval of their religion from the most powerful man in Tahiti. They got it too from Britain's Poet Laureate: Southey's supportive reviews of the missionaries' *Transactions* helped to give their actions respectability amongst the Anglican and conservative middle classes. Southey's Church and King nationalism effectively influenced the development of the muscular Christianity that became a vital force in Victorian imperialism. And if such an outcome seems both unlikely and ironic considering Southey's earlier idealisations of South Sea liberty, then it should remind us that Tahiti had, by 1830, been for many years one of the issues that led the once-radical writers of the 1790s to eat the words in which they had first formulated Romanticism.

CHAPTER 6

Exploration, headhunting and race theory: the skull beneath the skin

In this chapter, we examine the field that, along with botany, benefited most powerfully from exploration – the study of living creatures. Armed with the host of specimens that Banks and others had placed at their disposal, natural historians were able to move their field into new areas. After exploration had stocked their centres of calculation, they could access the skin and bone they needed to slot the animals of new regions into their universal systems of nature. And they did not just leave those specimens in drawers, but began to build new methodologies, and ultimately disciplines, upon them. Georges Cuvier in France, John Hunter in Britain, and J. F. Blumenbach in Germany became the leaders in the technique of comparative anatomy. Poring over the bones that Banks and other men of science retrieved from Australia, Tahiti and North America, they learned to infer the shape and scale of the whole skeleton. Examining the internal organs too, they discovered a new way of arranging animals. Displayed in the anatomists' museums, the similarities and differences of a range of bodily structures revealed a rank order in nature.

Empowered by their technique, natural historians scrutinised not only the animals but also the indigenous people whom explorers had encountered. They began to collect and measure their bodies and their bones and, on the basis of their figures, to divide humankind into a catalogue of races. Many of them came to agree that 'Caucasians' were distinct from and superior to other races and the 'negroes' were nearer than others to animals. Racial theory and the related disciplines of ethnology and craniometry (the measurement of skulls) gained authority because explorers had encountered native peoples and because men such as Banks had the networks to ship these people back to Europe in the form of specimens for study – alive or dead. Race theory, which often placed black people at the bottom of a rigid hierarchy, also depended on an international trade in the body parts of recently discovered 'natives'. Here we examine the positions of different theorists, so as to focus the early nineteenth-century debate about race with clarity as well as to reveal its hitherto obscure relationship with the material expropriation of indigenous people's bodies.

Race theory changed Britons' perceptions of the peoples of its empire. Here, we assess how Coleridge's views were altered as he researched the ideas of Blumenbach, Hunter and their successors. Under their influence Coleridge developed a theory of his own, one that differed significantly in one respect – it approached the question of human variety through a Romantic historicism. Seeing racial difference as the organic development of spiritual forces, Coleridge added a new, sinister, element to British discourses on race. And, as was the case with his changing view of Tahiti, he moved from asserting black people's human equality in the 1790s to asserting the 'fact' of their inferiority in the 1820s. In this area, his response to exploration and to race science turned him from an anti-imperialist radical into a (in today's terms) racist advocate of a colonialist mission to 'civilise'.

'It is', wrote Thomas Carlyle in 1828, 'the age of machinery, in every outward and inward sense of that word.'[1] All over Britain, time and space were being measured out in the rhythms of new contrivances: power looms, steam engines, hydraulic presses, telegraphs and treadmills, to name but a few. Natural philosophy was embracing technology, and people's lives would be transformed. It would, in the words of the industrialist Josiah Wedgwood, 'make machines of men as cannot err'.[2]

Turning men into automatons suited Wedgwood's dream of efficient factory production. To realise the dream, however, men had accurately to be known – and this proved harder than Wedgwood expected. Nevertheless, as his friend Banks knew, philosophers across Europe were using new methods to make such knowledge possible. One of these philosophers was the Dutch anatomist Pieter Camper, and he also drew inspiration from machines. In 1794 he displayed a new one to the public. It consisted of 'an horizontal quadrangular table, upon which was placed a perpendicular frame, that was also quadrangular. In the laths which completed this frame a number of holes were bored parallel to each other; so that threads could be drawn through them, and be fastened in every direction required'.[3]

Camper's device was not an instrument of torture – not for live bodies anyway. The ghost to be trapped in it was the mind[4] – in particular the mind of the 'negro' and the 'native'. The mind was to be pinned down by measuring the skull. By the power of his measuring table, Camper would measure and classify the varieties both of mankind and animals. He would subject humans to a hierarchy, a rank-order fixed in their heads. At the top of Camper's hierarchy was the idealised cranium of ancient Greek statuary, at the bottom the bird. Black people's heads put them nearer the animal than the Greek gods:

When in addition to the skull of a negro, I had procured one of a Calmuck, and had placed that of an ape contiguous to them both, I observed that a line, drawn along the forehead and the upper lip, indicated this difference in national physiognomy; and also pointed out the degree of similarity between a negroe and the ape. By sketching some of these features upon a horizontal plane, I obtained the lines which mark the countenance, with their different angles. When I made these lines to incline forwards, I obtained the face of an antique; backwards, of a negroe; still more backwards, the lines which mark an ape, a dog, a snipe, &c. This discovery formed the basis of my edifice [Fig. 13].[5]

Camper's edifice became apparently objective evidence for the natural inferiority of the 'negro'. Through his 'facial angle', geometry seemed to prove racial hierarchy. He emphasised his methodological independence of human bias: his machine did away, he claimed, with the fallible and subjective human observer. It was transparent – not a device to be admired for the ingenuity of its operation, but a frame through which one saw things as they were.[6] He designed it to make science trustworthy, to let it escape from the dubious authority of travellers' impressions. Mr Webber, artist on Captain Cook's voyage, had, he complained, 'too much of the mannerist'; his portraits of islanders could not be accepted as accurate recordings of nature.[7] Camper himself could not visit Tahiti or meet islanders, but he did the next best thing – he went to that part of the original portable and sturdy enough to be brought to Europe intact.[8] In 1786 he sketched a Tahitian skull carried back to Britain by Cook's voyagers.

Let us turn from the science of Europe to an island in the West Indies. In 1787 Alexander Anderson wrote from St Vincent to Banks in London.

I am sorry that as yet I have been able only to obtain one Carrib's skull for you which I now send; it is a very difficult thing to get the Craniums of the Yellow Carribs, or Aborigines; the greater part of them has been extirpated by the Black Carribs: at present there is only two familys of them existing in the most remote part of the Island. Their burial places, (which is always the Hut in which they die) are not easily found; and any attempt to disturb the ashes of their ancestors they regard as the greatest of crimes. (*DTC*, vol. VI, p. 159)

Grave robbing was a crime in Britain too, as Banks knew. Yet despite the islanders' resentment and Anderson's qualms, Banks continued to seek crania.

Banks wanted skulls because natural historians wished to replace their reliance on travellers' tales with a discourse that seemed to be an objective

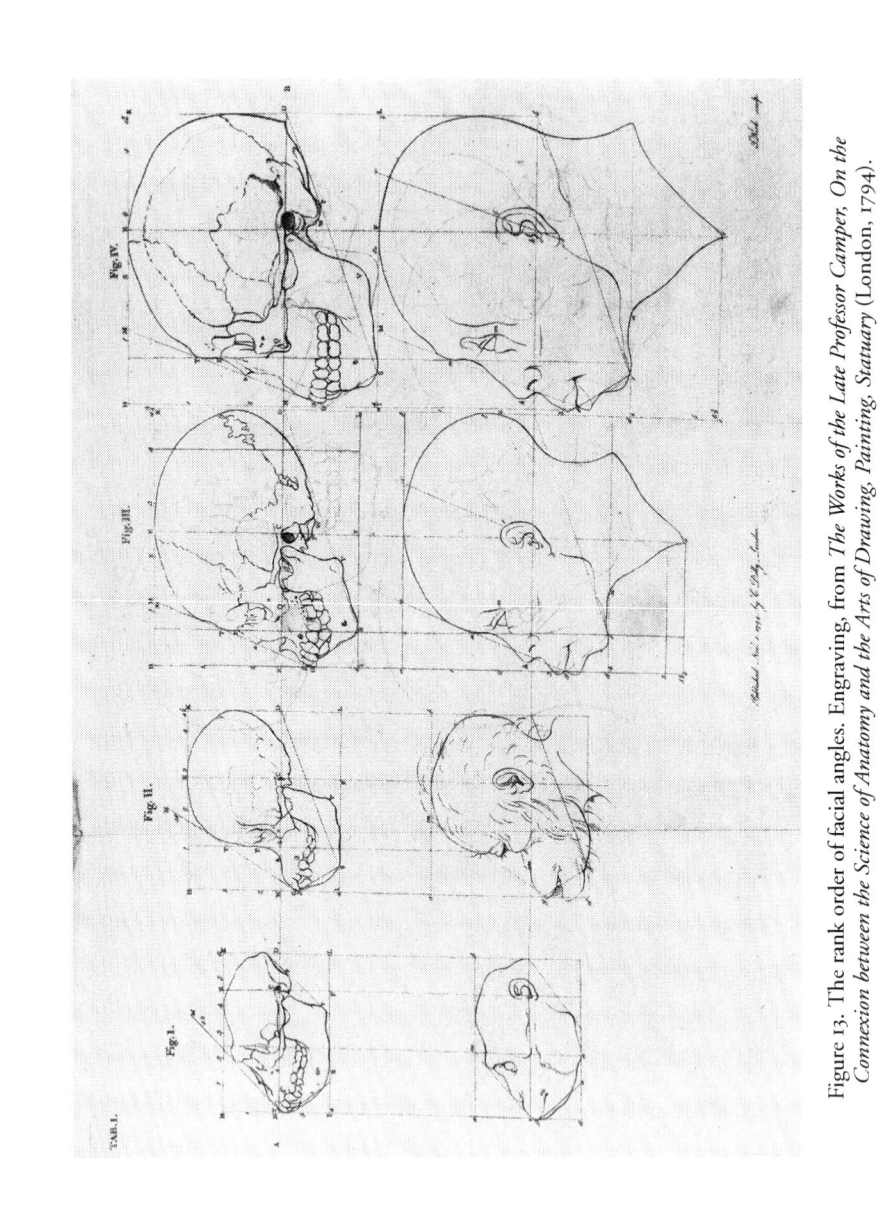

Figure 13. The rank order of facial angles. Engraving, from *The Works of the Late Professor Camper, On the Connexion between the Science of Anatomy and the Arts of Drawing, Painting, Statuary* (London, 1794).

observation of fact. They required empirical evidence to persuade themselves – and their fellow men of science who were also trained to trust empiricist method – that they had proved their ideas about race.[9] To do so they became headhunters in the name of science.[10] This created a trade, one that reveals colonial commerce at its most exploitative and grisly. One of the chief headhunters was Blumenbach who, in 1787, asked Banks to supply a Tahitian skull. Banks's reply shows how anatomists and natural historians created an ever-increasing demand for native skulls, and tried to locate new suppliers because they rapidly became subject to the profiteering of those who possessed the raw material:

I wish it was in my power to procure for you the cranium you enquire after but since Dr Hunter here & Dr Camper in Holland have written so much on that subject those who have possession of the crania of the South Seas have set a high value upon them. (BL Add MS 8096, ff. 387–8)

Banks used his network to ensure Blumenbach's needs were satisfied. Captain Bligh brought one back for him in 1791. Science was, in this case, fostering a macabre trade in which capitalist laws of supply and demand operated with little regard to morality.

Blumenbach's goal was to extend human knowledge by basing classification of the animal realm on the similarities and differences of a combination of bodily features, internal as well as external. By this means he avoided the reliance on external appearance and subjective impressions that had limited Linnaeus's *Systema naturae* (1748) and Georges Buffon's *Histoire naturelle* (1749). Both these writers had divided mankind into racial groups. In doing so, they had given the term 'race' a new set of contexts. Prior to their work (and still to some extent after it), the word was used interchangeably with terms such as 'nation', 'tribe' and 'peoples'.[11] Used in this sense, the term was a historical and a diachronic one that described familial descent and *not* physical features or appearance. One's race was one's ancestors. But in Linnaeus and Buffon the word 'race' was used interchangeably with 'variety' – a synchronic term describing external appearance and not descent, stock or lineage. The pioneering natural historians made 'race' signify empirically observable variations within the human family of races – a family viewed in its distribution over space, rather than through time.

Linnaeus classified creatures binomially according to their genus and species. In the tenth edition of his *Systema naturae* (1758) he divided the species *Homo sapiens* into six diurnal varieties and one nocturnal: *ferus* (four-footed, mute and hairy); *americanus* (red, choleric, erect); *europaeus* (white ruddy muscular); *asiaticus* (yellow, melancholic, inflexible); *afer* (black, phlegmatic, indulgent); *monstrosus* (several deviant forms). *Homo nocturnus* was exemplified by *Homo sylvestris* (man of the woods or orang-utan). In the division between men and the apes there was doubt on which side of the line Pygmies, Hottentots and orang-utans belonged.[12] Linnaeus's system was essentially another version of the Great Chain of Being, demonstrating gradation in nature but static and unable to account for change.

It was also unable, in the opinion of Blumenbach, to account for the true differences between races. The problem was the observation: both Buffon and Linnaeus seemed too impressionistic, taking too few of the characteristics of a species into the purview of their classification. In particular, Linnaeus was thought to have given anatomical features too little place, a neglect which Hunter, Georges Cuvier and others sought to rectify by comparing the anatomical features of different animals and peoples. Everard Home's description of Hunter's collection reveals the importance of anatomical specimens to the comparative methodology of the new classificatory science: 'All the organs of an animal body are arranged in distinct series, beginning with the most simple state in which each organ is met with in nature, and following it through all the variations in which it appears in more complex animals.'[13]

Like Hunter, Blumenbach needed organs and bones. As an empiricist project, natural history acquired its power through the belief that it exactly fitted the world, from observation of which it had been constructed. And so the theorist required not just drawings and descriptions of crania, but the skulls themselves. Blumenbach acquired the world's largest collection of heads, to ensure that his science could be based, and be seen to be based, on the real objects that it represented. His family called it 'Golgotha'. Coleridge examined it while studying in Göttingen in 1799; it contained 70 or 80 skulls, a number which later rose to 120. Blumenbach became a connoisseur of crania, a headhunter-by-proxy, enhancing his power and prestige as a man of science by his possession of more and more skulls. His language reveals the avidity of the obsessive collector rather than the detachment to be expected of the natural historian: 'how numerous already my collection of skulls of different nations is, & how enthusiastic desirous I am to make it more and more compleat' (BL Add MS 8097, f. 132).

The more general Blumenbach aimed to make his racial science, the greater the number of individual real skulls he needed to possess. Skulls were vital to his scheme, because they were the ultimate hard facts on which the claims of science could be founded. When he received the skull harvested in St Vincent by Anderson he told Banks: 'On the first view I found out the real Caribbean physiognomy by the . . . high & flat eye-holes, & then by the flat backward falling forehead' (BL Add MS 8097, ff. 134–5). He could only arrive at his idea of the generic traits of each racial group by comparing several skulls from that group, so as to eliminate merely individual or accidental characteristics. And so, like the tribesman regarded by Europeans as 'savage', Blumenbach fetishised the objects of his desire. That he did so is in one sense unsurprising: the bones of the dead gave him power – the power that stems from society's perception that one is able to explain the mysteries of life.

Blumenbach's Golgotha gave him more scientific power than Camper ever acquired through his skull-measuring device since Camper, in the opinion of his fellow anatomists, had too few skulls to put in it. Lacking the raw materials, his data were too scanty for his hierarchy to be reliable. And Blumenbach himself criticised the 'facial angle' as being too limited and variable a measurement to sustain the classification that Camper based on it. Camper's empiricism was not thorough enough to satisfy his fellow empiricists.

The lesson that natural historians drew from Camper was that more skulls, and more techniques of measurement, were needed. Georges Cuvier provided the latter. He replaced the 'facial angle' with measurement of cranial capacity (brain size) in relation to facial area. He expressed this measurement as a ratio in which the intellectual was judged against the sensitive. In Europeans, he decided, the ratio of skull area (intellect) against facial area (sense) is 4 to 1. In 'negroes', it is '4 to 1.2'. Blacks, he concluded, were naturally endowed with better senses and smaller intellects than whites.[14]

Blumenbach strove for better techniques of measurement. He replaced the 'facial angle' with description of as many features as possible, chiefly the form of the frontal and superior maxillary bones. And, crucially, he moved to establish his scientific authority by reproducing his collection, so as to demonstrate to all the full extent of the evidence on which his conclusions rested. His science rested on possession of the real, but depended for acceptance on dissemination in virtual form. He could only demonstrate the anatomical basis of his racial categories by publishing his skulls. He had his collection drawn, engraved and published with commentary in the language which all European men of science could read, under the title *Decas collectionis suae craniorum diversarum gentium illustrata*.[15] But the *Decads* were dependent on Banks's rate of production and so, therefore, was the success of Blumenbach's racial science. In 1791 Blumenbach was still begging Banks for a Tahitian skull: 'the moment I shall have one of them in my possession I will immediately publish the 2nd Decad'

(BL Add MS 8097, ff. 362–3). By 1795 he had one, and acknowledged Banks's 'generosity' by prefacing his *De generis humani varietate nativa* with a letter of thanks.[16] Sir Joseph's transoceanic collection network had received its public place in European science's systematic effort to locate racial types in nature – an effort that, despite the fact that it led Blumenbach to make enlightened endorsements of the full humanity, artistic prowess and technological expertise of non-Caucasians, was later to be used to justify the clearance of indigenous peoples from the lands desired by white settlers.[17]

Possession of a hundred and more skulls allowed Blumenbach to achieve a more ambitious and more authoritative theory than had Camper. Having received the Tahitian skull, he had the missing link he desired. He had it drawn and engraved in his published *Decad* because it allowed him to confirm his five-fold classification of humanity into different races. This classification was pre-Darwinian: it stressed not evolution by natural selection but a process of human degeneration from a perfect, Adamic, original man. It was, that is to say, reconcilable with scripture even while it claimed empirical accuracy. Racial variety, it asserted, had been produced as the original men had gradually separated – and descended, influenced by environment and climate – into the different races found on earth in the present day. These races were all human, and all degenerate by comparison with the Adamic original. Some, however, were more degenerate than others. The Caucasian (a term Blumenbach coined) had degenerated least, the 'Negro' most. Tahitians were part of the fifth, Malayan, race:

Of a brown colour, from a clear mahogany to the darkest clove or chestnut brown; with thick, black, bushy hair, a broad nose and wide mouth. To this class belong the South Sea Islanders, or inhabitants of the fifth part of the world; of the Marianne, Philippine, Molucca, and Sunda Isles, &c., with the true Malays.[18]

Here Blumenbach echoes Linnaeus in his dependence on impressions of skin colour. But his 'Golgotha', illustrated in print, allowed him to argue that 'the Caucasian must, on every physiological principle, be considered as the primary . . . of these five principal Races'.[19] His Tahitian skull was evidence that the Malayan race was a 'transition' between the primary Caucasian and the most degenerate – the Ethiopian. Race relations – and distinctions – became matters of fact when founded on the skull beneath the skin.

Or so it seemed, for Blumenbach's craniometric scheme founded what became the most influential racial classification of the nineteenth century before Darwinism. But in fact Blumenbach's empiricism, like that of Camper before him, was vitiated by his own aesthetic idealism. In their search for more objective, and so more authoritative, science, neither man was alive to another fact – that their predilection for classical ideals of beauty shaped their whole approaches to the issue of race. Camper organised his cranial hierarchy so that all skulls aspired to a facial angle that never existed in life, the angle measurable on Greek statuary. The further removed from that angle, the more animal-like a race was. Blumenbach also took his ideals from Greek art, approving of the skull of a Georgian woman because 'the form of this head' corresponded 'exactly to that of the marble statue of a nymph in the collection of the late Mr Townley'.[20]

Neo-classical aesthetics became an altogether more torrid influence when transplanted to the islands of the Pacific, where many of Blumenbach's and Camper's skulls had been collected. They coloured the views and actions of the collectors in unexpected ways, ways that then impacted upon what the natural historians thought they saw in their piles of heads. Blumenbach saw in his skulls the characteristics that travel narratives had preconditioned him to see. His Tahitian cranium looked relatively degenerate because it fitted a description of living Tahitians that he had read. He quoted the naturalist on Captain Cook's second voyage, Georg Forster: 'their features were very irregular, and in general very ordinary'. The skull reminded him of Forster's description of the island women: 'artless nymphs in whom youth supplied the want of beauty'.[21]

Behind this aesthetic was male sexual desire. The gentlemanly explorers of Tahiti had indulged in promiscuous sexuality with the women they viewed as nymphs (often, in fact, these women were prostituted by their menfolk in return for iron tools). Banks had enjoyed himself in this way when on Tahiti, as we mentioned in chapter 1. He had selected women for their beauty and dallied with several at once, giving gifts of European manufacture as 'payment'. Viewing Tahiti as a 'new Cytherea', the explorers and skull collectors looked through Ovidian eyes. They dallied with and quarrelled over the island women like Greek gods with dryads. Blumenbach adopted their views. Sitting in Göttingen examining his skulls, he mirrored Banks and Forster viewing the 'artless nymphs': anatomical science followed the excited gaze that had led in Tahiti to carnal knowledge. Thus the scientific idea that Tahitians were racially more degenerate than Caucasians was complicit with a self-serving and exploitative sexual fantasy. This fantasy positioned island women as primitive nymphs so that European men would be able to enjoy them without consequence to themselves.

Shaped by fantasies about the living, Blumenbach's science was less objective than it pretended. Fashioned also by a fetishisation of the dead, it was less different from the 'primitive' knowledge of the Tahitians than he

Figure 14. John Webber, watercolour, 'A Human Sacrifice at Tahiti' (1777). BL Add MS 15513.16.

realised. In fact, Blumenbach's collection was uncannily like those of Tahiti, for the island chiefs' power and reputation also depended on assembling a collection of skulls in one place. The islanders collected the skulls in great shrines (*marae*). These sites were *tabu* (taboo) areas, places of spiritual power where the chiefs, but not the ordinary people, officiated in ceremonies (Fig. 14). The chief's power was demonstrated by his ability to approach the *marae*, and by evidence that the ancestors blessed his actions. Banks had participated in such a ceremony in Tahiti: first he 'was stripped of his European clothes, and a small piece of cloth being tied round his middle, his body was smeared with charcoal and water, as low as the shoulders, till it was as black as that of a negroe'.[22] In appearance a native, Banks stepped into the role of a Tahitian chief. He encountered at first hand the sacredness of the dead: so *tabu* was the procession that everyone whom they passed hid himself under the first shelter that he could find.

Cook and Banks soon realised the immense importance of the dead body in Tahitian culture. They witnessed the veneration accorded to the skulls of chiefs[23] and they contrasted the reverence of the Tahitian favourably with that of the Briton:

The Marae . . . is at once a burying ground and a place of worship, and in this particular our churches too much resemble it. The Indian, however, approaches his Marae with a reverence and humility that disgraces the christian, not because he holds anything sacred that is there, but because he there worships an invisible divinity, for whom, though he neither hopes for reward, nor fears punishment, at his hand, he always expressed the profoundest homage and most humble adoration.[24]

Attentive to the islanders' beliefs, Cook forbade his men to plunder the *marae*.

Despite Cook's sensitivity, many commentators regarded the Tahitians as superstitious because they venerated skulls; Blumenbach's dependence on them, on the other hand, was simply seen as proper scientific method. Sure of the rightness of their own beliefs and the superiority of their civilisation, the Christian missionaries whom Banks later helped to establish in the Pacific destroyed the *marae*, having convinced the chief Pomare of the greatness of their own God. Robert Southey recorded approvingly how the priest of Huahine, Patii,

tore off the sacred cloth in which they were enveloped from vulgar eyes, and stripped them of their ornaments; then, one by one, he threw the idols into the flames, sometimes pronouncing its name and fabled pedigree, expressing his own regret that he had ever worshipped it, and calling upon the spectators to behold that these objects of a false worship were not able to help themselves.[25]

Having led his agents to remove skulls from the island, Banks had then indirectly aided in the destruction of the sacred sites in which skulls were laid to rest.

As Blumenbach's principal supplier of skulls, Banks was the impresario of scientific discussion of race, a natural history of mankind that became increasingly accepted as the nineteenth century progressed. That natural history, it follows, depended on a network that supplied centres of calculation in the European metropolises and universities.[26] Banks's skulls, assembled at Göttingen, allowed Blumenbach to bring fragments of not just one but many indigenous peoples under his analytic eye. Possessing the small and desiccated relics of those peoples, he could compare them, as nobody within any one of those peoples could (or would seek to) do, for his own and his scientific peers' satisfaction. At the centre of calculation, he could make dead fragments 'prove' – or rather justify – a new European understanding of where Europeans stood in relation to whole peoples, and where those peoples stood in relation to each other. His division of the world into races, that is to say, was the universalisation of a data-accumulating process that began with an act as particular as the division of skull from skeleton. Apparently all-embracing, his race science actually concealed its own partiality, its reliance on the few pieces of native life small and stable enough to be carried on shipboard back to Europe. Living 'natives' tended to die of disease if brought back (hence the eagerness of Hunter and Blumenbach to measure Omai). And Blumenbach, like the other race theorists, had not himself travelled. In the absence of even brief contact, he was conjuring with the bones of the dead. But it was the headhunting network of Banks, feeding the continued European faith in empiricism, that led to men of science believing in the trick. In the eyes of Blumenbach's peers, the Göttingen Golgotha blossomed into a world-wide classification; a few dry bones lived again as universal truth.

Truth is rarely as universal in practice as is claimed when first put forward. Natural historians, comparative anatomists and race theorists did not all read the same signs in their skulls, and a vigorous debate developed, in which white men argued about the bodies of black people. It was an intricate debate, and one we need to be clear about if we are to understand accurately the origins of contemporary racial stereotypes and to see clearly the roles of different Romantic-era writers in defining (and also contesting) those stereotypes. In what follows, we discuss some of the participants in the debate, beginning with the extreme position set out by polygenesists, before examining their opponents – including Coleridge, whose distinct and Romantic contribution to the debate we investigate in detail.

On one side of the debate was the Manchester surgeon Charles White who, in his *Account of the Regular Gradation in Man* (1799), argued that 'everyone who has made natural History an object of study, must have been led occasionally to contemplate the beautiful gradation that subsists amongst created beings, from the highest to the lowest. From man down to the smallest reptile . . . Nature exhibits to our view an immense chain of beings'.[27] So far, so Linnaean. At the top of the chain was the European, seen through Camper's neo-classicist aesthetics as well as the Platonic notion of the archetype:

Where shall we find, unless in the European . . . that nobly arched head . . . the perpendicular face, the prominent nose, and round projecting chin? Where that variety of features, and fulness of expression; those long, flowing, graceful ringlets; that majestic beard, those rosy cheeks and coral lips? In what other quarter of the globe shall we find the blush that overspreads the soft features of the beautiful women of Europe, that emblem of modesty, of delicate feelings, and of sense? . . . Where except on the bosom of the European woman, two such plump and snowy white hemispheres, tipt with vermillion?[28]

Like the explorers of Tahiti, this anatomist disguised in a racialised aesthetic the swelling of sexual desire.

White stared at white women's breasts with his mind's eye; he also drew up black people's bodies with tape and pencil. Over fifty Africans resident in Britain submitted to his measurements. On the basis of these he concluded not only that the 'Negro' 'seems to approach nearer to the brute creation than any other of the human species' but also that 'various species of men were originally created'.[29] Blacks were a different race in the new sense that they were a different, *non-human*, type or species of life. They were more like orang-utans than people. White was putting the skull science pioneered by Camper, Hunter and others[30] to a new sinister use – lending scientific authority to the self-interested arguments of slave-owners and their apologists that blacks were not human. He was also, he thought, proving from the hard facts of skull and skeleton the arguments of historians of human civilisation such as Lord Kames, who had merely relied on Banks's and Solander's impressionistic descriptions of Tahitians' behaviour to generalise about their essential racial characteristics.[31]

Few contemporary anatomists agreed with White. Most thought their skulls proved blacks to be the lowest variety of a human family in which whites were at the top but in which different races shaded into each other.

For most, race meant a variety within one family, rather than separate species. One who did not think so was a surgeon in several ways White's heir, Dr Robert Knox, author of the phrase sometimes taken to represent nineteenth-century racism in general: 'Race is everything: literature, science, art, in a word, civilisation, is traceable solely to the race to which the individual or nations belong.'[32]

Cynical, radical, atheistic, Robert Knox was, in fact, in no way a typical voice for early nineteenth-century Britain. In *The Races of Men* (1850) he emphasised the iconoclastic nature of his views, 'opposed to all the received opinions of the day'.[33] The iconoclasm had particular causes: a distinguished anatomist in Scotland until 1828, Knox lost his reputation through a scandal that other skull-seeking anatomists had only narrowly avoided. He had been obtaining cadavers for dissection from William Burke and William Hare who, it transpired, had been murdering people for the purpose. Although cleared of any complicity, Knox was widely attacked and burnt in effigy. Embittered and angry, he eventually left Edinburgh, finally settling in London, where he lectured and wrote on human anatomy and physiology.[34] Always closer to the traditions of French scientific materialism than the mainstream of the more religiously orthodox British science, Knox espoused the cause of 'Transcendental Anatomy', which maintained that the history of life forms, from extinct vertebrates upwards, was the unfolding of an organic (not divine) principle, thus linking man with the apes.[35] Knox's adherence to the ideas of Etienne Geoffroy Saint-Hilare marked him out as one of a group of radical, free-thinking philosophers. His study of human variety, *The Races of Men* (1850), re-established him as a celebrated figure in the guise of a prophet of a European race war who had foretold the interracial conflicts of the 1848 revolutions in his earlier, unnoticed lectures.

For Knox, like White, the word 'race' designated not a variety (the usual scientific use of the word 'race') but a permanent type which is not convertible and which is *not* to be confused with nationality. The races of men were clearly distinct with 'remarkable organic differences', including mental and psychological ones, which were innate and had not altered over human history. Knox firmly rejected scriptural chronologies and with them the theory of 'monogenesis' or the common origin of mankind, descended from Adam. He argued that the races of men differed from the earliest known historical period and they had always so differed. The causes of these differences were not external: neither climate nor diet had any bearing on them. And so, for Knox, racial difference was effectively permanent and unchanging. It was also fundamental: he traced 'human character, individual, social, national, to the all-pervading, unalterable, physical character of race' and explained human history as 'the war of race against race'.[36] He was most concerned to establish and demarcate the European races of Saxon (or Scandinavian) and Celt. Knox argued for the natural and psychological inferiority of the 'dark races' as he called them, believing that the antipathy between them and the Saxon races 'is greater than between any other'. He prophesied their extinction.[37] Although he was a marginal figure before the publication of *The Races of Men,* Knox became influential when his ideas were taken up by James Hunt, who founded the Anthropological Society of London in 1863.[38]

Influence came late to Knox, for he remained at the extreme. On just about every major point relating to human variety and culture Knox was in total opposition to what we might call the major theories of race in the early nineteenth century. Knox rejected completely the work of Blumenbach. He also had contempt for the major English development of Blumenbach's Christian scheme: the thought of James Cowles Prichard. Prichard, like most theorists in Britain, also depended on anatomical specimens but drew different conclusions from them. He never accepted that racial difference should be equated with separate species and unchanging types.[39] Species, too, Prichard recognised, was a fluid rather than absolute category, having no ultimately fixed boundaries.

Prichard came to Bristol as a student in 1802 and returned in 1810, being elected surgeon to the Bristol infirmary in 1816. He also married the daughter of Coleridge's erstwhile patron, the Unitarian minister John Prior Estlin. In 1813 he brought out his important *Researches into the Physical History of Mankind* (a work he changed substantially in several later editions). The *Researches* was a book made possible by British imperial power. It not only made use of the anatomical studies that Banks's skull collecting had set in train, but also responded to the work of William Jones and the Asiatic Society on Oriental languages and cultures. Prichard began by revising Blumenbach, accepting Blumenbach's notion of degeneration but arguing that the original primary race was black, as black races occasionally produced white offspring. In making this argument he effectively replaced, with the principle of heredity, Blumenbach's suggestion that racial change occurred as a result of environmental influences (principally climate). He argued that racial variety occurred through the accidental eruption of new variations in humankind.

For Prichard race was never a rigid category and he stressed the variability of groups, nations and tribes, eventually more or less abandoning the concept altogether. He came to argue for the impossibility of defining racial types and denied that there was such a thing as the 'negro' race: 'it is by no means evident that all those nations who resemble each other in the shape of their skulls, or by any other peculiarity are of one race, or more nearly allied by kindred to each other than to tribes who differ from them in some particulars'.[40] His view of variety thus became a nominalist one, for he denied that there were any essential biological differences. The biological argument for racial difference was for him largely analogical and he argued for the necessity of tracing affinities between different nations in terms of language, religion, political institutions and manners.

Prichard was associated with the evangelical wing of the Church, and his Christianity shaped his theory. He believed passionately in the unity of man, accepting the truth of the creation story and believing that all other religions were corruptions of the original Christian dispensation. Like the scholar Jacob Bryant, he regarded all mythology as a corruption of an original and primitive monotheist, Trinitarian, divine revelation, preserved by the Hebrews after the deluge. The aim of his scientific work was to trace, on the basis of linguistic and cultural similarities, the origin of mankind in a single family that had been dispersed over the face of the earth after the flood. To this end he accumulated a mass of ethnological data from scientific and travel accounts – including, as we showed in chapter 4, Banks's protégé Mungo Park. In his last work *The Natural History of Mankind* (1843), he distinguished between the three great families of man deriving from scripture: the Semitic (Syrio-Arabian), the Japetic (Indo-European) and the Hamitic (African). Prichard's eventual abandonment of race theory altogether was a move away from the territory of physical anthropology to something much closer to contemporary cultural anthropology or ethnography, the very discipline that Knox reacted so strongly against.

Prichard's thought had greater centrality in early nineteenth-century Britain than Knox's. In his acceptance of Biblical authority, modified but not supplanted by the latest empirical techniques, Prichard suggests that race theory remained, for many, reconcilable with Christianity. In this he mirrors the pre-eminent British palaeontologist William Buckland and the one literary Romantic to consider matters of race at length – S. T. Coleridge.

Coleridge's writings on race were not influential directly – he left them unpublished. But they affected his and his followers' published arguments about colonialism and Britain's historic role with regard to other peoples. They are worth discussing here, then, not just as examples of a well-informed idealist modification of Blumenbach's and Prichard's theories, and not just as evidence for an enquiry into whether Romantic writers were racist, but as contributions to the developing Victorian discourse about a national imperial mission.

Coleridge defined his own position in the race debate in opposition to the materialism associated with Knox and with Louis-Antoine Desmoulins's *Histoire naturelle des races humaines* (1826) which put forward a 'polygenesist' classification of man into sixteen distinct species, then divided these into 'races' or subspecies, making race a subspecific category. As a materialist, Desmoulins, like Knox, rejected the scriptural account of the genesis of man. He also, like Knox, detected racial difference in the European group itself, conflating ideas of nation and race. Coleridge's response was characteristic: 'This work is quintessential French – and Desmoulins's the pure & *intense* Frenchman. No other nation could have produced the author of this work.' Coleridge objected that Desmoulins had banished God and Providence from the system. His challenge to Desmoulins was to show 'any instance of five or six aboriginal Species in the whole Catalogue of the Mammalia so slightly distinguished from each other or passing so imperceptibly into each other, as in this 5 or 6 Races of Man'. That is, that the difference between humans was so comparatively slight in comparison to differences in the animal kingdom that they could not be classed as distinct species. Coleridge's imperative was to maintain the symbolic truth of 'the necessary idea' of the narrative of the dispersal of Noah's sons: Shem, Ham and Japhet. This prevented him from countenancing explanations which accounted for human difference in terms of separate species (*CM*, vol. II, pp. 176–7).

Coleridge's own explanation was closest to his former tutor Blumenbach's. He came to regard Blumenbach's physiology as a theistic alternative to the scientific materialism of French thought and he was captivated by Blumenbach's notion of a formative force or vital principle divinely implanted and developing in response to external stimuli, a notion first developed by John Hunter and Immanuel Kant.[41] But his own theory was not a copy of Blumenbach's, but a significant development that tried to supersede Blumenbach's reliance on empirical data with an idealist organicism. This theory appeared as a series of notes to be used by his friend and follower J. H. Green in a course of lectures at the Royal College of Surgeons in 1828. These notes revise Blumenbach's work along the lines that Prichard was simultaneously pursuing. As well as accepting Blumenbach's hypothesis of the formative force, Coleridge also completely concurred with the monogenist notion of there being one species of humanity radically different from all other animals. This species was variegated along Blumenbachian lines into five distinct races, determined by degeneration from a primary race. The difference between races was thus one of degree. For Coleridge, 'variety' was a different term from 'race' (the words had been synonymous for Blumenbach) and related to 'minor, more fugitive and accidental differences' (*SWF*, vol. II, pp. 1388–90). He also suggested that the concept of 'race' is a semantic necessity and not an absolute category: 'What are differences of Kind as opposed to differences of degree – & who is to be judge what difference in degree is equivalent to a difference in Kind?' (*SWF*, vol. II, p. 1389).

Coleridge's differences of degree were hierarchical. Man stood at the top or 'ultimate intent' of organic creation, incorporating the attributes of lower beings as he rose above them (*SWF*, vol. II, p. 1397). This hierarchical model led him to revise Blumenbach in a more disturbing way. Where Blumenbach had preferred the Caucasian race on grounds merely aesthetic, Coleridge wished to see the Caucasian or Indo-European race as the summit of human development: Blumenbach, Coleridge noted, had made no distinctions 'in respect of intellectual faculties, and moral predispositions'.[42] Yet a moral superiority was evident, for the Caucasian retained more of the ideal humanity of the primary, historic race from which all had degenerated than did the others: in the Caucasian we 'find the moral beauty, the cui bono or final cause of the Fact – that the Human Species consists of ONE *historic Race*, and of *several* others' (*SWF*, vol. II, p. 1402). The greatest moral degeneration was revealed by 'the wretched state of the Boschesman in the wilds of Caffari or the New Hollanders' (*SWF*, vol. II, p. 1401). Here, Coleridge used the concept of degeneration in a pejorative rather than in Blumenbach's neutral sense.

Coleridge agreed with some of Blumenbach's followers in thinking that anatomy could apparently reveal not just physical but mental inferiority. In 1827 he observed 'certain remarkable coincidences between the moral qualities and the configuration of the skull' (*TT*, vol. II, p. 116).[43] His views (in this area at least) resemble those of William Lawrence, whose *Lectures on Physiology, Zoology and the Natural History of Man* he read shortly after their publication in 1819.[44] Lawrence also argued from Blumenbach's skulls in ways that Blumenbach himself eschewed. He referred 'the varieties of moral feeling, and of capacity for knowledge and reflection, to those diversities of cerebral organisation, which are indicated by, and correspond to the differences in the shape of the skull'.[45] Blacks, it turned out, were 'proved' by their skulls to be inferior: their 'natural inferiority' was 'clearly evinced by the convincing evidences of anatomical structure and experience'.[46] The 'negroes' of the Congo, Lawrence thought, show 'the most disgusting moral as well as physical portrait of man'.[47] Whilst blacks were clearly of the same species as whites, separate from apes, they were nevertheless measurably nearer 'the monkey' in terms of their cranial capacity. What they needed,

Lawrence concluded, was 'kindness and indulgence' from Europeans who, being of 'superior endowments', should colonise rather than enslave them. Caucasians must 'extend the blessings of civilisation' to Africans.[48]

Like Lawrence, Coleridge began to dispute Blumenbach's view that differences in skin colour and anatomy might be explicable by climatic variation. Also like Lawrence, and *contra* White and Knox, he argued for the 'resemblance' of some blacks to apes but denied that this showed that blacks were a different species from whites. Indeed, he was, at least on occasion, more enlightened than Lawrence in this debate, attributing the supposed 'resemblance' not to racial but cultural factors (*CN*, vol. IV, entry 4984).

Most importantly, Coleridge differed from both Blumenbach and Lawrence in trying to derive race, and natural life in general, from its origins in the divine creativity. Coleridge added to empiricist natural history a characteristically Romantic organicism dedicated to demonstrating the growth of man and nature from God. Blumenbach's skulls became grist to the Coleridgean mill of an *Opus Maximum* that was intended to reconcile the Biblical account of mankind's origins with the latest scientific evidence. Coleridge combined Biblical hermeneutics (learnt from Blumenbach's Göttingen colleagues[49]) with comparative anatomy as he tried to explain how 'the Hebrew Tradition, whether it be interpreted historically or mythical[ly] . . . the idea of Shem, Ham and Japhet . . . will be a guide in the attempt to connect the scheme with Historical Events & Facts' (*SWF*, vol. II, p. 1457). He would revise Blumenbach's theory of racial difference, he asserted, into a form 'that 1. . . . is founded on history, at all events on an ancient and justly venerated tradition: 2. that . . . leaves room for historic combinations, to be judged by the canons of credibility . . . 3. . . . escapes the error of attributing to the Climate and the accidents of Circumstance a larger share of influence than either sound Philosophy or the Facts themselves will admit' (*CM*, vol. I, pp. 540–1).

If Coleridge's scheme resembled Prichard's in its Christian bias, it differed from it as Coleridge adopted an idealist methodology derived from Kant. In the process Coleridge not only offered a teleology for racial categories, but implied that racial inequalities were part of God's providential scheme working itself out through nature and history. He substituted the term 'historic race' for Blumenbach's usual 'central race'. Degenerate mankind had not yet dragged itself up to the stage in which the historic race would again walk the earth, but of all the presently existing races, only the Caucasian was moving towards it. Caucasians alone had a vision of racial progress, in which the degenerate races of the day would eventually be reunited as the divine spirit worked, through history, towards a renewal of the original unity of man (*SWF*, vol. II, p. 1406). Coleridge contrasted Caucasians with 'inferior Races' who were tending towards a 'Catastrophe of Destruction' via a 'judgement', after which only 'the crowning Products that formed the final cause of the preceding Epoch were carried over to the new Ledger or Page' (*SWF*, vol. II, p. 1405). In this millenarian scenario, providence would naturally select, for survival and renewal, the races capable of forming (and acting on) abstract ideas, in particular the abstract idea that history moves in a gradual progress, through multiplicity, towards unity. At present, the Caucasian race seemed the only one capable of such ideas.

In face of this apocalyptic judgement, what was to be done? Because the Caucasian race had degenerated least from the historic original, as was revealed by its ability to form and act on abstract ideas, it was its divinely appointed task to lift the others from a degeneracy that was intellectual and moral, as well as physical – like 'a central Sun relatively to the Planets, communicating Light, heat . . . ameliorating them even where it leaves them in their peculiar orbit' (*SWF*, vol. II, p. 1402). Europeans had to civilise the peoples of other continents, Coleridge decided, for 'it is possible that certain climates are inhabitable without physical degeneracy only by the animalising changes brought about by moral degeneracy' (*SWF*, vol. II, p. 1404). As an example he pointed out the black skin of the Negro. The Negro had become animal-like in an attempt to cope with hostile climate, but white Caucasians would cope by their superior moral strength and scientific knowledge: 'a far higher state of moral and intellectual energy in the central Race, with the scientific powers & resources of that far higher state, might enable the Masters of the world to reside unharmed on any part of their Estate' (*SWF*, vol. II, p. 1405). Here Coleridge set out the sinister ideology (and anticipated the very language) used by those who did conquer black peoples' land to justify their white supremacist policies. And his phrases are uncomfortably close to those used in Germany by Nazi race theorists.[50]

Where, in Coleridge's scheme, did blacks' inferiority come from? It was, as the Bible showed, ordained by God to allow the historic race to fulfil its civilising and Christianising mission. The 'children of Ham', he declared, interpreting Genesis 12. 1–2, 'seem by Providence to have been impelled to the south, and there as the inhabitants of Africa, to bear witness to us of that awful prophecy which Christianity, the universal redeemer, has been lately, to the undying glory of this nation, at once fulfilling, and healing the unhappy slaves that were to be servants to their elder brethren till that time when the servant should be as the master and the master as the servant before the eye of the common Lord'.[51] Britons, Coleridge implied, could congratulate themselves that they had begun to fulfil Providence by abolishing the slave trade and by converting unwilling slaves into willing servants – servants of Jesus and of the men who spoke of Jesus. Like Lawrence, Coleridge then arrived at a practical proposal; for him the knowledge-systems of the Bible and of science justified a racial solution based not on extermination or exclusion, but on colonisation and conversion: 'I dare challenge the most industrious research to supply only one single instance of a tribe, that ever by their own unassisted efforts under the most favourable circumstances of nature without the influence of more civilised and cultivated states have ever raised themselves from a savage or even from the rudest forms of the pastoral state' (*SWF*, vol. II, p. 1415). In face of this, Coleridge declared in 1833, 'Colonisation is not only a manifest expedient – but an imperative duty on Great Britain. God seems to hold out his finger to us over the sea' (*TT*, vol. I, p. 369).

Coleridge never travelled to 'pastoral' Tahiti. He never explored 'rudest' Africa. Nor did Blumenbach, Camper or Prichard. They did not need to; they could theorise human nature and history through the schemes provided by philosophy and theology – when they were supplemented by the 'facts' brought back by travellers and colonists, 'facts' they could build into the new classificatory science. That science was not monolithic – there was no simple racist position in the early nineteenth century, but a debate in which the word 'race' was contested and positions differed sharply (and with them, attitudes to black people). Men such as Blumenbach and Prichard were humane and innovative, developing the terms that their own culture made available to them so as to accept the common humanity of all people and to honour the intellectual and artistic achievements and potential of Africans. Men such as White and Knox were not, for they used the same methodology of measurement to erect permanent barriers and to justify war upon and enslavement of people they judged to be non-Caucasian. Others, including Lawrence, were different again, for they rejected Christian schemes and opted for a materialist account of difference, but still argued that all races were of the same human species.

Nevertheless, the fact that there was considerable dispute, and a range of more and less condescending arguments towards peoples who did not seem white, should not blind us, now, to the fact that natural history seized upon bodies, dead and alive, so as to establish paradigms of difference that were written, as natural signs, all over the skin and deep in the bone. This was the contemporary scientific paradigm within which every informed writer on human natural history had to work, whether they were materialist or Christian. And it often brought with it its own methodological equivalent of

Camper's wooden measuring frame (with which we began this chapter), in which prejudice and partiality achieved the appearance of objectivity. There were exceptions – men such as Prichard, Gall and Spurzheim who, on the evidence of comparative anatomy, dismissed the notion of essential mental differences between various human groups – yet the Revd Richard Watson was right when he argued in 1824 that, on the whole, the real enemy of racial equality was the anatomist *per se*. 'The minute philosophers', wrote Watson, 'who take the gauge of intellectual capacity from the disposition of the bones of the head, and link morality and the contour of the countenance'[52] – these men militated by their use of their discipline against the acceptance of racial equality.

Sir Joseph Banks promulgated no race theory of his own, yet all those who did were indebted to him: to his influence in building an empire of knowledge on the foundation of a network for importing objects. Race debate was ultimately dependent on a mastery of materials, a mastery that it went on to promote as it 'proved' racial inferiority and thereby legitimised colonisation. For Lawrence and Coleridge were not alone in arguing that colonisation was a moral mission for Britain and not just a commercial opportunity. By 1833 Evangelicals and Utilitarians had formed an alliance, supported by the 'scientific' authority that natural history and comparative anatomy appeared to provide. This alliance was strong enough to force a reluctant East India Company, by act of parliament, to aid the Christianisation of British India. Men of religion and men of reason, men such as Wilberforce and Mill, united in the belief that blacks had been proved to need education and government by Caucasians. This truth, after all, was written not just in the Bible but on and in black people's bodies.

But this 'truth', which sent white men to Africa, India and the Pacific to rule and 'civilise' the native people, was a product – the end-product of a trade that was already imperial, a trade that exported explorers and men of science across the world and imported their findings to London and Paris. The new science depended on the appropriation of foreign cultures at the levels of objects and bodies (living and dead) as well as the levels of information and images. Exploration fed race theory skulls, as well as signs, and race theory, in its turn, legitimised the imperial domination that increasingly followed exploration. But race theory rested on desires and obsessions it did not acknowledge – on the desire for power through knowledge and on the obsession with possession of the object that could root that knowledge in the real. In the process, the skull became the holy grail of the nineteenth-century creed of Romantic race theory.

CHAPTER 7

Theories of terrestrial magnetism and the search for the poles

The focus of this chapter is on the development of the science of terrestrial magnetism, the hypotheses and theories it gave rise to, and the literary and political uses of its metaphors in Mary Shelley's *Frankenstein* (1818) and S. T. Coleridge's writings. This was a time when a series of theories were put forward as researchers including Biot, Euler, Aepinus, Gauss, Coulomb, Oersted, Hansteen and Alexander von Humboldt developed notions about the earth's magnetic properties and began the process of detailed measurement on sea and land, mapping the globe with a series of isogenic lines, lines as significant and important as the boundaries attached to states and nations. These maps depended on voyages of exploration, which spawned further writing – both theoretical and fictional. We discuss the magnetic research of Banks and Cook in the context of earlier British work in the field, and assess their legacy in the nineteenth-century polar explorations, culminating in James Clark Ross's location of the North Magnetic Pole in 1831 and his search for the South Magnetic Pole in 1839–43.[1] In the British context, Banksian science was once more crucial, and after Banks's death the Royal Society and the Royal Navy continued the co-operation in scientific exploration that he pioneered.

It became apparent very early in European history that measuring the earth's magnetism was not a straightforward venture. This phenomenon came to be measured in three ways. First, it had been noted, at least by the time of Columbus, that a suspended magnet did not, in fact, always and in every location point to the geographic north as determined by celestial observations. This fact seems to have been well known by the fifteenth century, as the variation was marked on some compasses by 1450. It became understood that the divergence between the two points was a universal phenomenon and one that varied in different parts of the globe. The angle between the meridian of the compass needle and geographic north came to be known as 'variation' and later 'declination'. It came to be measured by the azimuth compass in which a mariner's compass was combined with an instrument for the astronomical measurement of geographic north by taking the azimuth of the sun.[2] The importance of the phenomenon to mariners was quickly grasped; if the declination was a constant then it would be possible to determine the fugitive value of longitude at sea. If the magnetic poles were fixed like the geographic poles, then the angle between the two would depend on one's position on the east–west axis, thus if these angles were tabulated they could then be used to determine longitude. The first Englishman to publish a tract on compass variation was William Borough, whose *A Discours of the Variation* appeared in 1581.[3]

The second important magnetic measurement was that of inclination. It was noted that the compass needle if freely suspended would point down from the horizon at the north end in the northern hemisphere and at the south end in the southern hemisphere. This became known as the 'dip' or 'inclination'. To measure this the compass needed to be placed in a vertical rather than horizontal plane. In 1576 the London instrument maker, Robert Norman, constructed a dip-circle or inclinometer and began the process of the systematic mapping of the earth's magnetic inclination.[4] Norman concluded that the needle would align itself vertically at 90° to the horizon and that it would be 0° horizontally at the North Pole. In London he found that the north pole of the needle inclined to 71° 5′ below the horizon. Norman's observation disproved the common hypothesis that the compass pointed to some magnetic feature like a mountain on the earth's surface. Such a magnetic mountain featured on Gerard Mercator's famous projections of the earth's surface. The point of attraction must be to something inside the earth itself, what he called the 'point respective'.[5] It also became apparent by 1634, after sustained observations in London and Paris by Henry Gellibrand among others, that both the dip and the variation changed over time; awareness of this 'secular variation' led to less confidence that terrestrial magnetism could be a safe navigational aid.[6]

With the awareness of the phenomenon of secular variation, it became necessary to refine magnetic theories of the earth if the problem of ascertaining longitude was to be solved. Previously, ignorance of the phenomenon had hampered attempts such as that of the Frenchman Guillaume de Nautonnier. In 1602 de Nautonnier had argued that the earth was, in fact, a tilted dipole on which the geographic and magnetic poles did not coincide. Observing the angle of variation would, therefore, give a longitude. De Nautonnier's argument thus became the origin of magnetic longitude schemes. Unfortunately de Nautonnier, like Gilbert, did not know of the magnetic field's secular variation, so his scheme could not possibly work and the longitude problem would remain to perplex the eighteenth-century navigator and natural philosopher.

In 1682 it was noted that the compass variation altered on a daily rather than secular basis.[7] The following year a new account of the earth's magnetism appeared, by the brilliant young astronomer Edmond Halley, discussing the variation of the compass and the problems this occasioned for the art of navigation. Halley rejected theories which claimed that the earth had two magnetic poles on an axis, as this would mean that variation would be uniform when it patently was not. Halley was thus led to hypothesise that the earth had not two, but four magnetic poles, two in each hemisphere, each pair moving in a not yet determinable way.[8] In another paper of 1692, Halley refined his argument: two of the poles were situated at the ends of the axis of an outer magnetic shell and two on the ends of the axis of an inner shell. These shells, separated by an effluvium, had slightly different periods of diurnal rotation: 'the External Parts of the Globe', he commented, 'may well be reckoned as the Shell, and the Internal as a Nucleus or inner Globe included within ours, with a fluid medium between'.[9] The cycles of rotation would probably overlap every seven hundred years or so. Halley even suggested that it was possible that additional shells might exist between the outer shell and the core if his hypothesis failed to account for new observations. This hypothesis is illustrated in the paper Halley holds in his portrait at eighty years of age, painted in 1736 and attributed to Michael Dahl (Fig. 15). Halley's four-pole model of the earth's magnetism was widely accepted and regarded as scientific orthodoxy for many years; in the Romantic period figures like Erasmus Darwin and S. T. Coleridge regarded it as an interesting speculation.

Halley wanted to turn speculation into fact and so, in 1698, he was given command of HMS *Paramore* in order to chart the variations of the magnet and to 'improve the knowledge of the Longitude and variations of the Compasse'.[10] This voyage, unlike those of Cook a century later, was to be confined to the Atlantic and, as well as the taking of measurements, was also to search for the location of *terra australis incognita*. Halley took a substantial number of observations of the magnetic variation, using azimuth compasses as well as other astronomical observations to determine longitude. His second voyage (in 1699) was much more successful, although he did not take any measurements of the magnetic inclination, an omission for which he was criticised when returning to Britain.[11] The *Paramore* sailed southward to the equator before skirting the east coast of South America. From Rio de Janeiro the ship sailed south to 52° 24′ encountering the iceberg-infested waters of the South Atlantic.

Figure 15. Michael Dahl, 'Edmond Halley (1656–1742)'. Halley at the age of eighty holds a diagram illustrating his theory of terrestrial magnetism.

On his return Halley produced a chart of variation for the Atlantic. This chart was the first to feature isolines of magnetic force (or Halleyan lines as they were also known). This chart (Fig. 16) was published in 1701, and expanded in 1703 to encompass the entire globe.[12] Halley's map was to remain in use till the end of the eighteenth century to correct compass

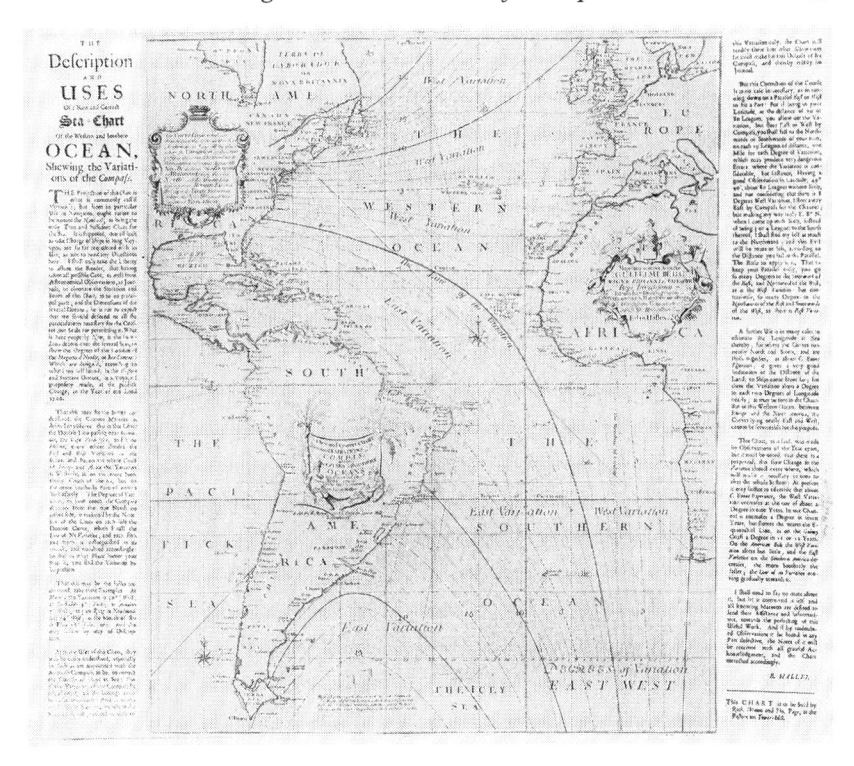

Figure 16. Halley's Atlantic Chart of 1701, illustrating magnetic variation.

bearings, although the hope of using variation to find longitude had long since been abandoned.

Halley had clearly demonstrated the benefits of government-sponsored scientific expeditions and his argument that the most accurate means of measuring the earth's distance from the solar body was to chart the transit of Venus across the sun (an event he predicted would occur in 1761 and 1769) would provide the impetus for Cook's first voyage. More than this, in Halley's magnetic charts there was a large blank in the region of the Pacific where no readings had yet been taken. As well as observing the transit of Venus, Cook, William Wales and others would be obliged to fill in Halley's omissions with magnetic readings of their own some seventy years later.

Throughout the eighteenth century, tables of magnetic variation were published in the *Philosophical Transactions of the Royal Society*. A feature of the narratives of later explorers is the substantial tables of magnetic and other measurements that sometimes interrupt the flow of the narrative and that were later banished to weighty scientific appendices. The great Enlightenment endeavour of the measurement of the earth was well under way – fuelled by the natural philosophers of the Royal Society. Not only would the earth be mapped in terms of its coastlines but it would also be encompassed with figures and formulae describing the extent of its various forces. Cook's three voyages were the epitome of this approach. They had clear, official objectives, the first to measure the transit of Venus, the second to prove the existence or non-existence of the fabled *terra incognita*, and the third to investigate the possibility of finding the Northwest Passage from its western approach. An important feature of all of the voyages was the diurnal taking of observations of the magnetic dip, inclination and, later, intensity. These observations, when represented in print, thus demonstrate what Mary Louise Pratt refers to as 'the imperial eye' of the traveller in action, with its epistemic ordering of the earth's geography and peoples, surveying the world with a 'planetary consciousness'.[13] Pratt points out that this process of representation granted the eighteenth- and nineteenth-century travel account an authority which was never possessed by the explorers, and which was read back into their achievements. Pratt, along with Barbara Stafford and Bruno Latour, regards natural history in general, but specifically Linnaean botany, as the dominant epistemological paradigm of the period.[14] This seems to us correct, yet the science of terrestrial magnetism and the discipline of measurement were also key discourses.

Global certainty rested on the accumulation of data. Halley, for instance, was uncertain about how the magnetic declination operated but was confident that once sufficient observations had been accumulated it would be possible to attain certainties such as the determination of longitude by magnetic means. Getting the data became a priority.[15] James Cook's voyages resulted from the official acceptance that field recordings might make Halley's hopes come true. Cook, along with his successors, generated vast quantities of data. Between 1783 and 1788, Buffon published a volume listing over 7,000 observations made between 1767 and 1780. Cook's voyages thus came at a crucial moment in the development of the science of terrestrial magnetism and are a part of the construction of that European self which mapped the globe in pursuit of universal – and useful – knowledge.

But data turned out not to equal knowledge. Mapping led to less certainty than the magnetists had hoped, for observations did not lead to complete clarification of the phenomena observed. Despite the mass of figures that the travellers scribbled down in the cramped cabins of their ships, despite the hypotheses that theorists spun from those figures, the totalising aims of finding the longitude and developing more efficient methods of navigation receded further into the distance. Part of the problem was instrumentation: taking readings on a rocking and spray-dashed deck or in a humid and hostile country was far from easy, yet the data had to be precise.[16] Few of the instruments, however, were built for the rough and tumble of exploration. Mariners thus had different requirements from the natural philosophers who stayed at home and the two groups came to differ over what constituted the best kind of instrumentation for their joint endeavours. The difference was exacerbated by the fact that many philosophers of magnetism had a complex and self-interested relationship with the makers of the instruments that the explorers were to use. The success of Gowin Knight is a case in point. As Patricia Fara has shown, Knight made his name by successfully marketing powerful artificial magnets in the mid-century. This led to the manufacture of more precise measuring instruments. Knight was also well known for modifications of the traditional steering and azimuth compasses.[17] With their use of hard steel needles, not subject to rust, and their brass casings, Knight's new scientific compasses became the ones fitted by the Royal Navy to all ships engaged in foreign service.

The Royal Navy gave magnetists power and wealth. Compass makers vied for lucrative contracts to supply it, for it was the largest corporate organisation in the world. Natural philosophers, meanwhile, steered a similar course: aiming, Fara shows, 'to demonstrate their mastery of the terraqueous globe through mensuration, they recruited maritime practitioners as research assistants and appropriated naval technologies of representation'.[18] Furthermore, by emphasising the value of technologically redesigned compasses in aiding navigation and thereby assisting trade and empire, magnetists like Knight created a public perception of the importance of scientific endeavour as applied to useful objectives. Thus the creation of a powerful body of public scientific knowledge was rooted in Britain's policy of maritime, mercantile expansion.

Cook was one of the mariners who had assisted Britain's imperial expansion, and he went on to test Knight's compasses, both the steering and the azimuth variety, while making magnetic observations on the *Endeavour* voyage.[19] He was also equipped with sextants made by John Hadley and an astronomical brass quadrant of one-foot radius made by John Bird. The Royal Society provided two astronomical telescopes, Gregorian reflectors with parabolic mirrors of polished speculum metal and a dipping needle to measure inclination. Astronomical clocks, thermometers, theodolites and a portable observatory were also supplied. Along with the hardware came a living magnetic expert – Charles Green, who was highly regarded by the

Royal Society and was one of the few people who could find the longitude by observations of the moon and the stars.[20]

Once under way, Cook took magnetic measurements on a daily basis and compared these with astronomical readings. On 25 October 1768 he noted that the declination of the compass was '2° 24′ West being the result of several very good Azimuths'. In actual fact the azimuth compass proved too delicate for making observations at sea, as did the dipping needle.[21] Cook also used Knight's needles to ascertain the rate of magnetic variation of the island of Tahiti:

> The *Variation of the Compass* I found to be 4° 46′ Easterly, this being the mean result of a great number of trials made by four of Dr Knights needles belonging to the Azimuth Compasses all of which I judged to be good ones, and yet when applied to the Meridion line I found them not only to differ one from a nother sometimes a degree and a half but the same needle would differ from it self more or less, the difference sometimes amounting to half a degree both at the same time and on different days. This will in a great measure account for the seeming errors that on a nice examination appears to have been made in observing the Variation inserted in the Course of this Journal.[22]

Cook's report to the Admiralty on Knight's compasses was critical. He comments how he 'never once was able to make use of the Compass in a troubled Sea'. He blamed himself for not knowing how to use the compass properly, but certainly found it 'by far too Complex an Instrument ever to be of general use at Sea'.[23]

Cook's first voyage demonstrated the impossibilities of finding longitude by observations of the variation, although he blamed this on the unreliability of his needles. He was not then aware, of course, of the ways in which iron on board ship would affect the ship's compass. At the end of his first voyage Cook believed that the lunar method for determining longitude was the surest. On his second voyage to search for *terra australis incognita* Cook was given Larcum Kendall's duplicate of Harrison's fourth chronometer to test as a means of determining the longitude.[24] Cook found Kendall's watch extremely accurate and a better solution than magnetism to the longitude problem. Nevertheless, magnetic observations were still made, by specially provided experts William Wales and William Bayly. Wales was given instructions to 'Observe, or assist at the Observations of, the variation of the compass, and to Observe the Variation of the Magnetic dipping Needle from time to time'.[25]

Once again Cook was to conclude that observations of the variation were 'not always to be depended upon'. He was at a loss to account for this unreliability, speculating that 'there must be some fault in the

Magnetism and the search for the poles

Compasses, or observations or the variation does not follow that uniform law one might reasonably expect'. Wales and Charles Clerke noted similar concerns. Wales claimed that 'almost all those [readings] which gave the least variation were made when the sun, in the morning, was on the Starboard side of the Ship, and those which gave ye most on the Larboard'. Cook's sarcastic response was that Wales was 'a Philosopher' to notice this. This time when determining the variation Knight's compasses were tested against those adapted by the compass maker Henry Gregory and a mean figure established.[26] Again the reason for this variation probably relates to the position of iron in the ship relative to the compass.[27] Wales took various measurements of the declination and dip on land at the temporary observatories at Resolution Port, Ship Cove and Vaitahu Bay. He noted their inaccuracy, attributing it to his failure to make the necessary adjustments to the instrument which 'is not convenient for a Voyage of this kind where we are continually moving from place to place & thereby changing the Dip very considerably'.[28]

Cook's second voyage was also a voyage to the Geographic South Pole. He achieved a furthest south on 30 January 1774, encountering pack ice stretching to the pole. Disproving the existence of the Great Southern Land, this ice, in Cook's opinion 'extended quite to the Pole or perhaps joins to some land, to which it had been fixed from the creation'. He recorded his position as latitude 71° 10′ S and longitude 106° 54′ W. The day before, he recorded a variation of 22° 41′ E.[29] Cook seems not to have speculated about the relevance of these readings to the existence of magnetic poles, but it is clear that he had a conception of the Geographic South Pole and also that his underlying assumption was that magnetic variation should be uniform, and that the differences in his compasses pointed to their unreliability or to some other cause which he could not ascertain.

The Cook voyages marked the end of a phase in the application of the science of terrestrial magnetism for navigational purposes, although they provided a mass of magnetic observations for processing. By the time of Cook's death the belief that variation and dip might hold the key to determining longitude was no longer generally held. John Harrison's chronometers, once they were available in less expensive but equally reliable versions, had won the argument for the best means of ascertaining longitude at sea. A new quantitative element of measurement of magnetic force was introduced by J. C. Borda in 1778, the notion of 'intensity', calculated by counting the number of oscillations taken by a magnetic needle to settle on the magnetic meridian. The focus shifted to an understanding of the nature of the phenomenon itself, practical navigation giving way to 'pure' science. Natural philosophers increasingly represented their data in the form of charts and diagrams as well as in lengthy tables of readings, allowing the performance of thought experiments to visualise where the inaccessible magnetic poles might be.[30] For instance, John Churchman claimed that 'two magnetic points' alone were necessary to understand the variation of the compass, provided one understood, as Halley had not, that the geographic poles of the earth were not magnetic. Churchman adopted the theories of the Swiss mathematician, Leonard Euler, and argued that the two magnetic poles, or points as he called them, were not diametrically opposite. Euler claimed that the magnetic poles moved from east to west, but Churchman argued that both magnetic poles moved round the poles of the earth from west to east. Churchman proudly printed in his *Magnetic Atlas* a letter from Banks of 1787 in which the President of the Royal Society provided information regarding the variation at the Society's London headquarters, and in which he expressed a 'reasonable hope, that science will derive real increase from your labours'.[31] For his part, Churchman hoped that expeditions might be sent by the US or British governments to locate the magnetic poles. In this he was remarkably prescient as the early nineteenth century saw the beginnings of such exploration. The quest for the discovery of the Northwest Passage and the conquest of the magnetic and geographic poles was to enter a new and more confident phase. Indeed, the world was becoming a global laboratory with the growth and development of co-operation between scientists and explorers. Banks was to prove a central figure in this development.

The gathering of magnetic data continued. Alexander von Humboldt made substantial magnetic observations during his expedition to South America, 1791–4, particularly of magnetic intensity. He concluded that magnetic intensity varied from place to place and, with Jean-Baptiste Biot, he established that it increased with latitude.[32] Humboldt was important both for the development of the international profile of terrestrial magnetism studies and for his cosmical theories concerning the unity of nature of which geomagnetism was an essential part. Collaborating with Humboldt in Paris after 1798, Biot developed his own theory of geomagnetism which postulated that the earth's magnetism originated from a small magnetic dipole at the earth's centre, its axis perpendicular to the magnetic equator.[33] After 1808, Humboldt began a series of experiments at the Paris Observatory in collaboration with the French astronomer, François Arago, commencing an extensive and systematic examination of the earth's magnetic field that continued until 1835. Humboldt became heavily influenced by Hans Christian Oersted's 1820 discovery that electric currents could induce magnetic effects, a discovery that linked the phenomena of electricity, magnetism and heat. This was cemented by Michael Faraday's revelation that magnetism can induce electric currents.

By this time there were so many conflicting theories of what the magnetic poles might be that writing about them necessarily assumed a kind of metaphoricity. Commentators disagreed about how many poles there were, where they were located, and whether or not they were moving or stationary. They also disputed the nature of the magnetic poles themselves. They could be seen as areas of convergence of magnetic forces to which the needle pointed, or the point at which the dipping needle achieved 90°, or points of maximum magnetic intensity.[34] In 1839 Carl Friedrich Gauss would argue that there were no magnetic poles or axes and that they played no part in causation or analysis of the earth's magnetism.[35] Gauss assumed that magnetism was distributed within the earth and over its surface, and that the concept of a magnetic pole was meaningless, as was the notion of a magnetic axis or meridian. He developed what is known as 'spherical harmonic analysis' to calculate the varying density of this magnetic fluid. Magnetic force at any point on the earth was thus a summation of the forces from all other points. For Gauss, the magnetic pole was a region where the horizontal magnetic force is zero. He predicted that these two places would be at 75° 35′ N 95° 39′ W and at 72° 35′S 152° 30′ E (later corrected to 66° S 146° E). It was to test Gauss's predicted position for the South Magnetic Pole that James Clark Ross set out in 1839.

By 1830 polar theories were numerous and contradictory and as well as Gauss, Peter Barlow and the astronomer John Herschel assumed that the magnetic poles were fictitious. Nevertheless, a series of expeditions was sent to the Arctic to locate the Northwest Passage or the North Pole and to study terrestrial magnetism.[36] The primary reason for the interest in the Arctic was material. Since the close of the fifteenth century, western explorers had attempted to locate a commercial sea route north and west around the American landmass to the profitable trading lands of the East. This desire was accompanied by anxieties regarding Russian and French expansion in the area. Russia was foremost in the exploration of the Bering Straits, and the growing predominance of her fur traders, voraciously harvesting sea-otter pelts, was a strong cause for concern. The British East India Company certainly had much to gain from the discovery of such a passage. The Company's China trade had increased tremendously in the eighteenth century, largely due to the enormous growth of tea imports.[37] In 1776 parliament offered an award of £20,000 for the discovery of a Northwest Passage, not only by merchant ships and by way of Hudson Bay (as had been offered since 1743), but also by any route and by any ship, including those of the Royal Navy. At the same time an award of £5,000 was offered to any ship approaching within one degree of the North Pole.

What existed at the geographic poles had the same mysterious allure that our unexplored solar system holds for us today.[38] Although it may seem absurd to us, the nineteenth-century consensus was that there existed an open polar sea at the North Pole. This belief was based on serious reasoning and unreliable information for there was no agreement or sure understanding about how ice and bergs were formed. Cook believed that the best explanation argued that ice was precipitated by land. From a study of North American and Siberian coastlines, men of science assumed that there was no landmass at the North Pole. If there was no landmass, they reasoned, the Arctic Circle itself should be free of ice. The main British propagandist for this view was the wealthy lawyer, antiquarian, naturalist and Fellow of the Royal Society, the Hon. Daines Barrington. Convinced by Engel of the existence of the open polar sea, Barrington studied the accounts of former voyages to the Arctic region and the records of the master whalers who had fished there, convincing himself that there existed at the North Pole an open sea that was navigable and under a climate less severe than generally maintained. He came to believe that a passage to India could be achieved by sailing from Spitzbergen, over the pole and south through the Bering Strait into the Pacific.[39]

This was a venture that the Royal Society would find irresistible. It was ever eager to assist the Royal Navy in its voyages of exploration, in the field of Arctic and Antarctic discovery.[40] Barrington convinced the First Lord of the Admiralty, Lord Sandwich, of the practicability of this idea and, in 1773, the government dispatched two ships, the *Racehorse* and the *Carcass*, to explore the possibility. The expedition was commanded by Banks's schoolfriend Constantine John Phipps; on board were the young midshipman Horatio Nelson and the former slave Olaudah Equiano (known then as Gustavus Vassa). Equiano, one of the first important black British authors, writes how he was 'roused by the sound of fame to seek new adventures, and to find, towards the North Pole, what our Creator never intended we should, a passage to India'.[41] Phipps also received advice concerning botany and zoology from Banks and from the anatomist John Hunter. He was instructed to find the North Pole and to turn back at 90°[42] but was stopped by an impenetrable 'wall of ice extending for more than twenty degrees between the latitudes of eighty and eighty-one, without the smallest appearance of any opening'.[43] Magnetic observations were taken with various compasses and Nairne and Blunt's dip needle.

Equiano, awed by the immensity and coldness of the Arctic and fearful of imminent death, may have been convinced that there was no open polar sea, but not so Barrington. He read a series of papers on the subject to the Royal Society, which included accounts (many of them hearsay, and few well authenticated) of mariners who claimed to have achieved very high latitudes. One of the results of his activity was the planning and organisation of Cook's third, fatal, voyage which had as its aim the seeking of the Northwest Passage by way of the northwest coast of America, after, that is, safely returning Omai to his South Sea birthplace. Misled by Jacob von Stählin's map of 1776 which pictured Alaska as an island, Cook's expedition hoped to find a way through the strait between it and the coast of North America and thence sail to the Arctic Ocean. From there they would enter the Atlantic by way of Baffin's Bay. The hopes proved illusory: Cook proved that Alaska was part of the mainland and not an island and, turned back by the pack ice at 70° N, realised that there could be no open polar sea.[44]

Neither Phipps's nor Cook's experiences of the ice barrier deflected Barrington from his beliefs, although he did have opposition. The Whitby whaler and Arctic expert, William Scoresby, rejected open polar seas as fantasy. Scoresby is an important figure in the history of polar exploration who, in contrast to armchair theorists like Barrington and John Barrow, had extensive personal knowledge of the Arctic.[45] In addition to pursuing his education, Scoresby also went to sea every whaling season. In 1806, as chief officer of the *Resolution*, he pushed as far north as 81° 30′. It was in 1807, at the age of eighteen, that Scoresby first made the acquaintance of Banks, whom he met at 32 Soho Square.[46] He subsequently became a regular correspondent and visitor. In 1811 he tested a device of Banks's invention for the ascertaining of deep-water temperatures in the Arctic. It was probably at Banks's suggestion that Scoresby began to study the natural history of the polar regions. Certainly he became Banks's chief authority on matters relating to the Arctic and an important part of his international network of science.

On his return from whaling off Greenland in 1817, Scoresby made known, through papers and correspondence, the remarkable and inexplicable melting of the polar ice fields that he had witnessed. Eighteen thousand square miles of ice had broken free from the polar cap and were gradually drifting southwards to the Atlantic. For the first time in many years, the east coast of Greenland at 74° N was accessible. This news was communicated to the President of the Royal Society. Banks, with his eye ever focused on the commercial implications of natural phenomena, was interested in the agricultural possibilities opened up by the recently improved climate. He wrote to Scoresby on 22 September 1817 requesting the fullest details. In reply Scoresby wrote that, had he been fortunate enough then to command a voyage of exploration rather than a whaling mission, 'the mystery attached to the existence of a north west passage might have been resolved'.[47]

Scoresby proposed that an expedition of discovery be mounted to take advantage of these new conditions.[48] The second secretary of the Admiralty, John Barrow, however, would not agree to a civilian command. The navy's experience of Halley's captaincy and of Banks's own behaviour prior to Cook's second voyage convinced them of the unwisdom of this course of action. Scoresby was also unpopular with Barrow because of his scepticism about the open polar sea which he considered 'too improbable to render it necessary to hazard any opinion concerning it', and he was dubious of the possibilities of any Northwest Passage, as he indicated to Banks.[49] Banks, now near the end of his career, regretted that Scoresby was not involved in the navy's expeditions. He continued to correspond with the whaler, eagerly soliciting all kinds of information about Arctic conditions. In 1817 he solicited Scoresby's expertise in the construction and testing of an improved dipping needle.

Disappointed not to command an expedition, Scoresby returned to whaling, continuing to study Arctic natural history, geography, meteorology and magnetism. He was something of an expert on the latter. In 1819 he contributed a paper to the Royal Society on the variations of the magnetic needle, which Banks read with great interest.[50] Scoresby's comments on terrestrial magnetism are mainly practical. He notes that magnetic force does not decrease with cold, as some had maintained, and discusses in detail the effects of the ship's iron on the compass.[51] In later life, Scoresby became one of the experts on the deviation of the compass especially as connected with the new iron ships and even invented a laminated compass needle.[52]

Scoresby and Banks provided the initiative for further co-operation between the Royal Navy and the Royal Society in a series of maritime and overland expeditions that sought the Northwest Passage and the poles. After Banks's death, Barrow, from his influential position at the Admiralty, organised further voyages, voyages whose history he subsequently wrote. Indeed, although Barrow himself never sailed into Arctic or Antarctic waters, he regarded polar exploration as his personal crusade and attempted to expunge the initiatives of Banks and Scoresby from its history.

Barrow had several reasons for promoting polar voyages. After the end of the Napoleonic Wars, he had many surplus officers on his hands doing little, so sending expeditions to the Arctic (as well as Africa) was a convenient option. It was also necessary to forestall the Russians, already a distinct trading presence in North America and now themselves explorers. In 1816, for example, Otto von Kotzebue had sailed north through the Bering Strait in search of a Northeast Passage. While charting the Alaskan coast, he located and named Kotzebue Sound.

The voyages that Barrow initiated were wide-ranging in incident and interest. They were geographic voyages of discovery but also scientific expeditions concerned with natural history, meteorology, hydrography and geomagnetism. They were rich in extraordinary events, encounters with previously unknown Innuit peoples, strange landscapes, extreme suffering, cannibalism and death. They were staffed by a range of naval officers: John Ross, John Franklin, William Edward Parry, Edward Sabine, James Clark Ross, Francis Crozier and many more. Here we wish to focus on the geomagnetic issues that the voyages raised and their implications for writing – factual and fictional – about the poles and polarity.

John Ross's 1818 expedition to Baffin's Bay famously concluded when Ross thought he saw a line of mountains blocking Lancaster Sound, and turned back. In fact the Sound, although this would not be proved for several years, was the actual entrance to the Northwest Passage. After his return, Ross was mocked by Barrow and others for his catastrophic blunder; nevertheless, his scientific accomplishments were substantial. Ross had been taught astronomy by William Wales and he was a competent leader of a scientific expedition. His ships were supplied with the best instruments the Royal Society could recommend, including four dipping needles, one by Nairne and Blunt, which was to prove the most reliable, and two azimuth compasses designed by Henry Kater FRS. Ross also had with him Edward Sabine, who would become one of the leading British experts on terrestrial magnetism. Ross was charged to observe 'the variation and inclination of the magnetic force' and to investigate the conundrum of whether or not the magnetic poles were 'singular, plural, stationary or moving'. His ships were floating laboratories equipped to test a variety of navigational instruments.[53] The expedition made substantial numbers of magnetic observations, recording variation, dip and intensity.

Ross's own magnetic speculations were not extensive. More effusive was his second-in-command, Lieutenant William Edward Parry, who, in a letter to his parents, commented excitedly on the extraordinary magnetic readings he was obtaining:

Since I wrote that paper, the variation of the compass has increased to 89°!! so that the North Pole of the needle now points nearly due *West!* The *Dip* of the needle is about 84° 40′. As the needle is supposed to direct itself constantly to the Magnetic Pole, it follows that this pole must now be West from us, and as the dip is not far from 90°, it follows that it must be placed somewhere not very far from us in that direction. The greatest variation observed by Baffin here 200 years ago . . . was 56°, so that an amazing increase has taken place during that interval.[54]

Parry clearly assumed that there was one Magnetic North Pole and that it was mobile and some distance south from the Geographic North Pole.

Parry was sceptical about the existence of the mountains that Ross thought he saw stretching across Lancaster Sound. His differences with Ross over this issue pleased Barrow, who subsequently appointed him to command the three major expeditions in search of the Passage. Parry's first voyage in command was a spectacular success, venturing through Lancaster Sound and reaching a furthest West of 110°. Here, Parry named the land he could see further to the west Banks Land (later Island) after Sir Joseph.

The scientific objectives of the voyage were similar to those of its predecessor and once more Edward Sabine was present. Among the usual scientific tasks, Parry was to record the 'magnetic influence in that neighbourhood, supposed to be so near the position of one of the great magnetic poles of the earth'. Once again Parry noted the sluggishness of the compass in high latitudes, with only the compass designed by Kater continuing to traverse at all effectively.[55] Only those compasses with lighter cards were sensitive enough to record even a limited degree of movement and even they needed extensive tapping. Parry landed ashore and recorded the dip as 89° 41′ 42″ and could now experience the uncanny phenomenon of passing north over the magnetic pole. On 28 August 1819 he wrote that they 'had undoubtedly passed over one of those spots upon the globe, where the needle would have been found to vary 180°, or in other words, where its north pole would have pointed due South'.[56] Sailing between the fixed Geographic North Pole and the moving Magnetic North Pole brought home to Parry's crew the strangeness of the polar regions where instrumentation became useless and odd relations existed between the elements. It was a world at the limit of human endurance where scientific theory and instrumentation risked its validity.

Parry was to venture twice more in search of the Passage in 1821–3 and 1824–5. He was also to lead an attempt on the North Pole with James Clark Ross in 1827, achieving over 82° and getting to within 500 miles of the pole. Magnetic observations continued on these voyages, as on the two overland voyages commanded by John Franklin. Scientific appendices to the voyage narratives recorded the massive accumulation of magnetic data, but little new was added to knowledge of the phenomena, except that on his third voyage Parry's observers noticed that variation changed according to a daily cycle, which led them to 'suspect an influence of the sun on the earth's magnetism'.[57]

The honour of finding the Magnetic North Pole eluded Parry. Ironically it was to be located by John Ross some twenty years after his initial foray into Baffin's Bay. Ross, blackballed by Barrow after his earlier failure, raised money from a wealthy gin distiller, and set off in the 85-ton paddle steamer *Victory*, with his nephew James Clark Ross among the crew. The expedition is famous for two things. First, Ross's men spent three winters in the Arctic before finally escaping (everyone at home considered them dead); second, James Clark Ross located the Magnetic North Pole, or at least the point of maximum vertical dip.[58] Ross's party set up winter quarters at Felix Harbour on the Boothia Peninsula. From his observations during the winter of 1830, James Clark Ross believed that the magnetic pole was located somewhere to the northwest of their quarters and, in May 1831, he set out with his party in search of it. Ross presents the journey as a quest in search of the 'mysterious spot', a place where 'no deviation from the perpendicular was assignable' for the needle. Finding the pole and placing the Union flag there would be the 'keystone of all these labours and observations'. After a gruelling journey, Ross's party arrived near the pole itself. He found the place unremarkable, commenting that he could have forgiven

one among us who had been so romantic or absurd as to expect that the magnetic pole was an object as conspicuous and mysterious as the fabled mountain of Sinbad, that it was a mountain of iron, or a magnet as large as Mount Blanc. But nature had erected here no monument to denote the spot which she had chosen as the centre of one of her great and dark powers; and where we could do little ourselves towards this end, it was our business to submit, and to be content in noting by mathematical numbers and signs, as with things of far more importance in the terrestrial system, what we could ill distinguish in any other manner.[59]

Here Ross romances the quest for the magnetic pole, contrasting the monotony of the landscape with the fantasies of the *Arabian Nights*. Nothing, however, marks the place where nature centres her 'great and dark powers' and the only indication Ross has of the place is the mathematical sign that his dipping needle reads 89° 59′, only one minute off the vertical and as near the pole as any scientific compass could then achieve. Ross recorded the spot as 70° 5′ 17″ N and 96° 46′ 45″ W. He regretted that he was only able to construct a modest sized cairn, rather than 'a pyramid as large as that of Cheops', though he went on to point out that in fact he had not located the precise point of 'that mysterious pole' which is in any case not a 'visible and tangible reality' but a series of mathematical signs.[60]

Not content with finding just one pole, James Clark Ross voyaged south in 1839, seeking the Magnetic South Pole (Fig. 17). By this time the science of terrestrial magnetism was dominated by the construction of magnetic observatories around the world and the collection of vast amounts of data. In particular Gauss and Wilhelm Weber set up the Göttingen observatory, co-operating with other international observatories that formed the Göttingen Magnetic Union in 1834, a worldwide network of observatories dedicated to Humboldt's scheme of simultaneous magnetic observations around the globe.[61] In the 1830s Gauss was gaining increasing influence with his theory that geomagnetism as a phenomenon should be limited to the surface of the earth which functioned as an indeterminate collection of magnets randomly disposed. British interest in geomagnetism also increased, especially with the formation of the British Association for the Advancement of Science in 1831, which gave Edward Sabine a platform to proselytise for further exploration. In 1834 the Association sponsored a magnetic survey of England (again using James Clark Ross).[62]

The new era of international collaboration produced more expeditions to the Antarctic, including the American expedition of Charles Wilkes (1838–42), the French expedition of Dumont D'Urville (1837–40) and Ross's British expedition (1839–43).[63] These expeditions searched for the Magnetic South Pole and took the extensive magnetic readings that Gauss needed to verify his general theory of terrestrial magnetism. The Ross expedition benefited from superior scientific instrumentation, especially the 'dipping needle deflector' of R. W. Fox, which measured declination, dip and intensity with greater accuracy at sea than any of its predecessors.[64] Gauss had predicted that the earth's Magnetic South Pole existed in latitude 66° S longitude 146° E, a position that no vessel had ever reached. On 11 January Ross sighted a mountainous, snow-covered land that blocked his path to the magnetic pole. He named this Victoria Land, some 500 miles southwest of the magnetic pole. On 17 February, after skirting the approach to the pole for over a month, Ross finally felt himself 'compelled to abandon the perhaps too ambitious hope I had so long cherished of being permitted to plant the flag of my country on both magnetic poles'.[65] Ross disproved Gauss's predicted position of the pole at 66° S and 146° E, locating it closer to 76° S. It now became clear that the theory of a simple magnetic axis did not fit the observed facts and that two terrestrial magnetic systems, one terrestrial the other cosmic, were at play.

Figure 17. John R. Wildman, 'Captain Sir James Clark Ross (1800–62)'. Visible in the right of the portrait is a dip-circle used in the venture to locate the South Magnetic Pole.

'TO STAND SELF-CENTRED ON THE ATTRACTIVE POLE': LITERARY IMAGININGS

It has long been known that the literary Romantics were obsessed with ideas of polarity. Romantic epistemologies as developed by Blake, Wordsworth, Coleridge and others were dependent on contrary forces, subjects and objects, opposites and reconciliation. Traditional accounts of Romantic thought, such as that of M. H. Abrams, have presented its writers as progressing through polarity towards a theodicy, a movement from innocence to experience and then to a higher plane of transcendent unity.[66] More recently, revisionist feminist scholars have identified this concern with a 'masculine' form of Romanticism, not shared by female poets and novelists in the period.[67] The material contexts of polar exploration and the science of terrestrial magnetism, however, have not yet been fully taken into account when discussing Romantic metaphors of polarity. Ideas about magnetism entered many discourses, literary, religious and visual. Here we want to concentrate on texts that adopted metaphors of polarity in the context of science and exploration, further establishing links between these subjects and the writing of the British Romantic period.

The poet Eleanor Anne Porden, most famous for her scientific epic, *The Veils, or the Triumph of Constancy* (1815), published *The Arctic Explorers* in 1818, inspired by the prospect of John Ross's first expedition. A woman fully informed as to recent scientific theory, Porden combined literary and scientific interests in the manner of Erasmus Darwin. In *The Arctic Explorers* she discusses terrestrial magnetism, providing a fully informed endnote about the phenomenon. Aware that one of Ross's objects is to discover 'the North Magnetic Pole', she describes its periodical revolution round the geographic pole. She also outlines the various theories about the number of the poles. Porden's poem is a *tour de force* which presents the Arctic as sublime, to be penetrated by the manly British explorers with the help of the magnet's feminine attractive powers:

> And thou, unseen Directress! Power unknown!
> Shrined darkling on thine adamantine throne,
> Who lov'st, like Virtue, still to shrink from view
> And bless a world, yet shun the glory due;
> While yet they seek thee o'er a trackless main,
> Guide of their course! befriend their poet's strain.[68]

Although the Arctic is gendered male, here Porden represents magnetic power as female, mysterious, shy, benign, modest and yet powerful. She is a being whom male science and exploration must possess and explain, one who suggests the exotic romance of the *Arabian Nights*.

> Go forth, brave Seamen, reach the fated shore,
> Go! Doomed to honours never reaped before,
> Nor fear strange tales that brooding ignorance teems,
> Wild fictions, borrowed from Arabian dreams;

> Fear not, while months of dreary darkness roll,
> To stand self-centred on the attractive Pole;
> Or find some gulf, deep, turbulent, and dark,
> Earth's mighty mouth suck in the struggling bark;
> Fear not, the victims of magnetic force
> To hang, arrested in your midmost course;
> Your prows drawn downward and your sterns in air,
> To waste with cold, and grief, and famine there.[69]

Porden summons up these 'strange fancies' of the Orientalist imagination only to contrast them with the real ills the explorers will face: cold, frostbite, snow blindness, avalanches and icebergs, the endless days or nights of the Arctic. Porden presents the pole as either affirming the self in a masculine, phallic, self-centredness, or alternatively as destructive, with a feminine chasm, holding the ship in an everlasting magnetic suspension.

It is a similarly primal and atavistic landscape that Robert Walton encounters in Mary Shelley's *Frankenstein* (1818), a novel of gothic excess and extremes, of poles and polarities, which also possesses the literal and figurative slipperiness that characterised scientific discourse about magnetism. The frame narrative of the novel is set in the Arctic seas (we do not get any navigational readings)[70] where Captain Walton and his crew are beset by ice. Walton presents himself as a natural philosopher and explorer, a man inspired by travel narratives to investigate the secrets of the magnet and search for a passage through the Arctic Ocean. He records reading with 'ardour the accounts of the various voyages which have been made in the prospect of arriving at the North Pacific Ocean through the sea which surrounds the pole', voyages which 'composed the whole of our good Uncle Thomas's library'.[71] Possibly he alludes to Richard Hakluyt's *Principal Voyages, Traffiques and Discoveries of the English Nation* (1598–1600) or its continuation in Samuel Purchas, *Purchas, His Pilgrims* (1625) or perhaps more recent accounts like those of Phipps and Cook. He may also refer to theorists like Engel, Barrington and Beaufoy. Certainly he accepts the hypothesis of the open polar sea:

I try in vain to be persuaded that the pole is the seat of frost and desolation; it ever presents itself to my imagination as the region of beauty and delight . . . the sun is for ever visible; its broad disk just skirting the horizon, and diffusing a perpetual splendour . . . there sailing over a calm sea, we may be wafted to a land surpassing in wonders and in beauty every region hitherto discovered on the habitable globe. (pp. 9–10)

Discussing *Frankenstein* in the *Quarterly Review* of 1818, John Wilson Croker attributed Walton's belief in this theory to the novelist's acquaintance with Barrington's and Barrow's ideas.[72] The most obvious predecessor of Walton's voyage is that of Phipps; it also pre-empts the major exploratory activity of Franklin, Parry and the Rosses. Mary Shelley's journal records her reading 'old voyages' in 1816, but does not specify which these were.[73] Walton is undertaking 'a voyage of discovery towards the northern pole' presumably hoping to sail across it. Only by 'undertaking such a journey', he tells his sister, 'can the secret of the magnet' be attained (*Frankenstein*, pp. 10, 10n, 17). It is quite possible that Walton is seeking to locate the North Magnetic Pole, discovering the causes of variation and dip.

What theories Walton may have regarding the 'secrets of the magnet' are not revealed by the text. That Mary Shelley was aware of such theories is, however, clear. Her husband Percy encountered the itinerant lecturer Adam Walker at Syon House Academy in 1802 and again at Eton. Walker lectured on astronomy, electricity and magnetism,[74] mediating the discoveries and theories of Humphry Davy, Erasmus Darwin and Luigi Galvani to Percy. From Percy, they spread to Mary.[75] Walker, influenced by the mystical philosophy of Jacob Boehme, rejected Halley's notion of a polar nucleus and argued instead that the sun was central to an understanding of terrestrial magnetism, which was the source of a universal circulating fluid, a solar ethereal fire, conducted through the earth by iron.[76]

Darwin was a source for Walker; it is also likely that Mary Shelley encountered magnetic theory in Darwin directly. Darwin's opinions featured in *The Botanic Garden*, and mostly derived from Aepinus and Halley. He explained that:

> The variation of the compass can only be accounted for by supposing the central parts of the earth to consist of a fluid mass, and that part of this fluid is iron, which requiring a greater degree of heat to bring it into fusion than glass or other metals, remains a solid, and the inertiæ of this fluid mass with the iron in it, occasions it to perform fewer revolutions than the crust of the solid earth over it, and this is gradually left behind, and the place where the floating iron resides is pointed to by the direct or retrograde motions of the magnetic needle.[77]

Darwin and Walker most likely influenced *Frankenstein*. Yet they do not appear explicitly in its pages. Captain Walton gives no indication of his own ideas about the earth's magnetism, or whether he favours Halley's and Darwin's notions of a central magnetic core, or Walker's hypothesis of a solar origin. Walton's magnetic science is shown, instead, as being analogous to Frankenstein's electro-chemistry. The 'secrets of the magnet' that Walton searches for resemble the secrets of feminine nature, which the masculine science of Frankenstein and his tutor Waldman must discover by penetrating her hiding places. This would seem to indicate that Mary

Shelley included terrestrial magnetism in what Anne Mellor has described as her 'feminist critique of science' in which the male scientist is shown to desire to dominate and control a female nature.[78]

Instead of discovering the open polar sea or the secrets of the North Magnetic Pole, Walton finds only the 'vast and irregular plains of ice' encountered by Phipps as his ship is surrounded and imprisoned by the elements. Threatened with his crew's mutiny, Walton reluctantly agrees to sail southward, if the ice will allow, and consequently he returns ignorant and disappointed. Accusing himself of 'cowardice and indecision', he may well have in mind how Henry Hudson, while exploring a Northwest Passage, faced mutiny and finally perished in 1611 after he and his son were set adrift in the bay named after him (*Frankenstein*, pp. 162–4). Phipps also was in the process of abandoning the ships and escaping in the boats before the loosening of the ice allowed him to depart.

What conclusions may we draw from the novel regarding competing theories of magnetism and polar exploration? If Walton's scientific exploration is analogous to that of Frankenstein's search for the origins of life, we might deduce that the novel regards such experimentation as reckless and dangerous, useless and self-destructive. Yet the novel remains ambiguous. The Creature keeps alive Walton's quest to reach the North Pole in his seeking out 'the most northern extremity of the globe' as the appropriate place to commit suicide, now his creator is dead. He does not wish to plant the Union flag there in patriotic pride, as Phipps and Parry hoped, but, instead, to destroy himself in a funeral pyre, an elemental combination of fire and ice which would return him to his origins. In leaping on to his ice raft and hoping to use this to attain the pole, the Creature shows that he does not share Walton's belief in a temperate open polar sea any more than Cook or Scoresby had done. He does not expatiate on his method of navigation but we must presume that it is celestial, and that measurements of variation and dip will not be taken on his journey, nor any record be bequeathed to posterity of these values at 90° North.

Mary Shelley acknowledged her debt to the 'The Rime of the Ancient Mariner', which she had heard Coleridge recite in 1806. Captain Walton declares that though he goes to 'unexplored regions, to "the land of mist/ and snow"', he 'shall kill no albatross' (*Frankenstein*, p. 14). It is a fitting tribute, for in making her fictional character allude to Coleridge's poem, Shelley grants it as much power over the explorer's imagination as the factual narratives by which Walton has been inspired. And Coleridge himself had been inspired by the voyage accounts of polar explorers. The debt of 'The Rime of the Ancient Mariner' to travel accounts in general, and those of the Cook voyages in particular, has often been discussed.[79] Coleridge also developed a philosophy of nature that was based on polarities analogous to the magnet. This also has been extensively discussed.[80] Here we wish to do no more than indicate how the science of terrestrial magnetism itself and the material history of polar exploration may have inflected his writings.

'The Rime of the Ancient Mariner' is, on one of its many levels, a poem about polar exploration. William Wales, Cook's astronomer on his second and third voyages, taught Coleridge mathematics at Christ's Hospital. One of the school's main emphases was on preparing boys for a career in the Canadian empire: navigation was an important subject and one of the pupils, James Robinson, had been seconded to serve as clerk on Phipps's polar mission in 1773.[81] Coleridge spent much time there learning to compose poetry but was nevertheless immersed in the milieu of scientific and geographic exploration. It was perhaps in affectionate remembrance of his school years that he later equated polar exploration with poetic composition, 'Parry seeks out the Polar ridge;/ Rhymes seeks S. T. Coleridge' (*CPW*, vol. II, p. 972). Certainly, much of the topography of the 'Ancient Mariner' is derived from the accounts of eighteenth-century as well as early modern explorers to the North and South Poles:

> Listen, Stranger! Mist and Snow,
>   And it grew wond'rous cauld:
> And ice, mast-high, came floating by,
>   As green as Emerauld.
>
> And thro' the drifts the snowy clifts,
>   Did send a dismal sheen;
> Ne shapes of men ne beasts we ken –
>   The Ice was all between.
>
> The Ice was here, the Ice was there,
>   The ice was all around:
> It crack'd and growl'd, and roar'd and howl'd
>   Like noises of a swound.[82]

The mariner's journey is circular; from Britain the ship voyages south, crossing the equator and from thence to the Pacific Ocean, the 'silent sea'. After the killing of the albatross (a common enough event on such voyages) the ship returns to the equator where the mariner undergoes a torment of heat and thirst and the crew of the ship expire. After his 'blessing' of the watersnakes, the mariner returns to the place from which he departed. The details of his return voyage are not described, as the mariner is placed in a trance. Presumably his return journey must either have been via an undiscovered Northwest Passage, or over the pole itself, either way a vindication of the open polar sea hypothesis. Throughout, the mariner does not direct his course by compass readings, but by celestial observation of the sun, stars and moon. The southern sea becomes the uncanny polar opposite of the safe harbour of his home; a place where self-identity is challenged and perceptions are altered.

In the 1790s, when Coleridge penned his poem of exploration, he regarded magnetic phenomena as being analogous to the divine power. In his 'Lectures on Revealed Religion' of 1795 he compared Christ's miracles with the 'rare and extraordinary Influence of Magnetism and Electricity', arguing that since the discovery of an evidential basis for these phenomena, their existence and reality is accepted, but there exists as much reason to doubt the testimony of their effects as to question scriptural eyewitness accounts of the miracles. Coleridge further described Stoicism's attempt to understand the divine essence as like that of 'a Mole [who,] after turning up a few Inches of Soil' might feel confident to 'describe [the] central fire, or the magnetic Nucleus of this Planet' (*Lects 1795*, pp. 112, 157). Coleridge's reference to the magnetic nucleus would here seem to indicate an adherence to Edmond Halley's model of the earth's magnetic shell whose powers are hidden deep in its interior, perhaps as transmitted to him by Erasmus Darwin. It was an idea he returned to in his essay *On the Constitution of the Church and State* (1829) when he played with Halley's speculation of multiple worlds within the globe while discussing the potential that exists in the present visible world:

The world in which I exist is another world indeed, but not to come. It is at present as (if *that* be at all) the magnetic planet, of which, according to the Astronomer HALLEY, the visible globe, that we inverminate, is the case or traveling-trunk – a neat little world where light still exists in *statu perfuso*, as on the third day of the Creation, before it was polarized into outward and inward, i.e. while light and life were one and the same.[83]

Science, and here magnetic science, gave Coleridge an underpinning for religious belief, in this case defending the truthfulness of scriptural accounts of miracles and providing reasonable grounds for faith.

Polarity, as adopted from the German *Naturphilosophie*, became one of Coleridge's most abiding principles. For the idealist philosopher Schelling, from whom Coleridge borrowed much of his thinking about this subject, nature was in a process of continual flux of opposed forces in a dynamic tension. Coleridge outlined this 'law of POLARITY' in *The Friend* in 1818 as 'the manifestation of one power by opposite forces: who trace in these appearances... the agency of positive and negative poles of a power essential to all material construction'. For Coleridge the powers of nature were two and these powers were in polar opposition. Such powers could only manifest themselves in nature by their opposites, each being interdependent as the poles of a magnet are opposite, yet part of a whole greater than themselves and known through the phenomena of attraction and repulsion. One power expands infinitely and the other contracts, giving us the universal and particular. Things in nature are thus the synthesis of opposing powers, and all nature strives to return to the state of unity. Coleridge summarised his understanding of these phenomena in *The Friend*:

EVERY POWER IN NATURE AND IN SPIRIT must evolve an opposite, as the sole means and condition of its manifestation: AND ALL OPPOSITION IS A TENDENCY TO RE-UNION ... *The principle may thus be expressed. The Identity* of Thesis and Antithesis *is the substance of all* Being; *their* Opposition *the condition of all* Existence, *Being manifested; and every Thing or Phænomenon is the Exponent of a Synthesis as long as the opposite energies are retained in that Synthesis.* (*Friend*, vol. II, p. 479, vol. I, p. 94)[84]

To this hypothetical universal law all forms of phenomena, including electricity, magnetism and chemical processes, correspond.

We have seen how ideas about the earth's magnetic field have always been imbricated in the material process of exploration and commerce. So too Coleridge's espousal of the *Naturphilosophie* and its law of polarity was infused with material and political implications.[85] One example of this can be seen in *On the Constitution of the Church and State*. The analogy between the political and the natural is explicitly made as Coleridge identifies the 'life and energy of the Nation' with 'the imponderable agents, magnetic, or galvanic, in bodies inorganic'. Coleridge thus uses the metaphor of terrestrial magnetism to construct his 'Idea' of a constitution of the Church and State which works through the laws of polarity, reconciling the interests of permanence and progression, just as this principle works throughout nature generally. Applying the same principles of polarity in a more Platonised manner, Coleridge argues that there exists an 'Idea' of the State prior to experience and not abstracted from any particular state, but that this 'Idea' can only be manifest in the works of individual nations and societies. The 'Idea' cannot exist in its pure rational state in the forms of men but it could be regulative of existing arrangements, which may or may not conform to it. The social State in ideal form reflects two forces, the interest of 'Permanence' and the interest of 'Progression'. The 'interest of permanence is opposed to that of progressiveness; but so far from being contrary interests, they, like the magnetic forces, suppose and require each other'. The interests of permanence are served by the landed classes, and the interests of progression by the commercial classes. The idea of the State approximates to that of the British parliament where the landed interest is represented in the House of Lords and the other in the Commons, the King 'in whom the executive power is vested' functioning as 'the beam of the constitutional scales' or balance of interests. There were, however, things that the State was not able to do, no matter how ideally constituted. The idea of the Nation, thus, includes both that of the State and of the 'National Church', 'two poles of the same magnet; the magnet itself, which is constituted by them, is the CONSTITUTION of the Nation'.[86]

Robert Walton, Victor Frankenstein and Samuel Taylor Coleridge approached the poles by different routes from those of Edmond Halley, James Cook, John Ross and their fellow explorers, but they were all interconnected in a metaphoric web of polarities that involved scientific administrators like Banks and Barrow, Arctic commentators like Scoresby and Barrington and magnetic theorists like Aepinus and Gauss, as well as navigators like Wales and instrument makers like Knight. The poles, both magnetic and geographic, proved elusive and they were surrounded by figure and fantasy. The attempts of navigators and scientists to master their secrets, from Halley's first scientific voyages under the auspices of the Royal Society and the Admiralty to later explorations also sponsored by those two bodies, are important elements in the construction of bodies of knowledge in the period.

PART II

British science and literature in the context of empire

CHAPTER 8

'Man electrified man': Romantic revolution and the legacy of Benjamin Franklin

In this chapter, we focus on late eighteenth-century Britain, investigating the context within which a long-established area of study – electricity – acquired new cultural meaning. We show that electricity came, in the 1790s, to be a symbol of revolution because it was associated with Benjamin Franklin, the statesman who had helped lead the American revolution against Britain. To a network of English natural philosophers, including Joseph Priestley and Erasmus Darwin, Franklin's success in winning independence made electricity a symbol of their belief that the liberty, equality and simplicity of American society was both more powerful and more natural than the hierarchy of British society. This network, dissenting, radical, provincial, was initially patronised by Banks but was dropped by him when its revolutionary politics became too controversial. And it was during these years of controversy that Priestley emigrated to the part of America that Franklin had recommended – the Susquehanna valley. Those who remained fostered the young Coleridge, Southey and Humphry Davy, shaping their social relationships and intellectual standpoints. The electrical network, indeed, helped determine the path – the very vocabulary – of their early Romanticism. Later, the pressure that Banks placed on that network helped push their Romantic discourses away from radicalism and away from the provinces. They redefined themselves and their work in a loyalist and metropolitan context. Banks, that is to say, was one of the causes of Romanticism's retreat from the language and politics of revolution.

When Joseph Banks returned from his voyage round the world, one of the first things he did was dine with two Fellows of the Royal Society. One of them was Benjamin Franklin, diplomatic representative of the American colonists as well as the distinguished pioneer of electrical science. Over their food and wine, the men discussed botany and navigation and the lightning conductors of Franklin's design that saved Cook's ship 'from Damage when a Dutch Man of War lying near them in the Road of Batavia was almost demolished'.[1] But what most fascinated Franklin were Banks's descriptions of the indigenous people he had met. The very next day, Franklin wrote to a friend that 'the People of Otahitee (George's Island) are civilised in a great degree . . . The Inhabitants of New Zealand were found to be a brave & sensible people, and seem'd to have a fine Country, the Inhabitants of New Holland seem'd to our People a stupid Race, for they would accept none of our Presents'.[2] Stupid though they seemed, it was nevertheless the New Hollanders (or Australians) who held Franklin's interest: 'We call this Stupidity,' he wrote, 'But if we were dispos'd to compliment them, we might say, Behold a Nation of Philosophers! such as him whom we celebrate for saying as he went thro' a Fair, How many things there are in the World that I dont want!'

Franklin's interest in the indigenous Australians is not altogether surprising. Not only was he a polymath, but he had for many years been studying the indigenous people of America with the eye of one looking for an alternative to the corruptions of British society. In 1784 he delivered to the public a lifetime of thinking about 'Indians' in his *Remarks Concerning the Savages of North America*. This book revealed Franklin's familiarity with the latest views on 'noble savages' – views including those he had heard first hand from Banks and those expressed by writers who had responded to the narratives of Cook and Bougainville. Like Diderot and the Abbé Raynal, Franklin valued the 'savages' for their freedom from the desires and vices of civilisation. His indigenous Americans, like the aboriginal Australians, 'don't want' and are admired for not wanting the tawdry goods that fascinate white people.[3]

It was their honesty and strong sense of justice that made Franklin see Indians as, in some respects, ideal Americans, models for a society seeking to establish its independence from Britain after its revolution. The Indians, Franklin recorded, resented settlers' hypocrisy. And missionaries would talk but not listen. When a Susquehanna Indian, after politely listening to a missionary, told him the Susquehannas' creation story, the missionary said:

'What I delivered to you were sacred truths; but what you tell me is mere fable, fiction, and falsehood.' The Indian, offended, replied, 'My Brother, it seems your friends have not done you justice in your education; they have not well instructed you in the rules of common civility. You saw, that we who understand and practise those rules, believed your stories, why do you refuse to believe ours?'[4]

In Franklin's hands, Indians become embodiments of virtues he hopes his fellow colonists, now the founders of a new nation, will live by – natural honesty, courtesy and self-reliance, coupled with an inherent suspicion of cant of all kinds, political as well as religious. They refuse to accept being cheated of their natural deserts; they will not tolerate hypocrisy or accept that they are inferior. In short, they have the very characteristics that the colonists had recognised in themselves when, during the 1770s, they had argued their cause against the British government. Franklin's Indians, that is to say, have a radical independence and rightful suspicion of the discourses that claim authority over them. They are coloured by his revolutionary ideology and, in turn, they serve to make that revolutionary ideology appear indigenous to the American continent. Embodied in the Indians, it was, apparently, always there, just as it was already there in what Banks had taken to be the stupidity of the New Hollanders.

It was a long way from the forests of America to the streets of Bristol, yet it is certain that when Robert Southey penned these lines in Britain's Atlantic port he had both Franklin's words and Indian deeds in mind:

> The electric truth shall run from man to man,
> And the blood-cemented pyramid of greatness
> Shall fall before the Flash.
> (Robert Southey, *Wat Tyler*, 1794)[5]

Here Southey's fictional character, the revolutionary leader John Ball, uses electricity to symbolise the spirit that freed men from the mental chains imposed by Church and State – chains he symbolises by the sacrificial altar of the Aztecs. 'The electric truth shall run from man to man,' he says: electricity puts 'truth' into action, making it an instantaneous force, capable of destroying 'greatness' as it links the common people in a circuit of power and issues in a flashing outbreak.

Southey's fictional character used electrical metaphors in allusion to a real revolutionary hero. The man who had famously drawn the magical 'fluid' down a kitestring from the sky and revealed its positive/negative polarity, was of course Franklin himself. 'The fable of Prometheus is verify'd,' declared one commentator on the kite experiment:[6] Franklin had captured fire from the heavens. He had linked earth and sky, mastering lightning – the very instrument of the gods' wrath – and showing it to be electrical. To the accompaniment of thunder, he could pass streams of electric blue 'fluid' across space, from cloud to kite to person. This stunning visual and tactile display made him a prototype of the Romantic genius, of the experimentalist who, like Prometheus, rebelled against the tyranny of despotic authority, putting 'that wonderful matter which Nature has kept hid from us' into the hands of man.[7] After the American Revolution, Franklin became the idol of radicals in France, where he was portrayed warding off lightning while a prostrate Britain lay defeated at his feet: 'he snatched the lightning from the sky and their sceptre from the tyrants' ran a revolutionary motto.[8]

For dissenting Britons, Franklin was a father of the kind of society they wanted to see at home. In 1785 Richard Price, Priestley's friend and fellow philosopher, declared:

> With heart-felt satisfaction, I see the revolution in favour of universal liberty which has taken place in *America*; – a revolution which opens a new prospect in human affairs, and begins a new aera in the history of mankind . . . Who could have thought, in the first ages of the world, that mankind would acquire the power . . . of subjecting to their wills the dreadful force of lightening.[9]

American republicanism was the hope of the world, as Franklin's 'subjection' of lightning proved. The harnessing of electricity, then, was evidence of the superiority of republican liberty to monarchical hierarchy, and of the independent to the colonial state. Franklin's scientific achievement vindicated revolution on the American model, for it showed it to have emerged from a culture both more vigorous and closer to nature than that of imperialist Britain.

Price made electricity a symbol of the blessings of republican liberty. So did Erasmus Darwin. In 1787 he addressed Franklin as a 'Philosopher and Friend . . . the greatest Statesman of the present, or perhaps of any century, who spread the happy contagion of Liberty among his countrymen; and . . . deliver'd them from the house of bondage, and scourge of oppression'. In the same letter, he informed Franklin of a new electrometer 'likely to be of service in detecting the small quantities of electricity given out in chemical processes'.[10] From here it was just a short leap to using electricity as a figure of revolutionary action as he did in *The Botanic Garden*:

> Led by the phosphor-light, with daring tread
> Immortal FRANKLIN sought the fiery bed;
> Where, nursed in night, incumbent Tempest shrouds
> The seeds of Thunder in circumfluent clouds,
> Besieged with iron points his airy cell,
> And pierced the monster slumbering in the shell.
> So, born on sounding pinions to the WEST,
> When Tyrant-Power had built his eagle nest;
> While from his eyry shriek'd the famish'd brood,
> Clenched their sharp claws, and champ'd their beaks for blood,
> Immortal FRANKLIN watch'd the callow crew,
> And stabb'd the struggling Vampires, ere they flew.
> The patriot-flame with quick contagion ran,

> Hill lighted hill, and man electrified man;
> Her heroes slain awhile COLUMBIA mourn'd,
> And crown'd with laurels LIBERTY return'd.[11]

In this passage Darwin pays tribute to his scientific father-figure, making Franklin a hero who destroys vampiric imperialism. Darwin turns the hilltop communication fires of the American revolutionists into an electric circuit, in which men are charged with patriotism and liberty. The 'electric fluid' acts here as a symbol of revolutionary ideas and emotions so powerful that they surge through the sinews, nerves and minds of all Americans, electrifying them into belief and battle. To put it another way, Darwin was imagining the spirit of liberty that formed the Americans' revolutionary ideology as the subtle, all-pervasive and animating fluid that Franklin had conducted from the skies. Franklin's political ideas – his affirmation of life, liberty and the pursuit of happiness – engender revolution through the power of his science.

It was precisely this kind of electrification that Coleridge looked for in the Britain of the 1790s, inspired by Franklin's discovery and the destruction of British imperialism that it symbolised. His Romantic poetry came into being, in part, as an articulation of nature as a republican anti-colonialist force, in terms derived from Darwin's verse, Price's rhetoric and Franklin's experiment. In his 'Ode to the Departing Year' he envisaged Africa being liberated from the 'strange, horrible and foul' evil of the slave trade that the 'thankless Island' of Britain imposed on it (lines 89, 94, *CPW*, vol. I, p. 165). The liberating force would be a natural and Franklinian one – the electrical discharge of lightning:

> Avenger, rise!
> For ever shall the thankless Island scowl
> Her quiver full, and with unbroken bow?
> Speak! from thy storm-black Heaven O speak aloud!
> And on the darkling foe
> Open thine eye of fire from some uncertain cloud!
> O dart the flash! O rise and deal the blow!
> The Past to thee, to thee the Future cries!
> Hark! How wide Nature joins her groans below!
> Rise, God of Nature! rise.   (lines 93–102)

In 1795, then, electricity was vital to the Romantic creed of nature as a revolutionary and anti-imperial power. In *The Watchman* Coleridge quoted Franklin's slogan 'rebellion to tyrants is obedience to God' (*Watchman*, p. 241). The American Revolution showed that despotic government only created in the people it repressed a righteous anger that made them formidable when they rose in rebellion. In the West Indies and in Britain itself, the government should beware provoking a revolution by people who believed they had God and nature on their side. The feelings of the democratic radicals, Coleridge concluded, had 'electric force' (*BL*, vol. 1, p. 199).

It was not just its association with Franklin that made electricity a powerful image of revolution, but also the theoretical explanation of its workings that Franklin's successors had elaborated. Chief among these was Joseph Priestley, who first met Franklin in 1765 when the American natural philosopher arrived in London to represent the interests of the colonies. Soon, Priestley began to pursue experimental researches. His *The History and Present State of Electricity* (1767) summarised and extended Franklin's work. It was to be followed by Priestley's discovery of oxygen[12] and photosynthesis – a discovery that led to his acknowledgement as one of the foremost men of science of the age. He was, in fact, invited to become the astronomer on Cook's second voyage of exploration, only for Banks, his sponsor, to inform him that the Church of England clerics at the Board of Longitude had vetoed the appointment of a dissenter.

Priestley's dissent was not just religious. He wrote on politics as well as the history and theology of Christianity. A Unitarian, he was excluded by his faith from university, church and state. His politics and his science were formed by this enforced position outside the established institutions of power and knowledge. He sought a natural philosophy that would comprehend spirit as well as matter, mind as well as body, and relate them to the Creator. Electricity was at the centre of his efforts. So was the philosophy of the Unitarian David Hartley, a philosophy Priestley edited and updated.[13] Hartley, in Priestley's version of his thought, gave electricity a vital role. It was one of the manifestations of a principle at work in forming not only 'natural bodies' but the mind too. This principle was a reworking of Isaac Newton's speculative account of ether; it consisted of a 'polar virtue' that set the corpuscles from which matter was made into a 'vibrating motion' resulting from their attraction to and repulsion of each other. This vibrating process existed internally, 'making the parts of bodies cohere' and shaping patterns of sensation and even thought.[14] It also existed externally – forces acted at a distance by making the imponderable ether that filled space vibrate.[15] Electricity, in his thinking, became one manifestation of the natural principle that shaped the world in unity, revealing mind and world, inside and outside, thought and matter to be organised by the same activity.

Priestley agreed, eagerly seizing on a philosophy that offered organic unity: 'matter', he wrote in 1782, is not that *inert* substance that it has been supposed to be; . . . *powers* of *attraction* or *repulsion* are necessary to its very being . . . And since it has never yet been asserted, that the powers of *sensation* and *thought* are incompatible with these . . . I therefore maintain, that we have no reason to suppose that there are in man two substances so distinct from each other.[16]

In Priestley's system, all was material, but matter was transformed from solid mass into a synthesis of dynamic powers. Men's minds were different vibrating combinations of the same powers that were also manifest in rocks and stones and trees. God was the creator of a unified world; attraction and repulsion were his agents.[17]

While Franklin had conducted electricity from the skies, others had fished it from the seas. When John Hunter published his dissections of the torpedo and gymnotus fish (in 1773 and 1775), the anatomical organs for transmitting electricity were laid open to the scientific world. They revealed, Hunter concluded, 'that the will of the animal does absolutely control the electric powers of its body; which must depend on the energy of its nerves'.[18] Hartley and Priestley soon incorporated Hunter's demonstration into their theories – if electricity could be transmitted at a distance through water, perhaps that was formed by a combination of electricity with other vital principles. The power of the fish, the medium through which it passed and the body receiving the shock must all be akin. Hunter noted that the 'oscillation' produced by the gymnotus:

may be so strong, as not only to check and overpower those in the part which touches the fish, but also to propagate themselves along the skin and up the nerves, to the brachial ganglion, and even to the spinal marrow and brain; whence the person would first feel the stupefaction ascend along the arm to the shoulder, and then fall into a giddiness.[19]

This gradual ascent of the electric charge suggested that the nervous system was itself electrical.[20] Electricity, it seemed, connected exterior and interior, for the two were organised on the same principles – shocks joined the body of the fish with the body of a person via the intervening water because they simply reversed the direction of a human nervous system that itself employed electrical vibrations to transmit the will from the brain to the limbs.

Such conclusions seemed to be confirmed when in 1791 Luigi Galvani claimed to have made the legs of a frog move by conducting electricity, through wires, from its nerves to its muscles. Galvani argued that this fluid was 'animal electricity'. Produced in the brain and transmitted to the muscles, it was the vital force, causing motion. Although it was unclear whether this 'galvanic' fluid was the same as the 'electrical fluid' traced in the nerves by Hunter, it was now even more strongly possible to identify electricity as the principle of vitality and will, within and without intelligent life-forms. In 1800, Southey did just that, writing that 'the galvanic fluid stimulated to motion . . . is the same as the nervous fluid'.[21]

Among those who made this identification was Priestley's friend Darwin. In *The Botanical Garden* 'The dread Gymnotus' appears, 'electric in his ire', and able to emit a stupefying shock whose 'power seemed to be determined by the will or anger'.[22] Electricity, then, was a natural force that some creatures could communicate at will. By a mental exertion they could transmit vibrations that effectively subdued, from a distance, other creatures. With electricity, they could subjugate others' bodies and control their minds:

> Starts the quick Ether through the fibre-trains
> Of dancing arteries, and of tingling veins,
> Goads each fine nerve, with new sensation thrill'd,
> Bends the reluctant limbs with power unwill'd.[23]

To Coleridge and Southey, Priestley and (to a lesser extent) Darwin were heroes. Coleridge praised Priestley and accurately summarised his development of the philosophy of Hartley:

> he first who mark'd the ideal tribes
> Down the fine fibres from the sentient brain
> Roll subtly-surging. Pressing on his steps
> Lo! PRIESTLEY there, Patriot, and Saint, and Sage.
> ('Religious Musings', lines 369–72; *CPW*, vol. 1, p. 123)

In December 1794 Coleridge announced that, like Priestley, he himself 'went further than Hartley' and believed in 'the corporeality of thought – namely that it is motion' (*CL*, vol. 1, p. 137). Although he had come to doubt this belief by mid-1796, in 1795 it underlay his understanding of the political situation in terms of an electric communication from mind to mind. In March 1795 he applied his reading about electric fish to current affairs, hoping that George Dyer would 'never suffer your feelings to be benumbed by the torpedo Touch' of 'that Fiend' 'misanthropy' (*CL*, vol. 1, p. 155). Later in the year he attributed the people's political torpor to 'the torpedo touch of extreme want' which 'benumbed' them into 'selfishness' (*Lects 1795*, p. 45). Like fish stunned by an electric ray, their own minds and wills had been stupefied by an electric charge surging up their nerves, overwhelming the proper mental motion proceeding 'down the fine fibres' from the brain. Apathy towards reform and revolution was, in this diagnosis, a mental sickness that was not of the people's own willing. They had been stupefied by the shocking power of the social climate that Pitt's government had engineered.

What was needed, Coleridge decided, was a triumph for a countervailing electric charge, a movement from mind, through the nerves, to the minds of others, powerful enough to overcome stupefaction. It was in acceptance of – and in tribute to – Priestley's work that Coleridge thought so. In the preface to his experiments on air Priestley declared 'this rapid progress of knowledge . . . will, I doubt not, be the means, under God, of extirpating *all* error and prejudice, and of putting an end to all undue and usurped authority in the business of religion as well as of *science*'. The 'English hierarchy', he continued, '(if there be anything unsound in its constitution) has equal reason to tremble at an air pump, or an electrical machine'.[24] Because the electrician could 'exhibit the operations of nature, that is of the God of nature himself', he would undermine false systems of knowledge and authority by showing them to be unnatural.[25] In a metaphor that became notorious for its invocation of the 1605 plot to destroy King and Parliament, Priestley declared that 'the propagation of the truth' upon which natural and moral philosophers were engaged resembled 'a train of gunpowder to which the match will one day be laid to blow up the fabric of error'.[26] 'Error', for Priestley and for Coleridge, included the contemporary parliament, corrupt and unrepresentative as it was. It also comprehended the established Church, which enforced subscription to superstitious corruptions of true Christianity, in which its venal clergy believed only for the sake of feathering their nests. Priestley's natural philosopher, armed with apparatus for capturing nature, was levelling his electrical fluid against Church and State – in the name of the 'common rights of humanity'.[27]

Conservatives saw the republican and revolutionary implications of this view of science at once. A cartoon of 1791 linked Priestley with Tom Paine's *Rights of Man*, with the French Revolution and with English rebellion – a picture of Wat Tyler's rebellion appears on the wall behind the man of science.[28] Edmund Burke, similarly, saw Priestley's science as a dangerous enthusiasm, an indulgence in innovatory ideas that threatened judgement, tradition and order:

> These philosophers are fanatics . . . they are carried with such an headlong rage towards every desperate trial, that they would sacrifice the whole human race to the slightest of their experiments.[29]

Conservative attacks culminated in the mob assault on Priestley's Birmingham house and laboratory in 1791. They were burnt to the ground, and

Priestley, deprived of his apparatus and fearful for his safety, emigrated to America in 1794.

In December of that year, Coleridge mourned Priestley's departure. Coleridge had reason to mourn: the trajectory of his intellectual development at that point was chiefly a result of his admiration for Priestley. He became a Unitarian, reading Priestley's works at university in Cambridge and later in Bristol. He began campaigning, as Priestley had, against the exclusion of Unitarians from public office. And he adopted an elitist brand of radicalism in which philosophers of nature and mind would lead people out of corruption towards a state of feeling, thinking and living at one with each other and with the world of which they were part.

What Priestley made possible in his laboratory and hoped in prose, Coleridge put into poetry. In 'Religious Musings', he claimed that the anti-establishment natural philosophers who were dedicated to liberty would keep the revolution on peaceful course, guiding the exploited masses towards millennial harmony. And chief among them would be Priestley's mentor Benjamin Franklin, wielding the natural electricity he had channelled from the heavens:

> From Avarice thus, from Luxury and War
> Sprang heavenly Science; and from Science Freedom.
> O'er waken'd realms Philosophers and Bards
> Spread in concentric circles; they whose souls,
> Conscious of their high dignities from God,
> Brook not Wealth's rivalry! And they, who long
> Enamoured with the charms of order, hate
> The unseeemly disproportion: and whoe'er
> Turn with mild sorrow from the Victor's car
> And the low puppetry of thrones, to muse
> On that blest triumph, when the Patriot Sage
> Called the red lightnings from the o'er-rushing cloud
> And dashed the beauteous terrors on the earth
> Smiling majestic.
>
> ('Religious Musings', lines 225–38; *CPW*, vol. 1, pp. 117–18)

Coleridge's scientific 'Sages' were all electricians, men who harnessed nature's secret power and explained matter and mind in relation to it. Coleridge went on to mention Newton, Hartley and Priestley as well as Franklin: these men would be rewarded for their wisdom and leadership in a new millennium in which 'the renovated Earth' would vindicate their loving knowledge of nature ('Religious Musings', line 365, *CPW*, vol. 1, p. 123).

By late 1795, however, that force had been effectively resisted: Pitt's crackdown on radical meetings and writings made opposition too dangerous for even brave democrats to dare. After the execution of Louis, the British public tolerated the silencing and exile of Franklin's sympathisers and successors because it feared that they, like the French, would turn American anti-imperialism into bloody regicide and terror. Even Banks was, by 1798, seeking to suppress all 'Jacobin innovations' in science, suspicious that the disciples of his now-dead friend Franklin – disciples including Coleridge's mentors Priestley and Thomas Beddoes – would bring about revolution on the French model.[30] 'Every town', Coleridge lamented, 'is insulated, the vast conductors are destroyed by which the electric fluid of truth was conveyed from man to man, and nation to nation' (*Lects 1795*, p. 313).

Dispirited by the repression, by the insulation of radicals from their fellow Britons, Coleridge and Southey considered following Priestley to America. They took advice from Priestley's friend Thomas Cooper and chose the area that Priestley had settled in as their destination.[31] Their intention was to realise on a small scale the millenarian society that Priestley's radical 'truth' had been unable to bring about in Britain. Pantisocracy, as they named it, would be a society living in harmony with nature. Members would dedicate themselves to philosophical researches as well as labour on the land. There would be no hierarchy, no priests either, and all property would be held in common. Remote from the corruptions of British society, and peopled largely by Unitarian intellectuals, Pantisocracy would be an ideal republic nurtured by the welcoming soil of the republic that had successfully freed itself from the grip of colonialist Britain.

Pantisocracy was the logical outcome not only of the failure of radicalism to gain popular support in Britain but of a virulent anti-colonialism that Coleridge and Southey inherited from – among others – Franklin and Priestley. In a 1795 pamphlet that numbered Priestley among the 'disinterested Patriots' 'who against corruption nobly stood/ For Justice, Liberty and equal Laws' (*Lects 1795*, pp. 38, 41), Coleridge attacked Britain as an imperialist exporter of war and misery across the globe (*Lects 1795*, p. 58). War with revolutionary France was part of an imperial pattern of evil exploitation and mass murder, evidenced not least by the use of Native Americans to scalp white American colonists fighting for independence. Coleridge's reference was to a notorious massacre of 1778 in which Indians employed by Britain killed and scalped women and children in the very place to which Priestley, and now the Pantisocrats, were emigrating – the Susquehanna valley. Behind his indictment of British imperialism, then, was resentment that he and his radical heroes could find nowhere, even in the independent

United States, unmarked by what Franklin had termed Britain's 'absolute despotism'.[32]

The Pantisocrats' interest in the Susquehanna area had Franklin as well as Priestley behind it. The Indians idealised by Franklin in his 1784 *Remarks Concerning the Savages* were from the Susquehanna tribe. It was Susquehannas who, according to Franklin, challenged the cant of the missionary who rejected their creation story as a falsehood. Coleridge and Southey were themselves trying to escape the cant of Christianity as it was established in the contemporary British Church. Their choice of the Susquehanna area reflected their hope that, despite the corrupting influence of the British in 1778, they would be welcomed by Franklinian Indians, models of hospitality, independence and natural religion. This hope, as well as their post-massacre anxiety, is evident in Southey's letter of 22 August 1794: 'Should the resolution of others fail, Coleridge and I will go together, and either find repose in an Indian wig-wam – or from an Indian tomahawk' (Curry, vol. 1, p. 70). It is evident too in Southey's poems of the time, in which Franklin's account of the Susquehannas is cited. Franklin, Southey notes in *Madoc*, wrote that

> There is in every village of the Susquehannah Indians, a vacant dwelling called the Stranger's House. When a traveller arrives within hearing of a village, he stops and halloos, for it is deemed uncivil to enter abruptly. Two old men lead him to the house, and then go round to the inhabitants, telling them a stranger is arrived fatigued and hungry. They send them all they can spare, bring tobacco after they are refreshed, and then ask questions whence they come and whither they go.

In Southey's verse, this passage turns into a scene in which Madoc, fleeing oppression in Britain, is welcomed by native Americans just as the Pantisocrats hoped to be welcomed:

> The elders of the land
> Came forth, and led us to an ample hut,
> Which in the center of their dwellings stood,
> The Stranger's House. They eyed us wondering,
> Yet not for wonder ceased they to observe
> Their hospitable rites; from hut to hut
> The tidings ran that strangers were arrived,
> Fatigued and hungry and athirst; anon,
> Each from his means supplying us, came food
> And beverage such as cheers the weary man.[33]

The Pantisocrats' idealisation of America as a place freed from subservience to Britain's Church and King, in which liberty fed and in turn fed upon advances in knowledge, derived from the impact of Franklin's views on Indians as well as from the British reception of his science.

Emigration to America remained a route that Coleridge and Southey would not take. They would not explore the American interior that Franklin's narrative had made so romantically appealing. They would stay at home, experiencing the consequences of government repression and the 'insulation' of radicals. These consequences were felt in the practice of science and literature as well as in the dissemination of political ideas. In fact, these discourses were so intertwined that to continue, in the era of anti-revolutionary fervour, in any one of them required a complicated reworking of one's practice as an intellectual. Writing politically, or even practising one's discourse in a network of like-minded men and women, was now difficult and dangerous.

To understand this situation fully there is no better example than the career of Humphry Davy, a man who, from the start of his experimentalist activities, was associated with radical and anti-establishment scientific and literary practitioners. Davy arrived in Bristol in October 1798 to work superintending the Pneumatic Institution of a friend and mentor of Coleridge and Southey – Thomas Beddoes. The Institution was a levelling one: it aimed to use newly discovered gases to heal the sick, taking medicine out of the hands of the profession. Beddoes was no less radical personally: he had left a fellowship at Oxford, unable to suppress his anti-Church beliefs, and become a fierce critic of the government. Like his friends Joseph Priestley and Erasmus Darwin, he mixed scientific with political publications and experienced increasing opposition from loyalists who feared the revolution in France would spread to Britain. The Home Office registered him as a 'Disaffected & seditious' person[34] and Banks closed the Royal Society to his work and refused to support the Pneumatic Institution. It functioned, instead, with the support of a network that Banks did not control (although he had supported it in pre-revolutionary times)[35] – a provincial network of middle-class dissenters, doctors and industrialists, 'new men' eager for reform. Davy soon became the bright star of this network, isolating new gases that Beddoes then publicised round the country. He had Coleridge and Southey breathe nitrous oxide and they, mightily impressed, decided Davy was a genius. Davy, in turn, absorbed their views, dedicating himself to the idea that poetry, philosophy of mind and natural philosophy were related means of comprehending the life-principle that animated everything. At Southey's behest, he published verse expressing the hope that the laws of nature would be revealed to a scientific genius:

> To scan the laws of Nature, to explore
> The tranquil reign of mild Philosophy;
> Or on Newtonian wings sublime to soar
> Through the bright regions of the starry sky.
>
> From these pursuits the Sons of Genius scan
> The end of their creation hence they know
> The fair, sublime, immortal hopes of man.[36]

In prose, Davy proposed the theory that light, heat and electricity were all modifications of the ether: 'the electric fluid', he suggested, 'is probably light in a condensed state'. Light formed chemical combinations with other forms of matter and thus helped compose living bodies. 'The different species [of matter] are continually changing into each other'; organic and inorganic nature, world, body and mind, Davy thought, might at root all be forms of one principle.[37]

By 1800 Davy was the great white hope of dissenting intellectuals. To Coleridge, for instance, Davy's ideas put chemistry at the forefront of the project to which he had dedicated himself, freeing thought and society from the repressive hold of those authorities who dominated Church and State. Like Priestley reborn, Davy promised to unravel the life-principle itself, to transform nature and man at once. This reputation, Davy discovered, was soon more a hindrance than a help. As the radicals' chief natural philosopher, as Beddoes's assistant, Davy was the prime target of loyalist attacks on revolutionary thinking. Both the nitrous oxide experiments and the theory of heat and light came in for savage satire in which Davy was pictured as a deluded fanatic addicted to brainclouding principles and wacky notions. He was smeared by association with his mentors and friends, his science belittled and his politics stigmatised.

It was in 1800 that there fell into Davy's hands a new device that would lead him away from Bristol and Beddoes, away from radical science and provincial networks and towards London, conservatism and the royal institutions of Sir Joseph. The device arrived in the forms of words, words transmitted via Banks, who communicated to trusted scientific friends and to the Royal Society a description sent him by Alessandro Volta. Volta had been checking out the theories of his compatriot Luigi Galvani. According to Volta, the electrical fluid that Galvani thought he was conducting from the bodies of dead beasts was actually being generated accidentally by Galvani himself. It was, Volta showed, the contact of two dissimilar moist metals that produced the flow of electricity. From this he deduced that placing many pieces of different wet metal together would allow him to generate electricity and that it was because it had such a mechanism within its body that the torpedo fish could give electric shocks. Volta then built his own torpedo-mechanism (the Voltaic pile) – and became the first man to have a technology for producing current electricity. Electrical science would no longer be reliant on gathering static electricity by friction machines; henceforth experimentalists would have in their armoury, as the military name for the pile – 'battery' – indicates, firepower.

Volta had made a breakthrough; it was Banks, however, who gave the breakthrough immediate influence. Receiving Volta's description in his capacity as President of the Royal Society, he put his network into action. In April 1800 he privately showed Volta's paper to the gentleman natural philosopher Anthony Carlisle even before publication. Seizing on the potential of the pile, Carlisle proceeded to decompose water into its elements. Chemists, it was clear, now had a tool strong enough to intervene in nature, breaking substances apart and revealing what they were made of. Davy, still in Bristol, still with radical Beddoes, got no private view of Volta's work from Banks. After its publication, however, he began experiments with a battery of the kind he had seen in Volta's article. In November 1800 he told Coleridge that he had made 'some important galvanic discoveries which seem to lead to the door of the temple of the mysterious god of Life'.[38]

By 1801 Davy was on his way to London. The instrument that would give chemists power had come via the metropolis, not via Beddoes's provincial network. Under pressure from satirical attacks, tarred by association with the French Revolution, that network was in abeyance. Isolated, reviled, Beddoes himself seemed, even to his friends, yesterday's man. Coleridge wrote in his notebook in the winter of the year, 'Beddoes hunting a Pig with a buttered Tail – his whole Life an outcry of Eureka and all eurekas Lies' (CN, vol. 1, entry 1034). Davy left for the scientific mainstream, knowing he needed more support and more funding than Beddoes could offer if he was to build a pile big enough to achieve the spectacular interventions in nature that he aimed at.

Going to London meant going, directly or indirectly, to Banks. It meant remodelling one's self and one's practice to suit the social and political context in which science was now pursued under Banks's aegis. Davy, not a gentleman of independent means, needed a job, and he took one at an institution Banks had just helped to create – the Royal Institution.[39] Coleridge feared for his friend in this fashionable and conservative environment: 'Davy', he noted in 1804, was 'more & more determined to mould himself upon the age in order to make the age mould itself upon him'.[40] These fears were justified, for Davy not only denounced the 'devouring flame of anarchy' spread by the French Revolution but accepted that 'the rich & privileged orders . . . are ultimately the guardians of refinement & civilisation & even of science'.[41] Davy turned electrical science away from the radical context that its association with American and French revolutionaries had given it. He caused a change in its symbolism in the process. After his Royal Institution years, electricity was no longer a figure for representing republican liberty or nature's revolutionary agency. Instead it stood for a depoliticised metropolitan hero – a remodelled Romantic experimentalist who, though a genius, as in Bristol, now worked in isolation before revealing his work to the world. Echoing Wordsworth,[42] Davy declared, 'The truly insulated individual can effect little or nothing by his unassisted efforts. It is from minds nourishing their strength in solitude, and exerting that strength in society, that the most important truths have proceeded.'[43] Davy, in short, made electrical research the hallmark of the experimentalist as sublime egotist.

Davy succeeded because he showed great flair in staging his research for consumption by the fashionable ladies and gentlemen who patronised the Royal Institution. In a series of demonstration lectures, Davy, as Jan Golinski puts it, 'converted the Voltaic pile . . . from an experiment into an instrument'[44] that he wielded to lever nature into revealing its constituent elements. He wooed an audience of socially powerful lay people with stunning sounds and sights: the fizz of escaping gas, the crack of a blue spark, and, rarest of all, the pure light of a new metal that burnt under water. He first decomposed the fixed alkalis, liberating sodium and potassium, then the alkaline earths. He showed that chemical affinities were related to electrical powers and that elements could be identified in electrochemical terms, sodium being the most electropositive, oxygen the most negative.

The science was brilliant; the presentation was just as impressive. Davy became the hottest ticket in town: subscriptions soared; money flowed into the Royal Institution coffers. The theatrical spectacle and the crafted oratory were matched by the cogent prose of Davy's written papers. The *Monthly Review* called Davy's 1807 Bakerian lecture to the Royal Society 'the history of one of the most brilliant discoveries of our times'.[45] The *Edinburgh* agreed Davy had 'made greater discoveries than any man has done since the days of Newton'.[46] Most significant of all, Banks was so impressed that when he agreed to sit for an official portrait as President of the Royal Society, he chose to be depicted holding a copy of Davy's 1807 Bakerian lecture. The former assistant of Beddoes had redeemed himself completely. Electrochemistry was now the discipline of which the British scientific establishment was most proud.

To Coleridge, Davy's work seemed a vindication of the Romantic project they had developed together in the 1790s, stripped of the political implications which had made both men distrusted in the Tory centres of metropolitan and national authority. Coleridge avowed that Davy's findings were 'more intellectual, more ennobling and impowering human Nature, than Newton's'.[47] Davy was still a sublime genius who promised to reveal the one law that powered both mind and matter. Electricity was one manifestation of this law, chemical attraction another, gravitation a third. When Davy had demonstrated the unity of these forces 'it will then', Coleridge concluded, 'only remain to resolve this into some law of vital Intellect – and all human knowledge will be Science and Metaphysics the only Science'.[48] Davy was all the more a hero for the Coleridge of 1807 because he seemed to renew the agenda of the 1790s in brilliant new terms *without* also renewing the radical context that the agenda had once possessed. And since Coleridge, like Davy himself, was working in London (for an increasingly Tory newspaper), he also wished to live down his revolutionary reputation. To this end, he made his enthusiasm for Davy public in his journal *The Friend* in a panegyric that made the chemist into the embodiment of a Romantic genius for an anti-Jacobin age – a man who was as worthy a cause for national pride as Shakespeare and a man superior to the 'mechanistic' natural philosophers of France, the nation Britain was still at war with. Coleridge put Davy in a deradicalised decontextualised pantheon of creative heroes, just as he was to do Wordsworth a few years later.

There were no literary responses to Davy more glowing than Coleridge's, but there was one more profound, one, moreover, that perfectly illustrates the different symbolic value that the electrical experimentalists had acquired in the wake of Davy's London achievements. Mary Shelley had grown up on Davy's brilliance: her father was an early supporter and her husband had constructed his own Voltaic pile at university. Indeed, Percy Shelley saw electrical researches as a way of harnessing nature's huge power, as T. J. Hogg remembered:

He charged a powerful battery of several large jars; labouring with vast energy and discoursing with increasing vehemence of the marvellous powers of electricity, thunder and lightning; describing an electrical kite that he had made at home, and projecting another and an enormous one, or rather a combination of many kites, that would draw down from the sky an immense volume of electricity, the whole ammunition of a mighty thunderstorm; and this being directed to some point would there produce the most stupendous results.[49]

Mary herself read Davy's electrochemical papers in late 1816; shortly afterwards she began working on *Frankenstein*. Anne K. Mellor and Maurice

Hindle, among others, have demonstrated that Victor Frankenstein is a hero made, in part, in the electrochemist's image.[50] His conversion from Renaissance alchemy to modern science comes in response to the classic experiment in which Franklin had conducted electricity from a thundercloud down the string of a kite, as he himself narrates:

I eagerly inquired of my father the nature and origin of thunder and lightning. He replied, 'Electricity;' describing at the same time the various effects of that power. He constructed a small electrical machine, and exhibited a few experiments; he also made a kite, with a wire and string, which drew down that fluid from the clouds.[51]

But Victor Frankenstein does not become, as Beddoes, Priestley and William Godwin had become, a member of an intellectual circle of equals dedicated to social reform. It is power that fascinates Victor, the power that electricity gives the lone experimentalist. Victor's teacher Waldman inspires him with this description of the 'masters' of science: 'They have acquired new and almost unlimited powers, they can command the thunders of heaven.' Victor is then seized with desire to 'explore unknown powers, and unfold to the world the deepest mysteries of creation'.[52] The man of science, he realises, is now an explorer of nature. This, as Mellor shows, was to echo the words of Davy that Shelley read in 1816, according to which the electrochemist has 'powers which may almost be called creative; which have enabled him to modify and change the beings surrounding him, and by his experiments interrogate nature with power not simply as a scholar, passive and seeking only to understand her operations, but rather as a master, active with his own instruments'.[53]

Victor Frankenstein is a would-be Davyan master, inspired by the exalted conception of the experimentalist that Davy had formulated in his writing and embodied in his public demonstrations. He is a new figure, a Romantic experimentalist armed with electricity but cut off from the social networks that would preserve his humanity and discipline his research. In this latter respect he is a critique of the remodelled Romantic genius, the master of nature operating alone, rather than in a society of equals. Victor represents, in other words, not only the power and the glory that modern chemists garnered after Davy, but also the dreadful dangers involved in separating science from the critical and emotional relationships provided by kinship with others (especially women). Shelley spelt out in Frankenstein the failings of egotistical Romantic masculinity, failings inherent in the Wordsworthian poet and in the Davyan experimentalist. It was because many scientists in the nineteenth and twentieth centuries lived out the scientific role as Davy defined it (but ignoring Davy's warnings about hubris and isolation) that her story became talismanic. But it was also because the politics of electricity in the 1790s became so suspect and because the power of Banksian patronage proved so strong that Davy defined the role in those terms. The scientist as master manipulator of nature working alone in his laboratory was a potent fiction born of the Romantics' forced retreat from the radical electricity of provincial dissent to the conservative electrochemistry of the Royal – and loyal – Institution and Society.

In 1795 such a change of position seemed unlikely. In that year Napoleon had still to come to power and Southey and Coleridge were still opponents of their government's war with revolutionary France. Transmutations of radicalism, and of the vocabulary in which it was expressed, were over the horizon of the nineteenth century. What mattered as the 1790s drew on was finding terms in which liberty and reform could be imagined, without incurring the opprobrium of a government and people opposed to all things revolutionary. Coleridge and Southey found those terms, in part, through explorations of another science, one that resembled electric medicine. Vaccination gave them a vocabulary that showed British civilisation, at home and abroad, as an empire of enlightenment, innovation and healing. But first, as we shall see, it had to be dissociated from radical science and revolutionary politics.

CHAPTER 9

The beast within: vaccination, Romanticism and the Jenneration of disease

Edward Jenner was, from the start of his career, a part of Banks's network. The first pupil of the anatomist John Hunter, he was recommended to Banks as the best person to dissect and mount the specimens brought back from the *Endeavour* voyage. So impressed was Banks by Jenner's skill that the doctor was invited to become the naturalist on Cook's second expedition. And although Jenner refused the risky offer, he remained in correspondence with Banks, sending him details of his experiments on the fertilising powers of manure and blood. Later, after his paper on the life-cycle of the cuckoo was read at the Royal Society, Jenner was elected to a fellowship. Banks, as President, congratulated him. Jenner had become an established and honoured member of the institutionalised science over which Banks presided.

So it seemed, at least, until 1798, when Jenner submitted another paper to the Royal Society, concerning the obscure rural sickness cowpox and the hope it offered for human health. To his chagrin, Banks rejected it: Jenner was refused access to the network; the Royal Society would not give his work its sanction. This chapter tells the story of why, and of how Jenner overcame Banks's disapproval, and, with the help of poets and journalists, got himself a public image that had been previously developed for explorers such as Cook and men of science such as Franklin, but that was dissociated from revolutionary politics.

With Banks's help and with the prestige produced by his publicity campaign, Jenner found ways to give his discovery imperial and international status, so that he became perhaps the most famous man of science in the world. By 1833 a discovery made in a rural backwater of provincial England had been spread across the globe as a symbol of the benefits of British rule. Jenner himself was portrayed as a benefactor of humankind who redeemed Britain from its imperial guilt. And yet, despite all this, vaccination remained tainted by its origin in the bestial: for many people in Britain and its colonies it was to be resisted because it both revealed humans' animality and symbolised the despotism of Britain's government.

Vaccination began in the British countryside and spread round the world but it built upon an Oriental medicine that Britain had imported and Anglicised. In China, in India, in Africa, people had long been taking jabs in the arm to guard them against the mostly deadly disease of all. In each of these countries, healthy folk were inoculated with mild doses of the full human smallpox. If the process worked, and they did not develop a severe case, then they suffered a slight infection but, afterwards, had lifelong immunity.

Little was known of inoculation in Britain and Europe, where medicine was less advanced than in the East, until the early eighteenth century. In 1713 and 1715 the Royal Society published reports on the practice by European medics living in Greece and Turkey. In 1716, in the American colonies, Cotton Mather's slave Onesimus told his master that inoculation was common in Africa. But it was not until an English woman returned from the East that the practice started to find root in Europe. Lady Mary Wortley Montagu had lived in Constantinople from 1717 to 1721 as the wife of the British ambassador. A keen observer of local customs, she wrote home about 'the invention of engrafting' prevalent in Turkey.[1]

Montagu had reason to know of smallpox's dangers in Britain, having lost a brother to the disease and having been severely scarred by it herself. In 1718, therefore, she had her son inoculated and, in 1721, her daughter. She then exhibited the still-healthy girl to the high-ranking Britons to whom her social status gave her access, including Sir Hans Sloane, the King's physician. With supporters this eminent, even the self-interested medical profession was prepared to test the import. On 9 August 1721 six death-row criminals were inoculated in the presence of the court doctors and members of the Royal Society and Royal College of Physicians. They survived, demonstrated their immunity, and gained their freedom. Impressed, Britain's scientific elite was now prepared to recommend inoculation to the most important members of British society. On 17 April 1722 the two daughters of the Princess of Wales were successfully immunised. Lesser aristocrats and other European royalty soon followed this example: Montagu's Orientalist enquiry had brought Europe the benefits of the East's superior medical knowledge.

When Edward Jenner looked out of the window of his comfortable doctor's house in Gloucestershire, he knew that Montagu's Turkish treatment had been Anglicised for over seventy years. But he also knew that it had its risks. If not properly performed, inoculation gave people the full fatal

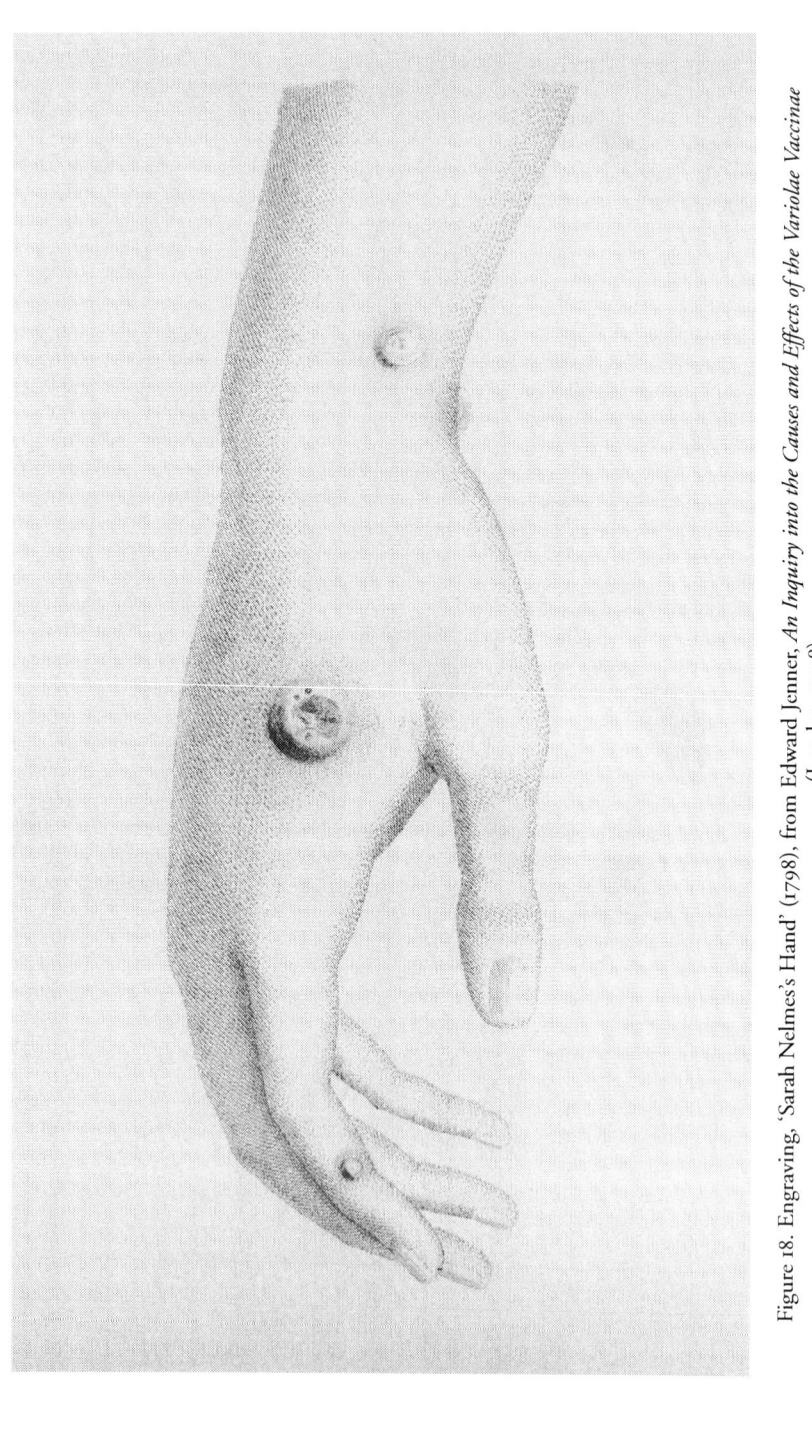

Figure 18. Engraving, 'Sarah Nelmes's Hand' (1798), from Edward Jenner, *An Inquiry into the Causes and Effects of the Variolae Vaccinae* (London, 1798).

disease and if quarantine wasn't strictly enforced, the inoculated patient infected others. Nevertheless, inoculation was the best that doctors could do. Or was it? As Jenner surveyed the cows grazing in the meadows that spread green almost to his door, he wondered if he had found a better way. For Jenner had read something significant in his neighbours' palms. What he saw is pictured here in an engraving published in 1798 – a refined whiteness blemished only by three intriguing spots (Fig. 18). Despite its pearly skin, this hand was not a gentlewoman's but a dairymaid's. It belonged to Sarah Nelmes, a local farmworker who had been infected with the disease called cowpox. It was an ordinary girl's hand but paradoxically carried both the blessing of world health and the curse of western imperialism in its elegant grasp.

Nelmes's hand was depicted in Jenner's 1798 treatise *An Inquiry into the Causes and Effects of the Variolae Vaccinae, A Disease Discovered in Some of the Western Counties of England . . . and known by the name of The Cow Pox*.[2] Jenner's *Inquiry* was beautiful in its simplicity. Unlike Montagu's, Jenner's vision was not rooted in royal courts but in milking parlours. It was not sanctioned by the proceedings of scientific societies but by the tales of rustic villagers. It came not from the Sublime Porte of Constantinople but from the cowsheds of Gloucestershire. Just over seventy pages in length, it presented a series of stories about dairymaids, paupers and manservants whose daily, pastoral activities brought them in touch with cows and cowpox, and thus made them immune to smallpox.

The most important case in the *Inquiry* was that of Nelmes. Jenner had noticed that dairymaids had something the general population lacked: beautiful skin. At this time, everyone knew that smallpox epidemics left thousands either dead with broken pustules oozing bodily fluids, or living for the rest of their lives blind and with severely disfigured skin.[3] Even milder cases, like Montagu herself, were disfigured for life. Not dairymaids, though, for they caught cowpox.[4] To Jenner (and others), the maids' beautiful skin was evidence that cowpox gave them some protection against smallpox. Nelmes became the subject of Jenner's most crucial experiment. Since she had, he reported, just been 'infected with matter' from one of 'her master's cows', an otherwise harmless beast named Blossom, he inserted her cowpox into the arm of 'a healthy boy, about eight years old'.[5] The boy barely took sick and was thereafter immune to smallpox, confirming Jenner's hunch: getting cowpox prevented smallpox.

As it turned out, this revolutionary work on smallpox by a provincial British doctor made a breakthrough that changed the course of medicine – and history. Vaccination was new, for nobody had previously succeeded in protecting people against one disease by infecting them with another. Jenner, however, did not adequately understand the process by which vaccination worked. It was Louis Pasteur, a century later, who theorised and extended Jenner's discovery to make vaccination applicable to diseases other than smallpox, but Pasteur named the process after Jenner's work: 'vaccination', meaning 'from cows'. One of the quaint ironies of epidemiology is that we derive our technology for fighting terrifying pandemics and threats of biological warfare from the diseased udders of a humble beast. Vaccination protected people by infecting them with animal disease, making the hope of world health dependent on the mark of the beast.

When Jenner realised the importance of his discovery, he wasted no time in trying to transport it to both the nation and the empire. After all, smallpox was the deadliest scourge in existence, killing vast numbers in Europe (including, during the eighteenth century, six European monarchs and an annual average of 300 per 100,000 persons in Britain). In the new world, spread by European colonists, it was still more devastating, wiping out whole indigenous peoples in the space of three generations in America. But despite the disease's terrible power, Jenner faced an uphill task, for the public was too busy and too sceptical to pay attention to stories of miracle cures from rural backwaters. In 1798, Britain was expecting invasion by French revolutionary armies. In this climate, the rural simplicity of the story of the dairymaid with a sore hand, like the rustic speech of that other volume of 1798, *Lyrical Ballads*, was too quiet, too bucolic, to find immediate understanding in a worried metropolis. After three months waiting in London to receive patients, Jenner retired to Gloucestershire. Not a single person had volunteered for vaccination. Jenner, like Wordsworth and Coleridge, needed to promote his work by explaining its innovatory significance – both to men of influence and to the reading public at large. The poets sent their volume to major politicians and added the polemical *Preface*; Jenner, likewise, launched a propaganda campaign designed to convince the socially powerful that Britain would benefit from the healing power of nature that he, a doctor who had 'sought the lowly and sequestered paths of life',[6] had harnessed. It was a campaign that, from the start, presented science through the medium of poetry. Jenner attracted the services of Romantic poets, who lent their verse to his efforts to create the taste by which his discovery might be enjoyed by the people. They helped him make his pastoral medicine seem socially and politically conservative as they sought public approval in a Britain dominated by war with revolutionary France. They helped him also to advocate spreading vaccination across the world – as a British salve for the disease of empire.

PASTORALISM AND THE BODY

The taste for Jenner's medicine was affected by the fact that vaccination threatened to break some of the most powerful social and cultural taboos of its time. Jenner's discovery turned the pastoral ideal, long elaborated in polite poetry, into a strange reality. It made the lore of cowherds and dairymaids, typically portrayed as being innocent and ignorant, into the saviour of the lives of their social superiors. Those who owned the land became dependent upon those Burke, in his attack on revolutionary politics, had called the 'swinish multitude'. Fellow doctors advised Jenner against publishing a theory that relied on 'vulgar stories', since 'the public opinion of his knowledge and discernment' would 'materially suffer'.[7] At the Royal Society Banks refused to publish Jenner's theories 'which appeared so much at variance with established knowledge, and withal so incredible'.[8] Denied access to Banks's networks of science and patronage, Jenner found that 1798 was not a good year for a Briton to be challenging the established order.

The *Inquiry* did more than invert the social order: it made the bodies of pastoralists, and ultimately the bodies of cows, essential to the nation's health. For vaccination differed from other medical advances: it penetrated the human body with matter derived from the bodies of beasts and, in so doing, it made people sick to make them well. Jenner asked of people something much more profound than simply to accept that cowpox prevented smallpox. He asked them to accept that cattle and humans had similar constitutions at a time when medical men, philosophers and politicians alike were drawing lines and creating categories not only between the human and the animal world, but within these worlds, as we showed in chapter 6. The *Inquiry into the Causes and Effects of the Variolae Vaccinae*, in fact, emerged from Jenner's training as a comparative anatomist. A pupil of the pioneering surgeon and naturalist, John Hunter, Jenner had long thought that examining the effects of disease on animals 'casts a bright and steady light over some of the most obscure parts of human pathology'.[9] He argued that diseases were not just similar in animals and humans, but that they spread from one to the other.[10] Cross-infection was rendered more likely when animals themselves had been crossbred into hybrids (Jenner himself had conducted experiments to determine whether foxes and dogs would mate and breed). 'The wolf, disarmed of ferocity', the *Inquiry* observed, had degenerated into the domesticated dog, often 'pillowed in the lady's lap'.[11] Such unnatural intimacy between the human and the interbred animal made humans susceptible to a wide variety of sicknesses.

Jenner believed that animals mutated through crossbreeding to inferior versions of their former selves. Humans, likewise, became vulnerable to disease through degeneration. Through a sort of unnatural crossbreeding with industry and luxury, they were in a constant state of 'deviation' from the state in which they were 'originally placed by nature'.[12] Sounding like Rousseau, Jenner identified the causes of human degeneration as 'love of splendour', the 'indulgences of luxury', and the association with 'a great number of animals'.[13] The upper-class lady with her lapdog, living a life of ease and luxury, was already to radical writers a symbol of moral degeneracy.[14] She became, in Jenner's theory, a medical danger to humanity. The *Inquiry* brought radical suspicion of aristocratic manners home to the body: luxury, Jenner's science suggested, tainted the blood. Pastoral simplicity, on the other hand, protected the body from corruption – and Jenner, as the engraving of Nelmes showed, had the hand to prove it.

Or did he? Jenner was an empiricist who believed that what separated science from speculation was the specimen. As a pupil of Hunter he wanted to found his medicine on the thing itself. Men of science accepted Hunter's procedure: body parts, pickled and displayed, were acceptable evidence. But it was exactly this evidence that vaccination did not satisfactorily produce. Vaccination's success showed only in the absence of smallpox pustules, in human bodies that stayed whole and healthy when all around them were disintegrating with disease. But this absence, this immunity, might stem from a myriad of other factors: Jenner's medicine gave doubters nothing to see or touch to prove its effects. The engraving of Nelmes's cowpoxed hand was as near as his *Inquiry* could come to producing the 'facts' that contemporary science trusted.

Without specimens to show, Jenner's stories sounded like the case histories printed by every peddler of miracle cures. With no adequate explanatory theory either, Jenner the pamphleteer simply seemed like Jenner the rural quack. And he was not the only one who could print pictures representing cowpox's effects in the flesh. James Gillray undermined Jenner with a caricature that reminded everyone that pictures were not necessarily reliable evidence about the body. In 1802 Gillray published a print imagining the 'wonderful effects of the new inoculation' (Fig. 19): in it he depicts vaccination as a wild orgy of transformation where a side-glancing doctor vaccinates subjects who then sprout cows from their limbs, buttocks, mouths and ears. One poor vaccination victim simply grows a giant cowpox pustule from the right side of her face. Satanic horns erupt through the skull of another. The print finds a graphic language to articulate widely shared anxieties about the power of new science in the hands of an increasingly

Figure 19. James Gillray, 'The Cow Pock, or, The Wonderful Effects of the New Inoculation' (1802).

assertive medical profession. The development of comparative anatomy, like the advances in galvanism and electrochemistry, threatened to invade and transform the human. Dr Jenner and his allies, like the later Victor Frankenstein and Dr Jekyll, metamorphose men into hybrids – a sort of turning inside out of 'normal' Britons – into grotesque miscreations who wear their animality on the outside instead of hidden deep in their hearts.

Jenner's pastoralised body bred as many fears as it answered. Fear of English men and women degenerating to cattle became the cornerstone of a powerful anti-vaccination campaign that played upon some of the deepest anxieties of polite society. By the end of the eighteenth century, one of the agreed markers of gentlemanliness was one's distance from beasts. Cowper, the most popular poet of the period, portrayed the civilised man as one who was sheltered in domestic comfort. Leisured and insulated from the outdoors, he contrasted with the shepherd and the waggoner, peasants defined by their contact with animals.[15] Wordsworth, of course, focused on shepherds and waggoners in his poetry, but met hostility and incomprehension from reviewers and readers who failed to see how gentlemen

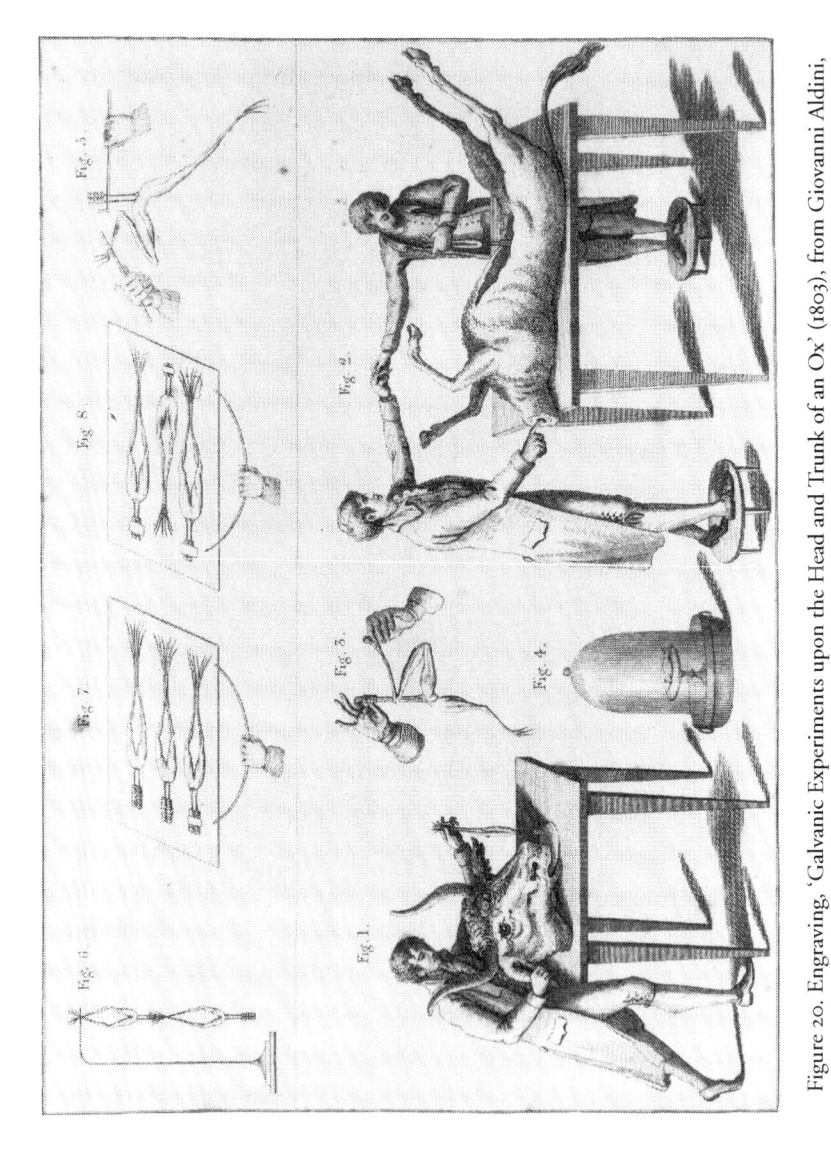

Figure 20. Engraving, 'Galvanic Experiments upon the Head and Trunk of an Ox' (1803), from Giovanni Aldini, *An Account of the Late Improvements in Galvanism* (London, 1803).

and women could learn conduct from peasants who reeked of the stable and the cowshed.[16] Jenner, however, practised a still more direct infusion of animal matter into the 'civilised' world and this violated the taboos of civility which gentlemen defined themselves by. He was rubbing gentlefolk's noses in the 'dirt' that hygiene could not clean up – the 'dirt' of their bodily similarity not only to peasants but to beasts.[17] At least it seemed so to Jenner's critics, who made fears of the British turning wildly brutish central to their opposition to him. Gillray was not the only one to reveal Britons' fear that vaccination would bring their animality out of the closet. In fact, many doctors were alarmed by Jenner's science in part because it reminded them of other scientific innovations that placed humans alongside beasts. William Rowley, for instance, attacked Jenner for infecting the medical profession with cowpox madness. Vaccination was simply the latest in a series of corrupt medical practices. Already 'electricity and galvanism mad', Rowley said, doctors were betraying their profession by endorsing science that made people like cows.

Like vaccination, galvanism was indeed the latest craze in medical advances. As we showed in chapter 8, Luigi Galvani amazed Europe because he seemed to draw a new kind of electricity from the body itself. The so-called galvanic fluid, unlike the static electricity previously manipulated by experimentalists, seemed to come from within and to be conductible from the inner fibres of one species to those of another. Galvani's nephew Giovanni Aldini revealed as much in a series of spectacular demonstrations in 1803. These demonstrations depended upon the corpses of cows, which Aldini used like gigantic electric batteries to recharge or reanimate dead things. 'Having obtained the body of an executed criminal,' Aldini reported, 'I formed an arc from the spinal marrow to the muscles, a prepared frog being placed between, and always obtained strong contractions' (Fig. 20).[18] Mary Shelley, who had read Aldini, took these experiments to their fictional extreme in *Frankenstein*: cows and criminality in the hands of these Promethean medical men had monstrous results. This is exactly how Rowley felt about Jenner's experiments. But Rowley's equivalent of Frankenstein's monster was, he believed, a matter of fact. He claimed to have treated a boy who, after being vaccinated, 'seemed to be in a state of transforming, and assuming the visage of a cow'.[19] This 'ox-faced boy', pictured in close-up at the beginning of Rowley's text, became a graphic warning of the dangers of the new science which threatened, like the French Revolution, to destroy the social and political order (Fig. 21). One ally of Rowley asked, 'are we to worship – to applaud – or even to submit to *Evil*, – to *Buonaparte* – or to *Vaccination*, . . . – No!'.[20] Resisting Jenner was like

Figure 21. Engraving, 'The Ox-Faced Boy' (1805), from William Rowley, *Cow-pox Inoculation No Security Against Small-pox Infection* (London, 1805).

resisting Napoleon, a divinely sanctioned mission against threats to established authority in Britain.

Rowley was part of a noisy campaign against Jenner led by Dr Benjamin Moseley, former surgeon to several powerful politicians of the time.[21] Moseley argued that vaccination could cause 'cow mania', and in this sense he articulated an earlier version of the present-day fear of BSE, or Mad Cow Disease.[22] Moseley adopted the position portrayed by Gillray's cartoon, that vaccination would turn patients into beasts. For Moseley, being injected with matter from cows brought the most dangerous form of sexuality – women's sexuality – into the open. As a result of vaccination, the bestial nature of women's desire led them to acts of animal madness: they mated with bulls. 'Can any person', Moseley went on, 'say what may be the consequences of introducing a bestial humour into the human frame, after a long lapse of years? Who knows, besides, what ideas may arise, in the course of time, from a brutal fever having excited its incongruous impression on the brain? Who knows, also, that the human character may undergo strange mutations from quadruped sympathy; and that some modern Pasiphaë may rival the fables of old?' Moseley's readers would not have had to be reminded that, in Greek legend, the gods caused Queen Pasiphaë to make love to a bull and give birth to the Minotaur, a monster with the body of a human and the head of a bull. Obviously, Moseley's invocation of this myth was meant to suggest that vaccination's blending of sexuality, power and beasts would have monstrous results.

Moseley's language was excessive, but it had its origin in elements of Jenner's own science. Relations between species were crucial issues in the new scientific discipline in which Jenner had been trained. Hunter's comparative anatomy became controversial because it demonstrated man's kinship with animals – particularly apes. In the later nineteenth century Hunter was suspected of having embraced the idea of evolution.[23] When his contemporary Erasmus Darwin expressed the idea explicitly in 1800, he found his morals and politics under vicious attack.[24]

Jenner did not embrace such radical views, but the language of the *Inquiry* brought them to mind anyway. 'Degeneration' and 'deviation' were charged terms; as we showed in chapter 6, Blumenbach argued that man had degenerated from the Adamic original.[25] And some races had degenerated more than others: blacks more than whites. The Negro, it was agreed, was more animal-like than the Caucasian. Crossbreeding, as Jenner argued about animals, produced further degeneration. People of mixed race, it was thought, were likely to be inferior to pure Caucasians. Crossbreeding threatened to lower Caucasians, by degrees, towards their ape-like black cousins.

Natural historians used crossbreeding as a key test. After Buffon, it was regarded as a way of distinguishing species.[26] If the offspring was always infertile, then it could be assumed that the parents were of different species. The mule showed the horse and donkey to be distinct. This theory got truly strange in the work of extreme racists. Unwilling to contemplate the mixing of whites and blacks, they applied the argument to people. Charles White and Edward Long, for instance, argued that black people were a different species from whites, and claimed as evidence the supposed 'fact' that mixed-race people were infertile.[27] Moseley, who was, like Long, an inhabitant of Jamaica and apologist for the plantation system, called Long 'the father of correct English–West-Indian literature'.[28]

In Moseley's extreme reasoning, Jenner's *Inquiry*, like comparative anatomy, threatened to undo the bodily distinctness upon which Long's arguments were founded. If animals were similar enough to people for their diseases to breed and spread in humans, then different races of men could hardly be organically separate, whether or not they were of the same species. And so it was no coincidence that Moseley portrayed vaccination in the figure of Pasiphaë mating with the bull. For him vaccination was an all too successful form of crossbreeding. It was an intercourse issuing in an offspring that was monstrous because it was fertile evidence that whites were not constitutionally different from blacks and from the beasts whom blacks were thought to resemble.

Moseley and Long had reasons for their need to make blacks and beasts different from whites. In the West Indian plantations where they had developed their thought, slaveholders had a vested interest in arguing that 'their' blacks were not fully human. In most plantation account books that have come down to us today, slaves and cattle were listed as pieces of property, side by side. Moseley himself associated slaves with animals.[29] Cow-like vaccination patients reminded him of the 'distortions from that terrible distemper, the yaws, in the African race, where there has been the resemblance of various animals'.[30] It was not simply fear of being infected with cow disease that sent shivers up Moseley's spine and obsessed his supporters, but the fear of discovering that they shared a common humanity with the slaves whom they wanted to believe to be bestial and inhuman so that they could exploit them with a clearer conscience.

PATRONS

If the profession and the public came gradually to accept vaccination, it was not by accident. Faced with Moseley's virulent parody of the pastoralism of the *Inquiry*, Jenner soon realised that he needed powerful supporters. Any radical implications to his theories about luxury were left behind as Jenner set out to cultivate the patronage of royalty and aristocracy. Jenner's neighbour, the Earl of Berkeley, used his influence at Court to gain an audience for the doctor. On 7 March 1800 Jenner was presented to the King, who gave permission for the second edition of the *Inquiry* to be dedicated to him.

It was through the characteristically eighteenth-century mechanism of patronage that vaccination first took hold in Britain. Vaccination was spread from the top down, not by government-organised campaigns but from royalty to aristocracy, and from aristocracy to their tenants. It was disseminated, that is to say, through the existing power-structure of Britain, which depended upon the manipulation of patronage, interest and obligation, on an informal basis, by the landowning elite. Jenner made himself an establishment man, astute enough to secure patronage. Suspicious of extreme democrats such as Tom Paine and William Cobbett,[31] he kept his oppositional politics private[32] and allied his science with high society – in conscious difference from radical experimentalists such as Erasmus Darwin and Joseph Priestley.[33] A crucial step was overcoming the suspicion of Banks, who not only headed the Royal Society, but was prominent in other organisations that Jenner hoped would help him. Moreover, as an adviser to the Admiralty and a consultant on overseas expeditions, Banks could, if he wished, promote vaccination in the empire. Ultimately, he did: Banks's network of correspondents, gardeners and officials in the colonies would receive and transmit the vaccine as they did botanical specimens and native skulls. But first he had to be convinced: Jenner achieved this by vaccinating a patient in a special demonstration that he put on for Sir Joseph's benefit. Reassured by the evidence of the controlled experiment he had personally witnessed, and convinced of its results, Banks gave his approval. Jenner had, by 1803, the social and scientific support to overcome his revolutionary reputation, to withstand Moseley's attacks and to resist the popular fear of his bestial medicine.

Jenner's path to fame and authority ran parallel to that of his fellow innovator of 1798. Wordsworth accepted the patronage of the Lonsdale family – as did Jenner himself. The Earl of Lonsdale was a Tory magnate with some of the most extensive landholdings in the country. In October 1800 he had Dr Robert Thornton vaccinate all four hundred inhabitants of the estate-village of Lowther. In the following weeks Thornton vaccinated about one thousand more locals who rented their homes and lands from the Earl. Both doctor and poet, then, overcame indifference to their versions of pastoral by making alliances with the aristocratic class of which they had first been implicitly critical.

PATRONISING A POET: JENNER AND ROBERT BLOOMFIELD

If Jenner sought patrons, he also acted as one. He encouraged a far more popular rural poet than Wordsworth to write verse praising vaccination.

Robert Bloomfield, who termed himself a 'writer of Pastoral poetry, and literally a Cow-boy',[34] was a former farm labourer and shoemaker who had taught himself verse-making after reading Thomson's *The Seasons*. Patronised by Capel Lofft and the Duke of Grafton, Bloomfield had published *The Farmer's Boy* in 1800. It had achieved immediate popular success on a scale made possible by the rapidly expanding book market. Twenty-six thousand copies were sold in fewer than three years, and translations appeared in French, Italian and Latin. To the poetry-reading public, Bloomfield was marketed as an authentic rustic voice, a peasant turned poet, whose pastorals were rooted in his childhood experience of sheep and cow herding.

Jenner showed an astute understanding of the possibilities presented by Bloomfield's success in the burgeoning public sphere addressed by poetry. He encouraged him to write on vaccination. After all, Bloomfield was not only the poet in vogue, and not only a former cowherd, but also a rustic who had suffered the effects of smallpox. His father had died of the disease when he was a year old. By July 1802 the gentleman-doctor, accustomed to writing pastoral verse himself, was inviting the labourer-poet to tea, with the intention of directing and correcting his vaccination poem. Bloomfield accepted the hospitality, but worried that Jenner was too pressing a patron.[35] Jenner was not a man to let the chance for favourable publicity from a fashionable writer go begging. He pursued Bloomfield until his vaccination poem was published. In 1803 he was writing to Bloomfield 'enquiring my determination as to the poem "On Vaccination," and expressing great interest in my welfare'.[36]

Bloomfield's poem *Good Tidings; Or, News From the Farm* appeared in 1804, with a dedication to Jenner. True to Bloomfield's public image as 'the farmer's boy', the poem spread the gospel of vaccination from the country to the town-based public. The poem begins with a pastoral scene of a kind familiar to readers of Wordsworth, Coleridge and Blake. It focuses on a simple, innocent child of nature at play.[37] But this child is blighted by smallpox: 'the boy is blind' (line 22). He is a pathetic figure, an embodiment of rural innocence and natural growth that is tainted by a disease spread from city to country: 'When last year's corn was green upon the ground:/ From yonder town infection found its way' (lines 48–9).

Bloomfield's poem is a powerful one because it is driven by his rhetorical efforts to resolve a tension that went to the very heart of his poetic authority as a 'writer of Pastoral poetry and literally a Cow-boy'. It was a tension that affected Wordsworth and John Clare too, for it arose from the attempt to claim that the idealisations inherent in the genre of pastoral poetry were observable in the lives of contemporary rural labourers. When, as was the case for Bloomfield and Clare, the poet's own position as a former labourer was one of the reasons for his fashionable success, the tension became threatening to his commercial prospects and to his sense of identity. Both Bloomfield and Clare suffered declining sales and increasing personal crises.

What is at stake in *Good Tidings* is the very continuance of a rural way of life upon which Bloomfield's poetic authority depends. He had made his reputation as a poet who, by virtue of his peasant upbringing (normally an insuperable disadvantage for a would-be poet), could uniquely root the pastoral ideal in the real. But smallpox threatened to uproot the ideal from the experienced world, to destroy innocence and peace as it wiped out whole families and blasted entire communities. Smallpox threatened Bloomfield's precarious poetic career because it exposed a fatal gap between the real world of farm labourers of which he had personal experience, and the idealised version of it to which his publication as a 'pastoral' poet committed him.

Bloomfield's sense of the danger his muse is in is evident in the dedication, which pleads that 'the egotism, so conspicuous in the poem . . . ought to be forgiven'.[38] In the poem itself, he again apologises for including grim details drawn from his real personal history, for these details undermine the pastoral poetic models to which he (and his readers) want to conform. Yet these details constitute the most powerful passage in the poem for they lend graphic realism to Bloomfield's account of smallpox menacing his family's domestic bliss:

> *Home*, where six children, yielding to its pow'r,
> Gave hope and patience a most trying hour;
> One at her breast still drew the living stream,
> And sense of danger never marr'd his dream;
> Yet all exclaim'd, and with a pitying eye
> 'Whoe'er survives the shock, that child will die!'
> But vain the fiat, – Heav'n restor'd them all,
> And destin'd one of riper years to fall.
> Midnight beheld the close of all his pain,
> His grave was clos'd when midnight came again;
> No bell was heard to toll, no funeral pray'r,
> No kindred bow'd, no wife, no children there;
> Its horrid nature could inspire a dread
> That cut the bonds of custom like a thread.
> (lines 179–92)

Apologising for relating the grim facts, Bloomfield asks for pity: if he sinks below the pastoral into 'tales of woe' it is because he was the child whose father died: 'Though love enjoin'd not infant eyes to weep,/ In manhood's zenith shall his feelings sleep?' (lines 211–12). Pathos, it seems, is the device by which Bloomfield will overcome the division between his own experience of rural life and the pastoral terms into which he is expected to translate it.

Pathos is not the poem's final solution to the tensions in Bloomfield's position: Edward Jenner is. Vaccination saved Bloomfield's muse because it made the pastoral ideal seem liveable – at least in one poem. It allowed it again to appear rooted in actual rural life. He said as much explicitly:

> Sweet beam'd the star of peace upon those days
> When Virtue watch'd my childhood's quiet ways,
> Whence a warm spark of Nature's holy flame
> Gave the farm-yard an honourable name,
> But left one theme unsung: then, who had seen
> In herds that feast upon the vernal green,
> Or dreamt that in the blood of kine there ran
> Blessings beyond the sustenance of man?
> We tread the meadow, and we scent the thorn,
> We hail the day-spring of a summer's morn;
> Nor mead at dawning day, nor thymy heath,
> Transcends the fragrance of the heifer's breath:
> May that dear fragrance, as it floats along
> O'er ev'ry flow'r that lives in rustic song;
> May all the sweets of meadows and of kine
> Embalm, O Health! this offering at thy shrine.
>
> (lines 79–94)

The sweet smell of success was the 'dear fragrance' of a cow's breath, now revealed not just as a feature of rustic song, but as nature's remedy for diseases bred in towns.

Briefly, Bloomfield's pastoralism offers to become socially radical. Not only is rural life preferred to urban but, as in *Lyrical Ballads*, rustics seem wiser than gentlemen. Jenner, Bloomfield tells us, had been dependent upon rural knowledge, on the local 'tradition' known to Gloucestershire pastoralists that contact with cows prevented smallpox infection. But if this seems to make professional medicine secondary to rustic experience, Bloomfield soon suggests that Jenner has raised pastoral lore to the status of scientific truth. In the process, in Bloomfield's heroic portrait, he becomes godlike, giving healing law to the whole world. By the poem's climax its pastoralism was neither radical nor levelling: vaccination did not lower men to the level of cattle; Jenner did not simply codify what cowherds already knew. Instead, through Jenner, the cowshed came to command the international stage:

> Forth sped the truth immediate from his hand,
> And confirmations sprung in ev'ry land;
> In ev'ry land, on beauty's lily arm,
> On infant softness, like a magic charm,
> Appear'd the gift that conquers as it goes;
> The dairy's boast, the simple, saving Rose!
> (lines 121–6)

In the image of the rose Bloomfield made the blister raised in the vaccinated arm into a symbol of natural beauty and fertility. Jenner, scattering vaccine roses, had become a Romantic hero – a godlike genius who harnessed the hidden virtue of nature. Vaccination killed the 'foul serpent' contagion and allowed villagers to 'Love ye your neighbours' without fear of infecting their own children (lines 237, 243). In other words, it restored Eden and allowed God's commandments to be lived out on earth. Jenner's 'victory' over smallpox was an apotheosis of the pastoral life that Bloomfield declared himself uniquely fitted to celebrate:

> Victory shall increase
> Th'incalculable wealth of private peace;
> And such a victory, unstain'd with gore,
> That strews its laurels at the cottage door,
> Sprung from the farm, and from the yellow mead,
> Should be the glory of the pastoral reed.
> (lines 365–70)

Jenner saved Bloomfield's pastoralism (at least in the short term) by allowing him to maintain the idealisations that his gentlemanly public expected. In return, Bloomfield helped Jenner's publicity drive, assistance which Jenner relished. After the poem was recited to a special meeting of the Royal Jennerian Society, he rewarded Bloomfield with a silver inkstand. Later, he sent a silver tea-caddy for Mrs Bloomfield.

THE DOCTOR AS ROMANTIC GENIUS: JENNER, COLERIDGE AND SOUTHEY

As university-educated gentlemen, Coleridge and Southey were not to be so easily patronised as Bloomfield. Yet as enthusiasts for the healing power of nature and subscribers to Rousseau's idealisation of childhood innocence, they were ready converts to the cause. As a father, Southey found ample reason to praise the discoverer of vaccination, declaring in 1802 that the nation should have awarded Jenner a greater sum of money for a discovery that protected innocent children so well. Coleridge agreed and gathered evidence from his reading to help Jenner prove his case for the 'the identity of the Small & cow pox' (*CL*, vol. III, p. 852). Southey also used his pen to aid the cause. He reviewed *Good Tidings* favourably, taking the opportunity to publicise vaccination.[39] Both writers were assisting Jenner to use the newly popular journals and reviews to seek validation of his discovery from the reading public. This was a departure from eighteenth-century scientific practice, in which discoveries' status as accepted science was typically decided by the Royal Society.

Like Bloomfield, the Bristol-based poets took vaccination beyond the scientific community. In so doing, they viewed Jenner in Romantic terms derived from their own experience of medical experimentation. It was in Bristol that they had become involved with Dr Thomas Beddoes, who, as we showed in chapter 8, was pioneering new forms of treatment (with Jenner's help) at his Pneumatic Institution and who became a strong supporter of Jenner.[40] Beddoes was a radical democrat, who pamphleteered against war with France and criticised aristocratic corruption in Britain's government.[41] His medicine had radical elements too, for he speculated that disease was caused by the fashionable and luxurious lifestyles of the rich. 'Fatal indolence' amongst the leisured classes weakened their constitutions, leaving them vulnerable to consumption.[42] Like Jenner, Beddoes proposed a remedy that seemed levelling in its social implications, for he too had been putting pastoral lore to experimental test. Interested in the tradition that 'stable-boys and grooms . . . are . . . but little liable to consumption', Beddoes sought to develop the healing powers of cows.[43] He had consumptive patients housed in cowsheds, hoping that the atmosphere produced by the cattle's breath and manure would effect a cure. Joseph Priestley's daughter was one who endured this 'stabling'. She wrote from her 'Cow-House' that despite the 'nauseous' stench and the 'successive generations of flies' she had become 'more than ever a friend to the cows'.[44] Others were less enamoured: Beddoes lamented one young lady who had died after refusing to spend a second winter closeted with cattle.

Beddoes's cowshed method exposed him to ridicule because it reduced well-to-do patients to the level of peasants living alongside beasts. Beddoes offered the alternative of introducing vessels containing cattle manure into the patient's apartment.[45] But this only rubbed respectable noses, already offended by Beddoes's politics, in the dirt. Beddoes found the reputation of his medicine tainted by the way it violated the taboos on which the social and political hierarchy depended. Still worse, it did not work, as the Bristol poets came to realise. Southey wrote in 1800: 'This is a place of experiments. We have consumptive patients, in cow-houses some, and some in a uniform high temperature – and the only result seems to be, that a cure may sometimes be effected, but very rarely.'[46]

Beddoes's cowshed method failed in practice, but so, argued Jenner's opponents, did vaccination. And in 1800 the medical profession was not capable of understanding theoretically how either would work. Based on rural tradition, the remedies of the two West Country doctors seemed not only similar in origin, but also similarly untested and unfounded on medical authorities. William Rowley attacked Jenner and Beddoes together – cowpox madness had infected a medical profession that was already 'Gas and vital air mad'. Jenner's medicine was like the 'fanciful and extravagant celestial visions' of the 'illuminati' (the mystical secret society suspected of fomenting political revolution).[47]

Jenner and his supporters drew lessons from such attacks. Not only did Jenner steer clear of Beddoes's radical politics, but his publicists also gradually replaced the levelling implications of his cow-medicine with an emphasis on the doctor as a genius of nature. Coleridge and Southey had another Bristol experimentalist in mind as they made that emphasis – the young Humphry Davy, Beddoes's assistant. Davy's discovery of nitrous oxide, they thought, heralded a new era in which a medicine, reformed by brilliant scientific work, would bring health to all.

With Jenner vaccinating in Gloucestershire and Davy developing nitrous oxide in Bristol, the West Country was suddenly at the forefront of science. In this heady atmosphere, it was the notion of genius that the poets created for Davy (and which he embraced) that they began to apply to Jenner too. Coleridge wrote directly to Jenner in 1811, telling the doctor that he congratulated himself that he had known men whom 'Providence has gifted with the power to acquire' true fame by doing 'what I could most have wished to have done' (*CL*, vol. VI, p. 1025). Amongst these men he named Humphry Davy and Jenner himself. They were benefactors of mankind who would be justly revered by future generations. Jenner had gained a place in the Romantic pantheon of creative geniuses. According to Coleridge's excited theories, the natural philosopher and the poet were engaged in a similar, prophetic, pursuit – harnessing the powers of nature by their imaginations, and so blessing mankind. Davy was a 'man who *born* a Poet first converted Poetry into Science and *realized* what few men possessed Genius enough to fancy' (*CL*, vol. V, p. 309; cf. *Friend*, vol. I, p. 471).

If scientific thought was a kind of realisation of poetry, poetry could be an exaltation of science. Convinced of Jenner's genius, Coleridge declared that he would lend his own poetic powers to the vaccination cause (*CL*, vol. VI, p. 1025). He never wrote the poem, but his enthusiasm for vaccination was sincere enough (his second son had died after complications following smallpox). But he was well aware that enthusiasm would promote the spread of vaccination, if published in influential places. He told Jenner that he intended to write articles on the discovery in *The Courier* as it was 'the paper of widest circulation, and, as an evening paper, both more read in the country, and read more at leisure than the morning papers' (*CL*, vol. VI, p. 1025). Jenner responded appreciatively to the prospect of such favourable publicity: 'his offer to me was very important'.[48]

POETIC CONQUEST: JENNER AS MILITARY HERO

Coleridge ceased working for *The Courier* before he could write his articles praising Jenner. But he had by then already singled the doctor out as an example to the nation. In his journal *The Friend* he declared: 'Pronounce meditatively the name of Jenner, and ask what might we not hope, what need we deem unattainable, if all the time, the effort, the skill, which we waste in making ourselves miserable through vice, and vicious through misery, were embodied and marshalled to a systematic War against the existing Evils of Nature?' (*Friend*, vol. II, p. 69). Jenner's science had become holy war: his conquest of evil offered an example, in Coleridge's moralising scheme, to redeem Britons, high and low, from lethargy and viciousness. Jenner came to believe in the truth, as well as the propaganda value, of publicity of this kind: by 1807 he saw himself as an inspired benefactor who deserved greater reward by the nation.

With Britain at war with Napoleonic France throughout the period in which Jenner was actively promoting vaccination, images of battle and conquest were not only current but patriotic. Portraying vaccination as a holy war ensured that Jenner's medicine appeared to the public as a cause for national pride. Bloomfield declared that, through Jenner, 'England strikes down the nation's bitterest foe' and, 'amidst the clangor' of Europe's war, ensures 'new germs of life sprung up beneath the sword' (lines 312–18). Jenner had become a military hero to make the nation proud of itself because it could fight the life-giving fight of vaccination as well as the life-destroying war with Napoleon. Vaccination became evidence of the value of the British civilisation which was currently being menaced by the French. Coleridge told Jenner that he thought the idea of vaccination had been 'inspired into you by the All-preserver, as a counterpoise to the crushing weight of this unexampled war' (*CL*, vol. VI, p. 1025).

War imagery of this kind performed two functions at once. It promoted Jenner's medicine by elevating him to the status of heroic victor (a peaceful conqueror in contrast to the warlike conqueror Napoleon). It gave Britons motives to fight France – the civilisation which produced and was protected by Jenner needed preserving from foreign political diseases. Vaccination thereby became enlisted as a key part of a nationalistic call-to-arms. Paradoxically, its very peacefulness became a cause for war. In the process, the patriotic loyalty of poet and doctor was established beyond doubt – a matter of no small importance for both Coleridge and Jenner because their past association with the democratic Dr Beddoes left them vulnerable to charges of pro-French Jacobinism.

VACCINATION AND THE FIGHTING FORCES

Publicising vaccination as a form of holy war would, of itself, have converted few to the cause had it not been so badly needed in the actual military campaigns Britain was launching against France. In 1797, Dr Thomas Trotter issued a pamphlet called *Medicina Nautica: An Essay on the Diseases of Seamen*, where he wrote:

The ravages which this fatal disease have made . . . in our fleets and armies, are beyond all precedent: the insidious mode of attack, the rapid strides at which it advances to an incurable stage, point it out as one of the most formidable opponents of medical skill. It has offered the severest obstacle to military operations, which the history of modern warfare can produce.[49]

Like its close cousin, yellow fever, smallpox was a contagion whose reputation arose from Britain's experience of war – particularly in the tropics, where deaths from disease exceeded deaths in battle by a ratio of eight to one. In the early part of the eighteenth century, doctors had believed that people contracted smallpox through inevitable changes to the 'innate seeds', which formed a part of every human's anatomy. As the period wore on, military doctors observed at close hand the circumstances in which it spread.[50] Smallpox and other diseases, they concluded, resulted instead from atmospheric changes or from small particles penetrating the body (perhaps an early version of germ-theory). Smallpox went from being a disease inside the body, to one outside it. This shift in perception turned the personal body political, and turned the purely medical, military. When pestilence stemmed from the body, people self-destructed. When it came from the earth and air, people were the victims of the environment. Military doctors branded it as an enemy whose methods for attack seemed beyond normal wartime decorum. Jenner himself referred to it with military terminology, as 'that formidable foe to health'.[51]

In fact, smallpox had waged its own biological warfare in the recent political past. In 1779, the French and Spanish sought to attack Britain in what historians refer to as the closest France had ever come to successful invasion. The hostile fleets had lined up in the English Channel and dominated it for three days. When the time for attack came, however, neither the French nor the Spanish troops could move a muscle. The crews were weakened by smallpox. So much so, that bodies reportedly piled up in the Channel at such an alarming rate that villagers would not eat the harbour fish for over a month. The remaining crews turned home in defeat.[52]

It was not only foreign troops who were weakened by disease. During the Napoleonic Wars the British military was desperate to recruit more men. The navy found it almost impossible to keep ships' crews at full strength, despite constant use of the press-gang. The army, likewise, needed soldiers after losing whole expeditions to disease in the West Indies. The Commander-in-Chief of the army was Jenner's patron, the Duke of York. Here the campaign to convert the powerful to the vaccination cause had direct results: the Duke ordered the compulsory vaccination of regiments in 1800. In the same year, Gilbert Blane, formerly Physician to the Fleet, introduced vaccination into the navy. In the armed forces, patrons rapidly made Jenner's desire to make war on smallpox come true. Vaccination first became institutionalised by the state in the hierarchical structure of the military, as part of reforms designed to impose mass hygiene on the ranks.[53] Winning the war against smallpox helped win the war against Napoleon and Jenner was praised for both.[54]

THE POWER OF JENNER'S EXAMPLE

By 1815 Jenner's campaign had been successful. He was no longer an obscure provincial doctor, but a man acknowledged as a benefactor of mankind and rewarded by parliament. He had overcome objections that vaccination was revolutionary, and defeated Moseley and the campaigners who had accused him of lowering humans to the level of beasts. His discovery had been adopted by the military, and spread round the globe.

Yet the civil population of Britain had not offered their arms to Jenner's lancet. In part, their reluctance was a result of the way in which the vaccination campaign was organised. Jenner and his publicists had preached to the educated reading public. They had allied vaccination with the ruling classes – royalty, aristocracy and gentry. Here they had been successful: by 1815 vaccination was widespread amongst these classes. But although these classes had the power of patronage, this itself had limits. In the country, the labouring classes were tied to the lords and squires by relationships of deference. In the burgeoning cities, this was not the case, as Jenner complained in 1805: 'in London my practice is limited to the higher orders of Society – In the Country, I can always find little Cottagers on whom I can introduce vaccine Virus in any form'.[55] Like Wordsworth, Jenner found the metropolis alienating because its social fluidity meant that his rustic vision was ineffective there. The lower classes in London could simply not be grasped, even when Jenner's notable patrons funded the Royal Jennerian Society to bring the benefits of vaccination to London's poor. By March 1805 it had performed only 6,924 vaccinations in London; by roughly the same period 145,840 people had been vaccinated in Madras. The Society had failed to vaccinate on a mass scale because it expected candidates for vaccination to conform to a bureaucratic discipline of form filling and regular attendance at specified centres. Workers were reluctant or unable to meet these conditions: the Society's expectations were simply alien to the lives of those it set out to help.

Jenner never won the hearts of Britain's labouring classes – ironically enough since it was with rural labourers that he had begun. In the later Victorian period parliament created a centralised state bureaucracy through which vaccination could be imposed on the population as a whole. Vaccination was made compulsory and fines and imprisonment were the punishments for those who refused. But compulsion only bred resistance and a campaign to take 'the parliamentary lancet out of the national arm',[56] involving street protests and mass rallies, was successful by 1908. Vaccination had become the epitome of established, state control. It was resisted as an infringement of civil liberties by those on whom the government tried to impose it.

The seeds of vaccination's later history were sown by Jenner's publicity campaign. He had sold his discovery to the existing political elite and had relied on their influence and patronage to spread it. He had addressed that elite in person, but also through publicists writing for the press. Those publicists had aligned it with the anti-Jacobin politics of much of that elite – a politics that, in Southey's hands, revealed a deep need to impose order on the labouring classes (a need Jenner had come to share). After 1800, then, vaccination was no longer simply imagined in the pastoral terms of the 1798 *Inquiry*. It was given a new public image as the divinely inspired discovery of a specifically British genius and as a holy war against infection – natural and political. It acquired a changed status in response to the need of Jenner and his allies to promote it (and to vindicate themselves) in a time of national and imperial strife with the forces unleashed by the French

Revolution. With the aid of the poets, vaccination had become a remedy for multiple 'infections'. Its discoverer had become a hero, to be revered (but also, by some, resisted) for his 'Jenneration' of both nature and politics.[57]

ROMANTICISING AND EXPORTING COW MEDICINE

Reverence and resistance were played out in different forms on the wider stage of Britain's empire. The military, which played a fundamental role in Britain's latest colonisation efforts, turned out to be Jenner's most important vaccination vehicle. For Britain wasted no time in using the navy to spread vaccination to the colonies, to Gibraltar and Malta in 1800, then to Ceylon, India, Canada, Africa and the West Indies. In 1803, to take just one example, vaccine was dispatched on the India-bound HMS *Wyndham* and *Walpole* with a detachment of the Royal Artillery.[58] Vaccine, soldiers and guns: from the start Jenner's remedy for the disease that plagued Britain's colonies was carried along with Britain's somewhat grimmer antidote to colonial rebellion. Jenner congratulated himself and 'all lovers of the Vaccine, on the introduction of our little *Pearl* into India'.[59] A remedy that had begun at the bottom, in the bodies of beasts and peasants, was now spread from the top down, from royalty to aristocracy, from aristocracy to their tenants and from the military to colonial subjects.

Just as Jenner was congratulating himself on vaccination's introduction into the empire, he was supervising a publicity drive designed to give it universal popularity. Verse gave Jenner's medicine the heroic role of imperial panacea. Robert Southey, who like Coleridge was fascinated with the relationship between imperialism, disease and imagination, told in his poem *A Tale of Paraguay* (1825) how 'this hideous malady . . . lost its power/ When Jenner's art the dire contagion stayed'.[60] Southey called smallpox the 'scourge' of 'the West', locating the origin of the disease in Africa.[61] Smallpox was Africa's revenge.[62] It had been sent forth to rebuke Britain for its brutish enslavement of native peoples, a sin that Jenner had atoned for. Southey wrote:

> Jenner! Forever shall thy honored name
> Among the children of mankind be blest,
> Who by thy skill hast taught us how to tame
> One dire disease, the lamentable pest
> Which Africa sent forth to scourge the West
> As if in vengeance for her sable brood
> So many an age remorselessly repressed.
>
> (canto 1, stanza 1)

For his part, Bloomfield linked vaccination and imperialism in similar Romantic terms. Jenner cured bodies, but he also cured all the ills of British commercial imperialism. Here is what Bloomfield had to say about India:

> Where India's swarthy millions crowd the strand,
> And round that isle, which crowns their pointed land,
> Speeds the good angel with the balmy breath,
> And checks the dreadful tyranny of death:
> Whate'er we hear to hurt the peace of life,
> Of Candian[63] treachery and British strife,
> The sword of commerce, nations bought and sold,
> They owe to England more than mines of gold;
> England has sent a balm for private woe;
> England strikes down the nation's bitterest foe.
> (*Good Tidings*, lines 303–12)

Poetry helped solidify the image of vaccination as saviour of public health and of Jenner as imperial hero – both against Napoleon and for ailing millions in the colonies. It turned heifer into hero: the lowly British beast, exalted by Jenner's transforming science, would atone for the sins of the nation's past and then bless that nation to go forward guilt-free into the imperial future.

The language of Jenner's poets was embraced by Britain's imperial governors, since as they tried to control native populations, romanticised vaccination gave them the ability to portray their colonial rule as a blessing. In India, for instance, vaccine entered the colony via one of Banks's correspondents, the surgeon James Anderson. But it was soon adopted by the Governor General himself. Richard Wellesley, who was responsible for vastly extending British territories through military conquest, said vaccination would 'have a salutary effect on the native' by showing that the government 'administered' on 'enlightened' principles.[64] Another British agent in India claimed it would bring 'good will from the people'[65] and the Governor of Madras predicted vaccination would 'bring an increase to the population and to the prosperity of the [East India] Company's territories in an incalculable ratio'.[66] Jenner's chief publicist at the time claimed that Jenner had turned imperialism from a threatening to a benevolent force in world politics: 'While our countrymen thus kindle the lamp of science in every clime, and shed the blessings of health and happiness around, they maintain the honour of Britain; who has rendered herself illustrious, by her achievements in the arts as well as arms.'[67] Britain's achievement in 'arms' – in both senses of that word – would, it appeared, create a stable and civilised empire in the colonies as it did in Britain itself.

COLONIAL RESISTANCE

Appearances can be deceptive, and it was in the colonies that further resistance to vaccination broke out. In India, high-caste Brahmins mirrored Moseley's anxiety about unclean bodies. They too feared that vaccination would link their bodies to those at the bottom of the social hierarchy – not to black slaves but to low-caste children, from whose arms serum was often obtained.

While contact with 'untouchables' threatened caste, ingesting matter from cows raised the spectre of breaking Hindu and Buddhist prohibitions about killing and eating animals. Vaccination actually threatened to be a doubly tabooed practice. The British were able to claim that vaccination did not involve the death of holy cattle, but Indians still resisted contamination. In the eyes of some, the mark vaccinators left in patients' arms were emblems of colonial rule. One Indian vaccinator reported being 'impeded in his progress by an old woman, who attempted to persuade the people that this was to be the means of enslaving them, and that they would be known by the mark in the arm, which she termed "The Company's chop"'[68] (which, according to *Hobson Jobson*, meant a seal or stamp that was placed on trade goods acquired by the East India Company). Indians did not view vaccination as a universal blessing the way poets like Robert Southey and colonial governors like Richard Wellesley had presumed. They resisted it because it violated their own religious taboos and because it marked them as property of a colonial government.

Besides, at this time Britain's colonies already had their own indigenous methods for dealing with smallpox. One was the worship of smallpox goddesses. In India, for instance, the principal goddess, Sitala, was honoured from Bengal to Gujarat, with village ceremonies and annual pilgrimages. Honouring her was designed to win her favour and gain protection from smallpox: angering her might lead to full infection and death. India's native inoculators, the tikadars ('mark-makers'), invoked Sitala.[69] They had long been practising smallpox inoculation (of the kind Montagu encountered in Turkey) in Bengal, Sind, Bihar and much of the Northwest, working within the religious and cultural context of the people. Tikadars were 'sought after and paid for by the people' and had 'long standing relations with client villages'.[70] Theirs was the native and dominant tradition. As late as 1873, their practices still far exceeded vaccinations in Bengal.

To successive British administrators, Indians' resistance was an indication of their cultural inferiority. The Superintendent-General of Vaccination for Bengal in the 1840s, for example, thought the Indians were in 'the trammels of a degrading religion, by which their thoughts are chained, their reasoning faculties hoodwinked'.[71] Thus vaccination became a means of justifying a stereotypical view of Indians as being rightly subject to British rule because they were, in the words of a sanitary commissioner responsible for vaccination, 'unreasonable' in their 'religious beliefs' and 'caste prejudices'.[72]

These views of Britain's colonial officials gained currency with the aid of literature. Like vaccination poetry, prose used Jenner's remedy to glorify British imperialism. The prose also hinted at an underlying anxiety about bestiality. In the writing of James Morier, one of Britain's first officials in Persia,[73] vaccination was a figure revealing imperialist stereotypes, colonial resistance and Britons' fears about their own bestial nature. Morier's popular novel *The Adventures of Hajji Baba* (1824)[74] influenced British views of how Persia was. Sir Walter Scott wrote enthusiastically about its 'fidelity' to Persian life.[75]

Morier made vaccination central to his story of *Hajji Baba*. Because the Persians resisted it, Morier treated them in his literary account as prejudiced, dishonest and superstitious. Vaccination became a marker of eastern inferiority. For example, this is what Morier has a Persian doctor say when a British physician arrives armed with vaccine:

He [the British doctor] pretends to do away with small-pox altogether, by infusing into our nature a certain extract of cow, a discovery which one of their philosophers has lately made. Now this will never do, Hajji. The small-pox has always been a comfortable source of revenue to me; I cannot afford to lose it, because an infidel chooses to come here and treat us like cattle. (p. 78)

As it turns out, the Persian doctor in this novel embodies the traits Morier found characteristic of the whole nation: cunning, wiliness, self-interest, love of power and conquest. Morier asked readers to reject the Persian doctor's fears of cultural contamination by Europe. After all, as all educated Britons knew, vaccination did not in fact contaminate people. It protected them from smallpox. Vaccination as a motif, in other words, confirmed British stereotypes about the people it tried to control.

But beneath Morier's stereotyping ran a deeper fear, a fear that haunted the British imperialists as well as those they tried to control. It was the fear of the beast within themselves. In the voice of the Persian doctor, Morier wrote:

There must be a great affinity between beasts and Europeans, and which accounts for the inferiority of Europeans to Mussulmans. Male and female beasts herd promiscuously together; so do the Europeans. The female beasts do not hide their faces; neither do the Europeans. They wash not . . . They live in friendships with swine; so do the Europeans . . . As for their women, indeed! What dog, seeing its female in the streets, does not go and make himself agreeable? So doubtless does the European. Wife, in those unclean countries, must be a word without meaning since every man's wife is every man's property. (p. 129)

This was not simply an Englishman's idea of Muslim prejudice. Morier's doctor ventriloquised the British fear of what they themselves might be made of – an animality which rendered them not superior but disturbingly like the colonised people whom they themselves regarded as bestial and unclean. Thus vaccination marked not only Britons' assumption of superiority but, paradoxically, their fear of similarity to their colonial subjects. Vaccination ('the blood of kine', according to Bloomfield)[76] revealed the beast-like nature of the British rulers because it imposed 'civilisation' through an injection of animality. Thus it made them insecure even as it seemed to confirm their superiority, and they were left trying to overcome that insecurity by forcing vaccination on their subjects[77] and then reading resistance as evidence of native superstition.

At home too, vaccination became a dirty marker of government imposition. British protesters declared they were fighting 'the battle of pure blood against experimental butchery upon their defenceless little ones'. They preferred 'salvation by sweetness' to 'salvation by filth'.[78] Likewise, Indians who objected to British rule saw vaccination as a symbol of cultural imperialism that subjugated and contaminated others in the name of reason. Because it brought state control home to the body, vaccination made colonial resistance a matter of flesh and blood. Gandhi, for instance, declared it a 'filthy process . . . little short of taking beef', and the Non-Co-operation Movement of the 1920s made refusal of vaccination part of its political campaign. It was not until the British had left that India implemented vaccination on a wide enough scale to eradicate smallpox. Before that time, the pastoral remedy that had begun in rustic Gloucestershire had been too British, too imperial for its own good. In India, the alliance of science with colonial authority – an alliance Banks had worked so hard to foster – met its match.

In 1798 the quiet country doctor could not have anticipated any of these global events. In that year, vaccination, like Wordsworth's and Coleridge's rural radicalism, seemed too low and too revolutionary for Banks and metropolitan medicine to countenance. It was remodelled, in one of the first sustained public relations campaigns, as a mark of Britain's scientific and cultural superiority, a token of national and imperial greatness. In part, it was literary men who remodelled it: Coleridge, Southey and Bloomfield used verse, newspapers and journals to rebrand Jenner, vaccination and, by association, their own rural discourses, as loyal and nationalist. With their assistance Jenner won over Banks and spread vaccination on Banks's networks, through the upper classes and across the empire. In an irony that is indicative of the distance the cure had travelled from its lowly roots, the common people of Britain and India – especially in the cities – continued, however, to resist it. Vaccination – the quintessential Romantic science – became, for the urban masses, an alien discourse which, though it wore a healthy face, carried the bestial soul of imperialism.

CHAPTER 10

Britain's little black boys and the technologies of benevolence

In this chapter we discuss another new technology and the social vision derived from it – a technology that Count Rumford derived from his theoretical work on the nature of heat. Like vaccination, this technology was embraced, by the governing classes, as a solution to the 'problem' of the poor. Like vaccination, it was, at first, romanticised by literary men keen to embrace a humanitarian science that was not associated with political revolution. Like vaccination too, it was resisted by the very poor it was designed to reform, as an attempt by their masters to discipline, rather than liberate, their lives. Later some of the writers who had hailed Rumford's achievements would think again, resisting, in poor people's names, the disciplinary uses to which Rumford's vision of technology was increasingly being put.

Rumford's heat-saving technology aimed to warm the poor and free them from their labour. In particular, it offered to eradicate the 'need' for boy chimney sweeps, a class of labourers created by the sheer number of narrow, twisting, soot-covered chimneys in Britain's mushrooming cities. Yet this domestic science was, we show, inflected from the start by issues arising in the empire. Borrowing the rhetoric of the abolitionist movement, campaigners hoped to move ordinary Britons to ban the little chimney-sweeping black boys just as they abolished the slave trade. They sentimentalised the sweeps in propaganda pieces that often borrowed heavily from popular Romantic poems. For writers such as Blake, William Hone and Charles Lamb, this sentimentalisation was part of the problem. We explore their response to the issue, showing that they not only opposed the exploitation of sweeps as a practice all too similar to colonial slavery, but also attacked the discourses on which the campaigners relied. They depicted sanctimony and sentiment as means of disciplining the poor, and attacked the regimentation that the social reformers wanted to impose on labourers. Rumford's work, we show, was an important part of this regimentation. He designed a totalised and technologised workhouse environment to control the poor – influencing Jeremy Bentham and pioneering the bureaucratised surveillance of the 'lower orders' by both government and philanthropic societies. In the process, he initiated the practices that Foucault and Ignatieff have seen as symbolic of the modern state. Romantic writers, to the extent that they opposed these practices by imagining the full and varied humanity of climbing boys and colonial slaves (as well as protesting about their exploitation), placed their fictions against the disciplinary politics that their fellow countrymen were developing out of the latest scientific discoveries and methodologies.

On a warm autumn day in 1797, an expatriate Englishman, raised in America, was sweating. It was not the weather making Count Rumford so hot but the progress of an experiment he was conducting at the Bavarian arsenal. On his orders, two horses were turning a mill which was connected by gears to a newly cast metal cylinder. As the horses walked round and round, the cylinder rotated against a stationary drill, which cut into the solid metal, creating a neat bore. Rumford, it would have seemed to a casual onlooker, was simply supervising the production of cannon for use against the armies of revolutionary France. The onlooker would have been wrong, for Rumford's differed from the standard method of cannon boring. Rumford had deliberately left the drill-bit blunt and encased the barrel in a tank of water. His apparatus was dedicated not to rearmament but to enlightenment – he was aiming not at France's soldiers but its natural philosophers.

For several years, Rumford had been devising experiments to test the nature of heat, a subject of considerable dispute among men of science. According to Lavoisier, the eminent French chemist, heat was a subtle fluid (*caloric*) that was squeezed out of a body when it was mechanically acted upon. Compressing a gas pushed caloric out of it, giving off heat. Hammering an iron bar knocked caloric out of it by percussion; rubbing metals together produced heat as caloric was squeezed from their surfaces. Heat, Lavoisier supposed, was a material substance, which drained out of one body into another. Rumford was convinced that Lavoisier's 'supposition is quite unnecessary' and he set his horses to work to prove it.[1] The gun barrel and the blunt drill would produce intense heat by friction. He would measure it by recording how long it took to boil the water in which the barrel was immersed. If heat really was a fluid, then over time the quantity present inside the barrel would begin to run out. In the later stages of the experiment less heat would be produced than at the start, as the caloric in the cannon was drained away until little or none was left.

Rumford put his horses and his thermometer into action and found that, however long they laboured at the mill, the time taken to boil the water was the same. Far from diminishing over time, the heat produced by the rubbing of drill and barrel 'appeared evidently to be inexhaustible'. Heat, he concluded, 'cannot possibly be a *material substance*'.[2] Lavoisier was wrong: heat was no caloric fluid but a form of 'MOTION'.

Rumford communicated his findings to Banks and, with his approval, they were read to the Royal Society on 25 January 1798. Endorsed by having received this hearing, they were published and soon Rumford was famous: his experiment was reported in Germany, Switzerland and France and he became the champion of anti-caloric theorists all over Europe. And the fact that what he meant by calling heat 'motion' was unclear gave others opportunities to develop his results. By the 1840s, after work by Humphry Davy, William Herschel and Thomas Young,[3] it was accepted that heat was a form of energy or work. In 1849, James Prescott Joule went back to Rumford's experiment and showed that the Count had been close to making a precise determination of the mechanical energy equivalent to the heat produced. Rumford, thereafter, was hailed as the great researcher who first showed that heat was equivalent to work.

While, in Rumford's experiment, two horses did the work to make the heat, on the other side of Europe, single boys as young as five were labouring to make others warm. They were apprentice chimney sweeps – 'climbing boys' – and many were worse off than Rumford's ponies, for, as campaigner David Porter noted, they got cold comfort for their labour:

If we would see this poor apprentice as he really is, let us view him in a wintry morning, exposed to the surly blast or falling snow, trudging the streets half naked, his sores bleeding, his limbs contracted with cold, his inhuman master driving him beyond his strength, whilst the piteous tears of hunger and misery trickle down his cheek, which is, indeed, the only means he has to vent his grief; follow him home, and view him in his gloomy cell, and there will be found misery unmasked: we shall see this poor boy in a cellar, used as a soot warehouse on one side, and his lodging room on the other; I would have said his bed-room, but he has seldom any other bed than his sack, or any other covering than his foot cloth: in this comfortless state he shiveringly sleeps, or rather passes over the chilly hours of night.[4]

The rich and famous man of science and the cold and filthy climbing boy seem worlds apart. Rumford spanned Europe; climbing boys were a specifically English phenomenon. He had authority; they had none. His influence was relatively brief; their exploitation continued until 1875. But climbing boys, though lacking social agency themselves, became as newsworthy through the agency of others as Rumford did through his own efforts. The powerless and frozen climbing boy, ironically enough, became a rhetorical figure of great force. Lacking a public voice himself, he gave doctors, reformers, philanthropists and poets voices to articulate the deepest underlying fears of a nation that was exploiting people at home and abroad in its pursuit of wealth and comfort. He, like the black slaves to whom he was compared, also opened a route towards social reform. He acquired social agency – at least as a symbol – by bringing into focus the social evils of the manufacturing and commercial system that produced him. He highlighted the corruption of many of the Britons who benefited from that system – local officials, rentier aristocrats, slave traders, factory owners. On the image of London's cold and stunted little black boys was founded a campaign to end child labour and poverty, a campaign which took many of its terms from a vision of science and technology developed by Rumford. After Rumford, Britons began to believe science could redeem the nation from its social ills.

CHIMNEYS

Rumford said nothing explicitly about climbing boys. Indirectly, however, his vision of science was to change their lives, for his work and theirs came into an unlikely proximity. Rumford's experiment showed on a natural level what the boys demonstrated on a social one – that heat was not a material resource but was produced in the expenditure of energy. It demanded an equivalent amount of work. And in the process, the heat-giving body would be effectively consumed. Like the coal whose soot they cleaned off chimney flues, the climbing boys were kept in freezing cellars till their energy was needed and they were used up by their labour, their bodies fragmented. Broken by deformity and disease, few lived to adulthood. Climbing boys were victims of a technology. Rumford, by contrast, became its master. A reluctant theoretician, he preferred to make science useful: 'I can conceive of no delight like that of detecting and calling forth into action the hidden powers of nature! – Of binding the Elements in chains, and delivering them over the willing slaves of man.'[5]

It was over fire that Rumford sought to rule, and he applied the lessons of his experiments on heat to the design of fireplaces. His scientific power and the climbing boys' predicament came to depend on the same thing – on offering a solution to the problems of an eighteenth-century technology. Tall chimneys had gained in popularity as the century went on, in response to the crowded living conditions in cities that demanded higher houses.

Figure 22. Engraving from the *Report of the Royal Commission on the Employment of Children in Mines and Manufacturies* (1842), XVII.

Such chimneys fed on coal, which began to be commercially mined on a large scale, bringing massive profits to the gentle- and noblemen on whose land the pits were dug. These pits, that is to say, extracted heat and profit for the wealthy from the work of the miners, many of them children. The few observers who went below ground were shocked to see English children work 'black and filthy' like adult 'negroes'. A Royal Commission reported: 'this is certainly a wretched and slave-like mode of labour; but stern necessity and habit have reconciled these children of poverty to all its fatigue and inconvenience' (Fig. 22).[6]

If child colliers worked at the start of a process of heat production, climbing boys laboured at the end of it. Coal-burning chimneys needed a stronger draught, and therefore a narrower flue, than wood-burning ones, particularly in grander houses where the air passage was hindered as the flue turned through several angles to reach a central stack. Only small boys could squeeze through the twists and turns of the chimneys, some only nine inches square, to be found in the palaces of the Bishop of London and the King himself. Such chimneys rapidly filled with soot and needed frequent cleaning. Yet they were impassable to brushes. The comfort of the rich, Mr Bennet told the House of Commons in 1818, depended on the labour of the poor.

The climbing boys were certainly poor. Master sweeps bought five-year-olds, the thinner the better, from workhouses, orphanages and destitute widows. Having paid a few shillings to apprentice them, they sent them round the streets by night, crying their trade. They forced the boys up chimneys till their bleeding sores hardened into calluses. Soon, legs and pelvis became deformed. Often, ingrained soot led to cancer of the scrotum or mouth. Some boys fell to their deaths from damaged chimney pots. Others were suffocated or burnt alive. It was, all too often, the roasted flesh of infants that kept the home fires burning. Callous indifference was part of the trade. The former sweep David Porter recorded that London climbing boys commonly lived in 'a cellar, sometimes without a fire-place, but mostly without a fire, in the coldest weather'.[7]

Roasted and frozen by turns, the climbing boy was never warm. He was not wealthy enough to afford the heat that he laboured to produce for others. The philanthropic Rumford, fresh from his successful experiments, was determined to bring him, as one of the labouring poor, the comfort of the hearth. In doing so, he brought science out of the laboratory and into the home. In the process, he changed it, turning theory to technology and making technology a power in the political realm. In Rumford's hands, fire was to save the working classes from the sweated labour and the domestic poverty that the climbing boy and the child miner so pathetically symbolised. It was, that is to say, to address two of the socio-economic problems that made governments fear that the 'lower orders' would turn, as they had in France, to revolution. Rumford's science, he hoped, would spread the warmth of ease and wealth to workers, thereby thawing their resentment of their masters. 'Nothing', he wrote, 'would tend more powerfully to quiet these commotions of civil Society which have been produced by those dreadful passions which have been let loose during the late political Revolutions.'[8] By giving them the means to heat their houses and cook their food efficiently, Rumford would reduce their fuel consumption, making a warm home an affordable commodity. 'Those', he asserted, 'who have never been exposed to the inclemencies of the seasons – who have never been eye-witnesses to the sufferings of the poor in their miserable habitations, pinched with cold and starving with hunger – can form no idea of the importance to them of the subject.'[9]

The subject was especially important to climbing boys, since reduced coal consumption meant less chimney cleaning and therefore a greater chance of survival. But how exactly did Rumford come to harness fire for the benefit of British people, or at least for the preservation of the social order? In autumn 1795 he had travelled from Munich to London to publicise his theories. The contrast between the cities astounded him, for Britain's capital was overshadowed by a 'dense cloud ... composed of *unconsumed* coal' which turned its pasty-faced inhabitants into 'negroes': 'it falls in a dry shower of extremely fine black dust to the ground, obscuring the atmosphere in its descent, and frequently changing the brightest day into more than Egyptian darkness'.[10] The darkness of Egypt, according to the Bible, was caused by clouds of pestilence that tainted people with famine and disease. London, in Rumford's analysis, had bought its economic success at the price of a pollution that alienated it from the European civilisation it claimed to lead. Coal turned the heart of England into a corner of darkest Africa. It drenched civilised Englishmen in the dirt that they thought confined to primitive foreigners.

Rumford's reaction to London was shared by other observers.[11] For William Blake in 1794, the pall of soot that darkened the city's buildings registered the miserable exploitation of the climbing boys whom coal had brought into being: 'the chimney sweeper's cry/ Every black'ning church appals'.[12] London's pollution was symbolic of the corruption created by its relentless commercialism: like Rumford's Egyptian darkness, Blake's sooty atmosphere spreads diseases. It taints not only the poor chimney sweep, but the 'youthful harlot' who 'blights with plagues the marriage hearse'.

For Wordsworth too, London's smoke stank of death. A 'black wreath' hung over the city.[13] When he arrived in 1791 its enclosed courtyards seemed 'gloomy as coffins', unrelieved even by the few 'straggling breezes of suburban air' that freshened the wider streets.[14] Pollution symbolised London's moral darkness; its diseased state was embodied by the poor streetwalker:

> ... at late hours
> Of winter evenings, when unwholesome rains
> Are falling hard, with people yet astir,
> The feeble salutation from the voice
> Of some unhappy woman now and then
> Heard as we pass, when no one looks about,
> Nothing is listened to ...
> (*Prelude* (1805), book VII, lines 365–71)

By 1812 Wordsworth had made London's foul air a symbol of the moral and social danger posed by an urbanised labouring class: 'the lower orders', he wrote, 'have been for upwards of 30 years accumulating in pestilential masses of ignorant population'.[15]

In 1802 De Quincey was to experience a similar alienation as, homeless and poverty-stricken, he searched unavailingly in the London streets for Ann, the child prostitute who had befriended him. Unable to find her amongst the crowds of unknown faces, he made Londoners' indifference seem as ingrained in them as the soot-filled air they breathed. The 'outside air . . . of London society is harsh, cruel and repulsive'. Ann, for all he could see through the obscuring crowd, might have been sucked into the 'central darkness of a London brothel'.[16] Like Wordsworth, he rejected the city, and looked yearningly towards the green woods and blue skies of the rural north.

Rumford, on the other hand, was convinced that he had the means to overcome London's alienating atmosphere. If economic and technological organisation, on an unprecedented scale, had made the city filthy as well as wealthy, then technology would clean it up. For Rumford, the answer to London's darkness was not to return to the pastoral virtues and rural economics of Grasmere. It was to progress further into a culture of manufacture, guided by science. In 1796 he invented a device designed to keep Londoners clean and white as well as warm. The Rumford fireplace, as it became known, dramatically increased the efficiency of the open hearth. After a series of tests, Rumford proved that smoking chimneys and wasted coal were a result of ignorance about the way a fire heated a room. A large and deep fireplace simply sucked air from the room up the chimney, preventing the smoke from the fire itself from escaping. The smoke then blew back into the room. Furthermore, too much heat was lost in convection when the smoke and vapour did travel up the flue. What was needed, Rumford discovered, was greater radiant and less convected heat. He achieved this by bringing the back of the fireplace forwards and by building its sides at angles of 130, rather than 90 degrees. By these means, radiant heat was reflected back into the room. He also narrowed the throat of the chimney just over the fire, inserting a smoke-shelf. This reduced the aperture available for air from the room to be sucked into the chimney and caused a temperature difference between hot air rising at the front of the flue and colder at its back. This colder air itself helped feed the necessary draught to the fire that had formerly come from the room.

Rumford's fireplace was a neat solution. A Rumford chimney applied more of the work done by combustion to its social purpose, heating the room rather than the chimney and the sky above it. It cut the soot deposited, saving the energies of climbing boys. It also cut the need for coal, saving labour in the mines. It would, Rumford concluded, be 'of great relief to the poor', 'for the less demand there is for any article in the market, the lower will be its price'.[17] If Rumford's chimneys were widely adopted, climbing boys would no longer freeze in cellars because they could not afford fuel for a fire. Excited at his ability to master nature on behalf of humanity, Rumford called his fireplace scheme 'the sublime in science'.[18]

Rumford's ardour paid off. A man of flaming zeal in his own cause, he gave his invention power by marketing it with the flair of a Josiah Wedgwood or a Matthew Boulton. No other-worldly theoretician, Rumford cultivated the rich, respectable and powerful. He introduced his chimneys first to the home of the leaders of Whig politics and fashionable society, the Duke and Duchess of Devonshire. In case their imprimatur proved insufficient, the baronets who dominated Britain's scientific institutions were also recruited. Sir John Sinclair, President of the Board of Agriculture, and Banks fitted Rumford chimneys in their houses. We know that they did because Rumford was careful to announce the fact: he traded on their names in the essays he published, essays he was careful to advertise in appropriate newspapers.

His publicity techniques worked: endorsed by men of science, used by the most fashionable aristocrats, his fireplaces became as desirable as Rumford the salesman could wish. Caricatures poked fun at the invention, but further spread its fame. James Gillray's 'The Comforts of a Rumford Stove' takes literally the Count's offer to bring rosy cheeks to the people of Britain (Fig. 23).

Rumford became very rich as his advice was sought all over the kingdom. But status was a stronger motive than money. He became a humanitarian hero because he was determined to make his device cheaply available to the poor. He refused to patent it, and he invited masons and bricklayers to copy the prototypes on display at his house, so that it would spread rapidly amongst the trade.

Rumford was initiating one of the founding features of nineteenth- and twentieth-century capitalism – the reform of the domestic sphere by technology that is derived from the latest scientific research. His labour-saving devices aimed to extend an idealised vision of middle-class life – of an ordered hearth and home – to labourers. But in fact they altered both lower- and middle-class domesticity, for they made the home part of a mass-producing economy, moving labour out to the workshops where Rumford's fireplaces, and also his stoves and roasters, were made. These would become the agents of social reform, replacing the 'bad' sweated labour of miners, climbing boys and domestic drudges with the 'good' labour of bricklayers,

Figure 23. James Gillray, caricature, 'The Comforts of a Rumford Stove' (12 June 1800).

masons and ironmongers. 'Order' and 'economy', that is to say, were social goals that Rumford was setting, goals to be reached by making 'the poor industrious' in a way of which gentlemen could approve.[19]

The wealthy classes, if Rumford's schemes worked, would no longer have to feel either menaced by the spectre of an idle, indigent and rebellious poor, or conscience-stricken over their sufferings. Fed and warmed by his devices, the labourers, in Rumford's vision, would have energy and health enough to become willing and able mechanics. They would contribute to an economy understood as a universally beneficial process of constructing and circulating manufactures.

Rumford's refusal to patent his inventions was a key reason for his reputation. Eschewing exclusive profit, he reaped his reward in kudos, especially with social and political reformers. William Wilberforce resolved to move 'the House of Commons to get my System adopted throughout the kingdom', Rumford reported.[20] Thomas Jefferson had Rumford fireplaces fitted in his home at Monticello. So did writers who shared Jefferson's liberal principles: in December 1796 Coleridge was asking 'is there any *grate* in the House? – I should think, one might Rumfordize one of the chimneys' (*CL*, vol. 1, p. 288).

Coleridge had, in fact, already done his best to advance Rumford's reputation. In his political journal *The Watchman* he made a poetic tribute to the Count. Rumford's 'triumphs', Coleridge announced, 'adorn/Fitliest our nature, and bespeak us born/ For loftiest action' (*Watchman*, p. 175). Rumford was a hero of the kind Coleridge had been waiting for. Like the radical natural philosopher Joseph Priestley, he seemed to show that scientific innovation could solve the injustices that Britain's reactionary politicians were ignoring. As we showed in chapter 8, Priestley had gone into exile, defeated by those politicians and the mobs they manipulated into burning his laboratory. Rumford filled the gap, and Coleridge declared himself proud of this new immigrant, since his determination to free the poor from forced labour compensated for Englishmen's rejection of the bill to abolish the slave trade. In Coleridge's prose, Rumford became a prototype of the man of science as Romantic hero: he shaped a role that Edward Jenner and Humphry Davy were later to fill.

Such was Coleridge's and Rumford's hope. They faced, however, one major difficulty. England's domestic slaves could not be freed unless they, and their masters, came to hear about the scientific solution. Coleridge intended to solve the problem by distributing pamphlets detailing Rumford's ideas in the cities. Rumford, though, lamented that 'those who might profit from his labours will not read and others cannot'.[21] A print-based promotion simply did not reach the poor it was intended to help. The labouring classes had little chance to obtain, and still less inclination to trust, Rumford's science as it appeared in the gentlemanly form of the essay. Instead, it was their employers, the mill-owners, who read and applied Rumford's words. Benjamin Gott was one of these. Gott, a manufacturer of woollen cloth, had heated several dyeing vats with the steam from one boiler after reading Rumford's seventh essay. He cut his fuel costs by two-thirds; soon other Yorkshire dyers followed suit. In 1800 Gott, by then Lord Mayor of Leeds, welcomed Rumford on behalf of a grateful woollen industry. It was the owners of Britain's burgeoning factory-system, not the labourers who worked long hours in that system, who expressed their thanks to the Count. His innovations were aiding the industrialist in the factory rather than the poor in their homes.

Hoping to bring warmth to all, Rumford took steps to reach the people who would not read his works. In early 1796 he proposed an institution that would house, feed and alert the poor to the benefits his inventions would bring them. It must, he wrote, contain 'something to *see* and to *touch*'.[22] And so he proposed to the philanthropic Society for Bettering the Condition of the Poor that it form a 'grand repository of all kinds of useful *mechanical inventions*'.[23] Model fireplaces and kitchens would be on display, with details of the manufacturers from whom they could be purchased.

What Rumford was proposing amounted to a major departure for eighteenth-century philanthropy. The Society was, like many such, composed of priests, aristocrats and independent gentlemen. Such men had experience in raising subscriptions and organising institutions. But they had little familiarity with science and technology. In February 1799 they told Rumford that his repository was beyond the Society's remit, but encouraged him to seek backing for a separate, independent, institution. He did so in a revised proposal that envisaged an even more radical departure. His *Proposals for Forming By Subscription in the Metropolis of the British Empire A Public Institution* (1799) aimed to unite 'experimental philosophers' and 'those . . . engaged in arts and manufactures' in 'general diffusion of the knowledge of all new and useful improvements'.[24] In Rumford's scheme, gentlemanly munificence would no longer relieve the poor directly but would enable technology to reach the masses, introducing them to a culture of improvement through industry. Rumford, in other words, modelled his understanding of human nature and social change on the market for machines. Abandoning the language of sentiment and duty that had driven eighteenth-century charity, he introduced a technologised version of utilitarianism. The people, he expected, would be so impressed by the usefulness of the devices to which he would give them access that they would strive to be more useful themselves. They would use machines to save themselves labour and, in the process, become like those machines. Rumford, in effect, wanted to manufacture souls as efficiently as Britain's industrialists manufactured inventions, and he wanted an institution to help him do so.

What he got was as big an innovation in science as it was in philanthropy. The existing scientific institutions were mostly elite bodies, controlled by gentlemen of independent means. As President of the Royal Society, Banks was dedicated to maintaining the authority of Europe's most prestigious scientific body. He did so by dissociating it from those who advocated radical social and political change. Rumford, having been praised by radical reformers such as Coleridge, needed Banks's backing for his new institution. He met and planned the institution with Banks at Soho Square: it would be another of the 'centres of calculation' affiliated to Banks's network, and Banks would be on the committee appointed to run it. By March 1799, Banks's involvement had secured the scheme's success. With Sir Joseph's impetus, the King became patron and the Earl of Winchilsea president. The Royal Institution, as it is known to this day, had, by July of that year, moved into premises in central London.[25]

For all his initial approval, Banks had reservations about Rumford's social engineering. These came to a head in 1800 as it became clear that Rumford conceived of the Royal Institution as a means of educating, as well as benefiting, the labouring classes. With the help of his Clerk of Works, Thomas Webster, Rumford designed not only a repository of useful inventions that artisans might inspect, but a school for eighteen to twenty young 'working mechanics'.[26] This school was to be in the same building as the repository and lecture theatre, with the young men housed in rooms in the attic. It was to teach geometry, mathematics and hydrostatics, leading to specialisation in architecture, mathematics, physics and chemistry. Graduates, it was hoped, would become skilled and innovative tradesmen, spreading the culture of technological improvement more widely among the labouring classes. Such, at least, was the plan. Soon, however, Webster found himself forced to show Sir Joseph that he did not intend to move labourers 'like hot-bed plants out of the sphere in which they are so useful'.[27] The President of the Royal Society welcomed applied science only so long as it did not construct an engine for social instability. Labourers, for Banks and many of the Institution's other gentlemen managers, might be relieved and comforted but were not to be given knowledge and power.[28] To men of Banks's class and conservatism, it seemed obvious that such knowledge would only make the labouring classes disenchanted with a social position that left them to work mines, till fields and clean chimneys. Despite Rumford's enthusiasm, the school scheme foundered on the political and social fears of Banks and the other gentlemen of science. Scientific schemes, it proved, could not easily run without the approval of Banks and the organisations that he influenced and controlled.

If the school scheme collapsed, so did the repository of useful manufactures. The design exhibition, centrepiece of Rumford's proposals, fell foul not of Banks's networks of patronage, influence and philanthropy, but of the very manufacturers whose work it was aimed to promote. In their enthusiasm to spread a culture of invention, Rumford and his supporters had forgotten that industrialists were motivated by profit and that profit often depended on secrecy. When Rumford sought to display a working steam engine, Boulton and Watt, the leaders in the field, were downright hostile. Rumford might, if he wished, eschew patenting his fireplaces, but Boulton jealously guarded his design. To the pioneer of the steam age, Rumford's understanding of manufacturing society was naïve. It was the flawed vision of a man who did not know the value of money because he had always been supported by the inherited wealth of the aristocracy. Rumford was playing at industry, unaware of the discipline of capital.[29]

Boulton and Watt made their opposition clear and no working steam engine was exhibited. The Royal Institution survived and flourished, but as a scientific club where a gentlemanly audience heard lectures on the latest research, some of which was carried out in its laboratories. There, Humphry Davy and Michael Faraday announced their startling breakthroughs in areas of science of which Rumford knew little. Symbolically enough, the steam-heating system that Rumford had designed to warm their audience had, by Faraday's time, broken down. The Count himself had long gone, first to Bavaria then to France, and the poor stayed dirty, cold and overworked in a London whose chimneys belched out clouds of soot.

CAMPAIGNING

The child prostitutes, miners and climbing boys remained after Rumford's departure. So, however, did elements of his scheme to make their labour a thing of the past. Rumford's technological utilitarianism had changed the face of British philanthropy. It continued to influence what became the longest and most obsessive philanthropic campaign in the nineteenth century – the campaign to abolish climbing boys. The campaign had begun in 1770, with Jonas Hanway, the opponent of the slave trade, who in 1785 published *A Sentimental History of Chimney Sweepers, in London and Westminster, Shewing the Necessity of Putting Them Under Regulations to Prevent the Grossest Inhumanity to the Climbing Boys*. Here, in print, Hanway attempted to move the public into taking action using a rhetoric that mixed Christian piety with fashionable sentimentalism. '*Pity* and *Compassion*', he wrote, 'join their pious prayers and most tender wishes' on behalf of the 'chimney-sweeping soot-boy and the miserable negroe-slave, the ignorant poor child, – and the sinner of every class!'[30]

Hanway moved enough people for parliament to pass an act regulating the trade in 1788. But without means of enforcement, it failed to end the boys' suffering. And so in 1792 Hanway's friend David Porter, an ex-climbing boy himself, again asked readers to pity the 'forlorn orphans' who were 'suffered to live in the grossest ignorance of religion and morality'.[31] Porter's Christian outrage resembled Hanway's but had a different, albeit indirect, effect. It put the campaign on a new footing by attracting the attention of the wealthy and powerful reformers who had been so impressed by Rumford. After publication, Porter was visited by Thomas Bernard, the founder of the Society for Bettering the Condition of the Poor – the society to which Rumford had proposed his institution scheme. Bernard took Porter up as he had Rumford. He promoted his publication and wrote one of his own. He mobilised his connections among the clergy and nobility and organised a new Society for the Protection and Instruction of Chimney Sweepers' Apprentices (1800). When this collapsed, Bernard became prime mover in its successor, the Society for Superseding the Necessity of Climbing Boys (1803). Like Rumford's Royal Institution, of which Bernard was a manager, the Society boasted the sort of social support that Bernard could deliver and that gave it authority in the land. The Prince of Wales was patron, the Bishop of Durham president and various dukes, lords and MPs vice-presidents. Several, including William Wilberforce, occupied similar positions in the Royal Institution. Many too were active in the campaign against the slave trade.

The 'Society with the affected name', as Charles Lamb called it, became the driving engine of the campaign for the next seventy years.[32] From the start, it favoured technological solutions over the tearful sentimentalism of Hanway. With Bernard active on its committee and running the Royal Institution after Rumford's return to Europe, the Society searched for an invention that would not simply relieve the boys' suffering but remove the need for them altogether. With an eye to profit, inventors and engineers strove to offer it one. In the Society's first year, G. Orr published details of his answer. He approved Rumford's method of narrowing the bottom of the chimney to make it draw better, but advised fitting a pulley too, with a continuous chain and brush attached. By these means, there would be 'no necessity to send for those dirty fellows . . . who, with their soot-bags and other implements always make a filthy mess'.[33] Later inventors further improved on Rumford's ideas. J. W. Hiort advocated a circular flue surrounded by air tunnels and Seth Smith patented his metallic chimney lining. A tube to be inserted in existing flues, it was a means to prevent the 'employment of climbing boys' that 'is deemed *odious*'.[34]

Reconstructing chimneys was expensive and so the Society confined its interest in these heirs of Rumford to lobbying for legislation requiring improved designs in new buildings. It gave its full support to a technology cheap and portable enough to be adopted by all – the chimney-sweeping machine. That support took the form of patronage. In 1803, with the Society's co-operation, the Royal Society for the Encouragement of Arts, Manufactures and Commerce awarded a gold medal to George Smart for his invention of 'the most simple, cheap, and proper apparatus . . . for cleansing Chimnies from soot, and obviating the necessity of children being employed'.[35] Smart had produced a design that is still the basis of chimney sweeps' brushes today. A series of hollow sticks were linked by a cord running within. When pulled, the cord expanded a circular brush.

Having become Smart's patron, the Society set out to push his machines down every English flue. Testimonials were sought from satisfied gentlemen, recommendations from fire insurance companies were produced. The Society struggled hard to give the humble brush social sanction and official approval. Its methods reflected its own composition: wealthy gentlemen and peers assumed that the machine could be pushed into society from the top down. If Smart's stiff bristles were to succeed where Hanway's soft sentiments had failed, it would be with the sanction of the elite. The Society paraded gentlemen and philanthropists before a committee of the House of Lords. It also persuaded Smart to be a witness, and duly published his testimony. The approval of the peers of the realm seemed vital not only for securing new laws but for making machines respectable.

Gradually, the Society realised that the example of the elite was not changing the habits of ordinary city dwellers. It directed its efforts lower down the social hierarchy. In 1805 it gave a reward for the chimney sweep who cleaned most chimneys by machine. It began publishing an annual list of machine-using sweeps to enable readers to find one in their area. When it had the funds, it provided machines free to willing sweeps, to help make the change from using boys who cost them almost nothing. Progress continued to be slow but this only increased the Society's belief in a mechanical answer. In the industrial town of Sheffield, James Montgomery was a prime mover for the Society. His words best express the campaigners' fixation on technological solutions. Replacing climbing boys by machines was a matter of patriotic pride, a way in which a commercial nation might redeem itself from the evil exploitation that accompanied the manufacturing system –

What! shall it be said of this free, this noble England, that it can produce machinery which in commerce shall keep the world at bay, and cannot circumvent this odious practice: by the power of levers, and the power of steam, can we work wonders beyond the extent of human calculation, yet not make a machine that shall sweep a chimney? Machines for making stockings, and for making shoes; let me see a machine for preserving legs! (*CSF*, p. 395)

It was because Britons prospered by using children like machines – at home and in the West Indies – that machines had to save the children. Faith in commercial and industrial Britain depended on it. Montgomery, a Moravian minister with mill-owner friends, kept his. But it was a faith far removed from the weeping piety of the campaign's father Hanway.

Desperate to reconcile Christian morality and industrial capitalism, Montgomery spoke for many in the middle class. Their conscience-salving investment in removing climbing boys, like their involvement in abolishing slavery, made the issue an overdetermined one. It meant more, and meant differently, to them than it did to the labourers themselves. The campaigners, in fact, created the boys as victims but knew little of their lives or those of their fellow workers. The campaign only increased philanthropists' class suspicions and prejudices, for they came to blame labourers for the slow spread of chimney- (and conscience-) sweeping brushes. In June 1817, George Reveley told a committee of the House of Commons of the 'extraordinary' fact that master sweeps were reluctant to replace their boys with machines. He could only explain it by assuming they were dishonest: 'when they send a boy up they can make him sweep just as they please, either sweep the chimney clean or leave it half done . . . in order to have to do them more frequently' (*CSF*, p. 214). The Society had soon created a stereotypical master sweep, feeding the nineteenth-century myth that the working classes were dishonest, obstructive and idle. 'The machine', stated the Society's fourteenth report, 'requires the labour of the master . . . to make it perform its operation, whereas a child ascends without putting the master to the slightest pain or trouble.' The boys, apparently, were victims of labourers who did not want to labour. To their masters, the Society concluded, 'the climbing boy is a broom which when once taught . . . works of its own accord, and costs little or nothing to keep or to repair'.[36]

The master sweeps' resistance was real but its causes were more complex than the Society's propaganda suggested. One was economic. Boys were cheaper than machines, and most master sweeps were themselves so poor that they could not afford to change. Moreover, they risked losing customers since many householders still preferred boys to brushes. They also feared that, like handloom weavers, they would be superseded by technology.

Smart overheard one master sweep declare: 'if this Business was suffered to go on . . . every Gentleman who had got a left-off Coachman or Footman would be introducing him as a Chimney Sweeper, and recommending him to his Friends, and . . . they who had served Seven Years to so dreadful a Business might go and rake the Streets'.[37] This remark mixes professional pride with the camaraderie of survivors – most master sweeps, though the Society was loath to say so, were themselves former climbing boys. It shows most powerfully, however, labourers' resentment that their trade, and therefore their lives, were at the convenience of gentlemen. For the master sweeps, the philanthropy of their social superiors was an insult and a threat. The climbing boy was bringing class hostility into the open.

The hostility increased. From 1816 the Society, realising it would not succeed simply by promoting machines, pressed parliament to ban the use of boys. Learning from the campaign against the slave trade, they demonised the masters. They scoured the newspapers for reports of injuries and deaths, and collected the most horrific stories. They made, in effect, a book of martyrs, calculated to provoke enough parliamentary pity to make MPs act. Where Hanway had been general in his sentimental appeal, the Society gave the graphic details. Masters treated children worse than brutes, said the *Observations on the Cruelty of Employing Climbing Boys in Sweeping Chimneys* (1829).[38] T. Young, the Society reported, had burnt straw and lit gunpowder underneath a climbing boy who had jammed in the flue that Young had forced him to climb. When the boy still couldn't free himself, Young tied a rope to one leg and pulled with a crowbar. Eventually he freed the boy, by now a mangled corpse.

Torture stories galvanised the House of Commons. But it was not wholly persuaded that technology was the answer to such abuses. Pressured by Luddite protests in 1819, MPs feared that labourers' resentment of mechanisation would lead to revolution. Suddenly, many gentlemen MPs found themselves sympathetic to the master sweeps. Sir J. Yorke declared it to be 'notorious that the use of machinery had already thrown a number of people out of employment, and it was obvious that the adoption' of chimneysweeping machines would have the same effect.[39] Rumford's vision of new inventions bringing ease, health and wealth to the poor seemed, in the year of the Peterloo massacre, limited and naïve.

It was the House of Lords that prevented the Society's new brooms from making a clean sweep of the country. Time and again, peers delayed and watered down bills passed by the Commons. Their reluctance meant that it was not until 1875 that effective measures were taken. It stemmed from self-interest. Peers were afraid of huge expenses in modifying the complex chimneys of their grand houses to suit the new machines. They also feared passing social legislation that might hamper the commercial system that was so profitable to them. And many lords were indifferent to the language of the campaigners. Conservative peers, used to regarding both labourers and manufacturers with hauteur, wept neither for the abused boys nor for the machine-wielding sweeps. The Lords neither accepted the demonisation of master sweeps nor bought the Society's mechanical solution. The campaign had not spoken to peers' concerns, fears or experience. The campaigners left Westminster defeated and disheartened.

POEMS

It was from Sheffield, rather than London, that new impetus came. Samuel Roberts, a mill-owner, and James Montgomery, poet, journalist and minister, realised that a different discourse was needed if the campaign was to win hearts and minds in parliament and beyond. Poems and stories might be better brush salesmen than the Society's reports, minutes and testimonials. In 1824 Montgomery published *The Chimney Sweeper's Friend and Climbing Boy's Album*. Montgomery included his own poems and verse from his Sheffield friends alongside offerings by established authors including P. M. James, Allan Cunningham and W. L. Bowles. Charles Lamb sent him a poem by the little-known William Blake.

The contributions were various, but Montgomery united his miscellany by a central analogy, repeated everywhere in the volume. The dedication to the King made the point at the outset: 'may these little oppressed ENGLISH SLAVES call upon *George the Fourth* to break their fetters' (*CSF*, p. 3). The climbing boy, black with soot, bonded to his master, was 'the only slave/ That breathes old England's air' (*CSF*, p. 6). Britons, added writer after writer, were shamefully tolerating in their own country the slave trade they had abolished in their colonies:

> Poor wretched sufferer! is this freedom's shore?
> Are there no slaves in England? Never more
> Let Britain boast that hers is freedom's land
> While foot of infant slave pollutes her strand.[40]

Britons prided themselves that their nation was superior to others because freedom under the law extended to everyone.[41] But their pride gave Montgomery an opportunity. He set out to humble his countrymen by showing that it was the law which they so revered that bonded apprentice sweeps as slaves.

The force of this argument was increased by its political context in the Britain of the 1820s and 1830s. For many years, radical leaders had been telling the labouring classes that their lot was worse than that of plantation slaves. William Cobbett declared in 1821: 'When *master* and *man* were the terms, every one was in his place, and all were free. Now . . . it is an affair of *masters* and *slaves*.'[42] And in 1831, as hungry labourers burnt ricks across southern England:

The *words* rights, liberty, freedom, and the like, the *mere words* are not worth a straw; and frequently they serve as a cheat. What is the sound of liberty to a man who is compelled to work constantly and who is still, in spite of . . . his vigilance, his frugality, half naked and half starved! In such a case the word liberty is abused: such a man is a slave, whatever he may call himself.[43]

Comparisons of this kind frightened the government and its supporters because they seemed to foment rebellion. If workers accepted they were slaves, what would they have to lose by riot and revolution? Politicians refuted the comparison by interpreting the law but Montgomery insisted that the climbing boy did not partake of legal protection. The laws that apprenticed him were effective; those intended to relieve his suffering were not. As black as a 'negro', the climbing boy was visible proof that West Indian slavery flourished in Britain.

The boy's sooty colour made him a rhetorical figure with which radicals could prise open the consciences of those who had blinded themselves to the exploitation of labourers. Both Leigh Hunt and William Hone were such radicals. Both men had attacked the government for its massacre of labourers at Peterloo. Both had been prosecuted in an attempt to silence them. Both printed the following remarkable story:

a Mrs. P. arrived at Bristol, from the West Indies, she brought with her a female Negro servant, mother of two or three children left in that country. A few days after their arrival, and they had gone into private lodgings, a sweep-boy was sent for by the landlady to sweep the kitchen chimney. This woman being seated in the kitchen when little *Soot* entered, was struck with amazement at the spectacle he presented; and with great vehemence, clapping her hands together, exclaimed, 'Wha *dis* me see! La, la, dat buckara *piccaninny*! So help me, nyung Misse' (addressing herself to the housemaid then present,) 'sooner dan see *one o'mine* picaninnies *tan* so, I *drown* he in de sea'. The progress of the poor child in sweeping the chimney closely engrossed her attention, and when she saw him return from his sooty incarceration, she addressed him with a feeling that did honour to her maternal tenderness, saying, 'Child! come yaw, child', (and without waiting any reply, and putting a sixpence into his hand;) 'Who *you* mammy? You hab daddy, too? Wha *dem* be, da la you go no chimney for?' and moistening her finger at her lips, began to rub the poor child's cheek, to ascertain, what yet appeared doubtful to her, whether he was really a *buccara*, (white.) I saw this woman some time after in the West Indies; and it was a congratulation to her everafter, that *her* 'children were not born to be sweeps'.[44]

The story brings anti-slavery rhetoric home from the Caribbean. The woman has authority as a witness since she has seen both the West Indian colonies and England. Her words thus 'prove' the similarity of climbing boy and slave. She recognises the sweep as a black child who deserves her care because he is even worse off than the black children in the slave plantations. But she reminds us that the colonies are places of oppression, places where maternal care might mean killing a child to save it from a life of exploitation. The lot of the climbing boy and the lot of the West Indian slave, we conclude, are truly dreadful. They involve not just oppression but the destruction or perversion of the most fundamental relationship of all — that of mother and child.

Against the odds, the black woman has preserved her maternal instincts. She is a better mother to the climbing boy than any of the Englishwomen he has encountered. Samuel Roberts thought so too. His contribution to Montgomery's *Chimney Sweeper's Friend* stated, 'the poor African negro is kidnapped and sold, but it is by strangers, or by foes. These children are kidnapped and sold, and that by their own countrymen, and by their own parents' (*CSF*, p. 12). Climbing boys, in Roberts's rhetoric, reversed the polarity of civilised and savage through which Britain justified its colonisation. The assumed superiority of white man over black was undermined by the enslaved little boys whose black complexion masked their white skin.

Roberts, Montgomery and most of his contributors made the climbing boy a child with power. No longer just a victim, he had, in their rhetoric, the ability to turn Britain into its colonies, to translate commerce into slavery. They used the climbing boy to play on Britons' colonial guilt and fear, creating an unwelcome resemblance between Britons and slave traders and between climbing boys and slaves so as to provoke readers into eliminating that resemblance. In an extraordinary 'vision', Roberts imagined a hellish scene whose location could be a West Indian slave plantation or an English town by night:

A lurid light faintly and fitfully illumines the awful deep and rugged vale. Strange frightful Imps of darkness, young crippled and deformed, black as the clouds, almost as shapeless too, people the horrid gloom. Inhuman fiends, with rods and scourges armed, torment the affrighted black unsightly creatures.[45]

Readers were implored to act with care and compassion, relieving the boys as they had African slaves. The slave trade had been abolished in 1807, and agitation to ban slavery altogether was gaining momentum by 1824. A significant influence in the abolition campaign had been poetry that pricked the consciences of the middle classes by insisting that, beyond racial difference, blacks and whites shared a common humanity. 'Am I not a man and a brother?' were the words supposedly uttered by the supplicating slave. Brotherhood, however, was not to be made too close. The abolitionists preferred parental protectiveness to equality. In the campaign medal issued by Wedgwood, the slave was pictured on his knees, imploring upright Britons to show him pity. Samuel Roberts put the sooty climbing boy in the same position, hoping for the same effect.

The *Chimney Sweeper's Friend* took advantage of the pity for black people produced by abolitionist verse. In turning the boys into slaves, Montgomery hoped to repeat the trick of making readers feel so guilty that they would demand abolition. If readers had imagined that black men could be their brothers, then they might believe that the boys, so dark and filthy that they seemed utterly alien, were also kith and kin. J. C. Hudson told 'the mistresses of families' to treat the climbing boy as if he were one of their family. His alienating blackness was not even skin-deep: 'he partakes in some degree of the fate of the negro: we lose, in his sooty complexion, all sympathy with him as a fellow-creature; forgetting that he was ever one of ourselves, or, that a single plunge into a bath would restore the relationship' (*CSF*, pp. 76–7). If Britons could remember their fellow humanity with real blacks, how much easier to discover it with those who could be washed whiter than white? Truly 'one of ourselves' underneath, the climbing boy was a 'black' who symbolically purged Britain's real anxiety about the races it was exploiting in the East and West Indies. He was a token black who could be scrubbed, cleaning up Britons' fears of the dark races of its empire. And he was a black who was a child. Acknowledging him as a fellow creature did not require one to accept him, or the colonial subjects whom he symbolised, as equals. He and they, the implication was, were in need of benevolent parental authority.

Fear could only be replaced by paternalism if the climbing boy was indeed 'scrubbed' (i.e. abolished). And not only the climbing boy. Entering every house, the boy sweeps were the visible representatives of the masses of child labourers hidden in Britain's 'dark Satanic mills' and mines. Their symbolic 'negritude' (to borrow Lamb's noun for their figurative state) enabled campaigners to make other working children seem like slaves too. The argument that had aroused such opposition when Cobbett made it (that Britain's labourers were worse off than slaves) became a staple even of conservative humanitarians who regarded radicals with fear and loathing. At least, it did in so far as children were concerned. This was no coincidence. Children, by definition, needed paternalism. Lacking independence, they could be conceived as passive targets of reforming benevolence in a way adult labourers could not. A gentleman could acknowledge boys' similarity to slaves without feeling that the acknowledgement would encourage them to rebel. Unlike their parents, boys would not strike or riot if they thought themselves slaves. They would not form political clubs, organise mass meetings or march on parliament. They would neither preach defiance nor practise revolution. Their position could be acknowledged without political consequences. And so they appealed to many who felt opposed to the exploitation of labourers in mill, mine and field but who had no wish to give those labourers power. Coleridge and Southey both came into that category by 1818. They wanted radical journals banned and political agitators like Cobbett locked up. Both campaigned against the use of child labour in cotton factories. According to Coleridge, defending the children's employment was like opposing the relief of climbing boys – tantamount to supporting slavery. The mills brought profit for a few, but created poverty and disease for the many. They resembled slave colonies, the child workers white slaves. Southey too saw climbing boys as part of a 'negro trade' that illustrated the 'evil' that had 'unavoidably arisen from the manufacturing system'.[46]

Seeing children as slaves opened people's eyes. It changed perceptions, and a mass campaign against child labour grew steadily in power. But it was the little black boy who made that insight possible. It was on him that the slave analogy rested. On the back of the crippled chimney sweep, the successful rhetoric of a movement of social change was carried. Yet if that movement was major, it was also narrow. Child labour reform salved the consciences of the middle classes about the exploitation produced by the manufacturing system. It did save children, but it also armed the powerful against the claims of the children's parents. Confident that they were doing good to infant labourers, Victorian legislators resisted adult workers' efforts to represent and organise themselves.

Those legislators were reflecting the priorities of the middle and upper classes, priorities that were implicit throughout Montgomery's *Chimney Sweeper's Friend*. Yet the book was not merely symptomatic of the emerging attitudes and insecurities of nineteenth-century Britain. It helped to define them. And it deployed them for effect. The poems in the collection adapted the language of Romanticism. They borrowed the forms and styles that, in Coleridge's, Wordsworth's and Blake's hands, had registered so sensitively the hidden anxieties of the age. But Montgomery's borrowings registered different anxieties – those of the comfortable middle classes. And they sketched out easier and cheaper solutions to those anxieties.

Montgomery's campaigning poetry sought to move well-off parents at their cosy firesides. It was a sentimentalisation of Romanticism. 'The Dream' borrows, at the verbal and formal level, from Coleridge's 'Ancient Mariner'.[47] It is a narrative poem in which a physical journey is also a mental one. The reader travels with the climbing boy out into the cold and into extremes of anguish.

> The snow – I never saw such snow –
>   Raged like the sea all round,
> Tossing and tumbling to and fro;
>   I thought I must be drown'd.
>
> Now up, now down, with main and might
>   I plunged through drift and stour;
> Nothing, no nothing baulk'd my flight,
>   I had a giant's power.
>
> Till suddenly the storm stood still
>   Flat lay the snow beneath;
> I curdled to an icicle,
>   I could not stir – not breathe.

White snow and white moonshine represent an extreme of alienation – the cold purity of death. But the boy is not allowed to die;

> My master found me rooted there;
>   He flogg'd me back to sense,
> Then pluck'd me up, and by the hair,
>   Sheer over ditch and fence, –
>
> He dragg'd, and dragg'd, and dragg'd me on,
>   For many and many a mile;
> At a grand house he stopp'd anon;
>   It was a famous pile.

Where the snow was white, the house is black. It represents a different kind of death – the life-in-death of the boy's terror:

> Up to the moon it seem'd to rise,
>   Broad as the earth to stand;
> The building darken'd half the skies,
>   Its shadow half the land.
>
> All round was still – as still as death;
>   I shivering, chattering stood;
> And felt the coming, going breath,
>   The tingling, freezing blood.

Throughout, Montgomery plays light against dark, hot against cold. The frozen boy is forced up the chimney, gets stuck, finds his master has lit a fire under him to force him out of the flue. He escapes, only to go on an imaginary journey to 'the flames of hell' and then up to a single bright star.

> Through the blue heaven I stretch'd my hand
>   To touch its beams, – it broke
> Like a sea-bubble on the sand;
>   Then all fell dark. – I woke.

Here the poem ends, leaving readers, like the boy, in the dark of a workday and the gloom of a hopelessness from which even dreams offer no escape.

CHANGELINGS

In March 1818 the campaigner Dr Lushington told a committee of the House of Lords that 'it is a frequent and ordinary practice in this country, to kidnap and steal boys for the purpose of employing them in this trade . . . several individuals have been so carried off, and . . . their parents have not known for some time, indeed in one instance some years, what had become of them' (*CSF*, p. 126). Lushington's 'facts' were, unbeknown to him, part of a communal fiction, an urban myth that gained the status of fact because people wanted to believe a story which encoded their hopes and fears so intriguingly.

Montgomery and the contributors to *The Chimney Sweeper's Friend* did not just perpetuate the myth but also set themselves to reshape it for propaganda purposes. Montgomery reprinted George Reveley's evidence to a committee of the House of Commons 'because it comes home to the better sort of persons in higher life' (*CSF*, p. 219). Reveley told MPs of 'a stolen child' who was sold to a master sweep for £8 8s. Sent to sweep the chimneys of a well-to-do family, his black disguise was penetrated because he showed himself acquainted with the property of the wealthy: 'when he was shown a repeating watch, he used to say his father had such a thing; or silver forks, he used to say the same' (*CSF*, p. 219). The boy's family was never found, though advertised for, but 'some lady took the child and educated him'.

Reveley's version plays on gentlemanly fears: abolish climbing boys is his message, lest you lose without trace your sons and have no heirs to inherit your property. His climbing boy is disturbing because he reminds gentlemen how fragile are the lines of blood and property that separate them from the labouring poor. If white sons could become filthy labourers and black slaves before anyone noticed the difference, then the distinctions between high and low, rich and poor, home and colony seemed dangerously weak.

Montgomery, by this point in the *Chimney Sweeper's Friend*, had made the climbing boy a figure provoking multiple anxieties. Montgomery's climbing boy forced readers into a double movement. First, he was an outsider moving in – a black slave and filthy labourer who came into the home. He made the hearth into an uncanny space through which the Englishman's castle was infiltrated by forces it was designed to keep out. The central symbol of domestic enclosure was opened to the cold winds of economic forces on which the gentry were dependent. Hearth and home, the climbing boy reminded the comfortably-off, rested on the bodies of labourers, labourers who, in Britain and the West Indies, only *seemed* alien, their blackness merely disguising their common humanity.

But Montgomery's boy, paradoxically, was also an insider moving out, a gentleman's son kidnapped, undermining inheritance and legitimacy. And if that gentle boy returned home as a brutalised, blackened sweep he might be so changed as to be unrecognisable, reminding gentlemen that nothing except their property distinguished them from the grimy sons of toil.

Montgomery's achievement was to concentrate social fears in the image of the climbing boy so that readers could never rest assured – and therefore never put him out of mind. Montgomery created a complex symbol, a contradiction on stunted legs, a cripple who, because he mixed black and white, inside and outside, Briton and African, gentleman and labourer, embodied too many social tensions to be tolerated. He would have to be abolished, and Montgomery brandished Smart's brush as the way to abolish him.

But Montgomery also gave readers some relief from the fears he provoked. The idealised gentlewoman came to their (and the boys') rescue, clutching hymn book and Bible. Samuel Roberts's 'The Chimney Sweeper's Boy' recounted the story of 'Edwin', a gentlewoman's beloved child. Abducted by a gypsy, he is sold to a sweep. Lost without trace, he returns one day to sweep the household's chimneys. His parents do not penetrate his black mask until they hear him singing, in the chimney, the hymns they had taught him. The mother identifies her son: '"The *sweep*!" Nerina shriek'd, with transport wild, / "Alcander! 'tis my *child*, my *child*! my *child*!"' (*CSF*, p. 61). Christian piety, runs the moral, will be rewarded. The God who restores the son to his mother will uphold the propertied classes against labourers and gypsies, provided that they and their children worship him piously and gratefully.

This version of the myth reassures, then. Indeed, it acts as a palliative for the anxiety of the wealthy. It offers emotional balm for guilt about and fear of the poor, by suggesting that class division can be overcome in a recognition of shared humanity. The myth of the restored changeling lets the wealthy imagine themselves taking the poor to their bosoms, without requiring them actually to do it. Having made well-to-do readers afraid, Montgomery was now making them feel good.

FORCEFEEDING

The Chimney Sweeper's Friend did not, of course, end the trade overnight. Nor did it campaign singlehanded. But it gave abolitionists a new language to graft onto the earnest prose in which they had recommended a mechanical solution. And the grafting process was easier than might be imagined, for the dissenting Christianity of Montgomery had more than at first appeared in common with the technologised benevolence that was Rumford's legacy. Both men wanted to reform the habits, as well as the occupations, of the labouring classes. Both men made them objects to be organised, disciplined and institutionalised by their social superiors. What Rumford aimed to do under the aegis of science, dissenters and Evangelicals did in the name of God. They would shape the minds of the poor, so that they would become more like the wealthy imagined themselves to be – ordered, sober, useful, industrious.

Rumford had been welcomed by Britain's philanthropists not just because of his fireplaces. Nor was his work on caloric the original cause of his fame. In Munich, he had been experimenting with people, on a huge scale. His aim was nothing less than to rid Bavaria of poverty, and his methods were draconian. On 1 January 1790, a day when Munich's citizens traditionally gave alms to beggars, Rumford sent the infantry into action. In 'less than an hour', he boasted, they had cleared every beggar off the streets.[48] They had cleared them into a newly commissioned workhouse that Rumford had taken over. Such workhouses were already familiar in Britain. It was not the institution, but Rumford's methods, that opened a bright new vision to philanthropists in London. For Rumford put a meticulously planned regime into operation. It was designed to replace the 'bad' labour of the streets with 'good' labour in the house of industry. It was designed also to make idle beggars and dissolute prostitutes into happy and willing weavers: Rumford's scheme would reform not just their work but also their minds.

To reform their minds, it was necessary to know them. Rumford had no doubt that he did. The poor would place their affections in the overseers of the workhouse, who must be 'persons of gentle manners, humane dispositions'.[49] They would do so because they saw it to be in their interest to do so. Rumford's was not to be a house of love, but of '*rewards* and *punishments*', 'the only means by which mankind can be controlled and directed'.[50] He based his practices on those of animal trainers. Watching men break horses 'suggested . . . many ideas which I afterwards put in execution with great success, in reclaiming those abandoned and ferocious animals in human shape which I undertook to tame and render gentle and docile'.[51] Men were animals, or children, to be 'controlled' by an artificial environment designed to make work attractive:

The children in the House of Industry at Munich, who, being placed upon elevated seats round the halls where other children worked, were made to be idle spectators of that amusing scene, cried most bitterly when the request to be permitted to descend from their places and mix in that busy crowd was refused; but they would, most probably, have cried still more, had they been taken abruptly from their play and *forced* to work.[52]

Here Rumford introduces a system in which discipline is produced through surveillance. By a process of organised mental torture, leisure is turned into idleness. Children are offered only different kinds of regimentation – the voyeuristic isolation of the excluded, or the mass labour of those allowed to work.

Here, Rumford's ideas were influential. Jeremy Bentham planned to adopt a similar supervisory and voyeuristic scheme in prisons, schools, factories and workhouses. This regime of inspection was represented architecturally by the Panopticon, a building in which a central supervisor commanded a view of all the inmates in their separate cells. According to Foucault and to Ignatieff, Bentham's Panopticon heralded – and acts as a symbol of – the bureaucratic and disciplinary state that capitalism produced in nineteenth-century Europe, a state that enforced conformity by inspection. If so, then Rumford stood behind Bentham, for the latter's Poor Panopticon was a system of workhouses designed on Rumford's lines. They were to use the Rumford diet and Rumford stoves. They would use inspection to make 'good subjects' out of foundling children.[53] They would feature a director, able to view from his central position all the activities of each institution. And that director, wrote Bentham, should be a man 'beyond all example fitted for the conduct of a business of this nature . . .

a man in whose [character?] genius and benevolence contend with each other . . . the man I am speaking of is Count Rumford'.[54]

Bentham's model was never taken up by the British government. Its mechanistic understanding of humans controlled by inspection, it was decided, left too little role for religious conscience. Rumford's model, on the other hand, was adopted – not by the government as such, but in the new schools. These introduced versions of inspection and surveillance closer to Rumford's Munich system than to Bentham's. In the Panopticon a warder commanded from a central point all the prisoners. In the Munich workhouse the punished were the watchers not the watched. Unwilling children were excluded from the work of their peers: their punishment was to watch in isolation, to wish to join in but be forced to remain voyeurs. Rumford, that is to say, produced discipline through a more subtle understanding of social dynamics than Bentham showed. By linking surveillance with exclusion and ostracism, he opposed watching to doing, individual to group, making labour desirable because it was the only route to social acceptance. It was a technique that Joseph Lancaster and Andrew Bell were to use in the monitorial school systems that they spread across the country.

Rumford's Munich house was a machine in which inspection encouraged industry. Safely out of view, regularly washed – unlike the beggars, streetwalkers and climbing boys – Rumford's poor laboured at looms for twelve to fourteen hours a day in return for shelter, food and a piecework payrate. They were constantly monitored: printed forms were used to record work done and material used, to issue free meals and detail absences. Rumford had, in fact, pioneered the development of social bureaucracy, replacing private charity by a state system that attempted to organise and survey a whole section of the people whom legislators had identified as a 'problem'. It was a model that derived from and in turn bolstered the factory system. Josiah Wedgwood had said that his factory would 'make machines of men as cannot err'.[55]

In a small country, Rumford ran his poor factory for the state. He acted on the Elector's behalf as an enlightened despot. He concentrated and centralised power in a way not possible in Britain's more complex society. Nevertheless, his Munich inventions proved exportable – and none more so than the soup kitchen. In his 1795 pamphlet *Of Food; and Particularly of Feeding the Poor*, Rumford told philanthropists how to feed as many as possible on as little as possible. By experimenting with ingredients, and measuring exactly, he had discovered that a pint and a quarter of soup, containing as little as $4\frac{3}{4}$ ounces of solid food, would satisfy the hunger of a grown person. The best ingredients were pearl barley, pease, potatoes, bread cuttings, vinegar, salt and water. Rumford had brought the disciplines of scientific empiricism to bear, pioneering the science we now call nutrition. With typical self-confidence, though, he pressed his claims too far. Water, Rumford noted, 'appears evidently to serve as *food*' for plants, so 'why should we not suppose it may serve as food' to people.[56] Science, if Rumford's suppositions were right, would feed the poor on even less than loaves and fishes.

Philanthropists in Britain were amazed by Rumford's totalised approach. He made it seem as if a marriage between science and the state could transform all aspects of poverty, creating an ordered, harmonious and happy society. Others, however, were less delighted. For William Cobbett, Rumford's soup and potatoes tasted of cant and coercion. They were a forcefed substitute for the real food which labourers would eat if they could – and once had eaten. The labourer's 'beer and bread and meat are now exchanged . . . for the cold and heartless diet of the potatoe plat. I can well remember when the very poorest of the people would not eat potatoes'.[57] Soup, meanwhile, smacked of the dependence to which once independent labourers had been reduced. It was a palliative, not a cure, dangerous if it left 'the *real causes* of the misery [to] be passed over in *silence*' and left 'the people . . . deluded . . . into a false hope of permanent relief'.[58]

Climbing boys were more dependent than most. Their masters, themselves poor, made them rely on handouts – on scraps from the tables of the houses whose chimneys they swept and on soup, provided at soup kitchens and at the Sunday Schools set up by campaigners. But Rumford's watery fare was supplemented, on May Day every year, by a charitable feast provided by Mrs Montague. Roast beef and plum pudding was the fare – the diet that, according to popular tradition, had made yeomen stout and Britain great.[59]

Charles Lamb described another annual feast held at Smithfield during St Bartholomew's fair. There too the menu was meaty and beery, with 'reeking sausages' and 'small ale' aplenty. The event, according to Lamb, was riotous – featuring jostling, shouting, and standing on tables. It was dedicated to the sensual pleasure of eating: Lamb watched the 'sable younkers lick in the unctuous meat'.[60] It was a day of gorging, compensating for the hard times experienced during the rest of the year.

Revelry and gourmandry did not appeal to Montgomery and his dissenting and Evangelical allies. From 1807, they instituted their own version of the climbing boys' annual feast in Sheffield. Montgomery knew that such feasts, like the fairs with which they were linked, were remnants of carnival. In his poem 'Easter Monday at Sheffield', his boy-narrator declares of the

Sheffield dinner: 'I thought the world turn'd upside down' (*CSF*, p. 427). But, in practice, Montgomery was not prepared to tolerate even a day's inversion of the social order. The Sheffield dinner featured roast beef and plum pudding, but the boys were fed morality, discipline and piety with their dinners:

> Books, pretty books with pictures in,
>   Were given to those who learn to read,
> Which showed them how to flee from sin,
>   And to be happy boys indeed.
>   (*CSF*, p. 427)

The books, and the dinner itself, were inducements to go to Sunday School. Both were parts of a supervisory regime aimed at moral reform, which Rumford would have recognised. Only the boys already learning to read at Sunday School got the books, so that those who did not were excluded, forced to look on as their peers enjoyed the pretty pictures. Once again, punishment took the form of an isolated voyeurism – looking at pictures that belonged to others. But reform was also a matter of inspection: it was by learning to look at books that the climbing boys would 'improve', as they linked pretty pictures with moral truths. Viewing books was the 'good' labour that would redeem the sweeps from the effects of their evil work.

The supposed 'depravity' of the little sweeps became a vital part of the abolitionists' case. Campaigners told parliament that boys who had neither schooling nor religion became young men given to theft and vice. The child-victim was potentially the hardened criminal. The boy raised the frightening spectre of a violent and disordered working class with no respect for property. His sooty skin symbolised the 'moral diseases' thought to emanate from the 'foul air' of the slums where he lived.[61] If he was a black slave, he was also an 'imp of fiendish make', a protégé of the adult devils of London's gloomy courts and rookeries.[62] He must be brought into the light, be taken from his murky haunts to institutions where improvement could be inculcated and inspected. The Christian philanthropists were as determined to sweep the streets as Rumford had been. Bernard wrote that reform of the poor's 'moral and religious character' was essential.[63] But the reform was to take place not in workhouses, but in Sunday Schools, for Bernard and his allies knew that British workhouses were so corrupt that many master sweeps recruited their climbing boys from them. What they did not know – or at least did not acknowledge – was that it was the very coerciveness as well as the corruption of those workhouses that made boys want to escape from them. Neither Rumford nor the philanthropists could see that, in trying to inculcate a culture of industry, order and morality into labourers, they were subjecting them to a mental, spiritual and physical imprisonment.

Technologised benevolence and evangelical Christianity alike treated working people as objects, to be ordered, disciplined and machined into usefulness and gratitude. Rescuing Britain's own black slaves, campaigners washed them white only to subject them to another kind of labour – the labour of becoming pious and 'good'. Sanctimony and science, in the hope of social 'improvement', replaced the forced work of climbing chimneys with the regimented task of moral improvement.

ROMANTIC CLIMBING BOYS

Montgomery had solicited poems from well-known Romantics. Walter Scott and Wordsworth had replied with words of encouragement but no verse. But their poetic lessons had been learnt by writers who did contribute. Montgomery's manufacturing friend Samuel Roberts actually quoted Wordsworth's 'The child is father of the man' when he argued that exploited boys became degraded adults. He also referred to the boys' 'human form divine', taking the phrase either directly from Blake or from its sources in Wesley, Pope and Milton.[64] Clearly, the campaigners had recognised the power of the Romantic idealisation of childhood as a state of holy innocence. Nevertheless, they buried the force of that idealisation beneath the suffocating assumptions, derived from evangelical Christianity, that the boy was a sinful object whose life led to evil. A slave, a demon, a changeling, a victim, trickster and talisman, the boy disappeared under the weight of discourses designed to make him provoke enough fears and induce enough hopes to stir the well-to-do into action. He was the subject of myths, tales of martyrdom, official reports and parliamentary debates, of scientific experiments, court cases and mass meetings, of press campaigns, medical procedures and workhouse discipline, of Sunday Schools and sentimental poems. He precipitated imperial anxieties and produced domestic changes: the great panoply of Victorian reform movements, their aims, methods, flaws and failures, were anticipated, and partly set in train, by the little sweep. The very length of the campaign meant that a carapace of words and images stuck to the boy, all tending to encase him in discourses of others' making.

Or nearly all. Some of the voices that spoke for the boys resisted the regimentation of body and mind that the social and religious reformers were imposing. Charles Lamb had reason to. Himself a charity boy, then a clerk, he knew what it was to drudge for little pay. He was not quite an independent gentleman, and gently mocked the moral earnestness of the gentlemen abolitionists. His 'The Praise of Chimney Sweepers' (1822), as his punning pen-name Elia/a liar suggests, is deliberately slippery.[65] Lamb's bizarre humour and archaic style make his portrait playful. As a result, readers can never assume a conventional emotional posture. Lamb's climbing boys resist the pity they invoke. They assume stereotypes only to throw them off unsettlingly:

> I reverence these young Africans of our own growth – these almost clergy imps, who sport their cloth without assumption; and from their little pulpits (the tops of chimneys), in the nipping air of a December morning, preach a lesson of patience to mankind.

Here, no sooner are the boys pitiable black slaves than they become tiny priests, mocking the pomposity of the Church. This comic subversion enables Lamb to make another quiet change – the boys preach, rather than, as in the Sunday Schools, being preached at. The joke of imagining chimney pots as pulpits allows Lamb to make a serious, and less reassuring, point than those made by evangelical philanthropists. The boys are not simply to be pitied but also to be admired. They teach endurance.

Lamb makes readers journey beyond their assumed superiority. He takes them on an imaginative journey, placing them in childhood again when the climbing boy seemed an epic explorer rather than a little victim:

> When a child, what a mysterious pleasure it was to witness their operation! to see a chit no bigger than oneself enter, one knew not by what process, into what seemed to be the *fauces Averni* – to pursue him in imagination, as he went sounding on through so many dark stifling caverns, horrid shades! – to shudder with the idea that 'now, surely, he must be lost for ever'.

Lamb's Latin alludes to Virgil's *Aeneid*. It makes the boy a hero, a new Aeneas exploring the hellish underworld to its very depths. The boy emerges brandishing his brush like 'a flag waved over a conquered citadel!' He is a comic version of Virgil's conqueror of Troy.

Lamb's heroic language is funny, but his point is the Romantic one that to the innocent imagination of children, many things that seem ordinary to jaded adults are full of extraordinary drama. He wants to tease readers into rediscovering that childhood imagination, so as to see the world afresh. New vision, he hopes, will see through old corruptions. After he makes readers see the boys through the eyes of childhood, he addresses them directly – 'Reader, if thou meetest one of these small gentry in thy early rambles, it is good to give him a penny.' Charity, here, results not solely from pity but also from admiration. It will be an informal and personal tribute, not an institutionalised dole for which the boy will have to accept sanctimony and surveillance.

Throughout his essay, Lamb's descriptions are offered self-consciously. His language works on the premise that he – and his readers – know that it 'only' fits its subjects humorously. He does not claim to represent the real with unvarnished accuracy. He does not presume to know the climbing boy in general as did most of the philanthropists. Lamb writes no case histories; he imposes no moral systems. Instead, his unlikely comparisons disturb the received 'knowledge' (indeed, disturb the very idea that there is such a thing as received knowledge). In the process, Lamb actually reveals some things about the climbing boys that are to be found nowhere in the abolitionist literature. He reveals some of their tastes – their likes and dislikes, their humour. And, characteristically, he does so in a digression, that turns out not to be a digression at all, about saloop, a drink made from 'the sweet wood yclept sassafras' and sold at roadside stalls throughout London. Its smell, Lamb says, is so pungent that he has never tried it. Nor will idle gentlemen, for it is a workman's drink: 'the rake who wisheth to dissipate his o'ernight vapours in more grateful coffee, curses the ungenial fume, as he passeth; but the artisan stops to taste, and blesses the fragrant breakfast'. Saloop and not Rumfordian soup is the labourer's meal of choice. Work makes sweet to him what their idleness makes sour to his social superiors. Saloop, that is to say, symbolises the 'hardhanded' labourer's difference from the gentleman, a difference based on work. Class difference, Lamb comically implies, is a matter of taste, but taste is a matter of labour.

Climbing boys turn Lamb's jokes nasty. They love saloop because of the particular kind of work that they do:

this composition is surprisingly gratifying to the palate of a young chimney-sweeper – whether the oily particles (sassafras is slightly oleaginous) do attenuate and soften the fuliginous concretions, which are sometimes found (in dissections) to adhere to the roof of the mouth in these unfledged practitioners.

Lamb's comically pompous vocabulary lets him avoid sentimental stridency. It lets him put an unpalatable argument without revolting readers. The climbing boys, in his opinion, like saloop because it softens the sooty cancers that, surgeons had shown, eat them to death from the inside out. Labour does indeed shape the taste. It also, grimly, rots the very mouths that do the tasting. Lamb brings readers up short as he turns aesthetics physical. A digression on liking an exotic drink turns out to be an analysis of the terrible bodily costs of manual work. Saloop, Lamb implies, is a small compensation for the sweeps, a 'sweet wood' with which Nature palliates the 'bitter wood' 'she has mingled' in their lot. Here 'bitter wood' perhaps refers to coal, the fossilised wood that necessitated their labour and that adhered to their mouths as soot. Lamb's metaphors keep unexpectedly and disturbingly collapsing into physical objects.

If saloop was a natural compensation, the climbing boys could not afford it. It was up to gentlemen to buy it for them:

Him shouldst thou haply encounter, with his dim visage pendent over the grateful steam, regale him with a sumptuous basin (it will cost thee but three half-pennies) and a slice of delicate bread and butter (an added halfpenny) – so may thy culinary fires, eased of the o'er charged secretions from thy worse-placed hospitalities, curl up a lighter volume to the welkin – so may the descending soot never taint thy costly well-ingredienced soups – nor the odious cry, quick-reaching from street to street, of the *fired chimney*, invite the rattling engines from ten adjacent parishes, to disturb for a casual scintillation thy peace and pocket!

Lamb's pseudo-religious diction gives his words the form of a mock-blessing. Gentlemen, he half-humorously suggests, should buy themselves absolution in the cup of saloop they purchase for the sweep who keeps their own soups and chimneys free of soot. The cost is small, but the symbolic value large. Guilt can be assuaged because charity, here, satisfies the tastes as well as soothes the wounds of those who labour for others' comfort. The climbing boy gets what his mind and body tell him he wants rather than what gentlemen think he should have.

Lamb's boys are never subalterns as they are in so much abolitionist writing. They are not reduced to case histories who have no questions to ask those who speak for them. Lamb's imagery is too curious and too telling for stereotyping to occur. He concentrates on the boys' mouths and pictures what goes into and comes out of the hungry lips that hide a sooty cancer within. What comes out is jocularity and mockery. The boys enjoy undermining the dignity of gentlemen:

In the last winter but one, pacing along Cheapside with my accustomed precipitation when I walk westward, a treacherous slide brought me upon my back in an instant. I scrambled up with pain and shame enough – yet outwardly trying to face it down, as if nothing had happened – when the roguish grin of one of these young wits encountered me.

The boy points the fallen and embarrassed Lamb out to the 'mob', helpless with mirth at the sight of a clean gentleman made as dirty as he is. His grin defines him and makes Lamb, and the reader, who remembers what may lie behind it, bear his insults:

the grin of a genuine sweep hath absolutely no malice in it – that I could have been content, if the honour of a gentleman might endure it, to have remained his butt and his mockery till midnight.

Lamb accepts the boy's pleasure at a superior being brought low: if, he implies, the boy is foul-mouthed towards gentlemen he has a cancerous reason to be. His taunts should be tolerated by those who, considering themselves above manual labour, benefit from his body.

The boys' mouths turn out to be contradictory places. Diseased within, they grin at gentlemen's discomfiture. But they reveal gentlemanly traits too:

The fine lady, or fine gentleman, who show me their teeth, show me bones. Yet must I confess, that from the mouth of a true sweep a display (even to ostentation) of those white and shining ossifications, strikes me as an agreeable anomaly in manners, and an allowable piece of foppery. It is, as when

A sable cloud
Turns forth her silver lining on the night.

The boys' teeth, so white against their black faces, confound the physical differences between rich and poor. Lamb makes readers see in close-up to force them to face the central, unspoken, question of his essay – is the social hierarchy inherent in nature, or written on the mind and body by labour? The irony in the above passage lies in the fact that the white teeth that the gentry prize as marks of their status seem to be found in climbing boys because the boys' faces are blackened by their work. Perhaps the bodily signs of gentility are misleading: certainly they are parodied in the mouths of the black sweeps.

Those very mouths lead Lamb to a comic fantasy – Elia's/a liar's version of the changeling myth. He recounts the story of a climbing boy found sleeping between the white sheets of a duke's bed at Arundel Castle. Such a boy was no ordinary pauper, but a kidnapped nobleman's son who had dim memories of his former ducal state. But for this boy, unlike the similar boys in the changeling stories of Montgomery and Roberts, there is no reconciliation. He is never restored to his parents. Lamb concludes that many of the white-toothed climbing boys were probably gentlemen's sons, 'irreparable and hopeless *defiliations*'. The difference between high and low, gentleman and labourer is thus thoroughly confused. What Lamb jokingly sees in the mouths of babes is the artificiality of social distinction – which depends neither on birth nor on rank but on work and what work does to body and soul.

The climax of Lamb's essay describes a ritual that is both gentlemen's reparation to the boys and a comic subversion of social hierarchy (like the essay itself). It is a ritual concerning mouths, mouths having their desires satisfied. The annual Smithfield feast, as Lamb describes it, is an occasion on which the social order is turned upside down. Gentlemen serve the boys, cramming their mouths with food. Lamb shows his friend Jem White force-feeding the boys what they want, mocking the delicacy of gentlemen in the process:

> how he would fit the tit bits to the puny mouths, reserving the lengthier links for the seniors – how he would intercept a morsel even in the jaws of some desperado, declaring it 'must to the pan again to be browned, for it was not fit for a gentleman's eating' – how he would recommend this slice of white bread, or that piece of kissing-crust, to a tender juvenile, advising them all to have a care of cracking their teeth, which were their best patrimony.

White parodies the formality and order of gentlemen's dinners. His table manners turn a supposed gentleman into a Falstaff dedicated to and consumed by the sensual pleasure of eating:

> standing upon tables, and prefacing every sentiment with a 'Gentlemen, give me leave to propose so and so', which was a prodigious comfort to those young orphans; every now and then stuffing into his mouth (for it did not do to be squeamish on these occasions) indiscriminate pieces of those reeking sausages, which pleased them mightily, and was the savouriest part, you may believe, of the entertainment.

Here White has achieved solidarity with the boys. His lips mock and his mouth eats as avidly as theirs. Status and superiority are parodied and then abandoned: the pleasures of the flesh unite gentlemen and boys. It is a far cry – or a loud belch – from the soup-fed, industrious and Sunday-Schooled vision that Rumford and the philanthropists advocated.

Lamb no sooner conjures up the Rabelaisian feast than he banishes it. 'James White is extinct,' he writes, 'and with him these suppers have long ceased.' The sudden entry of death breaks the anarchic comedy – and for more than one reason. Lamb is mourning the passing of an eighteenth-century attitude to the poor and its replacement by the institutionalised benevolence of Rumford's heirs. But he is also acknowledging guilt. Jem White was not, for all his mockery of gentility, one of the boys. He was paying for the Smithfield feast as a way of assuaging, for one day of the year, an exploitation which worked to gentlemen's benefit for the other 364. Lamb was not complacent enough to suggest that a day of licensed gorging and parody was more than a small symbolic restitution. He leaves us with an undercurrent of desperation – an image of White stopping the craving mouths of the boys with the sausages they liked because oily foods softened the cancerous soot that was glued to their palates. Within Lamb's benign humour is a fact he wants to make stick – not on our palates but in our throats.

Lamb's essay seemed uncontroversial. But its quiet subversiveness had access to a bigger and more immediate readership than much of the campaigning literature. Elia's pieces were popular features of the *London Magazine* and were influential upon the young Dickens. *Sketches by Boz* (1836) contains a discussion of climbing boys.[66] The piece takes its whimsical tone from Lamb's: 'The gradual decay and disuse of the practice of leading noble youths into captivity, and compelling them to ascend chimneys was a severe blow, if we may so speak, to the romance of chimney-sweeping.' If Dickens is humorously over-literal, he has a serious point, that the legends and customs which give labour its own dignity and (often subversive) value are being disciplined away by the respectable and timid. Such people feared the working classes, regarding their street culture as threatening rather than lively. Hogarth and Cruikshank had both celebrated the liberty supposedly natural to English people by drawing tumultuous London crowds in which climbing boys shared the common glee. Now such attitudes were being replaced by suspicion.

Dickens noted that the May Day festivities, in which climbing boys parodied ladies and gentlemen, were on the wane. These were 'signs of the times', signs confirmed when the master sweeps substituted an anniversary dinner where 'clean faces appeared in lieu of black ones smeared with rose pink, and knee cords and tops superseded nankeen drawers and rosetted shoes'. Even on May Day, the boys would have to conform to campaigners' demands for cleanliness and propriety. No black faces, drag acts or camp versions of the gentry were to be allowed. Riot, satire and outlandishness were off limits, to be replaced, Dickens concluded, by hypocrisy. The master sweeps and (he added in *Oliver Twist*)[67] the officials responsible for orphans and paupers would continue to buy and sell little boys for the trade. Later, Charles Kingsley would show the same thing, giving the abolition campaign new impetus by the power of his 1863 novel *The Water Babies.*

William Hone recorded the May Day festivities as part of his effort to show the social customs of the labouring classes to be manifestations of essential Englishness:

Here they are! The 'sweeps' are come! Here is the garland and the lord and lady! Poor fellows! this is their great festival … sometimes they wear coronals of flowers in their heads; their black faces and legs are grotesquely coloured with Dutch-pink;

their shovels are scored with this crimson pigment, interlaced with white chalk. Their lord and lady are magnificent indeed; the lord is always the tallest of the party selected from some other profession to play this distinguished character: he wears a huge cocked hat, fringed with yellow or red feathers, or laced with gold paper: his coat is between that of the full court dress, and the laced coat of the footman of quality; in the breast he carries an immense bunch of flowers; his waistcoat is embroidered; his frill is enormous; his 'shorts' are satin, with paste knee-buckles; his stockings silk with figured clocks; his shoes are dancing pumps, with large tawdry buckles: his hair is powdered, with a bag and rosette; he carries in his right hand a high cane with a shining metal knob, and in his left a handkerchief held by one corner, and of a colour once white. His lady is sometimes a strapping girl, though usually a boy in female attire.[68]

To this parodic ensemble a clown had recently been added, practising 'every antic and trick that his ingenuity can devise'. The climbing boy, as Hone commemorated him, was trickster as well as victim, at least for one day of the year.

Hone included advertisements for Smart's machine. He reprinted Lamb's essay. He recommended the *Chimney Sweeper's Friend* too, and excerpted from it the most profound poem of all on the subject.

> When my mother died I was very young,
> And my father sold me, while yet my tongue,
> Could scarcely cry, 'Weep! weep! weep!'
> So your chimneys I sweep, and in soot I sleep.
>
> There's little Tom Toddy,[69] who cried when his head,
> That was curl'd like a lamb's back, was shaved, so I said,
> 'Hush, Tom, never mind it for when your head's bare,
> You know that the soot cannot spoil your white hair'.
>
> And so he was quiet, and that very night
> As Tom was a sleeping, he had such a sight,
> That thousands of sweepers, Dick, Joe, Ned, and Jack,
> Were all of them locked up in coffins so black.
>
> And by came an angel, who had a bright key,
> And he opened the coffins, and set them all free;
> Then down a green plain, leaping, laughing, they run,
> And wash in a river, and shine in the sun,
>
> Then naked and white, all their bags left behind,
> They rise upon clouds, and sport in the wind;
> And the angel told Tom, if he'd be a good boy
> He'd have God for his father, and never want joy.

And so Tom awoke, and we rose in the dark,
And got with our bags and our brushes to work;
Though the morning was cold, Tom was happy and warm,
So if all do their duty they need not fear harm.[70]

Blake's Song of Innocence, in its context in Montgomery's collection, seemed similar to the poems that surrounded it. Like them, it opposed blackness to whiteness and spoke of God. Its final line must have seemed, to Montgomery and his evangelical collaborators, an orthodox expression of their views.

Blake's poem reads differently in its context in Hone. It follows a diagram of Smart's machine and a quotation from Montgomery calling the boys' lives 'unjustifiable personal slavery and moral degradation'. After this, Blake's text seems an examination of the workings of the moral degradation that slavery produces in the soul. The boy speaker of the poem has, like the boy sweep in 'London', 'mind-forg'd manacles'. His innocent and joyful energy has been perverted into worship of the forces that oppress them. His perversion is a matter of unwitting complicity, of passing on to other boys his own adaptation to slavery. He hushes Tom's cries at the loss of his lamb-like hair. He is making the best of a bad job, but he does so with such an unknowing will that he helps perpetuate what he is too innocent even to recognise as repression. The last verse is his interpretation of Tom's dream. It corrupts it. Tom's innocent hope is co-opted to make him a willing participant in his own oppression. But the oppression is not just that of a master sweep. It is that of Rumford, Bernard, Montgomery and the other abolitionists who offered the poor salvation if they learnt to love the gods of industry, duty and utility. Blake's 'evangelical' last line is in fact a quietly devastating exposure of the shallow sanctimony with which social reformers shaped the poor they helped. Blake's boy has been brainwashed.

When Blake himself published the poem in 1789, no philanthropists were yet advocating the abolition of climbing boys.[71] Hanway, Bernard and the Bishop of Durham wanted to relieve their suffering and reform their ignorance by sending them to Sunday School. In its context in *Songs of Innocence*, the poem is part of Blake's satire on the cant and hypocrisy of those who justified exploitation on earth by offering reward in heaven. Its imagery demonstrates the corruption of innocence in the repression of the body. The boy's hair that 'curl'd like a lamb's back' is shorn: he will have no 'white hair' to be blackened by soot. In 'The Echoing Green' 'white hair' is associated with the joyful laughter of 'Old John' (Erdman, p. 8).

And in other poems in the collection, the lamb is clearly a symbol of God's existence in bodily form, as in 'The Lamb', where to shear the lamb-child is to attack the bodily energy that is God.

The images of 'The Chimney Sweeper', in fact, are subtly linked to those of several poems in the collection. Not only is its 'green plain' reminiscent of the green that echoes to the joyful play of children ('The Echoing Green'; Erdman, p. 8), but its central opposition of black to white follows that of 'The Little Black Boy'. In that poem, the little African also imagines escaping his blackness:

> My mother bore me in the southern wild,
> And I am black, but O! my soul is white,
> White as an angel is the English child:
> But I am black as if bereav'd of light.
> (Erdman, p. 9)

This black boy, like Tom in 'The Chimney Sweeper', sees blackness as a deathly deprivation. He is 'bereav'd of light'; Tom is in a coffin of black. Both have a vision. He explores his feelings of inferiority to the white English boy as he imagines them both transformed into lambs joying in the golden light of God's presence:

> For when our souls have learn'd the heat to bear
> The cloud will vanish we shall hear his voice,
> Saying: come out from the grove my love & care,
> And round my golden tent like lambs rejoice.
> Thus did my mother say and kissed me.
> And thus I say to little English boy.
> When I from black and he from white cloud free,
> And round the tent of God like lambs we joy.

Tom Dacre also 'sees' himself transported from the black coffin (his body/the dark and deadly chimney) to 'shine' in the sun of God's energy. Blackness, that is to say, remains for these boys a condition that is to be metamorphosed into another that better reflects the divine energy of love. The little African is not able to view his colour in itself as a positive expression of that energy. It is, his mother tells him, 'but a cloud, and like a shady grove', allowing him to 'bear the beams of love'. It is a heat shield that leaves him better able to bear God's presence than can the white boy:

> I'll shade him from the heat till he can bear
> To lean in joy upon our father's knee.
> And then I'll stand and stroke his silver hair,
> And be like him and he will then love me.

By protecting the delicate-skinned white boy, the African hopes to be liked and to be similar. He has not been able to throw off the anxiety that makes him crave acceptance. Neither, it seems, have Tom Dacre and the friend who speaks for him in 'The Chimney Sweeper'. The joyful freedom of Tom's dream is all too easily converted into a willingness to work that would please their masters. Joy becomes duty just as, for the African boy, a vision of equality subsides into the hope of winning affection by serving.

Similarities to 'The Little Black Boy' make 'The Chimney Sweeper' an exploration of the psychology of one who struggles to liberate himself from complicity with his position, racially and socially, as an inferior and an other.[72] Similarities to 'Holy Thursday' make it a comment on the ideologies that regimented the poor in the names of charity, duty and industriousness. 'Holy Thursday' featured lamb-like children too, not sporting on the green but herded into St Paul's cathedral. These children are paupers, overseen by a 'grey headed beadle', the 'aged men wise guardians of the poor'. Their bodily energies disciplined, the children walk 'two & two' and are 'seated in companies' to hear sermons telling them how grateful they should be as objects of charity (Erdman, p. 13). The equivalent poem in *Songs of Experience* makes Blake's contempt for such charity clear.

> Is this a holy thing to see,
> In a rich and fruitful land,
> Babes reduced to misery,
> Fed with cold and usurous hand?
>
> Is that trembling cry a song?
> Can it be a song of joy?
> And so many children poor?
> It is a land of poverty!
> (Erdman, p. 19)

Charity, Blake implies, depends on the poverty it offers to relieve. In this context 'The Chimney Sweeper' of *Songs of Experience* is part of an attack on a system that is shown to be both social and psychological. Churchgoers perpetuate repression in the name of charity and pity. They satisfy themselves of their righteousness and propriety, thereby licensing themselves to enslave others:

> A little black thing among the snow:
> Crying weep, weep, in notes of woe!
> Where are thy father & mother? say?
> They are both gone up to the church to pray.

> Because I was happy upon the heath,
> And smil'd among the winters snow:
> They clothed me in the clothes of death,
> And taught me to sing the notes of woe.
> (Erdman, pp. 22–3)

The final line brilliantly concentrates Blake's criticism with biting irony – like his aphorism 'Pity would be no more / If we did not make somebody Poor'.

Blake's indictment is one of the most radical of any poetic statements. The simple lines crystallise, as no one else at the time was able to do so powerfully, the psychology of sanctimony and its connections with Church and State. The climbing boy, in Blake's verse, was a figure capable of exposing not only the cruelties of the commercial system, but the complicity of political institutions and religious reformers with that system. It is not surprising that James Montgomery printed only 'The Chimney Sweeper' from *Songs of Innocence*. Its subtle and oblique criticism might go unnoticed. But the poem in *Songs of Experience* leaves no doubt that the sanctimony of those who offered pity and charity to the poor was also Blake's target. The Sunday School abolitionists were, for all their good intentions, themselves part of a system that preferred pity to equality, discipline to freedom, utility to love, industry to energy, sin to joy. In Blake's world, the climbing boy became a radical figure whose 'innocent' words exposed them – a little black boy with much to show the whites. As one of the very few climbing boys made to speak against those who acted and campaigned on his behalf, he should have the last words, words the children labouring in Rumford's workhouse and on West Indian plantations might have echoed if they could:

> And because I am happy, & dance & sing,
> They think they have done me no injury:
> And are gone to praise God & his Priest & King
> Who make up a heaven of our misery.

Conclusion

With Sunday Schools and philanthropic technology we have moved a long way from the naval exploration of 1768 – moved towards the attitudes and trends that would characterise Victorian Britain. We have moved too, from the rural radicalism of early literary Romanticism to the campaigning sanctimony of its 1830s inheritors. We have moved, also, from a period when amateur gentlemen of science acted independently (Banks organising and funding Cook's scientific investigators personally) to a period when institutionalised science was officially dedicated to social reform. We have moved, in short, through the Romantic era into a world that Banksian projects (and the writings – literary as well as scientific – that influenced and were influenced by those projects) helped to create but also tried to resist. Thus, for example, Coleridge and Southey, excited by the power of new science, helped create the public figure of the researcher as national (but no longer revolutionary) hero, lionising Jenner and Rumford. Yet at the same time they resisted the idea that the kinds of technology that Jenner and Rumford had pioneered could counteract the social and moral effects, on the poorer classes of home and empire, of industrial and colonial capitalism. They found themselves, like Blake, objecting to the power of a new – and reactionary – social application of the science whose once-revolutionary implications had inspired them and whose discourse they had helped to define.

In 1768 Britain had been launched on a new voyage by Cook and Banks: now, in 1833, the course was altering. Exploration, and the impetus exploration gave to colonisation, to science and to technology, helped precipitate a bureaucratisation and technologisation of knowledge which Banks presided over but which, ultimately, led in directions that he did not himself take. One of these directions was the increasing specialisation and professionalisation of scientific enquiry itself. By the 1820s, full-time researchers in the developing mathematically based sciences, many of them middle-class, were openly campaigning to remove the power of the upper-class dilettantes (Banks's allies) in the Royal Society. Davy, Banks's successor as President, found himself abused as a stooge of 'royal' and *aristocratical* interest'.[1] For these new professionally minded experimentalists Banks's institutions, having pushed botany and natural history to new eminence on the back of exploration, had ossified. The Royal Society no longer provided adequate direction to science, which was now a body of knowledge of national consequence. The Royal Society and the universities, wrote Charles Babbage, must create a new professional class of researchers, or Britain would fall still further behind its European rivals.

By 1833 science and technology were increasingly viewed as a united activity, as a national achievement to be proud of and of utility in Britain's competition with other nations. It was in this spirit that a new institution was created to provide the impetus that, post-Banks, the Royal Society lacked – the British Association for the Advancement of Science. Together, the Association and the researchers who reported to it would take science beyond Banks's era and his legacy. They made sure, however, that they launched themselves on this voyage by a method to which Banks was accustomed: they invited literary writers to help mould the ideals to which they aspired. Coleridge came to the Cambridge meeting, embodying the continuing link between scientific and literary men, between Romantics of both kinds. But Coleridge did not simply bless the assembled researchers or greet them as his kin. Instead, the old admirer of Priestley and Davy told the gathering that the term 'philosopher' was no longer adequate 'to describe any student of the material world'.[2] In giving this advice he was implicitly accepting that his old 1790s hope for science would not be fulfilled. Natural science would not shortly discover the powers operating in the mind as well as in the physical world. The natural philosophers had taken a different, materialist, path: there was no immediate prospect that all science would become metaphysics. Consequently, a new name for them was needed. The term 'scientist' was proposed and, eventually, adopted. That we still use it today reflects the fact that, as Coleridge the veteran Romantic first saw, natural science had moved away from the Romantic aim of revealing 'the one life within us and abroad'. It was asserting its disciplinary unity by carefully separating itself from the spiritual and theological study of which it had once been part. This was a separation about whose dangerous consequences Mary Shelley had warned in *Frankenstein*; it remained for Coleridge, however, to bring about its formal and institutional designation.

Coleridge was not the only Romantic poet to help inaugurate the British Association. William Sotheby added his words to the Cambridge gathering of 'scientists', defining the aims and achievements of British science in celebratory verses written for the occasion. These verses reveal that, if poets were inspired by science, scientists benefited from the sublimity that poetry conferred upon their work. And they show, too, that Banks's legacy endured, for it was exploration, and the vision into space and time that came from exploration, that Sotheby found most fascinating. Listing Britain's scientific geniuses of recent years, he made them all inheritors of the processes Banks had stimulated and epitomised. He praised John Lindley for placing in 'lucid order' the 'bright flowers that bask beneath the Indian skies' and the fossil ferns of aeons past, 'now sculptured in the stone'.[3] He acclaimed Michael Faraday for decoding the northern lights that Banks's voyagers had described. He lauded Charles Lyell, whose 'advent'rous steps explored' the Alps until he understood how 'time's soft footstep wears the rocks away'.[4] But he reserved his deepest imaginative engagement for John Herschel, the astronomer sailing, like Banks, through the seas so as to find a better spot to explore the skies:

> On him may now propitious gales await!
> On him who to a far and foreign strand,
> A willing exile from his native land,
> Steers boldly on and seeks that southern clime
> Where he by science led, with skill sublime,
> Shall tell each star whose individual light
> Beams through the darkness of the Afric night,
> And weigh the worlds that traversing the sky
> Reserve their secrets for his searching eye,
> While the bright Cross illumining the whole
> With peerless splendour decks th'antarctic pole.[5]

Sotheby's words show that even the new generation of 'scientists' who differed from Banks in many respects owed much of their scope and reach to the knowledge and the networks that Banks made available. So too literary writers: Sotheby could not have written in these terms had Banks not done what he did. It remained the case, for all the difference of 1833 from 1768, that writers and researchers were responding to the information and to the contexts generated (in part) by Banks even when they questioned the uses to which Banks himself put them. Likewise, the earnest social reformers, though their moral utilitarianism differed from Banks's gentlemanly paternalism, owed some of their campaigning drive to the patronage of Banks and of the institutions he helped establish. Banks the Enlightenment gentleman was, in short, the part-progenitor of several of the related movements that shaped the age into a Romantic one – an age made not in his own image but an age that grew as it did because of his paternal legacy. Sir Joseph Banks was a founding father.

Notes

INTRODUCTION: BODIES OF KNOWLEDGE

1. Quoted in Carl Grabo, *A Newton among Poets. Shelley's Use of Science in Prometheus Unbound* (Chapel Hill, 1930), pp. 7–8. T. J. Hogg, *Life of Shelley*, 4 vols. (London, 1858), vol. 1, pp. 59–63.
2. As James Bruce and Commodore Byron both discovered (see chapter 2). On explorers' problems of credibility see Jonathan Lamb, *Preserving the Self in the South Seas, 1680–1840* (Chicago, 2001), pp. 80–2.
3. Thus, in *Biographia Literaria*, Coleridge included three scientific writers – Francis Bacon, Andrew Baxter and Erasmus Darwin – among the names of those whom he thought foremost in Britain's literature. Furthermore, as Roger Sharrock argues, Humphry Davy, close enough to Wordsworth to see his proofs through the press, may have influenced the theories set out in the Preface to *Lyrical Ballads*. See Sharrock, 'The Chemist and the Poet: Sir Humphry Davy and the Preface to *Lyrical Ballads*', *Notes and Records of the Royal Society of London*, 17 (1962), 57–76.
4. De Quincey's 1848 distinction, made in an essay on 'The Poetry of Pope', is reprinted in *De Quincey as Critic*, ed. John E. Jordan (London and Boston, 1973).
5. 'Natural philosopher' and 'man of science', as the cognate terms, will be used throughout this book, save where we refer to the new figure named in 1833.
6. With some very rare exceptions, women were excluded from experimental research in the period: it is in reflection of this exclusion that we use the cognate term 'men of science'. Nevertheless, some eminent women did, despite social restrictions, become active natural philosophers: Caroline Herschel, Jane Marcet and Mary Somerville being the prime examples in Britain. On women in science in the period, see *Uneasy Careers and Intimate Lives: Women in Science 1789–1979*, ed. P. Abir-Am and D. Outram (New Brunswick, N.J., 1987); *Natural Eloquence: Women Reinscribe Science*, ed. Barbara T. Gates and Ann B. Shteir (Madison, Wis., 1997); Londa Schiebinger, *The Mind Has No Sex? Women in the Origins of Modern Science* (Cambridge, Mass., 1989); Ann B. Shteir, *Cultivating Women, Cultivating Science: Flora's Daughters and Botany in England, 1760 to 1860* (Baltimore, 1996).

7. See 'Elegy on Captain Cook', lines 29–35, from Anna Seward, *The Poetical Works*, ed. Walter Scott, 3 vols. (Edinburgh, 1810), vol. II.
8. On the significance of collecting data from travellers in the seventeenth-century Royal Society, see Daniel Carey, 'Compiling Nature's History: Travellers and Travel Narratives in the Early Royal Society', *Annals of Science*, 54 (1997), 269–72. On the Royal Society before Banks see Marie Boas Hall, *Promoting Experimental Learning: Experiment and the Royal Society 1660–1727* (Cambridge, 1991) and M. Hunter, *Science and Society in Restoration England* (Cambridge, 1981).
9. David Philip Miller, 'Joseph Banks, Empire, and "Centers of Calculation" in Late Hanoverian Britain', in *Visions of Empire: Voyages, Botany, and Representations of Nature*, ed. David Philip Miller and Peter Hanns Reill (Cambridge, 1996), pp. 21–37 (p. 23).
10. On precursors of this approach, see Lisbet Koerner, *Linnaeus, Nature and Nation* (Cambridge, Mass., 1999).
11. Mai, the Tahitian name, was corrupted by the British explorers' misunderstanding of the language. We use the incorrect name because it was by this that Mai was known at the time of his visit to Britain.
12. See Jenny Uglow, *The Lunar Men* (London, 2003), for a recent discussion of these networks.
13. On Bentham, the Panopticon and its social purpose see John Bender, *Imagining the Penitentiary: Fiction and the Architecture of Mind in Eighteenth-Century England* (Chicago and London, 1987).
14. Banks oversaw the editing and preparation for the press of Cook's second and third voyage-narratives, which Cowper read.
15. Heather McHugh, plenary lecture at the 2001 conference of the North American Society for the Study of Romanticism, University of Washington, Seattle.
16. Carol Bolton, 'Taking Possession – Romantic Naming in Wordsworth and Southey', in *Silence, Sublimity and Suppression in the Romantic Period*, ed. Fiona L. Price and Scott Masson (Lewiston, Queenston, Lampeter, 2002), pp. 149–68 (pp. 154–5).
17. In *Lyrical Ballads. The Text of the 1798 Edition with the Additional 1800 Poems and the Prefaces*, ed. R. L. Brett and A. R. Jones, 2nd edn (London, 1991), p. 225.
18. Bolton, 'Taking Possession', p. 154.
19. *Orientalism* (London and Harmondsworth, 1985).
20. Pratt, *Imperial Eyes*; Peter Hulme, *Colonial Encounters: Europe and the Native Caribbean 1492–1797* (London and New York, 1986). Also, Stephen Greenblatt (ed.), *New World Encounters* (California, 1993); *Marvellous Possessions* (Chicago and Oxford, 1991); *Learning to Curse* (London and New York, 1990).
21. John Barrell, *The Infection of Thomas De Quincey: A Psychopathology of Imperialism* (New Haven and London, 1991); Nigel Leask, *British Romantic Writers and the East: Anxieties of Empire* (Cambridge, 1992); *Romanticism and Colonialism: Writing and Empire 1780–1830*, ed. Tim Fulford and Peter J. Kitson (Cambridge, 1998); *Romanticism, Race, and Imperial Culture 1780–1834*, ed. Alan Richardson

and Sonia Hofkosh (Bloomington, Ind., 1996). See also Nigel Leask, *Curiosity and the Aesthetics of Travel Writing, 1770–1840* (Oxford, 2002).
22. Abdul R. JanMohamed, 'The Economy of Manichean Allegory: The Function of Racial Difference in Colonialist Literature', in *'Race', Writing, and Difference*, ed. Henry Louis Gates, Jr. (Chicago and London, 1985), pp. 78–106.
23. Homi K. Bhabha, 'Signs Taken for Wonders', in *Europe and its Others*, ed. Francis Barker *et al.*, 2 vols. (Colchester, 1985), vol. I, pp. 89–106; 'The Other Question . . . the Stereotype and Colonial Discourse', *Screen*, 24.6 (Nov./Dec. 1983), 18–36.
24. In *Science in Action*. On Latour and travel writing, see Leask, *Curiosity and the Aesthetics of Travel Writing*, pp. 18–23.
25. H. B. Carter, *Sir Joseph Banks, 1743–1820* (London, 1988); David Mackay, *In the Wake of Cook: Exploration, Science and Empire 1780–1801* (London, 1985); John Gascoigne, *Joseph Banks and the English Enlightenment: Useful Knowledge and Polite Culture* (Cambridge, 1994); *Science in the Service of Empire: Joseph Banks, the British State and the Uses of Science in the Age of Revolution* (Cambridge, 1998).
26. Nicholas Thomas, *Entangled Objects: Exchange, Material Culture, and Colonialism in the Pacific* (Cambridge, Mass., 1991), *Colonialism's Culture: Anthropology, Travel and Government* (Cambridge, 1994), *Marquesan Societies. Inequality and Political Transformation in Eastern Polynesia* (Oxford, 1990), *In Oceania: Visions, Artifacts, Histories* (Durham and London, 1997).
27. Bernard Smith, *European Vision and the South Pacific 1768–1850* (Oxford, 1960). Many of the texts Smith discusses are easily accessible in *Exploration and Exchange. A South Seas Anthology, 1680–1900*, ed. Jonathan Lamb, Vanessa Smith and Nicholas Thomas (London and Chicago, 2000).
28. Philip Edwards, *The Story of the Voyage: Sea-Narratives in Eighteenth-Century England* (Cambridge, 1994) and Neil Rennie, *Far Fetched Facts: The Literature of Travel and the Idea of the South Seas* (Oxford, 1992). Also Rod Edmond, *Representing the South Pacific: Colonial Discourse from Cook to Gauguin* (Cambridge, 1997) and Vanessa Smith, *Literary Culture and the Pacific. Nineteenth-Century Textual Encounters* (Cambridge, 1998).
29. Greg Dening, *Mr Bligh's Bad Language: Passion, Power and Theatre on the Bounty* (Cambridge, 1992); see note 26 above for Thomas.
30. See Marshall Sahlins, *Islands of History* (Chicago and London, 1985) and Peter V. Kirch and Marshall Sahlins, *Anahulu: The Anthropology of History in the Kingdom of Hawaii* (Chicago and London, 1992), Gannath Obeyesekere, *The Apotheosis of Captain Cook: European Mythmaking in the Pacific* (Princeton, N.J., and London, 1992).
31. James Walvin, *Fruits of Empire. Exotic Produce and British Taste, 1660–1800* (Basingstoke, 1997), Henry Hobhouse, *Seeds of Change. Six Plants that Transformed Mankind* (London, 1999).
32. Hugh Thomas, *The Slave Trade. The History of the Atlantic Slave Trade, 1440–1870* (London, 1997), Philip D. Curtin, *The Image of Africa: British Ideas and Actions 1780–1850* (London and Madison, Wis., 1964), James Walvin, *Black Ivory: A History of British Slavery* (London, 1992).

33. Catherine Hall, *White, Male and Middle-Class. Explorations in Feminism and History* (Cambridge, 1992).
34. Barbara Stafford, *Voyage into Substance: Art, Science, Nature, and the Illustrated Travel Account* (Cambridge, 1984) and *Body Criticism: Imaging the Unseen in Enlightenment Art and Medicine* (Cambridge, Mass., 1991); Ludmilla Jordanova, *Sexual Visions: Images of Gender in Science and Medicine between the Eighteenth and Twentieth Centuries* (Hemel Hempstead, 1989); Londa Schiebinger, *Nature's Body: Gender in the Making of Modern Science* (Boston, 1993).
35. Stephen Jay Gould, *The Mismeasure of Man* (Harmondsworth, 1981) and 'The Hottentot Venus', *Natural History*, 91 (1982), 20–7.
36. Nicholas Hudson, 'From "Nation" to "Race": The Origins of Racial Classification in Eighteenth-Century Thought', *Eighteenth-Century Studies*, 29 (1996), 247–64, Robert J. C. Young, *Colonial Desire: Hybridity in Theory, Culture and Race* (London and New York, 1995), David Theo Goldberg, *Racist Culture: Philosophy and the Politics of Meaning* (Oxford, 1993), *Race: The Origins of an Idea, 1760–1850*, ed. Hannah Franziska Augstein (Bristol, 1996), David Bindman, *Ape to Apollo. Aesthetics and the Idea of Race in the Eighteenth Century* (London, 2002), Roxann Wheeler, *The Complexion of Race. Categories of Difference in Eighteenth-Century British Culture* (Philadelphia, 2000).
37. Schaffer, 'Natural Philosophy and Public Spectacle in the Eighteenth Century', *History of Science*, 21 (1983), 1–43 and 'States of Mind: Enlightenment and Natural Philosophy', in *The Languages of Psyche: Mind and Body in Enlightenment Thought*, ed. G. S. Rousseau (Berkeley, Los Angeles, Oxford, 1990), pp. 233–90; Golinski, *Science as Public Culture: Chemistry and Enlightenment in Britain, 1760–1820* (Cambridge, 1992); Patricia Fara, *Sympathetic Attractions. Magnetic Practices, Beliefs, and Symbolism in Eighteenth-Century England* (Princeton, N.J., 1996).
38. See Roy Porter (ed.), *Patients and Practitioners* (Cambridge, 1985), *Thomas Beddoes and the Sick Trade in Late-Enlightenment England* (London, 1992), and '"Under the Influence": Mesmerism in England', *History Today*, 35.ix (1985), 22–9 (p. 28).
39. Grabo, *A Newton among Poets*.
40. King-Hele, *Doctor of Revolution: The Life and Genius of Erasmus Darwin* (London, 1977); Knight, *Humphry Davy: Science and Power* (Cambridge, 1992).
41. Levere, *Poetry Realized in Nature: Samuel Taylor Coleridge and Early Nineteenth-Century Science* (Cambridge, 1981).
42. Bewell, *Romanticism and Colonial Disease* (Baltimore and London, 1999).

1 SIR JOSEPH BANKS AND HIS NETWORKS

1. For a positive assessment of Sloane's combination of many of the roles Banks was later to fill, see Maarten Ultee, 'Sir Hans Sloane, Scientist', *British Library Journal*, 14 (1988), 1–20. See also Arthur MacGregor, 'The Natural History Correspondence of Sir Hans Sloane', *Archives of Natural History*, 22.1 (1995), 79–90.

2. Coleridge quotes Banks in a letter of 17 February, 1803; *CL*, vol. II, pp. 933–4.
3. See John Gascoigne, *Science in the Service of Empire: Joseph Banks, the British State and the Uses of Science in the Age of Revolution* (Cambridge, 1998), p. 198.
4. See *Joseph Banks in Newfoundland and Labrador, 1766; His Diary, Manuscripts and Collections*, ed. A. M. Lysaght (London, 1971).
5. T. H. Watkins, 'Sir Joseph Banks: The Greening of the Empire', *National Geographic Magazine*, 190.5 (1996), 28–53 (p. 36).
6. Banks's descriptions of the voyage can be found in *The Endeavour Journal of Joseph Banks 1768–1771*, ed. J. C. Beaglehole, 2 vols. (Sydney, 1962).
7. Neil Chambers, 'Letters from the President: The Correspondence of Sir Joseph Banks', *Notes and Records of the Royal Society of London*, 53 (1999), 27–57 (p. 33).
8. See James L. Larson, *Reason and Experience: The Representation of Natural Order in the Work of Carl von Linné* (Berkeley, Los Angeles, London, 1971), pp. 109–15.
9. Later, however, Banks would prefer the 'natural' system of De Jussieu, which updated Linnaeus – incorporating more, and more naturally occurring, criteria for classifying plants. On this development see John Gascoigne, *Science in the Service of Empire*, p. 3.
10. Quoted in Watkins, 'Greening of the Empire', 47.
11. On correspondence and the development of the Royal Society see Marie Boas Hall, 'The Royal Society's Role in the Diffusion of Information in the Seventeenth Century', *Notes and Records of the Royal Society*, 28 (1973–4), 173–92, and Michael Hunter, *Establishing the New Science: The Experience of the Early Royal Society* (Woodbridge, 1989). On the importance of correspondence networks in developing seventeenth- and eighteenth-century forms of knowledge see Maarten Ultee, 'The Republic of Letters: Learned Correspondence, 1680–1720', *The Seventeenth Century*, 2 (1987), 95–112; Lorraine Daston, 'The Ideal and Reality of the Republic of Letters in the Enlightenment', *Science in Context*, 4 (1991), 367–86.
12. Banks's correspondence can be placed in context by comparison with the practices discussed by Anne Secord, 'Corresponding Interests: Artisans and Gentlemen in Nineteenth-Century Natural History', *BJHS*, 27 (1994), 383–408.
13. Letter of 1778; quoted in Lisbet Koerner, 'Purposes of Linnean Travel: A Preliminary Research Report', in *Visions of Empire: Voyages, Botany, and Representations of Nature*, ed. David Philip Miller and Peter Hanns Reill (Cambridge, 1996), pp. 117–52 (p. 129).
14. The *Florilegium* was never completed or published in Banks's lifetime, however.
15. Quoted in Patrick O'Brian, *Sir Joseph Banks: A Life* (London, 1987), pp. 168–70.
16. Reproduction, that is to say, would bring exotic colour to the abstract terms of the Linnaean system. It would not, however, illustrate the natural or cultural habitat in which the plants grew. What Paul Carter has termed the 'claims of locality', the 'subtler influences of climate, ground, and aspect' were absent from the pictures, which presented plants on a white background. Banks's botany would not, unlike the later botany of Alexander von Humboldt,

explore the specificity of a plant in its environment. See Paul Carter, *The Road to Botany Bay: An Exploration of Landscape and History* (Chicago, 1987), pp. 22–4.

17. See Alan Bewell, 'On the Banks of the South Sea: Botany and Sexual Controversy in the Late Eighteenth Century', in *Visions of Empire*, ed. Miller and Reill, pp. 173–96. Also, Colin Roderick, 'Joseph Banks, Queen Oberea and the Satirists', in *Captain James Cook: Image and Impact*, ed. Walter Veit (Melbourne, 1972), pp. 67–89.

18. Banks had a hand in the publication of, amongst others, Constantine John Phipps, *A Voyage towards the North Pole, Undertaken by His Majesty's Command, 1773* (London, 1774); James Cook, *Voyage to the Pacific Ocean . . . for Making Discoveries in the Northern Hemisphere* (London, 1784); William Bligh, *A Voyage to the South Sea, undertaken by command of His Majesty, for the purpose of conveying the Breadfruit Tree to the West Indies, in His Majesty's Ship the Bounty . . . Including an account of the Mutiny on Board the Said Ship, etc.* (London, 1792); *The Journal of Frederick Hornemann's Travels, from Cairo to Mourzouk, the Capital of the Kingdom of Fezzan, in Africa in the Years 1797–8* (London, 1802); Matthew Flinders, *A Voyage to Terra Australis, Undertaken for the Purpose of Completing the Discovery of that Vast Country, and Prosecuted in the Years 1801, 1802 And 1803, in His Majesty's Ship the Investigator, and Subsequently in the . . . Porpoise and Cumberland Schooner. With an Account of the Shipwreck of the Porpoise, Arrival of the Cumberland at Mauritius, and Imprisonment of the Commander . . . in that Island*, 2 vols. (London, 1814); Johan Ludwig Burckhardt, *Travels in Nubia; By the Late John Lewis Burckhardt* (London, 1819). See David MacKay, 'A Presiding Genius of Exploration: Banks, Cook, and Empire, 1767–1805', in *Captain James Cook and his Times*, ed. Robin Fisher and Hugh Johnston (Vancouver and London, 1979), pp. 21–39. Also, Glyndwr Williams, '"The Common Centre of We Discoverers": Sir Joseph Banks, Exploration and Empire in the Late Eighteenth Century', in *Sir Joseph Banks: A Global Perspective*, ed. R. E. R. Banks, B. Elliott, J. G. Hawkes, D. King-Hele and G. Lucas (London, 1994), pp. 177–91.

19. John Gascoigne, 'The Ordering of Nature and the Ordering of Empire: A Commentary', in *Visions of Empire*, ed. Miller and Reill, pp. 107–13 (p. 108). Also, David Philip Miller, 'Joseph Banks, Empire, and "Centers of Calculation" in Late Hanoverian Britain', in *Visions of Empire*, ed. Miller and Reill, pp. 21–37.

20. Robert Montgomery, *The Age Reviewed: A Satire in Two Parts*, 2nd edn (London, 1828), pp. 173–6.

21. Latour, *Science in Action*, p. 218.

22. Quoted in O'Brian, *Sir Joseph Banks*, pp. 168–70. This letter refers to the collection when it was located at Banks's house in New Burlington Street.

23. In H. B. Carter, *Sir Joseph Banks, 1743–1820* (London, 1988), p. 380.

24. Quoted in O'Brian, *Sir Joseph Banks*, pp. 168–70.

25. Douglas Oliver, *Return to Tahiti: Bligh's Second Breadfruit Voyage* (Honolulu, 1988), p. 97.

26. Carter, *Sir Joseph Banks*, p. 363.

27. On the importance of gardeners and gardens see K. W. Spence-Lewis, *Sir Joseph Banks. Royal Botanic Garden St. Vincent 1764–1820* (Seattle, London, St Vincent, 1994), and Ray Desmond, *Kew. The History of the Royal Botanic Gardens* (London, 1995), pp. 88–122.
28. Erasmus Darwin, *The Botanic Garden, a Poem. In Two Parts. Part I Containing the Economy of Vegetation, Part II. The Loves of the Plants*, 4th edn (London, 1799), canto IV, line 592.
29. Letter of 1 December 1815; *DTC*, vol. XIX, pp. 221–2.
30. Banks was well aware that in France his role was a government objective. Science and exploration were state-sponsored priorities there, as revealed by the expeditions of d'Entrecasteaux in 1791 and Baudin in 1801, sent by the Institut National to chart and collect in the South Pacific and determine the fate of La Pérouse's lost expedition of 1788. On this rivalry, see David Mackay, *In the Wake of Cook: Exploration, Science and Empire 1780–1801* (London, 1985), pp. 125–31.
31. Banks to James Wiles, 25 June 1791, *DTC*, vol. VII, pp. 218–26.
32. We are indebted to Neil Chambers, Curator of the Banks Archive, Natural History Museum, for this idea.
33. Quoted in Carter, *Sir Joseph Banks*, p. 26.
34. Letter of 3 March 1796; *DTC*, vol. X (1), p. 18.
35. Margaret Steven, *Trade, Tactics and Territory: Britain in the Pacific 1783–1823* (Melbourne, 1983), pp. 1–63.
36. Letter of 13 April 1786; *DTC*, vol. VII, p. 31.
37. Letter of 13 April 1786; ibid.
38. Letter of 16 April 1787; *DTC*, vol. VII, p. 47.
39. Ibid., vol. X, pp. 25–8.
40. On Banks and the Royal Society, see John Gascoigne, *Joseph Banks and the English Enlightenment: Useful Knowledge and Polite Culture* (Cambridge, 1994).

2 TAHITI IN LONDON; LONDON IN TAHITI: TOOLS OF POWER

1. Quoted in James Walvin, *Fruits of Empire: Exotic Produce and British Taste, 1660–1800* (Basingstoke, 1997), p. 158.
2. Quoted in ibid.
3. We use 'Polynesian' as the term that, by the 1830s and since, has most often been used in Europe to describe a group of peoples into which Society Islanders supposedly fell. More recently, as Nicholas Thomas shows, the term has been challenged as a European imposition on people of different backgrounds. See Thomas, *In Oceania: Visions, Artifacts, Histories* (Durham and London, 1997), pp. 133–55.
4. On coffee and tea and the culture arising from their import, see Henry Hobhouse, *Seeds of Change. Six Plants that Transformed Mankind* (London, 1999), and Anthony Farrington, *Trading Places: The East India Company and Asia 1600–1834* (London, 2002), p. 110.

5. Anna Laetitia Barbauld, *Eighteen Hundred and Eleven, a Poem* (London, 1812).
6. Walvin, *Fruits of Empire*, p. 190.
7. The name Omai was the explorers' misinterpretation of Mai. We use it because it was by that title that he was known by the British.
8. Our presentation of Omai's story is indebted throughout to E. H. McCormick's sensitive account *Omai Pacific Envoy* (Auckland and Oxford, 1977).
9. Louis Antoine de Bougainville had also returned to Europe from Tahiti with an islander on board: Aotourou, who had fascinated Parisian society. And Omai was preceded as a voyager to Britain by Tupaia, a Tahitian 'priest' who accompanied Banks on the *Endeavour*, only to die at Batavia before reaching his destination. On these visits see McCormick, *Omai*, p. 20, and Neil Rennie, *Far-Fetched Facts. The Literature of Travel and the Idea of the South Seas* (Oxford, 1992), pp. 109–25.
10. In interpreting Omai's words we are conscious that we rely on British transcriptions – either of his limited English or of translations of his Tahitian. All the evidence, then, is shaped by the British explorers and hosts of his visit. Remaining conscious of this fact, we do not claim unmediated access to Omai's views, but simply note that he is reported in similar terms by a large number of witnesses who encountered him at different times.
11. Burney's Private Journal, quoted in McCormick, *Omai*, p. 55.
12. Sarah S. Banks, 'Memorandums', quoted in McCormick, *Omai*, p. 105.
13. Georg Forster, *A Voyage Round the World*, 2 vols. (London, 1777), vol. 1, pp. 388–9. Quoted in McCormick, *Omai*, p. 53.
14. Quoted in Bernard Smith, *European Vision and the South Pacific 1768–1850*, 2nd edn (New Haven and London, 1985), p. 82.
15. According to Harriet Guest, the portrait 'privileges the exoticism rather than the Orientalism of the image' and 'inscribes its object with an acultural illegibility, isolated from any coherence of origin'. See Harriet Guest, 'Curiously Marked: Tattooing, Masculinity, and Nationality in Eighteenth-Century British Perceptions of the South Pacific', in *Painting and the Politics of Culture: New Essays on British Art 1700–1850*, ed. John Barrell (Oxford and New York, 1992), pp. 101–34 (p. 102). Caroline Turner has shown, however, that Omai is posed so as to be decipherable to European eyes, in dress that is an accurate representation of high-ranking Tahitians' clothes (and that, as Turner contends, he most likely brought to the sitting himself: see Caroline Turner, 'Images of Mai', in *Cook and Omai: The Cult of the South Seas* (Canberra, 2001), pp. 26–7).
16. In 'Curiously Marked', p. 112, Guest makes the *absence* of Omai's tattoo from the painting an intentional part of the artist's meaning. Turner, however (in 'Images of Mai' p. 26), summarises evidence to show that the tattoos were probably in the original painting, and were removed when it was cleaned in the twentieth century.
17. Blumenbach's letter to Banks, 8 January 1794. Quoted in McCormick, *Omai*, p. 331.
18. Lawrence had seen the painting by William Hodges held in the collection of artefacts that John Hunter had bequeathed. For the engraving and Lawrence's

racial theory see his *Lectures on Physiology, Zoology and the Natural History of Man*, 3rd edn (London, 1823), p. 489.
19. *The Endeavour Journal of Joseph Banks*, vol. I, p. 341.
20. Boswell, *Life of Johnson*, quoted in Rennie, *Far-Fetched Facts*, p. 127.
21. Sandwich's letter of 29 December 1774, quoted in McCormick, *Omai*, p. 131.
22. Fanny Burney's letter, quoted in McCormick, *Omai*, pp. 168–9.
23. Notebook of the Revd J. E. Gambier, quoted in ibid., p. 103.
24. Sarah S. Banks, 'Memorandums', pp. 15–17, quoted in ibid., p. 113.
25. Notebook of the Revd J. E. Gambier, quoted in ibid., p. 103.
26. Ibid.
27. *Seventeen Hundred and Seventy-Seven: Or, A Picture of the Manners and Character of the Age. In A Poetical Epistle From a Lady of Quality in England, to Omiah at Otaheite* (Dublin, 1777), pp. 22–3.
28. Quoted in Rennie, *Far-Fetched Facts*, p. 101.
29. As Iain McCalman has shown in his article 'Spectacles of Knowledge: OMAI as Ethnographic Travelogue', in *Cook and Omai*, p. 11.
30. Ibid.
31. Marina Warner, *Fantastic Metamorphoses, Other Worlds: Ways of Telling the Self* (Oxford, 2002), p. 143.
32. On these see Harriet Guest, 'Omai's Things', in *Cook and Omai*, pp. 32–3. Guest also reminds us that conservative and Evangelical Britons – William Bligh among them – regretted that nobody had instructed Omai, while in Britain, in Christianity or useful knowledge – so that he could convert and impress the islanders.
33. Cook's words, from *The Journals of Captain James Cook on his Voyages of Discovery*, ed. J. C. Beaglehole, 3 vols. (Cambridge, 1955–67), quoted in McCormick, *Omai*, p. 228.
34. J. Rickman, *Journal of Captain Cook's Last Voyage to the Pacific Ocean* (London, 1781), quoted in McCormick, *Omai*, p. 228.
35. Cook quoted in McCormick, *Omai*, p. 239.
36. *The Journals of Captain James Cook*, ed. Beaglehole, vol. III, p. 1059, quoted in McCormick, *Omai*, p. 236.
37. Letter of 6 October 1783 in *The Letters and Prose Writings of William Cowper*, ed. James King and Charles Ryskamp, 5 vols. (Oxford, 1979–86), vol. II, p. 168.
38. Letter of August 1784 in ibid., p. 271.
39. Letter of 16 August 1784 in ibid., p. 273.
40. *The Journals of Captain James Cook*, quoted in McCormick, *Omai*, p. 225.
41. Ibid.
42. *The Journal of James Morrison*, ed. O. Rutter (London, 1935), quoted in McCormick, *Omai*, pp. 271–2.
43. W. Ellis, *Polynesian Researches*, 4 vols. (London, 1853), quoted in McCormick, *Omai*, p. 293.

44. It should be pointed out, however, that contact between the servants of the East India Company and local rulers in Asia, where East–West relations had been in progress for centuries, was strikingly different from contact between Europeans and the peoples of North America or the South Pacific, where – as Peter Marshall discusses – 'cultures had been cut off from one another in historic times and had developed in very different ways'. See P. J. Marshall, 'The Legacies of Two Hundred Years of Contact', in *The Worlds of the East India Company*, ed. H. V. Bowen, Margarette Lincoln and Nigel Rigby (Leicester, 2002), pp. 223–37 (pp. 223–4).
45. Ahmat bin Adam, A Descriptive Account of the Malay Letters sent to Thomas Stamford Raffles in Malacca in 1810 and 1811 by the Rulers of the Indigenous States of the Malay Archipelago. September 1971. Unpublished manuscript, 11. MSS/EUR/C842, Oriental and India Office, British Library.
46. Ibid., pp. 62–3.
47. C. E. Wurtzburg, *Raffles of the Eastern Isles* (Singapore, 1954, [rpt 1984]), p. 421.
48. Banks corresponded extensively with Raffles on the natural history and ethnology of the East Indies. In the words of John Gascoigne, 'such studies provided Raffles with the familiarity with local conditions which enabled him to effect the purchase of Singapore Island for the East India Company in 1819, thus extending the effective reach of the British Empire'. John Gascoigne, *Joseph Banks and the English Enlightenment: Useful Knowledge and Polite Culture* (Cambridge, 1994), p. 182.
49. *The Autobiography of Munshi Abdullah*, trs. the Revd W. G. Shellabear (Singapore, 1918), p. 53.
50. John Bastin, 'Raffles the Naturalist', in *The Golden Sword: Stamford Raffles and the East*, ed. Nigel Barley (London, 1998), pp. 18–29.
51. Extending British influence in Java and Sumatra was the aim of Banks's correspondent Henry Colebrooke, who argued for keeping Java so as to provide 'a Mart for our Manufactures & an Emporium for our Trade'. Banks himself regretted that Java was handed back to the Dutch and hoped Britain would not give ground in Sumatra. See Gascoigne, *Science in the Service of Empire: Joseph Banks, the British State and the Uses of Science in the Age of Revolution* (Cambridge, 1998), p. 176, where Colebrooke is quoted.

3 INDIAN FLOWERS AND ROMANTIC ORIENTALISM

1. James Montgomery, *Poems*, ed. Robert Aris Willmott (London, 1855), pp. 251–3.
2. This impact is discussed in *Visions of Empire: Voyages, Botany, and Representations of Nature*, ed. David Philip Miller and Peter Hans Reill (Cambridge, 1996).
3. Banks's letter of 15 May 1787, in *The Letters of Sir Joseph Banks. A Selection, 1768–1820*, ed. Neil Chambers (London, 2000), p. 89.
4. See Mildred Archer, 'India and Natural History; the Role of the East India Company 1785–1858', *History Today*, 9 (1959), 736.

5. Kyd's letter of 15 April 1786, quoted in Kalipada Biswas, *The Original Correspondence of Sir Joseph Banks Relating to the Foundation of the Royal Botanic Garden Calcutta* (Calcutta, 1950), pp. 3–4.
6. Abstract of Kyd's proposal submitted by the Company to Banks for his opinion, *DTC*, vol. VII, p. 35.
7. *The Letters of Sir Joseph Banks,* ed. Chambers, p. 90.
8. Banks's memorandum to the Court of Directors of the East India Company, *DTC*, vol. VII, p. 31.
9. Banks's letter of 15 May 1787, *The Letters of Sir Joseph Banks,* ed. Chambers, p. 90.
10. Letter of 4 July 1794, *DTC*, vol. IX, pp. 52–6.
11. In her *Picturing Imperial Power: Colonial Subjects in Eighteenth-Century British Painting* (Durham and London, 1999), pp. 195–201, Beth Fowkes Tobin argues that the persistence of the particular in these Indian images subverts the generalising Linnaean project they were commissioned to aid.
12. Quoted in Deepak Kumar, 'The Evolution of Colonial Science in India: Natural History and the East India Company', in *Imperialism and the Natural World*, ed. John M. MacKenzie (Manchester and New York, 1990), p. 53. See also Satpal Sangwan, 'Natural History in Colonial Context: Profit or Pursuit? British Botanical Enterprise in India, 1778–1820', in *Science and Empires: Historical Studies about Scientific Development and European Expansion*, ed. P. Petitjean, Catherine Jami and Anne Moulin (Dordrecht, Boston and London, 1992), pp. 283–98.
13. On Banks at Kew see Ray Desmond, *Kew. The History of the Royal Botanic Gardens* (London, 1995), pp. 88–122.
14. Henry Jones, *Kew Garden. A Poem. In Two Cantos* (London, 1767), canto II, lines 111–12.
15. See *The Letters of Erasmus Darwin*, ed. Desmond King-Hele (Cambridge, 1981), pp. 109, 116, 122. *The System of Vegetables*, trs. The Botanical Society of Lichfield (London, 1783–5) and *The Families of Plants*, trs. The Botanical Society of Lichfield (London, 1787).
16. See the Prefaces to *The System of Vegetables* and *The Families of Plants*.
17. *The Botanic Garden, a Poem. In Two Parts. Part I Containing the Economy of Vegetation, Part II. The Loves of the Plants*, 4th edn (London, 1799), canto IV, lines 591–4.
18. On botanic gardens as symbols of a benevolent empire, see Richard Drayton, *Nature's Government: Science, Imperial Britain and the 'Improvement' of the World* (New Haven and London, 2000), pp. 115, 117, 121.
19. *The Botanic Garden*, p. 164.
20. For Darwin's career generally, see Desmond King-Hele, *Doctor of Revolution: The Life and Genius of Erasmus Darwin* (London, 1977).
21. Ann B. Shteir, *Cultivating Women, Cultivating Science: Flora's Daughters and Botany in England 1760–1860* (Baltimore, 1996); Janet Browne, 'Botany for Gentlemen: Erasmus Darwin and *The Loves of the Plants*', *Isis*, 80 (1989), 593–621. See also David Elliston Allen, *The Naturalist in Britain. A Social*

History (Harmondsworth, 1978). For Darwin's influence on feminist writers, see Luisa Calè, '"A Female Band despising Nature's Law": Botany, Gender and Revolution in the 1790s', *Romanticism on the Net*, 17 (February 2000), http://users.ox.ac.uk/~scat0385/17botany.html

22. In Desmond King-Hele, *Erasmus Darwin and the Romantic Poets* (Basingstoke, 1986); also Robert M. Maniquis, 'The Puzzling *Mimosa*: Sensitivity and Plant Symbols in Romanticism', *Studies in Romanticism*, 8 (1969), 129–55.
23. See Garland Cannon, *The Life and Mind of Oriental Jones: Sir William Jones, the Father of Modern Linguistics* (Cambridge, 1991) and *Objects of Enquiry: The Life, Contributions and Influences of Sir William Jones (1746–1794)*, ed. Garland Cannon and Kevin R. Brine (New York and London, 1995).
24. Letter of 22 September 1787, *The Letters of Sir William Jones*, ed. Garland Cannon, 2 vols. (Oxford, 1970), vol. II, p. 776.
25. First published in the *Asiatick Researches*. We quote it here from *The Works of Sir William Jones*, 13 vols. (London, 1807), vol. v, p. 1.
26. Edward Said, *Orientalism* (London and Harmondsworth, 1985); for further debate on this idea, see also John M. MacKenzie, *Orientalism: History, Theory and the Arts* (Manchester and New York, 1995); Rana Kabbani, *Imperial Fictions: Europe's Myths of Orient* (London, 1986); Mohammed Sharafuddin, *Islam and Romantic Orientalism: Literary Encounters with the Orient* (London, 1995).
27. Letter of 18 October 1791, *The Letters of Sir William Jones*, vol. II, p. 892.
28. *The Design of a Treatise on the Plants of India*, *Works of Sir William Jones*, vol. v, pp. 2–3.
29. *Botanical Observations on Select Indian Plants*, *Works of Sir William Jones*, vol. v, p. 63.
30. See *Sir William Jones. Selected Poetical and Prose Works*, ed. Michael J. Franklin (Cardiff, 1995), p. 214.
31. See *The Life and Mind of Oriental Jones*, p. 335; also Garland Cannon, 'Oriental Jones, Scholarship, Literature, Multiculturalism, and Humankind', in *Objects of Enquiry*, ed. Cannon and Brine, pp. 25–50.
32. Quoted in *Sir William Jones. Selected Poetical and Prose Works*, p. 213. On Jones's influence in Europe see Raymond Schwab, *The Oriental Renaissance: Europe's Rediscovery of India and the East, 1680–1880*, trs. Gene Patterson Black and Victor Reinking (New York, 1984).
33. Quoted in *Sir William Jones. Selected Poetical and Prose Works*, p. 213. Jones's effect on German philosophy and poetry is considered in E. S. Shaffer, *Kubla Khan and 'The Fall of Jerusalem': The Mythological School in Biblical Criticism and Secular Literature 1770–1880* (Cambridge, 1975), pp. 116–44.
34. *Sacontalá, or, The Fatal Ring*, in *Sir William Jones. Selected Poetical and Prose Works*, p. 388.
35. *Design of a Treatise*, *The Works of Sir William Jones*, vol. v, pp. 2–3.
36. *Botanical Observations on Select Indian Plants*, *The Works of Sir William Jones*, vol. v, p. 124.
37. *The Poetical Works of Robert Southey, Collected by Himself*, 10 vols. (London, 1838), vol. VIII, p. xv.

38. Ibid., pp. xvi–xvii.
39. Ibid., pp. 83–4.
40. In *Sir William Jones. Selected Poetical and Prose Works*, p. 102.
41. *Botanical Observations*, *The Works of Sir William Jones*, vol. v, pp. 139–40, quoted in *Sir William Jones. Selected Poetical and Prose Works*, p. 102.
42. On Southey's Orientalisation of the epic, see Marilyn Butler, 'Orientalism', in *The Penguin History of Literature: The Romantic Period*, ed. David Pirie (Harmondsworth, 1994), pp. 395–447. Also, Nigel Leask, *British Romantic Writers and the East: Anxieties of Empire* (Cambridge, 1992) and Javed Majeed, *Ungoverned Imaginings: James Mill's 'History of British India' and Orientalism* (Oxford, 1992).
43. *The Eclectic Review*, 8 (April 1811), 334–50; quoted in *Robert Southey: The Critical Heritage*, ed. Lionel Madden (London and Boston, 1972), p. 140; *Monthly Review* quoted in Southey's Preface to *Kehama*, *The Poetical Works of Robert Southey*, vol. VIII, p. xxi.
44. *Monthly Review* quoted in Southey's Preface to *Kehama*, *The Poetical Works of Robert Southey*, vol. VIII, p. xx.
45. Ibid.
46. *Selections from the Letters of Robert Southey*, ed. J. W. Warter, 4 vols. (London, 1856), vol. II, pp. 75, 96.
47. *Byron's Letters and Journals*, ed. Leslie Marchand, 12 vols. (London 1973–82), vol. III, p. 101.
48. See Majeed, *Ungoverned Imaginings*, pp. 93–100.
49. *The Poetical Works of Thomas Moore, Collected by Himself*, 10 vols. (London, 1844), vol. VI, pp. 153–4.
50. Thomas Medwin, *The Angler in Wales, or Days and Nights of Sportsmen*, 2 vols. (London, 1834), vol. II, p. 73. See Leask, *Romantic Writers*, pp. 155–6, for a discussion of this passage.
51. Wordsworth, *The Prelude* (1805), book XIII, line 442.

4 MENTAL TRAVELLERS: BANKS, AFRICAN EXPLORATION AND THE ROMANTIC IMAGINATION

1. As Ashton Nichols shows in his article, 'Mumbo Jumbo: Mungo Park and the Rhetoric of Romantic Africa', in *Romanticism, Race and Imperial Culture, 1780–1834*, ed. Alan Richardson and Sonia Hofkosh (Bloomington, Ind., 1996), pp. 93–113.
2. François Le Vaillant, *New Travels into the Interior Parts of Africa By the Way of the Cape of Good Hope in the Years 1783, 84, and 85*, 3 vols. (London, 1796), vol. II, p. 117.
3. Ibid., p. 143.
4. Quoted in Francis Masson, *Account of Three Journeys at the Cape of Good Hope 1772–1775*, ed. Frank R. Bradlow (Cape Town, 1994), p. 19.
5. He also found a new species of aloe and the unusual green ixia, *I. viridiflora*. On Masson's achievements, see Ray Desmond, *Kew. The History of the*

Royal Botanic Gardens (London, 1995), p. 95; see also Tyler Whittle, *The Plant Hunters* (London, 1970), pp. 63–4 and Toby Musgrave, Chris Gardner and Will Musgrave, *The Plant Hunters: Two Hundred Years of Adventure and Discovery around the World* (London, 1998), pp. 44–8.
6. Masson, *Account of Three Journeys*, p. 34.
7. Quoted in ibid., p. 38.
8. Quoted in ibid., p. 37.
9. 'An Account of Three Journeys from Cape Town into the Southern Parts of Africa undertaken for the Discovery of New Plants towards the improvement of the Royal Botanical Gardens at Kew', *Philosophical Transactions of the Royal Society*, 66 (1776), 268–317.
10. Letter of Masson to Banks, 13 November 1787, quoted in Masson, *Account of Three Journeys*, p. 57.
11. Ritchie was selected for the journey by Banks, who advised upon it and was informed of its progress, as letters from him to Charles Blagden make clear (13 October 1817 and 30 September 1819, Royal Society of London, Banks papers 63 and 78 respectively). Ritchie was supposed to answer the question that had vexed Banks for twenty years: where did the river Niger flow? Ritchie left in 1818 with naval officer George Francis Lyon as his companion. Though Ritchie died, Lyon returned and published *A Narrative of Travels in Northern Africa, in the Years 1818, 19, And 20, Accompanied by Geographical Notices of Soudan, and of the Course of the Niger* (London, 1821). Banks also helped publish the narratives of other explorers, including *The Journal of Frederick Hornemann's Travels, from Cairo to Mourzouk, the Capital of the Kingdom of Fezzan, in Africa in the years 1797–8* (London, 1802) and Johan Ludwig Burckhardt, *Travels in Nubia; by the Late John Lewis Burckhardt* (London, 1819).
12. Peter Brent, *Black Nile: Mungo Park and the Search for the Niger* (London, 1977), p. 4. On Park and African exploration in the period, see Christopher Lloyd, *The Search for the Niger* (London, 1973); E. W. Bovill, *Missions to the Niger* (Cambridge, 1964); Robin Hallett, *The Penetration of Africa: European Enterprise and Exploration Principally in Northern and Western Africa up to 1830* (London, 1965); K. Lupton, *Mungo Park: The African Traveller* (Oxford, 1979); Fergus Fleming, *Barrow's Boys* (London, 1998). Banks's role is examined in D. Middleton, 'Banks and African Exploration', in *Sir Joseph Banks: A Global Perspective*, ed. R. E. R. Banks, B. Elliott, J. G. Hawkes, D. King-Hele and G. Lucas (London, 1994), pp. 171–6.
13. Mungo Park, *Travels in the Interior Districts of Africa: Performed Under the Direction and Patronage of the African Association, In the Years 1795, 1796, and 1797* (London, 1984), pp. 1–2.
14. Ibid., p. 130.
15. Ibid., p. 131.
16. Bruce, *Travels to Discover the Source of the Nile in the Years 1768, 1769, 1770, 1771, 1772, and 1773*, 5 vols. (Edinburgh and London, 1790).
17. Bryan Edwards, *The History, Civil and Commercial of the British Colonies in the West Indies*, 2 vols. (London, 1793).

18. Letter of 9 October 1798; *Kew BC*, vol. II, p. 204.
19. Steven Shapin, *A Social History of Truth: Civility and Science in Seventeenth-Century England* (Chicago and London, 1994), pp. 122–4, 240–50.
20. Park, *Travels*, p. xxii.
21. Ibid., p. xxi.
22. Letter of 30 January 1799, in *Kew BC*, vol. II, p. 212.
23. Park, *Travels*, p. 74.
24. William Lawrence, *Lectures on Physiology, Zoology and the Natural History of Man* (London, 1819), p. 125.
25. James Cowles Prichard, *Researches into the Physical History of Man*, ed. George W. Stocking, Jr. (Chicago and London, 1973), p. 216.
26. Here we view Park from a perspective applied to Romantic poetry by Harold Bloom, 'The Internalisation of Quest Romance', *The Yale Review*, 58 (1969), 526–36. See also Mary Louise Pratt, *Imperial Eyes: Travel Writing and Transculturation* (London and New York, 1992), pp. 75–8.
27. Park, *Travels*, p. 104.
28. Ibid., p. 106.
29. Montgomery, 'The West Indies', part 3, lines 121, 117–18; in Montgomery, *Poems on the Abolition of the Slave Trade, by James Montgomery, James Grahame, and E. Beager* (London, 1809).
30. 'Lines, Suggested By The Uncertain Fate Of Mungo Park, The Celebrated African Traveller', lines 41, 34, 36, 7–10; in Mary Russell Mitford, *Poems* (London, 1810).
31. See Pratt, *Imperial Eyes*, pp. 75–80, for Park as a sentimental traveller.
32. Park made no explicit condemnation of the trade, however, perhaps because Edwards, who was not only his editor but the Secretary of the African Association who had employed him, was a firm opponent of the campaign to abolish it.
33. Park, *Travels*, p. 43.
34. 'Ode to Botany', lines 126–35, in William and Mary Howitt, *The Desolation of Eyam: The Emigrant, a Tale of the American Woods, and Other Poems* (London, 1827).
35. The draft is in MS W, published on p. 293 of vol. II of the *Thirteen Book Prelude*, ed. Mark L. Reed, 2 vols. (Ithaca and London, 1991).
36. Ibid., MS W 41v.
37. Francis Jeffrey, review of *Thalaba* in *The Edinburgh Review*, 1 (October 1802), 63–83, in *Robert Southey: The Critical Heritage*, ed. Lionel Madden (London and Boston, 1972), pp. 68–90 (p. 81).
38. Ibid., pp. 83–4.
39. Robert Southey, *Thalaba the Destroyer*, 2 vols. (London, 1801), vol. I, pp. 236–8.
40. Quoted in Carl Grabo, *A Newton among Poets. Shelley's Use of Science in Prometheus Unbound* (Chapel Hill, 1930), pp. 7–8.
41. *The Letters of John Keats, 1814–21*, ed. Hyder E. Rollins, 2 vols. (Cambridge, Mass., 1958), vol. II, p. 16.

42. *Endymion*, lines 810–11, in *Keats. Poetical Works*, ed. H. W. Garrod (London, Oxford, New York, 1970).
43. See Debbie Lee, 'Mapping the Interior: African Cartography and Shelley's *Witch of Atlas*', *European Romantic Review*, 8 (1997), 169–84 (p. 177).
44. 'To the Nile', lines 2–3, in *Shelley. Poetical Works*, ed. Thomas Hutchinson, corrected by G. M. Matthews (Oxford and New York, 1970).
45. 'To the Nile', lines 4, 11, in *Keats. Poetical Works*.
46. 'The Nile', lines 5, 9–11, in *The Poetical Works of Leigh Hunt*, ed. H. S. Milford (Oxford, 1923).
47. Quoted in Alan Bewell, *Romanticism and Colonial Disease* (Baltimore and London, 1999), p. 200.
48. See ibid., pp. 200–3.
49. Lines 41–5, quoted in ibid., pp. 202–3.
50. On *Alastor* and the costs of exploration, see Nigel Leask, *Romantic Writers and the East: Anxieties of Empire* (Cambridge, 1992), pp. 122–30; see also Saree Makdisi, 'Versions of the East: Byron, Shelley, and the Orient', in *Romanticism, Race and Imperial Culture*, ed. Richardson and Hofkosh, pp. 203–36, or, according to preference, the truncated version – 'Shelley's *Alastor*: Travel beyond the Limit', in *Romantic Geographies: Discourses of Travel 1775–1844*, ed. Amanda Gilroy (Manchester and New York, 2000), pp. 240–57.
51. Quoted in *Records of the African Association 1788–1831*, ed. Robin Hallett (London, 1964), pp. 168–9.

5 BANKS, BLIGH AND THE BREADFRUIT: SLAVE PLANTATIONS, TROPICAL ISLANDS AND THE RHETORIC OF ROMANTICISM

1. Quoted in Alan Richardson, 'Darkness Visible?: Race and Representation in Bristol Abolitionist Poetry, 1770–1810', in *Romanticism and Colonialism: Writing and Empire 1780–1830*, ed. Tim Fulford and Peter J. Kitson (Cambridge, 1998), pp. 129–47. Richardson cites Peter Fryer, *Staying Power: Black People in Britain since 1504* (London, 1984), p. 33. Bristol's dependence on the triangular slave trade for its prosperity is detailed in *Bristol, Africa and the Eighteenth-Century Slave Trade to America*, ed. David Richardson, 4 vols. (Bristol, 1986–96), vol. I: *The Years of Expansion 1698–1729*, and Madge Dresser, *Slavery Obscured: The Social History of the Slave Trade in an English Provincial Port* (Leicester, 2001).
2. Robert Southey, *Poems* (Bristol and London, 1797), Sonnets on the Slave Trade, iii, lines 9–14.
3. See Timothy Morton, 'Blood Sugar', in *Romanticism and Colonialism*, ed. Fulford and Kitson, pp. 87–106. Our account of the blood–sugar topos is indebted to Morton's excellent essay throughout.
4. For a discussion of the various accounts of the voyages to the South Seas in the period see Philip Edwards, *The Story of the Voyage: Sea-Narratives in Eighteenth-Century England* (Cambridge, 1994) and Neil Rennie, *Far-Fetched*

Facts: The Literature of Travel and the Idea of the South Seas (Oxford, 1992).
5. See Alan Moorehead, *The Fatal Impact: The Invasion of the South Pacific 1767–1840* (London, 1966), p. 51. See also Bernard Smith, *European Vision and the South Pacific 1768–1850* (Oxford, 1960), pp. 24–5.
6. *The Endeavour Journal of Joseph Banks 1768–1771*, ed. J. C. Beaglehole, 2 vols. (Sydney, 1962), vol. I, p. 341.
7. Coleridge, in fact, studied with Blumenbach himself, and viewed some of the specimens that Banks had sent him. See Trevor H. Levere, *Poetry Realized in Nature: Samuel Taylor Coleridge and Early Nineteenth-Century Science* (Cambridge, 1981), p. 210.
8. As, for instance, in J. F. Blumenbach, *A Manual of the Elements of Natural History*, trs. R. T. Gore (London, 1825), p. 37. See also *The Anthropological Treatises of Johann Friedrich Blumenbach*, trs. Thomas Bendyshe (London, 1865).
9. Georg Forster, *A Voyage Round the World in his Britannic Majesty's Sloop Resolution Commanded by Capt. James Cook, during the Years 1772, 3, 4, and 5*, 2 vols. (London, 1777), vol. I, p. 432.
10. John Hawkesworth, *An Account of the Voyages Undertaken by the order of His Present Majesty for Making Discoveries in the Southern Hemisphere*, 3 vols. (London, 1773), vol. II, pp. 80–6, 107.
11. *An Epistle from Oberea, Queen of Otaheite, to Joseph Banks, Esq.* (1774).
12. The Tahitian custom of tattooing, and the news that many of Cook's crew had let themselves be tattooed, also excited much comment after the *Endeavour* voyages were published. See Rod Edmond, *Representing the South Pacific: Colonial Discourse from Cook to Gauguin* (Cambridge, 1997), pp. 67–72.
13. Forster, *A Voyage*, vol. I, p. 213.
14. *Supplement to Bougainville's Voyage* (1772) in *Diderot's Selected Writings*, ed. Lester G. Crocker (New York and London, 1966), p. 228.
15. John Ellis, *A Description of the Mangostan and the Breadfruit* (London, 1775).
16. From a letter to the Royal Society proposing the scheme, quoted in Captain William Bligh, *The Log of H.M.S. Providence* (Guildford, Surrey, 1976), p. 18.
17. See H. B. Carter, *Sir Joseph Banks, 1743–1820* (London, 1988), p. 218.
18. Matthew Wallen, letter of 4 May 1787, BL Add. MS 33978, f. 117.
19. Banks's role in this and subsequent schemes is discussed in D. L. Mackay, 'Banks, Bligh and Breadfruit', *New Zealand Journal of History*, 8 (1974), 61–77.
20. William Bligh, *A Narrative of the Mutiny On Board Her Majesty's Ship Bounty and the Subsequent Voyage of Part of the Crew* (London, 1790), p. 10.
21. 25 June 1791; *DTC*, vol. VII, pp. 218–26a.
22. In James E. McClellan III, *Colonialism and Science: Saint Domingue in the Old Regime* (Baltimore and London, 1992), pp. 158–9.
23. Letter of 30 October 1788; Brinkman Collection, transcript in Banks archive, Natural History Museum, London.
24. Letter of Alexander Anderson, 30 March 1796; *DTC*, vol. X, pp. 25–6.

25. Alexander Anderson, report to Society of Arts (of which Banks was a member): quoted in K. W. Spence-Lewis, *Sir Joseph Banks. Royal Botanical Garden St. Vincent 1764–1820* (Seattle, London, St Vincent, 1994), p. 16.
26. From a manuscript essay intended for *The Courier*, September 1811. In *EOT*, vol. III, p. 235.
27. Southey, *Poems*, Sonnets on the Slave Trade, v, lines 13–14.
28. Our discussion of the poets and the *Bounty* is indebted to James C. McKusick, '"Wisely Forgetful": Coleridge and the Politics of Pantisocracy', in *Romanticism and Colonialism*, ed. Fulford and Kitson, pp. 107–28.
29. Ibid., p. 107.
30. 'Reflections on Having Left a Place of Retirement' (1795), lines 13 and 12, *CPW*, vol. I, p. 106.
31. James Watt, Jr., quoted in Jan Golinski, *Science as Public Culture: Chemistry and Enlightenment in Britain, 1760–1820* (Cambridge, 1992), p. 163.
32. 'The Very Probable Success of a Proper Mission to the South Sea Islands', *Evangelical Magazine* (July 1795), 264; *Sermons, Preached in London, At the Formation of the Missionary Society, September 22, 23, 24, 1795* (London, 1795), p. 170.
33. *DTC*, vol. XVII, pp. 334–45.
34. On these issues and the scholarly debates around them, see Peter J. Kitson, 'Sustaining the Romantic and Racial Self: Eating People in the South Seas', in *Eating Romanticism: Cultures of Taste/Theories of Appetite*, ed. Timothy Morton (New York, 2003), pp. 163–97.
35. *The Life and Correspondence of Robert Southey*, ed. Rev. Charles Cuthbert Southey, 6 vols. (London, 1849–50), vol. II, p. 243.
36. The missionary to Tahiti, William Ellis, credited Southey with ensuring the mission's success by publicising its endeavours in the *Quarterly Review*. In John Eimo Ellis, *Life of William Ellis Missionary to the South Seas and Madagascar* (London, 1873), p. 134.
37. Although of course in practice an empire of missionary Christianity often went hand in hand with one dedicated to profit.
38. A comprehensive assessment of the poem's relation to debates about the *Bounty* mutiny is given by James C. McKusick, 'The Politics of Language in Byron's *The Island*', *ELH*, 59 (1992), 839–56.
39. Byron swam the Hellespont in conscious emulation of the heroism of Leander. Torquil's final swim to freedom is likewise a heroic and individual escape to liberty and love.
40. As an undergraduate Coleridge wrote a Greek ode on the slave trade.
41. Said's *Orientalism* gave currency to such a model, and Abdul R. JanMohamed developed it into what he terms the 'Manichean allegory' of colonialist writing. Edward Said, *Orientalism* (London and Harmondsworth, 1985); Abdul R. JanMohamed, 'The Economy of Manichean Allegory: The Function of Racial Difference in Colonialist Literature', *Critical Inquiry*, 12.1 (1985), 59–87.
42. Quoted in Ellis, *Life of William Ellis*, p. 63.
43. Daniel Wheeler, quoted in Moorehead, *The Fatal Impact*, p. 88.

6 EXPLORATION, HEADHUNTING AND RACE THEORY: THE SKULL BENEATH THE SKIN

1. Thomas Carlyle, *Signs of the Times* (1828), in *Selected Writings*, ed. Alan Shelston (Harmondsworth, 1971), p. 64.
2. Wedgwood quoted in Michael Ignatieff, *A Just Measure of Pain: The Penitentiary in the Industrial Revolution 1750–1850* (London and New York, 1989), p. 68.
3. *The Works of the Late Professor Camper, On the Connexion between the Science of Anatomy and the Arts of Drawing, Painting, Statuary* (London, 1794), p. 34.
4. Camper's work had a parallel in J. C. Lavater's physiognomy, which claimed to be a method for reading character in the configuration of the face and head. Other materialist enquiries into the relation of skull, brain and mind followed, including Spurzheim's and Gall's phrenology, which claimed to analyse the mental disposition by interpreting the bumps and declivities of the skull. See J. C. Lavater, *Essays on Physiognomy; for the Promotion of the Knowledge and the Love of Mankind* (London, 1793), and J. C. Spurzheim, *Outlines of the Physiognomical System of Drs. Gall and Spurzheim, indicating the Dispositions and Manifestations of the Mind* (London, 1815). For Gall and Spurzheim's impact in Britain, see Roger Cooter, *The Cultural Meaning of Popular Science: Phrenology and the Organization of Consent in Nineteenth-Century Britain* (Cambridge, 1984). For a densely packed study of brain research at the start of the nineteenth century, see Alan Richardson, *British Romanticism and the Science of Mind* (Cambridge, 2001).
5. *Works of the Late Professor Camper*, p. 9.
6. Several historians of science have argued that, in the culture of late eighteenth- and early nineteenth-century science, experimentalists had to make their apparatus transparent in order for their demonstrations to be accepted as exhibitions of nature's laws; see, for example, Simon Schaffer, 'Natural Philosophy and Public Spectacle in the Eighteenth Century', *History of Science*, 21 (1983), 1–43, and I. Rhys Morus, *Frankenstein's Children. Electricity, Exhibition, and Experiment in Early-Nineteenth-Century London* (Princeton, N.J., 1999).
7. *Works of the Late Professor Camper*, pp. 27–8.
8. On Camper and South Sea people, see Bernard Smith, *Imagining the Pacific* (London and New Haven, 1992), pp. 186–7.
9. In arguing that empiricism was, at this time, a response by natural philosophers to their need to gain authority, an authority that was placed in doubt by reliance on the potentially untrustworthy travel narrative, we adapt arguments made about the seventeenth century by Steven Shapin, *The Social History of Truth: Civility and Science in Seventeenth-Century England* (Chicago and London, 1994), pp. 240–50.
10. 'Headhunters': Alan Bewell's appellation (private conversation).
11. See Nicholas Hudson, 'From "Nation" to "Race": The Origins of Racial Classification in Eighteenth-Century Thought', *Eighteenth-Century Studies*, 29 (1996), 247–64.

12. See David Theo Goldberg, *Racist Culture; Philosophy and the Politics of Meaning* (Oxford, 1993), p. 23; *Race and the Enlightenment: A Reader*, ed. Emmanuel Chukwudi Eze (Oxford, 1997), pp. 10–14; James L. Larson, *Interpreting Nature: The Science of Living Form from Linnaeus to Kant* (Baltimore, 1994); *Race: The Origins of an Idea, 1760–1850*, ed. Hannah Franziska Augstein (Bristol, 1996), pp. x–xvii; Harriet Ritvo, *The Platypus and the Mermaid and Other Figments of the Classifying Imagination* (Cambridge, 1997), pp. 120–1; David Knight, *Ordering the World: A History of Classifying Man* (London, 1981), pp. 58–81.
13. *Lectures on Comparative Anatomy; in Which Are Explained the Preparations in the Hunterian Collection, Illustrated by Engravings*, 6 vols. (London, 1814–28), vol. I, pp. 6–7. Quoted in Trevor H. Levere, *Poetry Realized in Nature: Samuel Taylor Coleridge and Early Nineteenth-Century Science* (Cambridge, 1981), p. 210. For an assessment of Hunter's importance see Stephen J. Cross, 'John Hunter, the Animal Economy, and Late Eighteenth Century Physiological Discourse', *Studies in the History of Biology*, 5 (1981), 1–110.
14. Georges Cuvier, *Lectures on Comparative Anatomy*, trs. William Ross, 2 vols. (London, 1802).
15. J. F. Blumenbach, *Decas tertia collectionis suae craniorum diversarum gentium illustrata* (Göttingen, 1795).
16. *De generis humani varietate nativa*, 3rd edn (Göttingen, 1795).
17. See Stephen Jay Gould, *The Mismeasure of Man* (New York and London, 1981).
18. J. F. Blumenbach, *A Manual of the Elements of Natural History*, trs. R. T. Gore (London, 1825), p. 37. See also *The Anthropological Treatises of Johann Friedrich Blumenbach*, trs. Thomas Bendyshe (London, 1865).
19. Blumenbach, *Manual*, p. 37.
20. Blumenbach's *Decas*, quoted in William Lawrence, *Lectures on Physiology, Zoology and the Natural History of Man* (London, 1819), p. 337.
21. Blumenbach, *Decas*, p. 12. On the Forsters' disenchanted view of Tahitian beauty, see David Bindman, *Ape to Apollo: Aesthetics and the Idea of Race in the Eighteenth Century* (London, 2002), pp. 123–50.
22. John Hawkesworth, *An Account of the Voyages Undertaken By The Order Of His Present Majesty, . . . for making Discoveries in the Southern Hemisphere, etc.*, 3 vols. (London, 1773), vol. II, p. 146.
23. Ibid., p. 236.
24. Ibid., p. 241.
25. Review of William Ellis, *Polynesian Researches*, in *Quarterly Review*, 43 (May 1830), 1–54 (p. 11).
26. Bruno Latour, *Science in Action: How to Follow Scientists and Engineers through Society* (Milton Keynes, 1987), pp. 217–48.
27. Charles White, *An Account of the Regular Gradation in Man, and in Different Animals and Vegetables* (London, 1799), p. 1. For White, see Kitson, *Theories of Race*, vol. VIII of *Slavery, Abolition, and Emancipation. Writings in the British Romantic Period*, general editors Peter J. Kitson and Debbie Lee, 8 vols. (London, 1999), pp. xii–xiii, xxv–xxvi, 215–64.
28. White, *Account*, p. 135.

29. Ibid., pp. 42, 125.
30. By, for example, Samuel Thomas von Soemmering, *Ber die korperlich Verschiedenheit des Mohren von Europer* (Frankfurt am Main, 1784) and *Ber die korperlich Verschiedenheit des Negers von Europer* (Frankfurt am Main, 1785); Lavater, *Essays on Physiognomy*; Edward Long, *History of Jamaica*, 3 vols. (London, 1774).
31. Kames cited Banks and Solander and expressed his belief in essential racial characteristics – and also that black people were a different, not fully human species, in *Sketches of the History of Man*, 2nd edn (Edinburgh, 1778), vol. I, pp. 37–40, 64–5. Recently, Robert Bernasconi has convincingly argued that Immanuel Kant was the originator of the essentialist view of race. See Bernasconi, 'Who Invented the Concept of Race? Kant's Role in the Enlightenment Construction of Race', in *Race*, ed. Robert Bernasconi (Oxford, 2001), pp. 11–36.
32. Robert Knox, *The Races of Men: A Fragment* (Philadelphia, 1850; reprinted Miami, Fla., 1969), p. 7.
33. Ibid., pp. 58–9.
34. For Knox, see Isobel Rae, *Knox the Anatomist* (Edinburgh and London, 1964), and M. D. Biddiss, 'The Politics of Anatomy: Dr Robert Knox and Victorian Racism', *Proceedings of the Royal Society of Medicine*, 69 (1976), 245–50.
35. See Adrian Desmond, *The Politics of Evolution: Morphology, Medicine, and Reform in Radical London* (Chicago and London, 1989), pp. 8–10.
36. Knox, *Races of Men*, pp. 7, 10, 12–13, 20, 24.
37. Ibid., pp. 151–3.
38. Hunt broke away from the Ethnological Society, a mainstream scientific body dominated by the liberal and Christian anthropology of the father of British anthropology, James Cowles Prichard, whose work both Knox and Hunt despised. See Robert J. C. Young, *Colonial Desire: Hybridity in Theory, Culture and Race* (London, 1995), pp. 118–43; George W. Stocking, Jr., 'What's in a Name? The Origins of the Royal Anthropological Institute (1837–71)', *Man*, 6 (1973), 369–90; Ronald Rainger, 'Race, Politics, and Science: The Anthropological Society of London in the 1880s', *Victorian Studies*, 22 (1978), 51–70.
39. Quoted in Michael Banton, *Racial Theories* (Cambridge, 1987), p. 29.
40. James Cowles Prichard, *Researches into the Physical History of Mankind*, 2 vols., 2nd edn (London, 1826), vol. I, pp. 237–9. For Prichard see Kitson, *Theories of Race*, pp. xx–xxii, 269–308; H. F. Augstein, *James Cowles Prichard's Anthropology* (Amsterdam, 1999) and *Race*, pp. 23–5; James Cowles Prichard, *Researches into the Physical History of Mankind*, ed. George W. Stocking, Jr. (Chicago and London, 1973), pp. ix–cxlix.
41. See Levere, *Poetry Realized in Nature*, pp. 205–12; see also Tim Burke, '"Humanity is Now the Pop'lar Cry": Laboring-Class Writers and the Liverpool Slave Trade, 1787–1789', *The Eighteenth Century*, 42.3 (2001), 245–63 (p. 247), and Denise Gigante, 'The Monster in the Rainbow: Keats and the Science of Life', *PMLA*, 117.3 (2002), 433–48.
42. Coleridge's manuscript notebook, no. 36, ff. 59v–60, held in BL Add. MSS.

43. He made this observation in the context of criticism of J. C. Spurzheim, in whose 'science' of phrenology he took an informed but critical interest. Spurzheim, he thought, had pressed his potentially useful method too far: when Spurzheim 'began to map out the cranium dogmatically, he fell into infinite absurdities'.
44. On Coleridge's dislike of Lawrence's materialism, see Levere, *Poetry Realized in Nature*, pp. 44–52.
45. Lawrence, *Lectures on Physiology*, p. 499.
46. Ibid., p. 364.
47. Ibid., p. 477.
48. Ibid., pp. 363–4.
49. See Martin Bernal, *Black Athena: The Afroasiatic Roots of Classical Civilization*, vol. I: *The Fabrication of Ancient Greece 1785–1985* (London, 1987), pp. 27–8, 215–30; E. S. Shaffer, *'Kubla Khan' and the Fall of Jerusalem: The Mythological School in Biblical Criticism and Secular Literature 1770–1880* (Cambridge, 1975), pp. 17–144.
50. A comparison made also by J. H. Haeger, 'Coleridge's Speculations on Race', *SiR*, 13 (1974), 333–57. In fairness to Coleridge, it should be remembered that he did not publish these speculations, and that he also reminded himself that race categories were not fixed essences, since races shaded into each other by degrees. For a judicious investigation of the matter, see Patrick J. Keane, *Coleridge's Submerged Politics: The Ancient Mariner and Robinson Crusoe* (Columbia and London, 1994).
51. *The Philosophical Lectures of S. T. Coleridge*, ed. Kathleen Coburn (London, 1948), p. 254.
52. Quoted by Philip D. Curtin, *The Image of Africa: British Ideas and Actions, 1780–1850* (London, 1964), p. 242.

7 THEORIES OF TERRESTRIAL MAGNETISM AND THE SEARCH FOR THE POLES

1. For our summary of the history of terrestrial magnetism we are indebted to the following: David R. Barraclough, 'Geomagnetism: Historical Introduction', in *The Encylopedia of Solid Earth Geophysics*, ed. David E. James (New York, 1989), pp. 584–92; Sydney Chapman and Julius Bartel, *Geomagnetism*, 2 vols. (Oxford, 1940), vol. II, pp. 899–937, 1004–7; A. Crichton Mitchell, 'Chapters in the History of Terrestrial Magnetism', *Terrestrial Magnetism*, 37 (1932), 105–46; 42 (1937), 241–80; 44 (1939), 77–80; *Geomagnetism*, ed. J. A. Jacobs, 3 vols. (London: vols. I and II 1987, vol. III 1989); J. A. Jacobs, *At the Earth's Core* (London, 1975); James D. Livingston, *Driving Force: The Natural Magic of Magnets* (Cambridge, Mass., 1996); Robert P. Multhauf and Gregory A. Good, *A Brief History of Geomagnetism and a Catalog of the Collections of the National Museum of American History*, Smithsonian Studies in History and Technology, no. 48 (Washington, D.C., 1987); Gerrit L. Verschuur, *Hidden Attraction: The Mystery and History of Magnetism* (Oxford, 1993); R. W. Home and

P. J. Conner, *Aepinus's Essay on the Theory of Electricity and Magnetism* (Princeton, N.J., 1979); Gregory A. Good, 'Follow the Needle: Seeking the Magnetic Poles', *Earth Sciences History*, 10 (1991), 154–67. For a recent discussion of the origins of the mariner's compass, see Amir D. Aczel, *The Riddle of the Compass: The Invention That Changed the World* (New York, 2001). See also A. R. T. Jonkers, *North by Northwest. Seafaring, Science and the Earth's Magnetic Field (1600–1800)*, 2 vols. (Göttingen and Baltimore, 2003); W. E. May, *A History of Marine Navigation* (London, 1973); Eva G. R. Taylor, *The Haven-Finding Art: A History of Navigation from Odysseus to Captain Cook* (London, 1956); Davis Waters, *The Art of Navigation in England in Elizabethan and Early Stuart Times* (London, 1956); Heinrich Winter, 'Who Invented the Compass?', *Mariner's Mirror*, 23 (1937), 95–102; C. Stewart Gilmour, *Coulomb and the Evolution of Physics and Engineering in Eighteenth-Century France* (Princeton, N.J., 1971).

2. Chapman and Bartel, *Geomagnetism*, vol. II, pp. 901–9. See also May, *Marine Navigation*, pp. 83–99.
3. Stephen Pumfrey, *Latitude and the Magnetic Earth* (Cambridge, 2002), p. 73.
4. Robert Norman, *The Newe Attractiue, Containyng a Short Discourse of the Magnes or Lodestone, and Amongst Other His Vertues, of a Newe Discouered Secret and Subtill Propertie, Concerning the Declinyng of the Needle, Touched There With Onder the Plaine of the Horizon* (London, 1581).
5. See Pumfrey, *Latitude*, pp. 73–7.
6. Stephen Pumfrey, '"O tempora, O magnes!": A Sociological Analysis of the Discovery of Secular Magnetic Variation in 1634', *BJHS*, 22 (1989), 181–214.
7. And in 1722 the London clockmaker George Graham proved that declination varied on a daily basis (a phenomenon known as 'non-secular magnetic time-variations'). Chapman and Bartels, *Geomagnetism*, vol. II, pp. 922–3.
8. Edmond Halley, 'A Theory of the Variation of the Magnetic Compass of the Most Ingenious Mr Edmund Halley, Fellow of the Royal Society', *Philosophical Transactions of the Royal Society of London*, 13 (10 June 1683), 208–20 (p. 216). See C. A. Ronan, 'Edmond Halley and Early Geophysics', *Geophysical Journal*, 15 (1968), 241–8 (p. 244); *The Three Voyages of Edmond Halley in the Paramore 1698–1701*, ed. Norman J. W. Thrower (London, 1981), p. 23; A. Armitage, *Edmond Halley* (London, 1966), p. 70.
9. Edmond Halley, 'An Account of the Cause of the Change of the Variation of the Magnetical Compass', *Philosophical Transactions of the Royal Society of London*, 17 (1692), 563.
10. Quoted Thrower (ed.), *Voyages*, p. 29.
11. For details of Halley's voyages, see ibid., pp. 15–55; Alan Gurney, *Below the Convergence: Voyages towards Antarctica 1699–1830* (London, 1998), pp. 69–85.
12. For the history of Halley's chart see Thrower (ed.), *Voyages*, pp. 55–66.
13. Mary Louise Pratt, *Imperial Eyes: Travel Writing and Transculturation* (London and New York, 1992), pp. 15–85.
14. Barbara Stafford, *Voyage into Substance: Art, Science, Nature, and the Illustrated Travel Account* (Cambridge, 1984); Bruno Latour, *Science in Action: How to Follow Scientists and Engineers through Society* (Milton Keynes, 1987).

15. See, for instance, John Harris, *Navigantium atque Itinerantium Bibliotheca: or, a Compleat Collection of Voyages and Travels, Consisting of above Four Hundred of the Most Authentick Writers,* revised by J. Campbell, 2 vols. (London, 1744–8). Quoted in J. C. Beaglehole, *The Voyage of the Endeavour, 1768–1771*. Volume I of *The Journals of Captain Cook*, 3 vols. (Cambridge, 1955–67), p. clxix.
16. In this respect, Jonathan Lamb has recently drawn our attention to the fragility of the European self and its scientific apparatus when faced by the unknown. The 'uncertainties that troubled the stability of the European self', Lamb writes, 'were intensified in the South Pacific'. The explorer could never be sure that his 'techniques of discovery, and the language in which he framed his discoveries, were thoroughly understood at home'. Jonathan Lamb, *Preserving the Self in the South Seas 1680–1840* (Chicago and London, 2001), pp. 5, 81.
17. Patricia Fara, *Sympathetic Attractions. Magnetic Practices, Beliefs, and Symbolism in Eighteenth-Century England* (Princeton, N.J., 1996), pp. 67–8; G. Grant and J. Klinkert, *The Ship's Compass* (London, 1970), p. 71; Joseph Bushby Hewson, *A History of the Practice of Navigation* (Glasgow, 1983), pp. 55–9; Alfred Hine, *Magnetic Compasses and Magnetometers* (London, 1968), p. 3; May, *Marine Navigation*. Also, Jan Golinski, *Science as Public Culture. Chemistry and Enlightenment in Britain, 1760–1820* (Cambridge, 1992).
18. Fara, *Sympathetic Attractions*, pp. 7–8.
19. 'Navy Board to apply to Dr Knight for his azimuth compass of a new construction, that experiments may be made of its utility'. Admiralty Minutes 3/76. Quoted Beaglehole (ed.), *Voyage of the Endeavour*, pp. 621, 622.
20. Beaglehole (ed.), *Voyage of the Endeavour*, pp. cxxxiii–cxxxiv.
21. Ibid., pp. 16, 61, 18.
22. Ibid., p. 138.
23. Ibid., p. 632.
24. J. C. Beaglehole, *The Life of Captain James Cook* (London, 1974), pp. 287–8.
25. J. C. Beaglehole (ed.), *The Voyage of the Resolution and Adventure 1772–1775* (1961). Volume II of *The Journals of Captain James Cook on his Voyages of Discovery*, p. 725.
26. Ibid., pp. 20, 76, 78, 104n, 780, 525–6.
27. Ibid., pp. 20, 89n, 104n.
28. William Wales, 'Journal', in ibid., pp. 830, 831–2.
29. Ibid., pp. 320, 323, 324, 643–4.
30. Fara, *Sympathetic Attractions*, pp. 112–17.
31. John Churchman, *The Magnetic Atlas or Variation Charts of the Whole Terraqueous Globe; comprising a System of the Variation & Dip of the Needle by which Observation being Truly Made, The Longitude may be Ascertained*, 3rd edn (New York, 1800), pp. xxiii, 53, 66–7. Euler's magnetic theory is described in his *Letters to a German Princess*, trs. Henry Hunter, 2 vols. (London, 1802), vol. II, pp. 209–86. See Home and Connor, *Aepinus's Essay*, pp. 145–8.
32. For Humboldt, see Alexander von Humboldt, *Cosmos: A Sketch of a Physical Description of the Universe*, trs. E. C. Otte, 5 vols. (London, 1848–58),

vol. I, pp. 176–93; vol. V, pp. 50–156; D. Botting, *Humboldt and the Cosmos* (London, 1973); Pratt, *Imperial Eyes*, pp. 111–200; Nigel Leask, *Curiosity and the Aesthetics of Travel Writing 1770–1840* (Oxford, 2002), pp. 243–98; John Cawood, 'Terrestrial Magnetism and the Development of International Collaboration in the Early Nineteenth Century', *Annals of Science*, 34 (1977), 551–87 (pp. 560–9).

33. A. von Humboldt and J.-B. Biot, 'Sur les variations du magnétisme terrestre à différentes latitudes', *Journal de Physique*, 59 (1804), 229–50; Cawood, 'Terrestrial Magnetism', 563.
34. Good, 'Follow the Needle', 162.
35. Carl Friedrich Gauss, 'Allegemeine Theorie des Erdmagnetismus' (1838). For Gauss, see Chapman and Bartels, *Geomagnetism*, vol. II, pp. 927–98; Good, 'Follow the Needle', 162–3; James Gabriel O'Hara, 'Gauss and the Royal Society: The Reception of his Ideas on Magnetism in Britain (1832–1842)', *Notes and Records of the Royal Society of London*, 38 (1983), 17–78; Cawood, 'Terrestrial Magnetism'; G. D. Garland, 'The Contributions of Carl Friedrich Gauss to Geomagnetism', *Historia Mathematica*, 6 (1979), 1–57.
36. The literature on this area is vast. Most useful for this discussion have been: Glyn Williams, *Voyages of Delusion: The Search for the Northwest Passage in the Age of Reason* (London, 2002); Pierre Berton, *The Arctic Grail: The Quest for the Northwest Passage and the North Pole, 1818–1909* (New York, 1988); Ann Savours, *The Search for the Northwest Passage* (London, 1999); Fergus Fleming, *Barrow's Boys* (London, 1998) and *Ninety Degrees North: The Quest for the North Pole* (London, 2001); Richard Vaughan, *The Arctic: A History* (Bridgend, 1999). See also Peter J. Kitson (ed.), *North and South Poles*. Volume III: *Travels, Explorations and Empires: Writings from the Era of Imperial Expansion*, ed. Tim Fulford and Peter J. Kitson, 8 vols. (London, 2001).
37. Williams, *Voyages of Delusion*, pp. 280–1, 290–1.
38. For these fantasies and the Gothicisation of the poles, see Francis Spufford, *I May Be Some Time* (London, 1996); William E. Lenz, *The Poetics of the Antarctic: A Study in Nineteenth-Century American Cultural Perceptions* (New York, 1995). See also John George Moss, *Enduring Dreams: An Exploration of Arctic Landscape* (Concord, Ont., 1996); Lisa Bloom, *Gender on Ice: American Ideologies of Polar Expeditions* (Minneapolis, 1993); Robert G. David, *The Arctic in the British Imagination, 1818–1914* (Manchester and New York, 2000); Eric G. Wilson, *The Spiritual History of Ice: Romanticism, Science and the Imagination* (New York and Basingstoke, 2003), and Erika Behrisch, '"Far as the eye can reach": Scientific Exploration and Explorers' Poetry in the Arctic, 1832–1852', *Victorian Poetry*, 41 (2003), 73–92.
39. Daines Barrington, *The Possibility of Approaching the North Pole*, 2nd edn (London, 1775; rpt London, 1818); 'Thoughts on the Probability, Expediency, and Utility of Discovering a Passage by the North Pole', in *Miscellanies* (London, 1781), pp. 63–77. See Williams, *Voyages of Delusion*, pp. 276–82.
40. For this aspect of the Royal Society's work, see Marie Boas Hall, *All Scientists Now: The Royal Society in the Nineteenth Century* (Cambridge, 1984),

pp. 199–215. See also Trevor H. Levere, *Science and the Canadian Arctic: A Century of Exploration 1818–1918* (Cambridge, 1993), pp. 1–33, 142–88.
41. Olaudah Equiano, *The Interesting Narrative and Other Writings*, ed. Vincent Carretta (Harmondsworth, 1995), p. 172.
42. For Phipps, see Constantine John Phipps, *A Voyage towards the North Pole* (London, 1774); John Barrow, *A Chronological History of Voyages into the Arctic Regions* (London, 1818), pp. 303–11; Ann Savours, '"A Very Interesting Point in Geography": The 1773 Phipps Expedition towards the North Pole', *Arctic*, 37 (1984), 402–28; Vaughan, *The Arctic*, pp. 142–4; Levere, *Science and the Canadian Arctic*, pp. 34–5.
43. Phipps, *Voyage towards the North Pole*, p. 74.
44. For Cook's third voyage, see Beaglehole, *Life of Cook*, pp. 472–688; Williams, *Voyages of Delusion*, pp. 287–334.
45. For Scoresby, see Tom and Cordelia Stamp, *William Scoresby: Arctic Scientist* (Whitby, 1975); Constance Martin, 'William Scoresby Jr (1789–1857) and the Open Polar Sea – Myth and Reality', *Arctic*, 41 (1988), 39–47.
46. For Scoresby and Banks, see Stamp and Stamp, *William Scoresby*, pp. 31–4; Harold B. Carter, *Sir Joseph Banks, 1743–1820* (London, 1988), pp. 505–12.
47. Quoted in Stamp and Stamp, *William Scoresby*, p. 66.
48. See Carter, *Sir Joseph Banks*, p. 508.
49. Quoted in Stamp and Stamp, *William Scoresby*, p. 52, 67.
50. William Scoresby, *Philosophical Transactions of the Royal Society of London*, 109 (1819), 96–106. Scoresby's data and conclusions are contained in his *An Account of the Arctic Regions*, 2 vols. (Edinburgh, 1820), vol. II, pp. 539–54.
51. Scoresby, *Account*, vol. I, p. 332; vol. II, pp. 376, 539–54.
52. Stamp and Stamp, *William Scoresby*, pp. 131–9.
53. John Ross, *Voyage of Discovery, Made under Orders of the Admiralty, in His Majesty's Ships Isabella and Alexander for the Purpose of Exploring Baffin's Bay, and Enquiring into the Probability of a North-west Passage* (London, 1819), pp. 10, xix; Appendix, p. cxxxiv. See Levere, *Science and the Canadian Arctic*, pp. 44–67.
54. Letter from W. E. Parry to his parents, 25 July 1819. Quoted in Levere, *Science and the Canadian Arctic*, p. 65.
55. William Edward Parry, *Journal of a Voyage for the Discovery of a North-West Passage from the Atlantic to the Pacific performed in the Years 1819–20* (London, 1821), pp. xxv–xxvi, cxxix.
56. Ibid., p. 62.
57. Parry, *Journal of a Third Voyage for the Discovery of a North-West Passage from the Atlantic to the Pacific in the Years 1824–25* (London, 1826), pp. 52–3, 56. See also Levere, *Science and the Canadian Arctic*, pp. 81–2.
58. For Ross's second voyage see M. J. Ross, *Polar Pioneers: John Ross and James Clark Ross* (Montreal and Kingston, 1994), pp. 119–64.
59. John Ross, *Narrative of a Second Voyage of Discovery in Search of a North-West Passage and of a Residence in the Arctic Regions during the Years 1829, 1830, 1831, 1932, 1833* (London, 1835), pp. 556–7.

60. Ibid., pp. 555, 556–7, 558–9. James Ross published a scientific account of his discovery as 'On the Position of the North Magnetic Pole', *Philosophical Transactions of the Royal Society*, 124 (1834), 47–52.
61. For this, see Cawood, 'Terrestrial Magnetism', pp. 576–8; Multhauf and Good, *Brief History of Geomagnetism*, pp. 11–22; J. G. O'Hara, 'Gauss and the Royal Society: The Reception of his Ideas on Magnetism in Britain', *Notes & Records of the Royal Society of London*, 38 (1983), 17–78.
62. John Cawood, 'The Magnetic Crusade: Science and Politics in Early Victorian England', *Isis*, 70 (1979), 493–518.
63. For Ross's expedition, see Ross, *Polar Pioneers*, pp. 215–54; G. E. Fogg, *A History of Antarctic Science* (Cambridge, 1992), pp. 73–93; Alan Gurney, *The Race to the White Continent* (New York and London, 2000), 203–69.
64. Multhauf and Good, *Brief History of Geomagnetism*, p. 20.
65. James Clark Ross, *A Voyage of Discovery and Research in the Southern and Antarctic Regions*, 2 vols. (London, 1847), vol. I, pp. 245–8, vol. II, pp. 446–7.
66. M. H. Abrams, *The Mirror and the Lamp: Romantic Theory and the Critical Tradition* (Oxford, 1953); *Natural Supernaturalism: Tradition and Revolution in English Literature* (London and New York, 1974).
67. Anne K. Mellor, *Romanticism and Gender* (London and New York, 1995).
68. Eleanor Porden, *The Arctic Explorers: A Poem* (London, 1818), p. 8, lines 13–18. For Porden see Edith Mary Gell, *John Franklin's Bride: Eleanor Anne Porden, 1795–1825* (London, 1930); Spufford, *I May be Some Time*, pp. 110–15, 118–19.
69. Porden, *Arctic Explorers*, p. 14, lines 79–90.
70. Recently Marilyn Butler in the introduction to her edition of *Frankenstein; or the Modern Prometheus. The 1818 Text by Mary Wollstonecraft Shelley* (London, 1993) and Spufford, in *I May be Some Time,* have located *Frankenstein* in the context of contemporary Arctic exploration. For the frame narrative see Andrew Griffin, 'Fire and Ice', in *The Endurance of Frankenstein*, ed. George Levine and U. C. Knoepflmacher (Berkeley, 1979), pp. 49–73; Richard J. Dunn, 'Narrative Distance in *Frankenstein*', *Studies in the Novel*, 6 (1974), 408–17; Anne K. Mellor, *Mary Shelley: Her Life, her Fiction, her Monsters* (New York and London, 1988), pp. 77–9, 109–11; Rudolf Beck, '"The Region of Beauty and Delight": Walton's Polar Fantasies in Mary Shelley's *Frankenstein*', *Keats–Shelley Journal*, 49 (2000), 24–92.
71. Mary Shelley, *Frankenstein or the Modern Prometheus*, ed. Nora Crook. Volume I. *The Novels and Selected Works of Mary Shelley*, 8 vols. (London, 1996), pp. 11, 9–10. Crook suggests several sources for Mary Shelley's knowledge of the open polar sea theory, including George Best in Richard Hakluyt's *Principal Voyages, Traffiques and Discoveries of the English Nation* (1589). It cannot be demonstrated that she actually read any, although Phipps and Barrington remain the most likely sources for her when composing the novel in 1816 (p. 10n). Further references will be to this edition of the novel and will be contained in the text.
72. 'Art. v. Frankenstein, or the Modern Prometheus, 3 vols. London 1818', *Quarterly Review*, 28.xxxvi (May 1818), 379–85.
73. *The Journals of Mary Shelley, 1814–1844*, ed. Paula R. Feldman and Diana Scott-Kilvert, 2 vols. (Oxford, 1987), vol. I, p. 146.

74. Richard Holmes, *Shelley: The Pursuit* (Harmondsworth, 1987), pp. 16–17; Desmond King-Hele, *Shelley – His Thought and Work* (London, 1960); Carl Grabo, *A Newton among Poets – Shelley's Use of Science in "Prometheus Unbound"* (Chapel Hill, N.C., 1930).
75. Mellor, *Mary Shelley*, p. 90.
76. Adam Walker, *A System of Familiar Philosophy: In Twelve Lectures*, 2 vols. (London, 1802). See Fara, *Sympathetic Attractions*, pp. 62, 64–5, 150, 182, 190, 194.
77. Erasmus Darwin, *The Botanic Garden* (London, 1789–91), note VII, p. 13; Desmond King-Hele, *Erasmus Darwin: A Life of Unequalled Achievement* (London, 1999), p. 267.
78. See Mellor, *Mary Shelley*, pp. 89–114.
79. See John Livingston Lowes, *The Road to Xanadu: A Study in the Ways of the Imagination* (Boston, 1927); Bernard Smith, *Imagining the Pacific: In the Wake of Cook's Voyages* (New Haven and London, 1992); Peter J. Kitson (ed.), *The South Seas and Australasia*. Volume VIII: *Travels, Explorations and Empires*, pp. ix–xxvii.
80. For Coleridge and *Naturphilosophie* generally, see Thomas McFarland, *Coleridge and the Pantheist Tradition* (Princeton, N.J., 1974); Raimonda Modiano, *Coleridge and the Concept of Nature* (London, 1985); Trevor H. Levere, *Poetry Realized in Nature: Samuel Taylor Coleridge and Early Nineteenth-Century Science* (Cambridge, 1981).
81. See Smith, *Imagining the Pacific*, pp. 135–92; Savours, '"A Very Interesting Point in Geography"', 411.
82. Samuel Taylor Coleridge, *Poems*, ed. John Beer (London, 1993), p. 218.
83. Samuel Taylor Coleridge, *On the Constitution of the Church and State*, ed. John Colmer (London and Princeton, N.J., 1976), pp. 174–7. This Appendix was originally sent as a letter to Edward Coleridge on 27 July 1826: see *CL*, vol. VI, pp. 593–601.
84. For an excellent elucidation of the principle of polarity see Levere, *Poetry Realized in Nature*, pp. 108–14.
85. For Coleridge, polarity and race theory see Peter J. Kitson, 'Coleridge and the Orang-Utan Hypothesis', in *Coleridge and the Sciences of Life*, ed. Nicholas Roe (Oxford, 2002), pp. 91–116.
86. Coleridge, *Church and State*, p. 31.

8 'MAN ELECTRIFIED MAN': ROMANTIC REVOLUTION AND THE LEGACY OF BENJAMIN FRANKLIN

1. Franklin's report of the meeting, quoted in I. Bernard Cohen, *Benjamin Franklin's Science* (Cambridge, Mass., and London, 1990), p. 133.
2. Franklin's letter, quoted in H. B. Carter, *Sir Joseph Banks 1743–1820* (London, 1988), p. 97.
3. *Remarks Concerning the Savages of North America*, in Benjamin Franklin, *Two Tracts: Information to Those who Would Remove to America*, 3rd edn (London, 1784).

4. Ibid., p. 33.
5. *Wat Tyler*, vol. II of *The Poetical Works of Robert Southey, Collected by Himself*, 10 vols. (London, 1838), act III, scene ii.
6. Quoted in Simon Schaffer, 'Priestley and the Politics of Spirit', in *Science, Medicine and Dissent: Joseph Priestley (1733–1804)*, ed. R. G. W. Anderson and Christopher Lawrence (London, 1987), pp. 39–53 (p. 40).
7. Quoted in ibid., p. 40.
8. Quoted in I. Bernard Cohen, *Science and the Founding Fathers: Science in the Political Thought of Jefferson, Franklin, Adams and Madison* (New York and London, 1995), pp. 184–5.
9. *Observations on the Importance of the American Revolution, and The Means of Making It a Benefit to the World*, rev. edn (London, 1785), pp. 1–2, 5n, quoted in Ian Wylie, *Young Coleridge and the Philosophers of Nature* (Oxford, 1989), p. 51. Our account is indebted to that of Wylie, as also to those of Shaffer (n6) and Golinski (n21). Also to J. L. Heilbron, *Electricity in the 17th and 18th Centuries. A Study of Early Modern Physics* (Berkeley and London, 1979).
10. *The Letters of Erasmus Darwin*, ed. Desmond King-Hele (Cambridge, 1981), pp. 166–7.
11. Darwin, *The Botanic Garden: A Poem in Two Parts. I, The Economy of Vegetation* (London, 1791), pp. 90–1.
12. Although Scheele is given priority by many of today's scholars, since Priestley accepted neither the term nor the concept on which it was based.
13. See Martin Fitzpatrick, 'Joseph Priestley and the Millennium', in *Science, Medicine and Dissent*, ed. Anderson and Lawrence, pp. 29–37; also Wylie, *Young Coleridge and the Philosophers*, p. 76.
14. David Hartley, *Observations on Man, his Frame, his Duty, and his Expectations* (London, 1791), p. 14.
15. Ibid.
16. *Disquisitions Relating to Matter and Spirit* (1782) quoted in Wylie, *Young Coleridge and the Philosophers*, p. 44. On Priestley's work on electricity, see John G. McEvoy, 'Electricity, Knowledge and the Nature of Progress in Priestley's Thought', *BJHS*, 12 (1979), 1–30; also Robert E. Schofield, *The Enlightenment of Joseph Priestley. A Study of his Life and Work from 1733 to 1773* (University Park, Pa., 1997), pp. 139–52.
17. For discussion of Priestley's materialism, see Erwin N. Hiebert, 'The Integration of Revealed Religion and Scientific Materialism in the Thought of Joseph Priestley', in *Joseph Priestley: Scientist, Theologian and Metaphysician*, ed. Lester Kieft and Bennett R. Willeford, Jr. (Lewisburg and London, 1980), pp. 27–61; also, John McEvoy, 'Causes and Laws, Powers and Principles: The Metaphysical Foundations of Priestley's Concept of Phlogiston', in *Science, Medicine and Dissent*, ed. Anderson and Lawrence, pp. 55–71.
18. 'Anatomical Observations on the Torpedo', *Philosophical Transactions of the Royal Society*, 63.2 (1773), 481–9.
19. Ibid., p. 77.
20. Ibid.

21. Quoted in Jan Golinski, *Science as Public Culture: Chemistry and Enlightenment in Britain, 1760–1820* (Cambridge, 1992), p. 205.
22. *The Botanic Garden* I, pp. 19–20.
23. Ibid., p. 35.
24. From the preface to Priestley's *Experiments and Observations on Different Kinds of Air* (London, 1774); quoted in Schaffer, 'Politics of Spirit', p. 40.
25. Quoted in ibid., p. 40.
26. Priestley's phrase, from his letters to the Revd Edward Burn, was quoted in horror by Burke in the House of Commons (*Parliamentary History*, 28 (2 March 1790), 438). See Schaffer, 'Politics of Spirit', p. 48.
27. Quoted in Schaffer, 'Politics of Spirit', p. 48.
28. W. Dent, 'Revolution Anniversary'. Reproduction in Golinski, *Science as Public Culture*, p. 182.
29. Edmund Burke, *A Letter from the Right Honourable Edmund Burke to a Noble Lord* (London, 1796), p. 26, quoted in Golinski, *Science as Public Culture*, p. 178.
30. James Watt, Jr., quoted in Golinski, *Science as Public Culture*, p. 163.
31. On Priestley and Cooper in America, see Jenny Graham, *Revolutionary in Exile: The Emigration of Joseph Priestley to America 1794–1804*, *Transactions of the American Philosophical Society*, 85, part II (1995).
32. Franklin had introduced this term into the Declaration of Independence in place of the milder 'arbitrary power' of the draft copy. See Alfred Owen Aldridge, *Benjamin Franklin, Philosopher and Man* (Philadelphia and New York, 1965), p. 260.
33. *Madoc*, part I, v, in *The Poetical Works of Robert Southey*, vol. V, p. 42 (note on pp. 153–4).
34. Quoted in Golinski, *Science as Public Culture*, p. 156.
35. As Jenny Uglow shows, before the alarm about Jacobinism Banks had supported the work of Priestley, Darwin, Josiah Wedgwood, James Watt and Matthew Boulton – the experimentalist and industrialist members of the Birmingham-based Lunar Society. Even after 1793, Banks remained a friend and ally of the less radical Boulton, Wedgwood and Watt. See Jenny Uglow, *The Lunar Men: The Friends Who Made the Future* (London, 2002), p. 125.
36. 'The Sons of Genius', in *Annual Anthology*, ed. Robert Southey, I (Bristol, 1799), pp. 93–9.
37. Both quotations from 'An Essay on Heat, Light and the Combinations of Light' (1799) in *The Collected Works of Humphry Davy*, 9 vols. (London, 1839), vol. II, pp. 28, 35 (quoted in P. M. Heimann, 'Ether and Imponderables', in *Conceptions of Ether: Studies in the History of Ether Theories, 1740–1900*, ed. G. N. Cantor and M. J. S. Hodge (Cambridge, 1981), pp. 61–83 (p. 79)).
38. Quoted in Trevor H. Levere, *Poetry Realized in Nature: Samuel Taylor Coleridge and Early Nineteenth-Century Science* (Cambridge, 1981), p. 32.
39. On the founding of this institution see Morris Berman, *Social Change and Scientific Organization: The Royal Institution, 1799–1844* (London, 1978).
40. Quoted in Levere, *Poetry Realized in Nature*, p. 30.

41. Quoted in Golinski, *Science as Public Culture*, p. 193.
42. On the mutual influence of the two men and their theories, see Roger Sharrock, 'The Chemist and the Poet: Sir Humphry Davy and the Preface to *Lyrical Ballads*', *Notes and Records of the Royal Society of London*, 17 (1962), 57–76.
43. Quoted in Golinski, *Science as Public Culture*, p. 188.
44. Ibid., p. 189.
45. 'On Davy's Bakerian Lecture', *Monthly Review*, 57 (November 1808), 225–7 (p. 225).
46. Henry Brougham, Review of Humphry Davy's 1807 Bakerian Lecture, *Edinburgh Review*, 12 (1808), 394–401 (p. 394).
47. Quoted in Levere, *Poetry Realized in Nature*, p. 33.
48. Quoted in ibid., p. 34.
49. T. J. Hogg, *The Life of Percy Bysshe Shelley*, 2 vols. (London, 1858), vol. 1, p. 33.
50. See Maurice Hindle's introduction to *Frankenstein, or the Modern Prometheus*, ed. Maurice Hindle (Harmondsworth, 1992) and chapter 5 of Anne K. Mellor, *Mary Shelley: Her Life, her Fiction, her Monsters* (New York and London, 1988).
51. *Frankenstein*, ed. Hindle, p. 221.
52. Ibid., p. 47.
53. Humphry Davy, *A Discourse Introductory to a Course of Lectures on Chemistry* (London, 1802), p. 16, quoted in Mellor, *Mary Shelley*, p. 93.

9 THE BEAST WITHIN: VACCINATION, ROMANTICISM AND THE JENNERATION OF DISEASE

1. Lady Mary Wortley Montagu, *Letters of the Right Honourable Lady M—y W—y M—e: Written During her Travels in Europe, Asia and Africa . . .* , vol. 1 (Aix, 1796), pp. 167–9; letter 36, to Mrs. S. C. from Adrianople, n.d.
2. (London, 1798), plate facing p. 32. All subsequent quotations from the *Inquiry* taken from The Harvard Classics, ed. Charles W. Eliot: *Scientific Papers. Physiology Medicine Surgery Geology* (New York, 1897), pp. 153–80.
3. On smallpox's prevalence see Donald R. Hopkins, *Princes and Peasants. Smallpox in History* (Chicago and London, 1983).
4. Jenner admitted taking his cue from the words of a local dairymaid. Others had preceded him in so doing. In 1774 Benjamin Jesty, a Dorset farmer, observing his dairymaids' immunity to smallpox, scratched cowpox into the arms of his family. Lacking Jenner's medical training and connections, Jesty could not develop his discovery on a national scale.
5. Jenner, *An Inquiry*, p. 153.
6. Jenner's letter of 29 September 1798, quoted in Paul Saunders, *Edward Jenner: The Cheltenham Years 1795–1823. Being a Chronicle of the Vaccination Campaign* (Hanover, N.H., and London, 1982), p. 72. Jenner's presentation of himself in pastoral terms is evident not only in comments such as this but in his refusal of the chance to cement his fame either by living in London or by exploring the Pacific with Captain Cook.
7. Dr Haygarth, letter of 15 April 1794, quoted in John Baron, *The Life of Edward Jenner*, 2 vols. (London, 1838), vol. 1, p. 134.

8. Baron, summarising a conversation with the Royal Society's President, in ibid., p. 168.
9. Quoted in ibid., p. 102.
10. Quoted in ibid., p. 136.
11. Jenner, *An Inquiry*, p. 153. Here Jenner explicitly followed what he advertised as Hunter's discovery.
12. Ibid.
13. Ibid.
14. Jenner's suspicion of aristocratic luxury echoes a widespread eighteenth-century fear, expressed forcibly by Gibbon, Cowper and Thomson amongst others. See John Sekora, *Luxury: The Concept in Western Thought, Eden to Smollett* (Baltimore, 1977). The lapdog is treated as a symptom of upper-class women's diseased sensibility in Sarah Scott, *The History of Sir George Ellison* (London, 1766) and Jonas Hanway, 'Remarks on Lap-dogs', in *A Journal of Eight Days' Journey* (London, 1756), pp. 69–70. For the medical argument that luxury was a danger to the body see George Cheyne, *The English Malady. Or, A Treatise of Nervous Diseases Of All Kinds* (London, 1733).
15. See Cowper, *The Task*, books I, II and IV, in *William Cowper: The Task and Selected Other Poems*, ed. James Sambrook (London and New York, 1994).
16. The radical Whig leader, Charles James Fox, told Wordsworth he thought blank verse unfit for such simple subjects. Wordsworth was guilty of undermining the status of poetic language, as Francis Jeffrey agreed when he regretted Wordsworth's derivation of 'lofty' conceptions from 'low' objects: 'nor is there anything, – down to . . . the evisceration of chickens, – which may not be introduced in poetry, if this is tolerated'. *Edinburgh Review*, in *Romantic Bards and British Reviewers*, ed. John O. Hayden (London, 1971), pp. 15, 21.
17. On 'dirt' as what we perceive to be out of place, something transgressing a boundary, see Mary Douglas, *Purity and Danger* (New York, 1970).
18. Giovanni Aldini, *An Account of the Late Improvements in Galvanism, with a Series of Curious and Interesting Experiments . . . Containing the Author's Experiments on the Body of a Malefactor Executed at Newgate* (London, 1803), p. 10.
19. William Rowley, *Cow-pox Inoculation no Security Against Small-pox Infection* (London, 1805), p. viii.
20. Mr Stuart, quoted in 'Review of Pamphlets on Vaccination', *The Edinburgh Review*, 15 (January, 1810), 322–51 (p. 343).
21. Moseley, like many of Jenner's medical opponents, had a lucrative practice in administering the inoculation method that Montagu had introduced. Details of the campaign, in which fifteen doctors joined Moseley in anti-Jenner pamphleteering, can be found in Saunders, *Edward Jenner: The Cheltenham Years*. By 1810, however, Moseley had lost, partly because the extreme rhetoric of his attacks on vaccination offended the proprieties of current scientific discourse. *The Edinburgh Review* complained of Moseley's language and summed up the debate conclusively in Jenner's favour: 'Review of Pamphlets on Vaccination'.
22. Quoted in Robert Thornton, *Vaccinae Vindicia; or, Defence of Vaccination* (London, 1806), p. 231.

23. Hunter's proto-evolutionary ideas were expressed more clearly in the work of his follower, William Lawrence. See William Lawrence, *Lectures on Physiology, Zoology and the Natural History of Man* (London, 1819).
24. For Darwin's views see his *Zoonomia; Or, The Laws of Organic Life*, 2 vols. (London, 1794–6), vol. I, pp. 105–7, and *Phytologia; Or the Philosophy of Agriculture and Gardening* (London, 1800), pp. 114–15. On attacks on Darwin see Alan Bewell, '"Jacobin Plants": Botany as Social Theory in the 1790s', *TWC*, 20 (1989), 132–9.
25. J. F. Blumenbach, *De generis humani varietate nativa*, 3rd edn (Göttingen, 1795) and *A Manual of the Elements of Natural History*, trs. R. T. Gore (London, 1825).
26. On Buffon see Philip C. Ritterbush, *Overtures to Biology: The Speculations of Eighteenth-Century Naturalists* (New Haven and London, 1964).
27. Charles White, *Regular Gradation in Man, and in Different Animals and Vegetables* (London, 1799) and Edward Long, *History of Jamaica*, 3 vols. (London, 1774), vol. II, pp. 51–83, 383.
28. See Moseley's *A Treatise on Sugar With Miscellaneous Medical Observations*, 2nd edn (London, 1800), p. 171.
29. Moseley's association of black slaves with wild beasts is apparent in his *A Treatise on Sugar*, 1st edn (London, 1799), pp. 169–80 and 2nd edn (London, 1800), pp. 167–8.
30. Rowley, *Cow-pox Inoculation*, p. viii.
31. In 1819 Jenner declared, 'I wish Cobbett would change places with Tom Paine [whose bones Cobbett had brought from America in a box] – I would travel many a mile in the snow to put him in the Box.' Quoted in Richard B. Fisher, *Edward Jenner 1749–1823* (London, 1991), p. 277.
32. In a letter of 29 April 1802 to his trusted friend, Henry Hicks, Jenner drew a caricature of Pitt with a forked tongue below these verses: 'And gentle Reader woulds't thou know/ What curs'd, what most malignant star,/ Produced the Income Tax and War/ Look at that Fellow's head below.' MS 5236 item 2, Wellcome Trust.
33. On Darwin see Bewell, '"Jacobin Plants"'; on Priestley see Simon Schaffer, 'Priestley and the Politics of Spirit', in *Science, Medicine and Dissent: Joseph Priestley (1733–1804)*, ed. R. G. W. Anderson and Christopher Lawrence (London, 1987), pp. 39–53.
34. From the Preface to *The Poems of Robert Bloomfield*, 2 vols. (London, 1809), vol. I, p. ii.
35. Letter to George Bloomfield, 21 July 1802; in *Selections from the Correspondence of Robert Bloomfield the Suffolk Poet*, ed. W. H. Hart (London, 1870 [facs. rpt Walton-on-Thames, 1968]), p. 29.
36. Letter to George Bloomfield, 2 August 1803; in ibid., p. 33.
37. From *The Poems of Robert Bloomfield*, vol. I, pp. 100–25.
38. Ibid., p. 100.
39. In the *Annual Review for 1804*, vol. III, p. 574. The *Monthly Magazine* said of the poem, 'Mr. Bloomfield's genius burns with undiminished lustre. Nature marked him for a poet in his cradle', 18 (1804), 594.

40. Jenner had speculated that tuberculosis might 'arise from our familiarity with an animal that nature intended to keep separate from man' – the sheep (see F. Dawtrey Drewitt, *The Notebook of Edward Jenner in the Possession of the Royal College of Physicians of London* (London, 1931), p. 41). He passed his experimental evidence to Beddoes, who incorporated it in his publications on using gases to treat tuberculosis. Jenner, that is to say, influenced Beddoes's cow-house cure by communicating his findings, as well as by example. Beddoes rapidly became a convert to vaccination and campaigned for Jenner to be given a greater reward by parliament.
41. See *An Essay on the Public Merits of Mr. Pitt* (London, 1796) and *Alternatives compared: or, What Shall the Rich Do To Be Safe?* (London, 1797).
42. Quoted in Roy Porter, *Doctor of Society: Thomas Beddoes and the Sick Trade in Late-Enlightenment England* (London and New York, 1992), p. 103.
43. Thomas Beddoes, *Essay on the Causes, Early Signs, and Prevention of Pulmonary Consumption For the Use of Parents and Preceptors* (Bristol, 1799), p. 60.
44. Quoted in Porter, *Doctor of Society*, p. 106.
45. Quoted in ibid.
46. *Selections from the Letters of Robert Southey*, ed. John Wood Warter, 4 vols. (London, 1856), vol. I, p. 93.
47. Rowley, *Cow-pox Inoculation*, p. 5.
48. Fisher, *Edward Jenner 1749–1823*, p. 156.
49. (London, 1797), p. 322.
50. Hopkins, *Princes and Peasants*, pp. 9–13.
51. Jenner, *A Continuation of Facts and Observations Relative to the Variolae Vaccinae, or Cow Pox* (London, 1800), in Harvard Classics, ed. Eliot, p. 231.
52. Hopkins, *Princes and Peasants*, pp. 73–4.
53. Blane and Thomas Trotter introduced vaccination to the navy as part of reforms instituted by Admiral St Vincent designed to impose sanitation on the fleet. It was through these reforms that doctors and surgeons increased their status in the navy, as they became officially responsible for inspection and supervision of crews. This official responsibility for imposing health through discipline anticipated the development of a similar role by civilian doctors. On the institutionalisation of health discipline in the navy see Christopher Lloyd and Jack L. S. Coulter, *Medicine and the Navy 1200–1900*, vol. III: *1714–1815* (Edinburgh and London, 1961), pp. 165, 349–52.
54. Thomas Alston Warren told his parishioners that 'our brave Seamen and Soldiers could successfully ply the ropes, direct the cannon, and handle the musket, whilst undergoing this new Inoculation. Our enemies did not like this at all'. In *An Address from a Country Minister to his Parishioners on the Subject of the Cow-Pox, or Vaccine Inoculation* (Oxford, 1803), p. 7. In parliament, Admiral Berkeley and General Tarleton agreed that vaccination was helping to win the war: Tarleton declared that 'in future ages, the glory of DR. JENNER'S fame will be superior to the trophied urn of the most renowned of warriors'. Charles Murray, *Debates in Parliament Respecting the Jennerian Discovery* (London, 1808), pp. 5, 78.

55. Fisher, *Edward Jenner 1749–1823*, p. 147.
56. Hansard 146, col. 722, quoted in R. M. MacLeod, 'Law, Medicine and Public Opinion: The Resistance to Compulsory Health Legislation 1870–1907', *Public Law* (1967), 107–28; 189–211 (p. 211).
57. Words used by the Victorian Anti-Vaccination League; quoted in ibid., 124.
58. Saunders, *Edward Jenner: The Cheltenham Years*, p. 118.
59. *Letters of Edward Jenner*, p. 19.
60. In *The Poetical Works of Robert Southey, Collected by Himself*, 10 vols. (London, 1838), vol. VII, canto i, stanza 3.
61. Coleridge argued that smallpox derived from Abyssinia whence it was carried by conquests, trade and the Roman armies to Constantinople and to Italy and France. And he asked Southey to inform Jenner that the Danes' successful control of an epidemic in cattle by inoculation of calves placed 'the identity of the Small & cow pox out of doubt': *CL*, vol. II, p. 852.
62. On Southey's images of African revenge for the slave trade see Timothy Morton, 'Blood Sugar', in *Romanticism and Colonialism*, ed. Tim Fulford and Peter J. Kitson (Cambridge, 1998), pp. 87–106.
63. Present-day Sri Lanka.
64. Quoted in the *Asiatic Annual Register* (1807), 19.
65. Quoted in David Arnold, 'Smallpox and Colonial Medicine in Nineteenth-Century India', in *Imperial Medicine and Indigenous Societies*, ed. David Arnold (Manchester and New York, 1988), p. 53.
66. Quoted in ibid.
67. J. Ring, *Treatise on the Cow-Pox Containing the History of Vaccine Inoculation* (London, 1801–3), p. 679.
68. Quoted in Thornton, *Vaccinae Vindicia*, p. 423.
69. See Ralph W. Nicholas, 'The Goddess Sitala and Epidemic Smallpox in Bengal', *Journal of Asian Studies*, 41 (1981), 21–44.
70. Quoted in Arnold, 'Smallpox and Colonial Medicine', p. 50.
71. Quoted in ibid., p. 53.
72. A statement made in 1878. Quoted in ibid., p. 53.
73. Morier served as secretary to the British embassies to Persia from 1809 to 1812, and as minister plenipotentiary in Tehran from 1812 to 1815. The narrative of his visit, published in 1810, became an authoritative work on Persia: it was translated into French and German.
74. All citations from *The Adventures of Hajji Baba of Ispahan* (London: Cresset Press, n.d.).
75. See the introduction to Sir Walter Scott, *The Talisman: A Tale of the Crusaders* (Edinburgh, 1871), p. 2.
76. *Good Tidings*, line 85.
77. In Britain the Vaccination Act of 1841 made variolation/inoculation illegal. A further act of 1853 made vaccination compulsory for all children within three months of birth. In 1861 Poor Law Guardians in each district of the land were permitted to appoint officers to enforce the law. And in 1867 parliament made those who refused vaccination punishable by repeated fines. In India,

Notes to pages 226–34

meanwhile, the native practice of tikadar inoculation was banned in Calcutta from 1804. Although this ban was ineffectual, it was succeeded by further bans until in 1880 the Vaccination Act made Jenner's system compulsory wherever the government of India chose to enforce it. Vaccination had become one of the chief means by which a fully centralised government sought to supervise the people. Medicine had become a bureaucratised discourse of state control, a means of imposing on the public the kind of order that their legislators thought was good for them. On hygiene and order see Michel Foucault, *The Birth of the Clinic: An Archaeology of Medical Perception* (London, 1989).

78. On 23 March 1885 over 20,000 Britons demonstrated against vaccination in Leicester. Their slogans are quoted in MacLeod, 'Law, Medicine and Public Opinion', 196, 201.

10 BRITAIN'S LITTLE BLACK BOYS AND THE TECHNOLOGIES OF BENEVOLENCE

1. Quoted in Sanborn C. Brown, *Benjamin Thompson, Count Rumford* (Cambridge, Mass., 1979), p. 195.
2. Quoted in ibid., p. 198.
3. Thomas Young, *A Course of Lectures on Natural Philosophy and the Mechanical Arts*, 2 vols. (London, 1807). Also, James Hutton, *Dissertation upon the Philosophy of Light, Heat and Fire* (Edinburgh, 1794), pp. 38–67; Joseph Black, *Lectures on the Elements of Chemistry, Delivered in the University of Edinburgh . . . now Published from his Manuscripts*, ed. John Robison, 2 vols. (Edinburgh, 1803), vol. I, pp. 115–35, 156–61. For an assessment of these and other scientific work in the area, see John Herschel, *Preliminary Discourse on the Study of Natural Philosophy* (London, 1830), pp. 315–23, and Mary Somerville, *On the Connexion of the Physical Sciences*, 3rd edn (London, 1836). For a more recent history of the subject see Robert Fox, *The Caloric Theory of Gases from Lavoisier to Regnault* (Oxford, 1971).
4. David Porter, *Considerations On the Present State of Chimney Sweepers With Some Observations on the Act of Parliament Intended for their Regulation and Relief, With Proposals for the Further Relief* (London, 1802), p. 30.
5. Quoted in Brown, *Thompson*, p. 195.
6. From the *Report of the Royal Commission on the Employment of Children in Mines and Manufactures* (1842), vol. XVII, pp. 63, 3.
7. Porter, *Considerations*, p. 35
8. Quoted in Brown, *Thompson*, p. 192.
9. *Collected Works of Count Rumford*, ed. Sanborn C. Brown, 5 vols. (Cambridge, Mass., 1970), vol. II, p. 311.
10. Quoted in Brown, *Thompson*, p. 167.
11. Princess Lieven wrote that it 'gives a vivid picture of chaos and the void. There is something positively hellish in the effect exerted by the sight of that opaque atmosphere'. Quoted in Venetia Murray, *High Society: A Social History of the Regency Period, 1788–1830* (London, 1998), p. 101.

12. 'London' from *The Songs of Experience*, Erdman, pp. 26–7.
13. 'Extempore Effusion upon the Death of James Hogg', line 30. *WPW*, vol. IV, pp. 276–8.
14. *The Prelude* (1805), book VII, lines 196–7, 208.
15. *Letters of William and Dorothy Wordsworth*, ed. Ernest De Selincourt, 2nd edn, rev. by C. L. Shaver, Mary Moorman and Alan Hill, 8 vols. (Oxford, 1967–), vol. III, p. 21.
16. Thomas De Quincey, *Confessions of an English Opium Eater and Other Writings*, ed. Grevel Lindop (Oxford, 1985), pp. 21, 23.
17. *Collected Works of Count Rumford*, vol. II, p. 311.
18. Quoted in W. J. Sparrow, *Knight of the White Eagle. Sir Benjamin Thompson, Count Rumford of Woburn, Mass.* (New York, 1965), p. 169.
19. *Collected Works of Count Rumford*, vol. V, p. 157.
20. Quoted in Brown, *Thompson*, p. 166.
21. Quoted in Sparrow, *Knight of the White Eagle*, p. 174.
22. Quoted in ibid., p. 109.
23. *Collected Works of Count Rumford*, vol. V, p. 139.
24. Ibid., pp. 443 and 455.
25. See Morris Berman, *Social Change and Scientific Organization: The Royal Institution, 1799–1844* (London, 1978).
26. Quoted in Sparrow, *Knight of the White Eagle*, p. 116.
27. Quoted in ibid.
28. As Morris Berman shows, many of the gentlemen behind the Institution were influential in the East India Company and preferred that the school should benefit empire by training engineers for the colonies in Bengal. See *Social Change and Scientific Organisation*, pp. 83–5.
29. Quoted in Sparrow, *Knight of the White Eagle*, p. 128.
30. *A Sentimental History of Chimney Sweepers, in London and Westminster, Shewing the Necessity of Putting Them Under Regulations to Prevent the Grossest Inhumanity to the Climbing Boys* (London, 1785), pp. ii–iii, xxvi–xxvii.
31. Porter, *Considerations*, p. xi.
32. *The Letters of Charles Lamb*, ed. E. V. Lucas, 3 vols. (London, 1935), vol. II, p. 425.
33. G. Orr, *A Treatise On A Mathematical and Mechanical Invention for Chimney Sweeping* (London, 1803), pp. 12–13.
34. J. W. Hiort, *A Practical Treatise on the Construction of Chimneys* (London, 1826); *Description of the Patent Metallic Lining and Damper for the Chimneys of Dwelling and Other Houses and Buildings Invented By Mr Seth Smith* (London, n.d.), p. 11.
35. Quoted in George L. Phillips, *England's Climbing Boys: A History of the Long Struggle to Abolish Child Labor in Chimney-Sweeping* (Boston, 1949), p. 14.
36. Fourteenth Report of the Committee of the Society for Superseding the Necessity of Climbing Boys (May, 1829), p. 6.
37. Phillips, *England's Climbing Boys*, p. 17n.
38. Ibid., p. 35.

39. *Parliamentary Debates*, 39 (1819), 448.
40. 'The Chimney Sweeper's Boy', by Samuel Roberts, *CSF*, p. 61.
41. The axiom 'there are no slaves in England' was founded on two eighteenth-century legal judgements made by Lord Mansfield. In 1771 Mansfield ordered the release from prison on grounds of habeas corpus of Jonathan Strong, a slave whose master wanted to resell him to a Jamaican planter. In 1772, in the case of James Somerset, an escaped slave whose master tried to reclaim and sell him, Mansfield ruled that his owner did not have the right to compel him to return to a foreign country. Somerset's liberty in Britain was effectively guaranteed, and the case was taken to have upheld the principle that a slave became a freeman once on English soil.
42. *Cobbett's Weekly Political Register*, 14 April 1821.
43. *Cobbett's Two-Penny Trash*, 5 January (1831), quoted in Raymond Williams, *Cobbett* (Oxford and New York, 1983), p. 37.
44. William Hone, *The Every-Day Book and Table Book*, 3 vols. (London, 1826–41), vol. I, p. 591.
45. *A Cry from the Chimneys; or An Integral Part of the Total Abolition of Slavery Throughout the World* (London, 1837), p. 10.
46. *Essays, Moral and Political*, 2 vols. (London, 1832), vol. II, p. 94.
47. James Montgomery, *The Climbing Boy's Soliloquies* (in *CSF*), pp. 396–428. 'The Dream' appears on pp. 402–13.
48. Quoted in Brown, *Thompson*, p. 125.
49. *Collected Works of Count Rumford*, vol. V, p. 117.
50. Ibid., p. 129.
51. Ibid., p. 128.
52. Ibid., p. 127.
53. Bentham's proposal quoted in Robin Evans, *The Fabrication of Virtue: English Prison Architecture 1750–1840* (Cambridge, 1982), pp. 218–20.
54. Bentham quoted from J. R. Poynter, *Society and Pauperism: English Ideas on Poor Relief, 1795–1834* (London, 1969), p. 133.
55. Quoted in Michael Ignatieff, *A Just Measure of Pain: The Penitentiary in the Industrial Revolution 1750–1850* (London and New York, 1989), p. 68.
56. *Collected Works of Count Rumford*, vol. V, p. 172.
57. *Cobbett's Weekly Political Register*, 32 (1817), 79.
58. *Cobbett's Weekly Political Register*, 31 (1816), 606.
59. See the popular song 'The Roast Beef of Old England': 'Then BRITONS be valiant, the moral is clear;/ THE OX IS OLD ENGLAND, THE FROG is MONSIEUR/ Whose puffs and bravadoes we never need fear/ O the Roast Beef of Old England/ And O the Old English Roast Beef.' Quoted in Ian Dyck, *William Cobbett and Rural Popular Culture* (Cambridge, 1992), p. 133.
60. 'The Praise of Chimney-Sweepers' (1822), in *The Works of Charles Lamb*, ed. Thomas Hutchinson (London, 1924), pp. 607–13.
61. Robert Southey's phrases, from 'On the Means of Improving the People' (1818) in *Essays, Moral and Political*, vol. II, pp. 134–5.
62. 'The Mother's Grave and Orphan's Purgatory', *CSF*, p. 352.

63. Quoted in Poynter, *Society and Pauperism*, p. 196.
64. Roberts, *An Address*, pp. 15 (Wordsworth), 14 (Blake). See Pope's translation of the *Odyssey*, book x, line 278, and see *Paradise Lost*, book III, line 44. Wesley quotes the *Paradise Lost* phrase in his hymn 'The morning flowers display their sweets'. Thanks to Paul Yoder and Kevin Binfield for tracing these sources.
65. In *The Works of Charles Lamb*, pp. 607–13.
66. *The First of May*, in Charles Dickens, *Sketches by Boz Illustrative of Every-Day Life and Every-Day People* (London, 1933), pp. 127–32.
67. See Charles Dickens, *The Adventures of Oliver Twist*, chapter 3.
68. Hone, *Every-Day Book*, vol. I, pp. 583–4.
69. Tom Dacre in Blake's self-published versions of the poem.
70. Hone, *Every-Day Book*, vol. II, pp. 625–6.
71. For an exploration of the poem in the context of the abolition campaign see Martin K. Nurmi, 'Fact and Symbol in "The Chimney Sweeper" of Blake's *Songs of Innocence*', *Bulletin of the New York Public Library*, 68 (1964), 249–58.
72. On these themes in 'The Little Black Boy' see Alan Richardson, 'Colonialism, Race, and Lyric Irony in Blake's "The Little Black Boy"', *Papers on Language and Literature*, 26 (1990), 233–48; David V. Erdman, *Blake: Prophet Against Empire*, 3rd edn (Princeton, N.J., 1977), pp. 226–42; D. L. Macdonald, 'Pre-Romantic and Romantic Abolitionism: Cowper and Blake', *European Romantic Review*, 4 (1994), 163–82; and David Bindman, 'Blake's Vision of Slavery Revisited', *Huntington Library Quarterly*, 58 (1996), 373–82.

CONCLUSION

1. Quoted in Jan Golinski, *Science as Public Culture: Chemistry and Enlightenment in Britain, 1760–1820* (Cambridge, 1992), pp. 244–5.
2. The philosopher of science William Whewell recorded that Coleridge 'stood up in Cambridge to forbid the British Association for the Advancement of Science the use of "philosopher" to describe any student of the material world. The word "scientist" was first proposed on that occasion.' Whewell's review of Mary Somerville's *On the Connexion of the Physical Sciences*, *Quarterly Review*, 51 (1834), 59–60, quoted in Trevor H. Levere, *Poetry Realized in Nature: Samuel Taylor Coleridge and Early Nineteenth-Century Science* (Cambridge, 1981), p. 73.
3. William Sotheby, *Lines Suggested by the Third Meeting of the British Association for the Advancement of Science, Held at Cambridge in June 1833* (London, 1834), reprinted in *Romanticism and Science 1773–1833*, ed. Tim Fulford, 5 vols. (London and New York, 2002), vol. III, pp. 217–26.
4. Ibid., p. 224.
5. Ibid., p. 223.

Index

Abdullah bin Abdul Kadir Munsyi 69–70
Abrams, M. H. 168
Abyssinians 42
Admiralty 33, 115, 156, 162, 175
Adventure HMS 49
Aepinus, Franz Maria Ulrich Theodosius 149, 170, 175
Africa 9, 42, 90–107, 109, 146–8, 222
   and Banks's influence 11, 44, 45
   and inoculation 199
   and slavery 17, 248
   and smallpox 222
   and travellers in 1, 3, 9, 11, 34, 38, 41, 163
   literary representations of 25
   penetration of by Britain 9
African Association 2, 11, 92–3, 106
Africans 47, 139, 260
African slave trade 97, 109–10, 117–18, 125, 183, 245
Aiton, William
   Hortus Kewensis 91
Alaska 9, 161
Aldini, Giovanni 207
American expeditions 166
American Revolution 179, 181, 183
Amra tree 81
Anderson, Alexander 44–5, 117, 129, 132, 223
Annals of Philosophy 5
Antarctica 9, 49, 160, 162, 166
Anthropological Society of London 141
Anti-Jacobin, The 119
Arabia 107
Arabian Nights 165, 168
Arago, François 158
Arctic 159–65, 168–9
Arundel Castle 263
Asiatic Society 79, 141
Asiatick Researches 79
'Atimucta' 81, 82
Atlas mountains 103
Augstein, Hannah 29

Aurungzebe 88
Australia 5, 14, 23, 38, 92, 127, 180
   and Banks's influence 11, 34
   and Cook's first voyage 5, 9
   and indigenous people 180
   British colonies in 9, 41, 42
   circumnavigation of 10
Azores 92
Aztecs 181

Babbage, Charles 272
Baffin's Bay 161, 163, 165
Ball, John (*Wat Tyler*) 181
Banks, Sir Joseph 8–9, 46, 62–3, 68, 164, 180, 181, 184
   and Africa 90, 91–5, 100, 103–7, 142
   and East Indies 69–70, 71–9
   Florigelium 112
   and imperialism 10–17
   and India 73–81, 226–7
   and influence on botanical science 87, 160
   and Jenner 198, 203, 211
   and magnetic research 149, 158, 175
   Objects of Natural History Illustrated 56
   and opposition to radical politics 179–80, 189, 191
   and Omai 48–57
   and polar exploration 161–2
   as President of the Royal Society 45, 119–20, 192–3, 194, 230, 240–1
   and race theory 127, 128, 129–31, 133–4, 139, 148
   and South Pacific 108, 112–17, 118
   scientific collection of 11–12, 41, 59, 68
   scientific networks of 12–15, 18, 20, 25, 33–5, 45, 223, 271–3
   in Tahiti 59, 135–8
   and travel narratives 9, 27–8
Banks Land 164
Barbary 34
Barbauld, Anna 47

Barlow, Peter 159
Barrell, John
 The Infection of Thomas De Quincey 26
Barrington, Daines 160, 161, 169, 175
Barrow, John 162–4, 165, 175
Bartram, William 4
Batavia 179
Bavaria 44, 241
Bayly, William 156
Beddoes, Thomas 15, 29, 119, 189, 191–3, 196, 216–17
Bell, Andrew 256
Bengal 71, 73, 74, 79, 224, 225
Bennett, Mr 233
Bentham, Jeremy 19–20, 229, 255–6
 Panopticon 19–20, 255–6
Bering Strait 159, 160, 163
Berkeley, Earl of 210
Bernard, Thomas 242, 258, 267
Bewell, Alan 105
 Romanticism and Colonial Disease 30
Bhaba, Homi K. 26, 60
Bible 146–7, 148, 253
Bihar 224
Bindman, David 29
Biot, Jean-Baptiste 149, 158
Bird, John 155
black people 138, 144–5
Blake, William 7, 17, 25, 167, 212, 250–8, 267–70
 and chimney sweeps 246
 and influence of Erasmus Darwin 78
 and London 234
 and opposition to propagandist sentiment 228
 and radical politics 271
 Songs of Innocence and of Experience 17
  'The Chimney Sweeper' (*Songs of Experience*) 269, 270
  'The Chimney Sweeper' (*Songs of Innocence*) 266–7, 268–9, 270
  'The Echoing Green' 267–8
  'Holy Thursday' 269–70
  'The Lamb' 268
  'The Little Black Boy' 268–9
  'London' 234, 267
Blane, Gilbert 220
Bligh, Captain William 3, 10, 23–4, 67, 92, 131
 and mutiny on HMS *Bounty* 116, 119
 and transportation of breadfruit 43, 115–16
Bloomfield, Robert 25, 212–16, 218, 223, 227
 The Farmer's Boy 212
 Good Tidings; Or, News From the Farm 212–16, 223
Blue Nile 42
Blumenbach, Johann Friedrich 14, 54, 113, 143–5, 147
 and comparative anatomy 127, 131, 132–8, 141
 and theories of racial degeneration 128, 209
 Decas Collectionis Suae Craniorum Diversarum Gentium Illustrata 133–4
 De generis humani varietate nativa 134–7
Blunt, Thomas 160, 163
Board of Agriculture 236
Board of Longitude 183–4
Boehme, Jacob 170
Bolton, Carol 22–3
Bombay 44
Book of Common Prayer 96
Boothia Peninsula 165
Borabora 67
Boraborans 48–9
Borda, J. C. 157
Borough, William
 A Discours of the Variation 150
botanic gardens
 at the Cape of Good Hope 92
 in Calcutta 44, 74–5, 79
 in St Vincent 44–5, 79
botany 13, 35–8, 71–89, 90–3, 108, 112, 116–17, 160
Botany Bay 35
Bougainville, Louis Antoine, Comte de 33, 180
Boulton, Matthew 236, 241
Bounty HMS 116, 118, 122
Bowles, William Lisle 246
Brazil 12
breadfruit 43, 56, 92, 108, 110–19, 120, 121–5
Bristol 16, 109–10, 117, 119, 120, 141
 and Beddoes 216
 and Coleridge 188
 and Davy 191, 192–3, 194
 and science 217
 and Southey 181
Britain 29, 189–90
 and Banks's influence 34, 43, 45
 and commerce 35, 44, 73
 and dominance in Europe 89
 and East Indies 70
 and fears of French Revolution 15, 16, 189, 233
 and inoculation 199
 and its colonial possessions 2, 9, 74, 224–5
 and reform 20
 and scientific progress 1–2, 5, 10–12, 16, 24, 25, 128, 271
 and slavery 183–4
 and visit of Omai 48, 49, 66
 and war with America 181–2
 and war with France 197, 202, 216, 218–20, 229
 and war with Spain 220
British Association for the Advancement of Science 5, 33, 166, 272–3

Index

British Empire 2, 6–9, 43, 77, 117, 123, 197, 198–9, 222–7
   and literary responses 6, 17–18, 63, 118, 124
   in Africa 106
   in India 73, 88–9
British explorers 3, 48
British manufactures 47, 66–8
British Museum 35, 41, 59
British parliament 175, 187, 242, 258
   House of Commons 175, 229–33, 238, 245–6, 252
   House of Lords 175, 243, 245–6
British 'slaves' 246–7, 252–3
Brougham, Henry 5
Browne, Janet 78
Bruce, James 42, 103
   Travels to Discover the Source of the Nile 93
Bryant, Jacob 142
Buckinghamshire 64
Buckland, William 142
Buffon, Georges-Louis Leclerc, Comte de 13–14, 154, 209
   Histoire naturelle 131–2
Burckhardt, Johan Ludwig 92, 106
Burder, George 120
Burke, Edmund 15, 119, 187, 203
Burke, William 140
Burma 9
Burns, Robert 109
Byron, Lord 23, 89, 107
   and concept of liberty 122
   and representation of the South Pacific 108–9, 121–3, 124
   and Southey's influence 86–7
   The Island 122–3
   Vision of Judgement 121–2

Calcutta 44, 74, 79, 241
Calicut 116–17
Calidasas *see* Kalidasa
caloric 229–30
Cambridge University 56, 188
Camdeo 84–5, 86
Camper, Pieter 128–9, 131, 133, 134–5, 139, 147, 148
Canada 9, 11, 47, 92, 172, 222
Canary Islands 92
Cannon, Garland 81
Cape of Good Hope 44, 90, 91–2
Carcass H.M.S. 160
Caribbean 6, 10, 108
   and race theory 133
   and slavery 17, 248
   British colonies in 23
   see also West Indies

Caribs 117, 129
Carlisle, Anthony 193
Carlyle, Thomas 128
Caroline of Brunswick, Princess of Wales 199
Carter, H. B. 27–8
'Caucasians' 14, 127, 134, 135, 144, 148, 209
   superiority of 144–6
Celt 141
Ceylon 222
Charlotte (Augusta), Princess of Great Britain 69
Charlotte Sophia of Mecklenburg-Strelitz, Queen of Great Britain 69
Chelsea Physic Garden 35
chemistry of heat 8
child labourers 249–50
chimneys 231–3
chimney sweeping machine 243–6
chimney sweeps 17, 228–9, 230, 241, 257–70
China 34, 38, 74
   and inoculation 199
   and tea 44, 75, 159
chocolate 46
Christian belief 96–8, 142, 148
Christian dissenters 254
Christian, Fletcher 122
Christian missionaries 73, 124–6, 137
Christ's Hospital 172
Church of England 184
Church Missionary Society 119–21
Churchman, John 158
   Magnetic Atlas 158
Clare, John 212–13
Clarkson, Thomas 8
Clerke, Charles 157
climbing boys *see* chimney sweeps
coal 232
Cobbett, William 211, 247, 249–50, 257
coffee 46
Coleridge, Samuel Taylor 23–5, 86, 141, 167, 171–5, 202, 212, 250–1
   and Davy 16, 17
   and drugs 34
   and education 215–19
   and electricity 183–4
   and empire 24
   and Erasmus Darwin's influence 78
   interest in science 8–9, 30, 186–97, 271, 272
   and magnetic research 149, 151
   and opposition to slavery 117–19, 124
   and race theory 24, 128, 132, 138, 142–7, 148
   and radical politics 15, 179, 226–7
   and relationship between poetry and science 4, 24–5
   and religious beliefs 173

Coleridge, Samuel Taylor (*cont.*)
  and representation of the South Pacific 6, 108–10, 112, 120–1, 123
  and Rumford 238, 240
  and study at Göttingen 113
  and William Jones's influence 82
  works:
    'Fears in Solitude' 110
    'Kubla Khan' 34
    'Lectures on Revealed Religion' 173
    Lyrical Ballads 22–8, 101–2, 202, 214
    'Ode to the Departing Year' 183
    On the Constitution of the Church and State 173, 174–5
    'Religious Musings' 186, 188
    'The Rime of the Ancient Mariner' 171–3, 251
colonial expansion 11, 34
colonialism 6–8, 90
colonisation 13, 121, 147, 148, 248
Columbus, Christopher 99, 149
compass variation 151–60
Congo 144
Congo, river 42
Constantinople 199, 201
Cook, Captain James 3, 5–6, 9, 18–19, 21, 22–3, 46, 119, 179, 180
  and Banks 271
  and magnetic research 149, 151, 155–7, 175
  and Omai 48–9
  and polar exploration 160, 169, 171, 172
  and scientific research 25
  and Tahiti 24, 27, 56, 110, 113, 137
  descriptions of the Society Islands 6
  first voyage of 4–5, 9–10, 35, 59, 112, 153–4
  second voyage of 91, 114, 135, 162, 184, 198
  third voyage of 42, 129, 161
Cooper, Thomas 189
Coulomb, Charles (Augustin de) 149
The Courier 218
Cowper, William 7, 18–20, 27, 34–8, 39, 47, 48, 62–6, 205
  and representations of London 62, 63
  The Task 18–19, 39, 47, 48, 62, 63–6, 79
cowpox 198, 201–2
Crabbe, George 78
craniometry 127
Crawfurd, John 47
creation theory 145–6
Creoles 117
Croker, John Wilson 169
Crozier, Francis 163
Cruikshank, George 265
Cunningham, Allan 246
Currin, Philip 29
Cuvier, Georges 14, 127, 132, 133

Dahl, Michael 151
Dampier, William 99
Darwin, Erasmus 4, 15, 30, 42, 168, 170, 186, 191
  and botany 77–9, 80, 81, 82
  and electricity 179, 182–3
  and evolutionary theory 209
  and heat experiments 230
  and magnetic research 151, 173
  and radical politics 211
  The Botanic Garden 77–9, 170, 182, 186
Darwinism 134
Darwinists 95
Davy Humphry 15, 16–17, 25, 30, 70, 170, 191–7
  and Coleridge 16, 17, 238, 272
  and experimental science 217
  in London 16
  as President of the Royal Society 271
  and radical politics 179
  and the Royal Institution 241
  and Southey 16, 17
'declination' *see* 'variation'
Delhi 88
de Nautonnier, Guillaume 150–1
Dening, Greg 28
De Quincey, Thomas 4, 235
Derby 5
Desmoulins, Louis-Antoine 143
  Histoire naturelle des races humaines 143
Devonshire, Georgiana Spencer Cavendish, Duchess of 57, 97, 236
  'Favourite Song from Park's Travels' 97
Devonshire, William Cavendish, Duke of 236
Dickens, Charles 265
  Oliver Twist 265
  Sketches by Boz 265
Diderot, Denis 114–15, 123, 124, 180
'dip' *see* 'inclination'
disease 219–20
Don Quixote 60
drugs 34
Durham, Bishop of 242, 267
D'Urville, Jules Sébastien César Dumont 166
Dutch 9, 68
Dyer, George 186

East India Company 11, 33, 35, 44, 68, 70
  and attempts to discover Northwest Passage 159
  and botanic gardens 44, 71, 73–5, 88
  and Christianisation of British India 148
East Indies 68–70, 71
Eden 215
Edinburgh 5, 140
Edinburgh Review 5, 194

Index

Edmond, Rod 28
Edwards, Bryan 93–4
  History Civil and Commercial of the British . . . West Indies 94
Edwards, Philip 28
Egypt 10, 103, 104, 234
electricity 1, 179–97
electro-chemistry 16, 194
Elia *see* Lamb
Ellis, John
  A Description of the Mangostan and the Breadfruit 115
Ellis, William 125
Endeavour, HMS 43, 45, 110, 155, 198
Enlightenment 112, 154
epic poetry 82, 85–6
Equiano, Olaudah 160, 161
Erdman, David 7
Estlin, John Prior 141
Ethiopia 105
Ethiopians 134
Eton 170
Euler, Leonard 149, 158
Europe 1–2, 14, 36, 42, 74
  and inoculation 199
  and knowledge of the world 5, 12, 20, 91, 138, 154
  and smallpox 202
  tours of 3
European civilization 114–15, 125, 149
European goods 47
Europeans 38, 63, 137, 139, 226
Evangelical Magazine 119

Faerie Queene 101
Falstaff 264
Fara, Patricia 29, 155
Faraday, Michael 159, 241, 273
Felix Harbour 165
'Feloops' 95
Flinders, Matthew 10
Forster, George 49, 59, 114, 118, 135
Forster, Johann Reinhold 49
Foster, John 86
Foucault, Michel 26–7, 229, 255
'Foulahs' 95
Fox, R. W. 166
France 9, 27, 35, 39, 112, 124, 181, 191, 195, 230, 241
Frankenstein, Victor (*Frankenstein*) 175, 196, 205
Franklin, Benjamin 1, 179–84, 185, 188–91, 196, 198
  Remarks Concerning the Savages of America 180–1, 190
Franklin, John 10, 163, 164, 170

French 43, 62, 75, 116
  colonial expansion 159
  expeditions 166
  philosophes 122–3
  Revolution 112, 118, 119, 187, 193, 194, 207, 221
  scientific materialism 140, 143
The Friend 173–4, 195, 218
Friendly Islands 42
Frogmore 69
Furneaux, Tobias 49

Gall, Franz Joseph 148
Galvani, Luigi 170, 185–6, 192, 207
galvanism 207
Gambier, J. E. 57–8
Gandhi, Mohandas Karamchand 226
Garrick, David 79
Gascoigne, John 27–8, 39
Gauss, Carl Friedrich 149, 159, 166, 175
Gellibrand, Henry 150
Genesis 146
Geological Society 5
geomagnetism 166
George III, King of Great Britain 56, 60, 116, 210, 233, 240, 246
George IV, King of Great Britain 242
German botanists 75
Germany 81, 230
Gibbon, Edward 88–9
  The Decline and Fall 89
Gibraltar 222
Gillray, James 204–5, 208
  'The Comforts of a Rumford Stove' 236
Gloucester, Duke of 56
Gloucestershire 214, 217, 226
Godwin, William 119, 196
Goethe, Johann Wolfgang 81
gold 106
Goldberg, David Theo 29
'Golgotha' 132, 134, 138
Golinski, Jan 29, 194
Gordon, Colonel 44
Gott, Benjamin 238–9
Göttingen 113, 132, 135, 138, 145, 166
Göttingen Magnetic Union 166
Gould, Stephen Jay 29
Grabo, Carl 30
Grafton, Duke of 212
Grasmere 235
Gray, Thomas 109
Greece 199
Greek statuary 128, 135
Green, Charles 155
Green, J. H. 143
Greenland 161

Greenwich 21
Gregory, Henry 157
Gujurat 224
guns 49
gymnotus fish 185, 186

Hadley, John 155
Hafiz (Kihwaja Shaus ud-Din Hafiz-i Shirazi) 87
Hakluyt, Richard
  Principal Voyages, Traffiques and Discoveries of the English Nation 169
Hall, Catherine 29
Halley, Edmond 151, 153, 154, 162, 170, 173, 175
Halleyan lines 152
Hampstead 103
Hansteen, Christopher 149
Hanway, Jonas 241–2, 243–4, 245, 267
  A Sentimental History of Chimney Sweepers, in London and Westminster, Shewing the Necessity of Putting Them Under Regulations to Prevent the Grossest Inhumanity to the Climbing Boys 241
Hare, William 140
Harrison, John 156, 157
Hartley, David 184–6, 188
Hastings, Warren Sir 74
Hawaii 9
Haweis, Thomas 119–20
Hawkesworth, John 38, 114, 118
Hayes, Charlotte 59
heat experiments 228, 229–30
heat-saving technology 16–17
Herschel, John 159, 230, 273
Hindle, Maurice 195
Hiort, J. W. 242
Hobhouse, Henry 29
Hogarth, William 265
Hogg, Thomas Jefferson 1, 195
Home, Everard 132
Home, Henry, Lord Kames 139
Homer 85
Homo sapiens 131–2
Hone, William 228, 247–8, 265–6
Hornemann, Frederick 11, 21, 92, 103, 106
hot air balloons 1, 103
Hottentots 132
Houghton, Daniel 92
Howitt, Mary 25, 98
Huahine 49, 67, 137
Hudson, Henry 171
Hudson, J. C. 249
Hudson, Nicholas 29
Hudson's Bay 47

Hulme, Peter
  Colonial Encounters 26
Humboldt, (Friedrich Heinrich) Alexander von 33, 149, 158–9, 166
Hunt, James 141
Hunt, James Henry Leigh 21, 103, 104–5, 247–8
Hunter, John 14, 54, 127, 128, 131, 132, 138, 139, 143, 160
  and comparative anatomy 204, 209
  and electricity 185
  and research into diseases 203

Ignatieff, Michael 229, 255
immunisation against smallpox 57
imperialism 3, 110
'inclination' 150
India 10, 34, 71–5, 85–7, 90, 107, 160
  and Banks's influence 44, 45
  and British colonies in 9, 10, 16, 23, 148, 222
  and British introduction of smallpox vaccination 224–5, 226
  and Christianity 148
  and importation of date trees 44
  and importation of tea 44
  and tradition of inoculation 199, 223, 224
  and travellers in 3
  and William Jones 79–89
'Indians'
  in Canada 47
  in London 47
  in North America 47, 180–1, 190–1
  in the South Pacific 6, 41, 62
indigenous objects 53
indigenous people 7–8, 47, 127–8
inoculation 199–201
Institut national 39
Irem 87

'Jaloffs' 95
Jamaica 210
James, P. M. 246
JanMohammed, Abdul R. 26
Java 47, 68–9, 71, 75
Jayadeva (Sri Jayadeva Goswami) 82
  Gitagovinda 82
Jefferson, Thomas 238
Jeffrey, Francis 3, 101–2
Jekyll, Henry, Dr.
Jenner, Edward 15–16, 25, 198–23, 227, 238, 271
  An Inquiry into The Causes and Effects of the Variolae Vaccinae, A Disease Discovered in Some of the Western Counties of England . . . and known by the name of The Cow Pox 201, 203–4, 221
Johnson, Samuel 11, 56, 79

Jones, Henry 75–7
Jones, Sir William 71, 79–89, 104, 141
    Botanical Observations on Select Indian Plants 80, 82, 85
    Design of a Treatise on the Plants of India 79
    Hymn to Camdeo 84–5
Jordanova, Ludmilla 29
Joule, James Prescott 230

Kailyal 86
Kalidasa 81, 82
    Sacontalá 81
Kames, Lord *see* Home, Henry
Kant, Immanuel 143, 145
Kashmir 87
Kater, Henry 163, 164
Keate, George 118
    An Account of the Pelew Islands 118
Keats, John 21, 103–5, 107
    Endymion 103
Kendall, Larcum 156
Ker, Charles 116–17
Kew Gardens 13, 34, 41, 42–3, 77, 79, 87, 91–2, 113
King-Hele, Desmond 30, 78
Kingsley, Charles 265
    The Water Babies 265
Knight, David 30
Knight, Gowin 6, 155, 175
    scientific compasses 155–6, 157
Knox, Robert Dr. 140–1, 142, 143, 145, 147
    The Races of Men 140–1
Kotzebue Sound 163
Kurtz 96
Kyd, Robert, Lieutenant Colonel 74

labouring classes 221, 236–8, 240
Labrador 35
Lake District 23, 109
Lamb, Charles 228, 242, 246, 249, 253–7, 259–65, 266
    'The Praise of Chimney Sweepers' 260
Lancaster, Joseph 256
Lancaster Sound 163, 164
Latour, Bruno 12, 26–8, 30, 48, 154
Lavoisier, Antoine Laurent 229–30
Lawrence, William 56, 95, 144–5, 147, 148
    Lectures on Physiology, Zoology and the Natural History of Man 144
Lear, King 100
Leask, Nigel
    Romantic Writers and the East 26
Ledyard, John 11, 92
Leicester Square 46, 59
Le Vaillant, François 90–1

Levere, Trevor H.
    Poetry Realized in Nature 30
Lincolnshire 41, 42
Lindley, John 273
Linnaean classification 79–80, 87, 154
Linnaeus *see* Linné, Carl von
Linné, Carl von 35–6, 77, 80–1, 82, 88, 89
    works:
        Families of Plants, The 77
        Florilegium 38
        Philosophica Botanica 79
        and race theory 134, 139
        son of 37–8
        System of Vegetables, The 77
        Systema naturae 36, 131
Linnean Society 5
Lofft, Capel 212
London 9, 44, 46–7, 73, 116, 129, 140, 150
    and anti-Jacobins 15
    Bishop of 233
    as 'centre of calculation' 39
    and chimney sweeps 231–3
    and Coleridge 195
    as commercial capital 46
    and criticism of the East India Company 74
    and Davy 192–3, 195
    as imperial centre 28, 148
    and importation of plants 13, 112
    and Jenner 221
    and Lamb 261
    and Royal Institution 240–1
    and Rumford 234–5, 254
    and sexual immorality 58–9
    and visit of Omai 14, 49–60
    in writing of William Cowper 62, 63
London Chronicle 56
London Magazine 265
London Zoo 70
Long, Edward 209–10
Longitude 150–1
Long Reach 42
Lonsdale, Earl of (Sir James Lowther) 211
Louis XVI, King of France 189
Louisiana 9
Lowther 211
Lucas, Simon 92
Luddite protests 245
Lushington, Dr 252
luxury 204
Lyell, Charles 273

Mackay, D. L. 27–8
Mackenzie, Daniel 75
Madras 44, 221, 223
Malabar 74

Malacca 70
Malaya 74
Malayan race 134
Malaysia 68–70
Malta 222
Manchester 139
Manchester, Duke of 57
'Mandingoes' 95
Maori 46
marae 137–8
Mariana Islands 134
Marlow 96
Marsden, William 69
  History of Sumatra 12, 69
Masson, Francis 3, 90, 91–2
  Stapeliae Novae; or, A Collection of several New Species of Genus; discovered in the Interior Parts of Africa 91
Mather, Cotton 199
McCalman, Iain 59
McCormick, Eric Hall 48
McCusick, James C. 118
McHugh, Heather 21, 22
Mechanics' Institutes 5
Medwin, Lieutenant Thomas 88–9, 107
  Angler in Wales, The 88–9
Mellor, Anne K. 171, 195–6
Mercator, Gerard 150
metaphors of polarity 168–75
Mexico 9
Mill, James 148
Milton, John 85, 259
Mitford, Mary Russell 97
  'Lines, Suggested By the Uncertain Fate of Mungo Park' 97
Molucca Islands 134
Montagu, Lady Mary Wortley 199–201, 224
Monticello 238
Montesquieu, Baron Charles-Louis de Secondat de
  Persian Letters 58
Montgolfier, Jacques Etienne 2
Montgolfier, Joseph Michel 2
Montgomery, James 25, 71–3, 88, 89, 243–4, 246–9, 257–8, 270
  'The Daisy in India' 71–3
  The Chimney Sweeper's Friend and Climbing Boy's Album 244, 246–9, 250–4, 259, 263, 266, 267
  'Easter Monday at Sheffield' 257
  The West Indies 97
Montgomery, Robert 39
  The Age Reviewed 39
Monthly Review, The 86, 194
Moore, Thomas 71, 82, 86–7, 88, 104–5
  Lalla Rookh 87, 104

Moors 96
Morier, James 225–6
  The Adventures of Hajji Baba 225–6
Morocco 34
Morton, Timothy 110
Moseley, Benjamin 208–10, 220, 224
Munich 234, 254–7
Munich house *see* workhouses
Mulgrave, Lord 56
Munsyi *see* Abdullah bin Abdul Kadir Munsyi

Nagkeser 85
Nairne, Edward 160, 163
Napoleon I (Bonaparte) 197, 208, 223
Napoleonic wars 162, 220
Native Americans 189
natural history 13–15, 127–48
Naturphilosophie 173–4
'negroes' 14, 127, 129, 133, 134, 139, 141, 146, 209
Nehru, Jawaharlal 80
Nelmes, Sarah 201, 204
Nelson, David 42
Nelson, Horatio 160
Neuha 122, 123
Newcastle 5
Newfoundland 35
New Holland *see* Australia
New South Wales 44
Newton, Isaac 22, 184, 188, 194–5
New Zealand 5, 9, 35, 49, 59, 180
Nicholson's Journal 5
Niger, river 42, 96, 97, 106
Niger valley 92
Nile 103
nitrous oxide 191, 217
Noah 143
'noble savages' 56, 110, 180
Norman, Robert 150
North America 10, 14, 36, 119, 127, 160, 161, 163
  and loss of British colonies 35
  and Pantisocracy 189–91
  British colonies in 9, 10, 13, 16, 179–84
  British expeditions to 12, 38
North (Geographic) Pole 34, 38, 150, 159, 160–5, 168, 171, 172, 173
North (Magnetic) Pole 149, 164–6, 168, 170, 171
Northeast Passage 163
Northwest Passage 9, 10, 154, 158, 159–60, 161, 162, 163, 164, 171, 173

Oberea 114
Obeyeskere, Gananath 29
Observations on the Cruelty of Employing Climbing Boys in Sweeping Chimneys 245
Oersted, Hans Christian 149, 158

Omai 14, 28, 45, 48–68, 79, 108, 138, 161
  and Banks 48–57
  and Cook 48–9
  in London 14, 58–9
Omai, Or a Trip Round the World 59–60
Onesimus 199
Orientalism 85–6, 87–8
Orr, G. 242
Otaheite *see* Tahiti
Ovid 135
Oxford University 191

Pacific islands 3, 5, 9, 16, 45, 113–14, 135
Pacific islanders 28
Pacific Ocean 160, 172
Paine, Thomas 211
  Rights of Man 187
Pantisocracy 118–19, 120, 189–91
Paramore, HMS 151
Park, Mungo 3, 4, 11, 21, 41, 90, 92–104, 106, 142
  Travels to the Interior Parts of Africa 94, 95, 103
Parkinson, Sydney 38
Paris 148, 150, 158
Parry, William Edward 10, 53, 163–5, 170, 171, 172
  'Omai, Banks and Solander' 53–4
Pasiphaë 209, 210
Pasteur, Louis 202
pastoralism 203
Patii 137
Pedas 68
Persia 44, 74
Peterloo 247
Petiver, James 33
Philippine Islands 134
Philology 81
Philosophical Magazine 5
Philosophical Transactions of the Royal Society 91, 153
Phipps, Constantine John 160–1, 169–70, 171, 172
Pilgrim's Progress 96
Pitt, William 4, 187
Plants of the Coast of Coromandel 75
Pneumatic Institution 191
polar exploration 149, 168
polarity 167, 173–5
political conservatives 187–8
polygenesis 143
Pomare 68, 125–6, 137
Pope, Alexander 79, 259
Porden, Eleanor Anne 168–9
  Arctic Explorers, The 168–9
  Veils, or the Triumph of Constancy, The 168
Porpoise, HMS 42

Porter, David 230, 233, 242
Porter, Roy 29
'power tools' 48, 67
Pratt, Mary Louise 12–13, 154
  Imperial Eyes 26
Price, Richard 182
Prichard, James Cowles 7, 95, 141–2, 145, 147–8
  Researches into the Physical History of Man 141, 142
Priestley, Joseph 4, 15, 77, 191, 192, 272
  and electricity 179, 184–90
  and radical politics 211, 238
  daughter of 216
  discovery of oxygen 184
  discovery of photosynthesis 184
  History and Present State of Electricity, The 184
Prometheus 181
Providence H.M.S. 116
Purchas, Samuel
  Purchas, His Pilgrims 169
Pygmies 132

Quarterly Review 169
Quebec 9

race theory 14, 127–8, 131–48
Racehorse, HMS 160
racial difference 94–5, 140–1, 143
racial prejudice 49–51
racism 140
radical politics 15–17, 86, 108–12, 119, 179–97, 247
Raffles, Sir (Thomas) Stamford 47, 68–70, 71
Raiatea 48, 67
Raja Ali 68
Ratu Gusti Wiyahan Karang Asam 68–9
Raynal, Abbé (Guillaume Thomas François) 56, 180
religious dissent 184
Rennie, Neil 28
Resolution, HMS 60, 66–7, 161
Resolution Port 157
Reveley, George 244, 252
Revesby Abbey 43–4
Reynolds, Joshua 11, 51, 53–6
Rio de Janeiro 151
Ritchie, Joseph 11, 21, 92, 103, 104–5, 106–7
  'A Farewell to England' 105
Robert Walton (*Frankenstein*) 169–71, 175
Roberts, James 43–4
Roberts, Samuel 25, 246, 248–9, 253–4, 259, 263
  'The Chimney Sweeper's Boy' 253–4
Robinson, James 172
Robinson, Mary 119
Robison, John 15
Robson, Francis 44
Romantic genius 181, 195, 196

Romantic imagination 112
Romantic poetry 102
Romanticism 30, 89, 90, 108–9, 167–8, 250–1
  and Banks's influence 6–9, 45, 71
  and exploration 6, 123
  and radical politics 15, 179
  and representation of childhood 259, 260
  and representation of nature 73
  as a new movement 101
Romanticism and Colonialism 26
Romanticism, Race and Imperial Culture 26
Ross, James Clark 10, 149, 159, 163, 164–6
Ross, John 163–4, 165–6, 168, 175
Rousseau, Jean-Jacques 122, 204, 215
Rowley, William 207–8, 217
Roxburgh, William 75, 79
Royal Academy 53
Royal College of Physicians 2, 199
Royal College of Surgeons 143
Royal Institution 16–17, 193–4, 197, 240–1, 242
Royal Jennerian Society 215, 221
Royal Navy 149, 155, 160, 162
Royal Society 2, 10, 12, 53, 56, 119, 162, 175, 194, 197
  and attempts to discover the Northwest Passage 162
  and Banks's influence 15–17, 33–4, 36, 113, 115, 149, 191, 203, 230, 271–2
  and inoculation 199
  and magnetic research 154, 155–6, 158, 160–1, 162
  and travel narratives 94
  Fellows of 179, 198
  transactions 91, 153
Royal Society for the Encouragement of Arts, Manufactures and Commerce 243
Rumford, Count, *see* Thompson, Benjamin
Rumford diet 255, 261
Rumford fireplace 235–7
Rumford stove 255
Russia 9, 159, 163

Sabine, Edward 163, 164, 166
Sacontalá 82
Sahara 103
Sahlins, Marshall 29
Said, Edward 80
  Orientalism 26
St Domingue 116
St George 60
St Helena 44
Saint-Hilare, Etienne Geoffroy 140
St Paul's Cathedral 269

St Vincent 44–5, 79, 117, 129, 132
saloop 261–2
Sandwich, John Montagu, 4th Earl of 57, 160
Sanskrit 79, 80
Saxon 141
Schaffer, Simon 29
Schelling, Friedrich Wilhelm Joseph von 173
Schiebinger, Londa 29
scientists 2–3
Scoresby, William 10, 161–2, 171, 175
Scotland 3, 109, 140
Scott, John 114
Scott, Walter 225, 259
'secular variation' 150–1
Seventeen Hundred and Seventy Seven; or, a Picture of the Manners and Customs of the Age. In a Poetical Epistle from a Lady of Quality 58
Seward, Anna 10
sexual desire 135
sexual freedom 56
shaddocks 42
Shakespeare, William 25, 81, 195
Shapin, Steven 94
Sheffield 243, 246, 257–8
Shelley, Mary 7, 169–71, 195–7, 207, 272
  Frankenstein 149, 169–71, 195–7, 207, 272
Shelley, Percy Bysshe 1–2, 21, 24, 25, 30, 88, 102–3, 104–5, 107
  and Robert Southey's influence 86
  and William Jones's influence 82
  interest in science 170, 195
  works:
  Alastor 105
  Defence of Poetry 25
  'Ozymandias' 88
  Prometheus Unbound 6
Ship Cove 157
Shteir, Ann B. 78
Siam 47
Siberia 160
Sinclair, Sir John 236
Sind 224
Singapore 9, 70
Sitala 224
skulls 128–31, 132–8
slave rebellions 44
slavery 1, 17, 108, 244, 246–50
Sloane, Sir Hans 33, 35, 199
smallpox 199–203, 212–16, 224
Smart, George 243, 245, 266
Smith, Bernard 28
Smith, Christopher 43, 116
Smith, Seth 242
Smithfield 264

Index

Snowdon 99
Society for Bettering the Condition of the Poor 239, 242
Society for the Diffusion of Useful Knowledge 5
Society for the Protection and Instruction of Chimney Sweepers' Apprentices 242
Society for Superseding the Necessity of Climbing Boys 242–6
Society Islands 6
Soho Square 34, 39–41, 42, 161, 240
Solander, Daniel 49, 53–4, 57, 139
Somerset 119
Sotheby, William 272–3
South America 9, 151, 158
South East Asia 9
Southern England 247
Southey, Robert 7, 15, 23, 30, 100–2, 112, 123–4, 186
  and colonialism 222
  and education 215–17
  and epic poetry 82, 85–6
  and Humphry Davy 16, 17
  and interest in science 271
  and labouring classes 221, 250
  and opposition to slavery 117–19
  and Pantisocracy 189–92
  and radical politics 179, 197
  and representation of America 181
  and representation of Britain 82
  and representation of the South Pacific 108–10, 120–1, 123, 126, 137
  and vaccination 224, 227
  and William Jones's influence 71, 82–9
  works:
    Curse of Kehama The 82–7, 89
    Madoc 190
    Tale of Paraguay, A 222
    Thalaba the Destroyer 100–2
    Wat Tyler 181
South Pacific 12
South (Geographic) Pole 157, 172
South (Magnetic) Pole 149, 159, 166
South Sea exploration 28–9, 48
Spain 9
Spitzbergen 160
Spurzheim, J. C. 148
Stafford, Barbara M. 29, 154
Streatham 56
sugar 46, 109–12
Sunda Islands 134
Sunday Schools 258, 260
Susquehanna Indians 180, 190
Susquehanna valley 119, 179, 189
Switzerland 230
Syon House Academy 170

Tahiti 5, 14, 23, 35, 38, 41–2, 110–16, 119–26, 127, 139, 180
  and Banks 45, 78, 108–9
  and British influence 60
  and Cook 9, 27, 241
  and Cook's first voyage 9
  and exportation of breadfruit trees 10, 92
  literary representations of 24, 124
  and magnetic research 156
  and Omai 48, 49, 51, 60–8
  and race theory 128, 129–31, 135
  and sexual immorality 58–9
Tahitian culture 59–60
Tahitian women 113
Tahitians 48, 54–6, 134
tea 44, 46
Terra incognita australis 151, 154, 156
terrestrial magnetism 149–75
Thames, river 42
Thomas, Hugh 29
Thomas, Nicholas 28
Thompson, Sir Benjamin, Graf (Count) von Rumford 1, 16, 33, 228–43, 254–7, 267, 271
  Of Food; and Particularly of Feeding the Poor 256–7
  Proposals for Forming By Subscription in the Metropolis of the British Empire A Public Institution 239
Thomson, James
  The Seasons 212
Thornton, Robert 211
Thousand and One Nights 101
Timbuktu 103
The Times 59
Tonga 66
Torquil 122, 123
'Transcendental Anatomy' 140
transit of Venus 153, 154
travel narratives 2–3, 38–9
Tripoli 92
Trotter, Thomas 219
  Medicina Nautica: An Essay on the Diseases of Seamen 219
Tupaia 49
Turkey 199, 224
Tyler, Walter (Wat) 187

Ulieta 67
Unitarians 184, 188, 189

vaccination 8, 15–16, 197, 198–227, 228
Vaipopoo 41–2
Vaitahu Bay 157
Vancouver, George 10–11

'variation' 149–50
Vauxhall Gardens 58
venereal disease 114–15
Victoria Land 166
Virgil
  Aeneid 260
Volta, Alessandro (Giuseppe Antonio Anastasio) 2, 192–3
voltaic pile (battery) 193, 194
von Kotzebue, Otto 163
von Stählin, Jacob 161

Wales 3, 109, 119
Wales, William 153, 156–7, 163, 172, 175
Walker, Adam 170
Wallich, Nathaniel 75, 77
Wallis, Captain Samuel 110
Walpole H.M.S. 222
Walvin, James 29, 47
war 219–20
Warner, Marina 59
The Watchman 183–4, 238
Watson, Richard Revd. 148
Watt, James 77, 241
Webber, John 59, 129
Weber, Wilhelm 166
Webster, Thomas 240
Wedgwood, Josiah 128, 236, 249, 256
Wellesley, Richard 223, 224
Wernerian Society 5
Wesley, John 259
West, Benjamin 51–3
West Country 109
West Indies 47, 65, 92, 115–17, 124
  and Banks's influence 45
  and botanic gardens 44
  and breadfruit as a food source for slaves 10, 43, 92
  and race theory 129
  and slavery 210, 244, 248, 253, 270
  British colonies in 10, 184, 222
  literary representations of 24
  see also Caribbean
Westminster 41
Wheeler, Roxann 29
White, Charles 139, 145, 147, 209
  Account of the Regular Gradation in Man 139
White, James 264–5
Wilberforce, William 148, 238, 242
Wiles, James 43, 116
Wilkes, Charles 166
Winchilsea, Earl of 240
Wollstonecraft, Mary 119
'Wooginoos' 42
Wordsworth, William 167, 194, 196, 211, 212, 250, 259
  and Coleridge 195
  and influence of Erasmus Darwin 78
  and innovations in poetry 86, 202
  and interest in exploration 21–3, 98–102, 104
  and interest in science 4
  and London 46–7, 221, 234–5
  and pastoral poetry 205, 211, 212
  and radical politics 226
  works:
    Excursion, The 6
    Lyrical Ballads 22–8, 101, 202, 214
    'Peter Bell' 98–9, 100
    'Poems on the Naming of Places' 22–3
    Prelude, The 21–2, 47, 99–100, 102, 234
workhouses 228, 254–7, 270
Wyndham, HMS 222

yellow fever 219
York, Duke of 220
Yorke, Sir J. 245
Young, Arthur 43
Young, Robert 29
Young, T. 245
Young, Thomas 230

Zoological Society of London 70
zoology 160

CAMBRIDGE STUDIES IN ROMANTICISM

GENERAL EDITORS
MARILYN BUTLER, *University of Oxford*
JAMES CHANDLER, *University of Chicago*

1. *Romantic Correspondence: Women, Politics and the Fiction of Letters*
   MARY A. FAVRET

2. *British Romantic Writers and the East: Anxieties of Empire*
   NIGEL LEASK

3. *Edmund Burke's Aesthetic Ideology*
   Language, Gender and Political Economy in Revolution
   TOM FURNISS

4. *Poetry as an Occupation and an Art in Britain, 1760–1830*
   PETER MURPHY

5. *In the Theatre of Romanticism: Coleridge, Nationalism, Women*
   JULIE A. CARLSON

6. *Keats, Narrative and Audience*
   ANDREW BENNETT

7. *Romance and Revolution: Shelley and the Politics of a Genre*
   DAVID DUFF

8. *Literature, Education, and Romanticism*
   Reading as Social Practice, 1780–1832
   ALAN RICHARDSON

9. *Women Writing about Money: Women's Fiction in England, 1790–1820*
   EDWARD COPELAND

10. *Shelley and the Revolution in Taste: The Body and the Natural World*
    TIMOTHY MORTON

11. *William Cobbett: The Politics of Style*
    LEONORA NATTRASS

12. *The Rise of Supernatural Fiction, 1762–1800*
    E. J. CLERY

13. *Women Travel Writers and the Language of Aesthetics, 1716–1818*
    ELIZABETH A. BOHLS

14. *Napoleon and English Romanticism*
    SIMON BAINBRIDGE

15. Romantic Vagrancy: Wordsworth and the Simulation of Freedom
CELESTE LANGAN

16. Wordsworth and the Geologists
JOHN WYATT

17. Wordsworth's Pope: A Study in Literary Historiography
ROBERT J. GRIFFIN

18. The Politics of Sensibility
Race, Gender and Commerce in the Sentimental Novel
MARKMAN ELLIS

19. Reading Daughters' Fictions, 1709–1834
Novels and Society from Manley to Edgeworth
CAROLINE GONDA

20. Romantic Identities: Varieties of Subjectivity, 1774–1830
ANDREA K. HENDERSON

21. Print Politics: The Press and Radical Opposition
in Early Nineteenth-Century England
KEVIN GILMARTIN

22. Reinventing Allegory
THERESA M. KELLEY

23. British Satire and the Politics of Style, 1789–1832
GARY DYER

24. The Romantic Reformation
Religious Politics in English Literature, 1789–1824
ROBERT M. RYAN

25. De Quincey's Romanticism
Canonical Minority and the Forms of Transmission
MARGARET RUSSETT

26. Coleridge on Dreaming
Romanticism, Dreams and the Medical Imagination
JENNIFER FORD

27. Romantic Imperialism: Universal Empire and
the Culture of Modernity
SAREE MAKDISI

28. Ideology and Utopia in the Poetry of William Blake
NICHOLAS M. WILLIAMS

29. Sexual Politics and the Romantic Author
SONIA HOFKOSH

30. *Lyric and Labour in the Romantic Tradition*
ANNE JANOWITZ

31. *Poetry and Politics in the Cockney School*
Keats, Shelley, Hunt and their Circle
JEFFREY N. COX

32. *Rousseau, Robespierre and English Romanticism*
GREGORY DART

33. *Contesting the Gothic*
Fiction, Genre and Cultural Conflict, 1764–1832
JAMES WATT

34. *Romanticism, Aesthetics, and Nationalism*
DAVID ARAM KAISER

35. *Romantic Poets and the Culture of Posterity*
ANDREW BENNETT

36. *The Crisis of Literature in the 1790s*
Print Culture and the Public Sphere
PAUL KEEN

37. *Romantic Atheism: Poetry and Freethought, 1780–1830*
MARTIN PRIESTMAN

38. *Romanticism and Slave Narratives*
Transatlantic Testimonies
HELEN THOMAS

39. *Imagination under Pressure, 1789–1832*
Aesthetics, Politics, and Utility
JOHN WHALE

40. *Romanticism and the Gothic*
Genre, Reception, and Canon Formation, 1790–1820
MICHAEL GAMER

41. *Romanticism and the Human Sciences*
Poetry, Population, and the Discourse of the Species
MAUREEN N. McLANE

42. *The Poetics of Spice*
Romantic Consumerism and the Exotic
TIMOTHY MORTON

43. *British Fiction and the Production of Social Order, 1740–1830*
MIRANDA J. BURGESS

44. *Women Writers and the English Nation in the 1790s*
ANGELA KEANE

45. *Literary Magazines and British Romanticism*
MARK PARKER

46. *Women, Nationalism and the Romantic Stage*
Theatre and Politics in Britain, 1780–1800
BETSY BOLTON

47. *British Romanticism and the Science of the Mind*
ALAN RICHARDSON

48. *The Anti-Jacobin Novel*
British Conservatism and the French Revolution
M. O. GRENBY

49. *Romantic Austen*
Sexual Politics and the Literary Canon
CLARA TUITE

50. *Byron and Romanticism*
JEROME McGANN, ed. JAMES SODERHOLM

51. *The Romantic National Tale and the Question of Ireland*
INA FERRIS

52. *Byron, Poetics and History*
JANE STABLER

53. *Religion, Toleration, and British Writing, 1790–1830*
MARK CANUEL

54. *Fatal Women of Romanticism*
ADRIANA CRACIUN

55. *Knowledge and Indifference in English Romantic Prose*
TIM MILNES

56. *Mary Wollstonecraft and the Feminist Imagination*
BARBARA TAYLOR

57. *Romanticism, Maternity and the Body Politic*
JULIE KIPP

58. *Romanticism and Animal Rights*
DAVID PERKINS

59. *Georgic Modernity and British Romanticism*
Poetry and the Mediation of History
KEVIS GOODMAN

60. *Literature, Science and Exploration in the Romantic Era*
Bodies of Knowledge
TIM FULFORD, DEBBIE LEE AND PETER J. KITSON

Printed in Great Britain
by Amazon